The Worlds of Victor Sassoon

The Worlds of Victor Sassoon

BOMBAY, LONDON, SHANGHAI, 1918–1941

Rosemary Wakeman

The University of Chicago Press   CHICAGO AND LONDON

The University of Chicago Press, Chicago 60637
The University of Chicago Press, Ltd., London
© 2024 by The University of Chicago
All rights reserved. No part of this book may be used or reproduced in any manner whatsoever without written permission, except in the case of brief quotations in critical articles and reviews. For more information, contact the University of Chicago Press, 1427 E. 60th St., Chicago, IL 60637.
Published 2024
Printed in the United States of America

33 32 31 30 29 28 27 26 25 24   1 2 3 4 5

ISBN-13: 978-0-226-83418-4 (cloth)
ISBN-13: 978-0-226-83419-1 (e-book)
DOI: https://doi.org/10.7208/chicago/9780226834191.001.0001

Library of Congress Cataloging-in-Publication Data

Names: Wakeman, Rosemary, author.
Title: The worlds of Victor Sassoon : Bombay, London, Shanghai, 1918–1941 / Rosemary Wakeman.
Description: Chicago : The University of Chicago Press, 2024. | Includes bibliographical references and index.
Identifiers: LCCN 2023052292 | ISBN 9780226834184 (cloth) | ISBN 9780226834191 (ebook)
Subjects: LCSH: Sassoon, Elias Victor, 1881–1961. | Capitalists and financiers—Biography. | International trade—History—20th century. | Globalization—Economic aspects. | Globalization—China—Shanghai. | Globalization—India—Mumbai. | Globalization—England—London. | Mumbai (India)—Commerce. | London (England)—Commerce. | Shanghai (China)—Commerce.
Classification: LCC HG172.S3 W354 2024 | DDC 332.092 [B]—dc23/eng/20231220
LC record available at https://lccn.loc.gov/2023052292

♾ This paper meets the requirements of ANSI/NISO Z39.48-1992 (Permanence of Paper).

For Michèle and Thierry

Contents

INTRODUCTION * 1

ONE
The Fortunes of Empire * 18

TWO
Bombay, Wonder of the World * 38

THREE
Bombay, Global Helm * 63

FOUR
London, Magnet of the World * 96

FIVE
London, Capital of Finance * 116

SIX
Enigmatic Shanghai * 144

SEVEN
Global Shanghai * 169

EPILOGUE * 193

Acknowledgments * 201
Notes * 205
Selected Bibliography * 233
Index * 245

✷ INTRODUCTION ✷

> Love, life, and laughter: poverty, wealth, starvation and despair,
> all mixed up together.
>
> HARRY JAMES GREENWALL, "Shanghai—City of Paradox" (1937)

Bombay, London, and Shanghai were among the most significant global cities of the 1920s and 1930s. As places, they were cutting-edge urban dynamos as well as crossroads in a global landscape of money and trade, culture and people. All three cities were great maritime ports. They were among the largest cities in the world and the densest. They shared a cosmopolitan spirit and were rhapsodies to modernity where a new middle class kicked up their heels in the Jazz Age. They were places of opulence and wealth. And at the same time, the three cities were symbols of extraordinary pathos, the cruelties of racism and sectarian violence, of poverty and despair. Bombay, London, and Shanghai were restless, shifting urban worlds entangled in the geopolitical crises of economic upheaval, war, and the political and territorial restructuring of empire. The sweeping flow of people, trade, and capital between them created polymorphic urban cultures dominated by global interaction. These global forces, which transformed and wove these cities together, sit at the heart of this book.

Tracking global-city status is a tricky maneuver for the interwar years. Statistics on cities tend to stop at 1900 or 1914, then skip to the post–Second World War era. One simple measure of global influence is population size. London was the biggest, wealthiest city on the planet in 1930, with over 8 million inhabitants in Greater London and over 13 million in the metropolitan area. It was the capital of the far-flung British Empire and the clearinghouse of the world economy. Only New York City reached these demographic heights, was overtaking London for first place on the world's statistical leaderboard in terms of not only population but also economic dominance. Shanghai's inhabitants reached 3.5 million by 1930. Just five years later, a massive influx of refugees pushed its population to 4 million. It was the fifth-largest city in the world. In Asia, only the Japanese colossi of Tokyo and Osaka (exceeding 7 million and 2.2 million people, respectively) outstripped it in terms of populace. Bombay claimed around 1.3 million inhabitants and was India's second-largest city after Calcutta. All these cities were "great choke points of human activity,"[1] as were Karachi and Rangoon. Singapore (population 567,000) and Hong Kong (population 840,000) also played pivotal roles as anchors for British power in both the South and East China Seas in the interwar years.

I have chosen to examine Bombay, London, and Shanghai in this book because they best exemplify the connectivity that characterized globalization in the 1920s and 1930s and how these forces impacted urban life. They were high-energy, high-traffic places—places of heightened global interaction. In the pages that follow, I seek to give us an understanding of how these three cities participated in and were shaped by these crosscurrents of globalization. All three were at the forefront of the dramatic changes taking place in the urban world. They thrived on industry, trade, and migration. They exuded the social and economic volatility of modernity and global capitalism, the mixing of cultures and people. They were ransacked for every conceivable urban imagery and use. The significance of the connections between Bombay, London, and Shanghai was particularly prescient amid their thorny restructuring away from the British Empire and toward the emerging contemporary global system. Bombay was London's "Gateway to the East," the "Urbs Prima" in India. It surpassed Calcutta in terms of trade and industry and population flows, and certainly in terms of connections with the imperial capital. Shanghai and Hong Kong were Britain's major commercial gateways to China. These two cities were also the main arenas for British investments in the Red Dragon. Bombay and Shanghai were the industrial powerhouses in Southeast Asia and the East. Only Tokyo's cotton industry compared. Lastly, Bombay and Shanghai, along with Hong Kong, were major entry points for the massive population streams flowing through Asia.

Most important to the framework of this book, Bombay, London, and Shanghai allow us to see how globalization played out at the level of cities. Global processes took place at ports, in banks and trade offices, in real estate deals, in mass entertainment venues, in strikes and riots. This is the "globalization from below" called for by historians. It avoids the simplifications often found in the planetary scale of analysis that has engaged much of the scholarly "global turn."[2] The three cities also provide a lens on global currents—but not just between metropole (London) and colonial city (Bombay), which has been the traditional schema of historians of empire. Instead, I follow the interlocking networks, trade webs, and information flows between cities in Asia (Shanghai) and Southeast Asia (Bombay), exploring their interdependence and the ways in which global influences worked out in both similar and dissimilar ways in different regions of the world.

Global Cities in the 1920s and 1930s

A nebulous concept, globalization in its broadest definition is about the interconnections that take place across a myriad of realms. Its origins and evolution, when and where it took place on the globe, all remain open to a variety of interpretations and ideological dispositions. For most theorists, globalization is a twentieth-century phenomenon distinct from that of empire. It is traditionally evidenced through economic indicators, especially trade and commerce, at the level of the nation-state or country. The features of globalization, according to this research, were in their infancy at the turn of the twentieth century. Then the First World War temporarily broke down these globalizing forces. The interwar years that followed are considered by economists as a period of "de-globalization" when world trade contracted from the instability caused by the war and the postwar geopolitical aftermath as well as by the Great Depression. In reaction, the major economies reoriented their trade patterns to protectionism and fell back to their own colonial systems. This version of events is wrapped around plenty of evidence at the level of individual countries.

Alongside these investigations into globalization, the idea of global cities is now a rich arena of scholarship. In the work of urban theorists, global cities—that is, cities connected by global business, common cultural and consumption patterns, the currents of labor and migration—arose with the rise of neoliberal capitalism in the late twentieth century.[3] These global places are where capital concentrates and accumulates. They are banking and financial centers, the headquarters for multinational corporations, nodal points in the global economy with highly specialized services and a fluid global labor force. A cadre of international elites controls how the world's resources and this concentration of capital are allocated and deployed. Global cities are communication, shipping, train, and air travel corridors. They knit global capitalism into webs of interdependence and symbolic cultural content. In this narrative, global cities are distinctively contemporary phenomena, even though there is little actual agreement on either the terrain or the temporality of globalization.

This book takes a broader viewpoint on the evolution of globalization and global cities. Despite the political instability and economic crises of the interwar years, the circulation of money, trade, people, and information was higher than ever before. Globalization was in full swing amid the glory years of the 1920s and even during the economic slump of the 1930s. Though dire poverty stalked cities and bloodthirsty scenes took place on the streets in many a global capital, profitable business carried on. Global trade made a remarkable recovery after the First World War. For example, the year 1929 marked the highest number of world exports ever recorded. Even after the worst years of the Depression, world trade quickly recovered.[4] The geopolitical changes after the First World War accelerated the internationalization of banking and intensified the relationship between banking and globalization. Multinational corporations continued to expand, as did their investments worldwide. When revenues took a downturn, as during the Depression, investors looked further afield and spatially opened up and widened the trading system in search of profits. Excess capital turned to financialization and ultimately to changing cities into speculative commodities.[5] The flow of money and goods continued unabated, as did the streams of refugees and labor for capitalist production. Even the financialization of everyday life that is distinctive of neoliberal capitalism can be evidenced in the intensity of the growing speculation in precious metals and currency.

Places did not experience the 1920s and 1930s equally, nor did they suffer the same during the Depression. Globalization is uneven. Worldwide exchange looks quite different if studied not by nation-states but by cities and their maritime networks. This urban aspect is only marginally included in standard economic analysis of the interwar years, even though cities and global capitalism are inextricably intertwined. From the vantage point of London, Shanghai, and Bombay, the interwar years were a period of rising global interactions aided by new communication technologies, complex maritime corridors, and expanding multinational corporations and financial networks. All three cities were the first ports of call for the swelling quantity and speed of news and information vital to global transactions. Print culture alone exploded with a myriad of English newspapers and periodicals as well as multivernacular books and press. The telegraph, wireless radio, and telephone vastly extended their reach across international borders. The revolutionary media of the interwar years has rarely been given its just due. Transportation was also on the cusp of revolution, this time with flight. Airboats, seaplanes, and zeppelins were testing the skies. Commercial air travel was beginning.

All these compressed time and space, and linked Bombay, London, and Shanghai together in a way that was unimaginable just a few years before.

Global elites shifted their resources into a web of finance and currency speculation, and they plowed capital into urban infrastructure. The FIRE industries—finance, insurance, and real estate—became the new frontiers of global trade. They were the triad that drove urban development. These globalizing forces were on the ascendancy throughout the interwar years. If anything, the bond between global capitalism and cities tightened. The reach of mass culture was unrelenting and was shifting urban life even in the farthest places to global forms.[6] Progress and celebration of the new were in the air. Spectator sports, consumer fashions, arresting art deco buildings, and glitzy nightclubs were a display of this deepening global connection.

As global cities, Bombay, London, and Shanghai had ties as close to distant shores as those to their hinterlands. They resembled one another more than they represented their individual countries. All this makes clear that the structure and spaces of global cities and contemporary globalization had a longer, more continual lineage than previously understood. This book helps fill in that past and complicates that temporality. It evidences the intricate overlaps between imperialism and globalization. In looking back over Shanghai's past, historian Jeffrey Wasserstrom signaled that "globalization is a process with a history." It is varied and uneven, shaped through junctures and disjunctures. In his recent study of the tea trade between China and India, historian Andrew Liu has also pointed to the need for "a more global conception of capitalism's history as a whole."[7] The present text argues that global cities were wrought in these dynamic ebbs and flows along with the expansive exchanges that took place across the twentieth century. The Second World War altered these globalizing processes. Postwar reconstruction and the Bretton Woods agreements on trade and capital flows made in the war's aftermath further shifted the global landscape, as did the neoliberal era of the late twentieth century.

It is not that Bombay, London, and Shanghai experienced smooth sailing. The idea of any "return to normalcy" after the First World War was nothing more than a pipe dream. The world economy gyrated like a spindle. Capitalism is by its nature turbulent, and world cities suffered economic convulsions with particular intensity. There was a "good times" boom immediately after the First World War, then a slump, and afterward a recovery in the Roaring Twenties. The value of money soared and plunged like a kite. There was a return to the gold standard, a silver crisis, then an abandonment of gold. The uncertainty and risk of global financial markets seeped into the fabric of urban life. Then the Great Depression reared its ugly head in 1929. World traders struggled with a glut of goods, falling prices, and fierce competition for markets. World trade declined; unemployment soared. Then the global economy picked up again by the mid-1930s, only to face the outbreak of the Second World War. Beyond this economic volatility were colonial expansions and contractions, vengeful civil wars and revolutions.

These last in particular drove major transformations in the global fabric. Global systems are, after all, dynamic historical processes. They undergo continuous change. When the armistice celebrations took place at the war's end in November 1918, the British Empire was still the pivot around which the global economy spun. London enjoyed extraordinary privileges as the capital of a vast territory. The empire stretched across a landmass of twelve million square miles populated by four hundred million people, reaching its geographical zenith as late as 1937. As a trade bloc, it was unassailable. The avalanche of British foreign investment capital was astonishing in scale, not just in its colonies but also in areas such as China outside its imperial domain. Funding across the globe by British banks continued right up until the Second World War.[8]

The book examines the urban bonds between Bombay, London, and Shanghai during these last fulcrum years of the British Empire. The British imperium was built on coal and cotton textiles—two stalwart commodities so instrumental to Britain's rise to global power but in decline by the interwar years. They were resistant to change, and Britain felt the impact. This was especially the case in the 1930s, when trading blocs offered a way out of the frenzied competition for global markets and Britain increasingly counted on the Commonwealth countries for stability. Britain's wealth became dependent on trade with its empire precisely when it faced a swell of voices for independence. London was increasingly influenced by and reliant on its colonies, especially India. It was no longer the maker of the world. It was also the moment when the imperial capital was relinquishing its role as primate city to New York.

For their part, Bombay and Shanghai were no longer simply colonial peripheries, nor were they just imperial or treaty ports. They were shifting into primate cities in their own right: tormented by the struggle for independence, yet massively inventive of urban modernity. Business networks across Asia had long circulated peoples and goods across the seas, even if they were doing so within the vectors of the British Empire by the 1920s and 1930s. In fact, trade within Asia was growing significantly faster than between Asia and the West. With their burgeoning commercial capital and "golden age" economies,[9] Bombay and Shanghai were increasingly assertive on the world stage. With the weakening of colonialism after the First World War, maritime trade routes no longer began and ended in London and the other European port cities. The cities of East and Southeast Asia were coming into their own as major hubs in an intricate web of waterborne global interaction, an account that has often been neglected in historical study. They were competing fiercely with one another for global markets. These connections between Bombay and Shanghai were transformative. The two cities attained modern global status, with a growing exchange between themselves (and other places) that belied the imperial capital.

This book explores the material foundations of urban society in Bombay, London, and Shanghai from the vantage point of this connectivity. The circuits between the three cities are something of a positioning device that allows us to examine the multifaceted connections, the layered processes of globalization and their interaction with the local. Historians have variously labeled cities at these critical junctures of globalization as global gateways and hubs or as at the nexus of empire. The term *portals of globalization* has recently been suggested as encapsulating the circulation of goods, ideas, peoples, and cultural transfers at specific sites on the world map. These currents overlapped, mutated, and competed at various levels and were framed by concrete historical actors.[10] I use the term *helm* interchangeably with this vocabulary. It denotes the commanding position of London, Shanghai, and Bombay in the global systems of the interwar years. Most important, this confluence of global influences made them not just hubs or junctures in a world network but vitally innovative centers of urban life. Thus, the term *helm* is meant to be expansive and to suggest the leading edge of urban transformation beyond commerce and trade to social and cultural dimensions and to the physical fabric of the city. Or perhaps better said, it places global "commerce and trade" directly into this wide-ranging urban milieu. At this critical moment of the 1920s and 1930s, the three cities were at the forefront of mass society and cultural invention, of social upheaval, of pioneering urban form and space. Bombay, London, and Shanghai were complex places in the collective imagination. They were agents of modernity in all its facets. They evoked empire and colonialism, the exotic East, the extremes of wealth and poverty. The contradictions, adaptations, and resistances in these complex urban places were razor sharp. The three cities were places of excess, of the mesmerizing forces of urbanity in all their spectacle and drama.

I use the figure of Sir Victor Sassoon (1881–1961) to weave the narrative of the three cities together. His life provides something of a plot to the story. The Sassoon family was among the wealthiest dynasties of the modern era. Part of an elite Jewish trading diaspora, the family fortune was made in opium, shipping, and the Bombay cotton mills.[11] As the heir to this fabled legacy, Victor Sassoon oversaw the far-flung Sassoon industrial and commercial enterprises and turned them into a global portfolio of commerce, finance and real estate, and start-up companies. The Sassoon headquarters was in the City of London, where Victor Sassoon managed his global investments. He moved to Bombay to manage the family's holdings and became one of that city's wealthiest and most influential business magnates. By the 1930s, he had shifted his fortune to Shanghai and transformed the city's International Settlement with a series of luxury hotels and apartment buildings that are still celebrated landmarks. He traveled worldwide, mixing his extensive business dealings in the three cities with the company of mid-twentieth-century glitterati, from tycoons and gangsters to Hollywood stars.

Tracing the Histories of Bombay, London, and Shanghai

Bombay, London, and Shanghai have storied pasts that have been authoritatively chronicled by scholars. The twentieth-century history of each city has been scrutinized and enriched from a variety of viewpoints. In the case of Bombay, much has been written on the colonial city at the turn of the twentieth century, and then on its new life as Mumbai in the century's later years. Scholarship on Bombay in the 1920s and 1930s generally focuses on the labor struggles in its textile industry, the birth of its celebrated motion picture industry, and its art deco architecture.[12] Scholarship on Shanghai has recently garnered an outpouring of interest that highlights the city's cultural glamour and its freewheeling atmosphere as a global meeting ground in the crazy years of the Roaring Twenties and the Chinese Republic.[13] As the imperial capital, mid-twentieth-century London has been treated through a host of prisms.[14] This book is not an attempt at a history of each city in one volume, an impossible task. Nor is it a comparative study. It focuses on a relational geography of entanglements across distance. It does not reduce these linkages to the one-way influence of imperial London on the colonial peripheries of Shanghai and Bombay. Instead, it concentrates on the open-ended interconnections between the three cities at a variety of levels—formal and informal, among the social elites and among the downtrodden. The narrative paints the urban texture that resulted from these entanglements and the ways in which the forces of globalization interacted with urban society.[15] This topologic framing matters, because it helps us understand how global capitalism works. It illuminates the urban cultures created by global interaction. It ties each city's cultural and spatial fabric directly to global interchange, to global commerce and finance. It speaks to the global modernities wrought in a moment of astonishing change.

The question at the center of *The Worlds of Victor Sassoon* is how these global forces impacted the three cities. The focus is on urban history. Though structured chronologically and sequentially from Bombay to London and then Shanghai, the chapters tack back and forth between all three places. The narrative begins with a brief historical description of the Sassoon family and the merchant capitalism that tied the three cities together in the nineteenth and early twentieth centuries. Then two chapters recount Victor Sassoon's Bombay in the 1920s and 1930s. Two chapters on London follow, and lastly two chapters on Shanghai. Here, the analysis also touches on Hong Kong, because it is impossible to understand Shanghai and the global circuits coursing through China without it. London is sandwiched in the middle of this narrative, because as imperial capital it played the most powerful role in the transmission of commercial information and resources across the British Empire and especially through Bombay and Shanghai. Its combination of financial power, entrepreneurialism, and cognitive capital was at the heart of global capitalism and its relationship to cities. And it was to London that Victor Sassoon went to transfer his wealth from Bombay to Shanghai, and ultimately across the globe.

The precise nature of these banking and financial transactions between the "Heart of Empire" in the City of London and places such as Bombay and Shanghai have not been considered in urban history. In general, urban economic culture in the mid-twentieth century has long suffered forfeit by scholars. This book attempts to fill that gap. Its lens is focused squarely on the global transactions in goods, bullion, finance and banking, and real estate. In the process, we see the workings of globalization at the ground level by the people who shaped it and the impact on urban life. By the end of the interwar period, we find Victor Sassoon in New York. It was evidence that the torch was passing. London was relinquishing its premier role in the struggle for global supremacy to the upstart across the Atlantic.

Taken together, the book forms an interpretative history of global urbanity in the 1920s and 1930s from the vantage point of three cities through which so many influences passed. It follows the flow of people, trade and capital, and cultural practices. Bombay, London, and Shanghai were cities of immigrants, of sojourners who stayed for a while or a lifetime. The age of steam-powered ships in the interwar years was the age of mass migration on a truly global scale. Millions of people were on the move, shuffled and reshuffled in the breakdown of empire and the redrawing of geopolitical maps after the First World War. The scale of this transoceanic migration was astonishing. They were refugees fleeing local conflict and ethnic violence. They were hundreds of thousands of free and bound laborers shipped across oceans. They were border-crossers, lost souls, war veterans, work hands and the skilled, people forging new identities. They clobbered their way through travel documents and inspection stations, or they went to places where none of that mattered and so they simply slipped into town.

In the early 1920s, global migration involved some 3.5 million people each year packing their belongings and moving elsewhere. This was the case even when restrictive laws and economic crisis depressed older immigration traffic in the West. Millions of Chinese and Indians still swept across Southeast Asia and the Far East in the 1920s, a preponderance of them through the gateways of Bombay and Shanghai. These diasporas and labor migrations that continued well into the 1930s kept the numbers of immigrants into the millions despite the Depression.[16] This "human face of global mobility"[17] was partly explained by colonial empire but just as much by the rapidly expanding global economy. Bombay, London, and Shanghai were crucibles for these tides of humanity, which explains their massive population growth. They articulated a geography of circulation that wove urban life deeply into the global fold. They were dream cities where somehow aspirations could come true. You could see and feel this diversity on the surface of each city, in its streets and daily life.

Bombay, London, and Shanghai were major world ports. A globalized world was only possible because of waterborne transportation, and all three cities had wide-ranging positions in the maritime world economy. The rise of British shipping from the mid-nineteenth century onward was an extraordinary globalizing force. The opening of the Suez Canal in 1869 was both a potent symbol and the basis of the new global connectivity. It cut the journey between London and Southeast Asia and the Far East by months. With the advent of the steamship with its screw propeller and iron hull, shipping lines began to operate not just regionally but worldwide. Passenger shipping reached a global peak in the interwar years. The steamers did a roaring business in transoceanic travelers, their holds packed with cargo. The cost of long-distance freight carriage was only a third of what it had been before the First World War. Global supply chains were increasingly concentrated along major maritime trunk routes from one large-scale port to another. This made London the primary imperial market, with Bombay and Calcutta in South Asia, as well as Shanghai and Hong Kong in the East, pivotal junctures for commerce and trade, giving them extraordinary prominence as global gateways. Shanghai became one of Asia's principal financial and trading centers. Its maritime economy boomed even in dark times. Historically, Bombay was the most important commercial gateway for Arabian Sea traffic. Once the Suez Canal was opened, India became the pivot of British commercial traffic in

Asia, with Bombay the premier gateway to the vast Asian market for British goods.

During the age of steam, ports were the heart of the city and its everyday life. The harbors teeming with huge steamers and a myriad of vessels were deeply rooted urban spaces and one of the foremost urban spectacles. The arrivals and departures of the cruise ships were grand occasions reported in the press. Harbors were living and working environments for diasporic communities, for the urban poor as well as for the better off. Dockworkers were among the most evident of urban classes. There was a visible coherence to this urban fabric of dock areas, whether it was Bombay or Shanghai, London or Liverpool, Hong Kong or San Francisco.[18] There were warehouses, foreign banks and stock exchanges, shipping companies and mercantile offices. These infrastructures and communication technologies tied to port commerce were integral not only to the spaces of the city but also to the built fabric, and to material and social structures. In particular, the spaces of finance and commercial exchange—that is, the banks and stock exchanges, the business headquarters, the insurance companies essential to commerce and the movement of capital—have largely been overlooked in urban history. *The Worlds of Victor Sassoon* explores these indelible ties between ports, these financial institutions, and city life, and how they reflect the intimate bond between urbanization and globalization.

Global cities were the sites of spectacular accumulation. As pivots in the global economy, they were the foci of international capital flows. Money poured in. Land and the built environment in Bombay, London, and Shanghai became intensely commodified. As David Harvey has explained, pouring surplus capital and labor into real estate and vast infrastructure projects stretches back to the modernization of cities in the nineteenth century.[19] What had changed by the interwar years was the global scale at which this took place and how it reconfigured urban space and architecture. Urban property and the built fabric constituted a speculative market tied to the mobilization of capital from all corners of the world. This was where urban development and global finance intersected. Financialization and reinvestment in real estate and infrastructure became particularly attractive as opportunities in trade and production declined during the Depression. Building booms were a fabulously profitable business that made millionaires. Art deco trophy buildings and grand development projects from Bombay's Back Bay and Ballard Estate to Shanghai's Bund signaled the power of this global finance. The aesthetic exuberance of art deco captured the privileged affluence, the spirit of excitement, and the new. It made cities into lavish beacons of modernity and celebrated a contemporary public culture unique to Jazz Age global cities in the interwar years.

At the apex of global business was a capitalist oligarchy that flouted borders and pulled the levers of international finance. This book brings to light the overlooked members of this group who manipulated global finance within a lush cultural economy. Displays of status and hierarchy, as well as racial exclusion, were always central to the imperial global economy. And it can certainly be argued that elites at these altitudes had few personal ties or political accountability to any particular urban place. They reveled in a sophisticated internationalism — yet they clearly functioned within explicit urban milieus. What distinguished the interwar years was the flowering of mass culture and the cult of celebrity. In all three cities under study, capitalist oligarchs played at the summit of urban society and indulged in the zany eccentricities of the Jazz Age — the costume parties, the nightclubs and grand hotels, and the horse-racing scene. This was the height of glamour. They capitalized on the mass press and curated their public images with the precision of media stars. The "Who," as English journalist Malcolm Muggeridge called them, survived well into the Thirties even when the tone of urban life was changing.[20]

The Worlds of Victor Sassoon investigates the cultural dimensions of their lives as the nexus between global wealth and mass culture. Culture is an elusive topic, but one essential to understanding the habits, the rituals, and the praxes that underlay trade and commerce of the interwar period. Global business operated across a wide spectrum of formal and informal alliances and associations. Unwritten rules and assumed cultural practices girdled the identity of globe-trotting bankers and financiers.[21] Some conduct was inherited from colonialism; other aspects were built on the diasporic cosmopolitanism of global business. There was a seamlessness to the flow between company offices, clubs and restaurants, the charity circuit. This latticework of relationships was essential to global business operations. It fused business into leisure society and media culture, especially the mass press. The pages that follow excavate this cultural cartography, the role it played in local urban society and its ties to the global economy.

The 1920s and 1930s produced a storm of cultural innovation in Bombay, London, and Shanghai that we associate with twentieth-century modernity. The three cities were "switching points" in the global circuits of ideas, people, and cultures and generated immense surplus value within the cultural logic of global capitalism. They were extraordinarily cosmopolitan places, cities of illusions and myths. The new technologies of communication and newspapers, music and motion pictures shaped the possibilities of both individual and collective agency. They brought the latest news from distant corners of the globe and shaped new modes of living. There was a consciousness of living in an integrated world, something legible on the city streets in a variety of forms that interacted with local circumstance. In this sense, I treat globalization not just from an economic point of view but as a regime of social and cultural practices. This approach allows us to examine the distinctive cultural forms that globalization took.

While the cultural glamour of Shanghai in the Twenties is well known, its relationship to global finance and the city's speculative urban development has not been well explored. This is also the case for London, and even more so for Bombay in the interwar years. The salaried masses—the white-collar and office workers who toiled away in banks and insurance companies as well as in corporate headquarters in all three cities—were knotted together by globalization. They represented an entirely new class of worker,[22] a new kind of self-consciously modern "middle class." Historian Su Lin Lewis has written that the 1920s and 1930s were a landmark moment for the formation of an outward-looking middle class in Asia's port cities.[23] We see these same processes in Bombay as well as in London. The jobs of its members involved the new technologies of communication and a new speed of information and global connectivity. Not only were their duties in tune with the rhythms of global trade. They, too, were urbane, and enthusiastic about the latest international styles of consumption, fashion, film, and leisure. A shared middle-class idiom crossed oceans and territorial boundaries. It was a cultural web spun largely by market capitalism. Modern city life in the crazy years of the Roaring Twenties and even the Thirties meant jazz clubs and wild costume parties. While the nightclubs and jazz scenes in London and Shanghai have garnered a great deal of interest, that scene in Bombay is only now being studied. Stylish young men and women imbibed the latest crazes. They filled luxurious movie theaters, prowled through department stores stocked with consumer fads, and fixated on the doings of the rich and famous reported in the tabloids. The Twenties and Thirties meant newspapers, radios, and newsreels, the sound of airplanes overhead, and a day at the racetrack.

Bombay, London, and Shanghai evoked the rise of leisure society. Spectator sports and flashy amusement parks were mass entertainments enjoyed by hundreds of thousands of thrill seekers. People mingling in crowds with others from all walks of life, of different ethnicities and cultures, made these sites into tableaux of common identity and experience. Such mass cultural events of the age have not been given their full due in scholarship. Horse racing was an engrained part of this world, though it is not a leisure pursuit normally associated with city life. But in the 1920s and 1930s, the turf was a massively popular spectator sport and a supreme urban spectacle. It was the haunt of the privileged and the zenith of mass entertainment. In Bombay and Shanghai, the racetracks were prime real estate smack in the middle of the city. In Britain, they were the first suburban forms of mass spectator sport. In both cases, the races were one of the most important arenas for collective urban life and a sign of a shared cosmopolitanism. They brought together people of all social strata in a carnivalesque setting and played a significant role in collapsing distinctions between high and low culture. Horse racing was also one of the first spectator sports to be heavily mediatized and shared by millions of enthusiastic fans in newspapers and over the radio. Hence, it is one of the key prisms through which to view the materiality and cultural power, and the social complexities, that framed urban experience.

Global interconnectedness was deeply embedded in the urban tissue of each city, touching nearly every aspect of life. Yet the contradictions of globalization made Bombay, London, and Shanghai into landscapes of both extraordinary ethnic diversity and intense racial and ethnic rivalries and social inequalities. The consequent tensions between escalating global interconnectedness and the volatile social relations brought about by sweeping change marked the interwar years.[24] This book highlights these societal dimensions and the disparities of the era. The newly arrived along with the homegrown suffered the irony that these urban worlds were both inclusive and exclusionary. Extremes of flamboyant wealth and crushing poverty were on full view. "Love, life, and laughter: poverty, wealth, starvation and despair, all mixed up together," author Harry Greenwall wrote of Shanghai. He could easily be describing Bombay and London, or any of the other world cities he observed and wrote about in the interwar years.[25]

The splendors of the city existed alongside the poverty on which its wealth was based. Bombay, London, and Shanghai concentrated and illuminated the growing discrepancies in wealth and power, and the social frictions underlying global capitalism. The migratory waves floating through these cities made up a diverse and fluctuating workforce. They existed in dynamic relation to the global economy, taking jobs at the ports and the shipyards and toiling in a host of industries and services, from finance to food markets, the sex trade to taxi driving, and everything in between. Throngs of laborers hired themselves out for the day or the week, for however long they could get paid. Conditions were often brutal in the cotton mills and factories as well as along the waterfront. Whole districts of floating peoples and the dispossessed emerged in these three cities. Millions lived in obscurity and endured extreme social stratification along class and ethnic lines. Many were nomads drifting in and out of these urban areas with the seasons or to escape economic crises. They formed a global network of their own in search of work. Their migratory flows shaped their own cosmopolitan existence in the underbelly of Bombay, London, and Shanghai. The banished areas in which they lived were far from the glamorous districts in terms of not only space but also ethnicity, language, faith, hardship, and circumstance. The social tensions were born of tradition, of colonial policy, and of the inequities of international capitalism.

Confrontations between labor and capital erupted in many parts of the world. But the struggle was particularly intense in these crossroad cities. Bombay, London, and Shanghai were fields of intervention for actors and practices at both the highest and the lowest levels.[26] Wealthy global elites on the one hand and the marginalized and poor on the other made the three cities into strategic sites of collective action and social ferment. Underground revolutionary networks spread out across the globe and found willing listeners among the downtrodden. Strikes and riots permeated the everyday worlds of all three places.[27] Marginalized groups made claims to urban spaces and resources and influenced the success or failure of key industries. There were winners and losers in these globalizing processes. Bombay and Shanghai shared a violent and unstable history. They revealed the sharp contradictions, the contested versions of globalization and modernity. In all three cities, these visible paradoxes and contradictions formed the spectacularity of the urban whirlwind, making them the best places to trace the relationship between city life and the forces of globalization.

On the Trail of Victor Sassoon

The figure of business tycoon Victor Sassoon (1881–1961) is the wayfinder through this wide-ranging global urban geography. He was one of the most powerful figures of the mid-twentieth century. My purpose in weaving his portrait into the narrative is multifold. Tracing his trajectories across the world suggests the magnitude of the connections between Bombay, London, and Shanghai. It grounds the history of cities and their global connectivity in both specific places and specific individuals. The diffusion of business elites, their material assets, and the urban cultures they wove together in the three cities are an essential part of this investigation. Imperialism involved control over the global economy by monopolistic companies and their entrepreneurial magnates. Wealthy moguls turned the wheels of commerce and flaunted their influence at the heights of urban society. Hence Victor Sassoon's deal-making offers a view on colonial urbanity coupled with global trade and finance.

FIGURE 1. *From left:* Lili Damita, Mrs. Peabody, Sir Victor Sassoon, Contessa de Frasso, Marlene Dietrich. Sir Ellice Victor Elias Sassoon Papers. (DeGolyer Library, Southern Methodist University, Dallas)

We can feel the pulse of this world in Sassoon's meticulously kept diaries, his letters, and the articles about his doings in social rags and newspapers. He was a "carrier of capital" and at the center of a global cosmopolitanism that controlled extraordinary material and cultural resources. The values and expectations, even the language and dress of globalism were mediated by the individuals who controlled the banks and trading companies stretched across the world. This book "follows Sassoon's money" in order to understand the role of financialization and how banking and currency markets were turned into real estate speculation. It traces how these global financial transactions impacted both the economic and the social realities of ordinary people. This investigation fills in the gaps in scholarship on the history of urban economics and the determining influence it had on city growth and character.

Scholars have long attended to the impact of production in the city, especially industrialization and deindustrialization. And indeed, the Sassoon cotton mills are an important part of this book. But the link between urban history and economic history has generally been weak. Trade and finance have been given little attention by urban historians. In the same sense, private real estate is foundational to the development of modern cities. But built spaces as artifacts of global operations are largely without history.[28] In the same sense, although information is understood as a vital aspect of globalization, the technology and infrastructure of global communication have not been treated at the urban scale. Examining Victor Sassoon's industrial, financial, and real estate enterprises in Bombay, London, and Shanghai as a case study offers the opportunity to bring all these aspects into the fold of urban history.

The book also offers a look into the wealth and power of global dynasties such as the Sassoons with origins in India and the Far East. It expands our understanding of how the strategies and portfolios of these non-Western magnates shaped global capitalism. It offers a lens on how global business was conducted in the cosmopolitan cities of the interwar years, and how it shaped the urban fabric. Following Victor Sassoon's flamboyant escapades and feats on the social scene illuminates the cultural spectacle that filtered through the three cities in the Jazz Age. His battles over trade and currency policy provide clear-cut forays into global commerce under British dominion. His response to labor conflicts and strikes in the Sassoon mills and to the violent struggles in Shanghai offer insight into the searing social disparities that plagued these cities. Thus, the global forces that shaped urbanity in the 1920s and 1930s and linked London, Shanghai, and Bombay together in a global metropolitan panorama will be highlighted in the pages that follow.

☀ 1 ☀
The Fortunes of Empire

> I am now convinced that occult powers, *Kings of the World*, exist.
> JEAN COCTEAU, *My Journey round the World* (1958)

In the summer of 1936, the luxury ocean liner the SS *President Coolidge* set sail from Shanghai to San Francisco. It was the largest passenger ship yet built in the United States—a floating resort for holiday makers and the rich and famous seeking adventure in the Far East. The ship was spectacular and one of the fastest vessels on the high seas. While its mighty engines danced the great hull across the water, passengers meandered among its nine luxurious decks. They amused themselves with fine dining and dancing, dips in the swimming pools, the comforts of lavish staterooms. Leaning over the ship's railings, voyagers relished the windswept skies and salt air of the Pacific. The crises engulfing China and the drumbeat of news about political turmoil in Europe seemed far away. The sea and the reveries aboard ship lulled passengers into an occasion free of care.

On board were the glitterati of Hollywood's golden age—Charlie Chaplin and Paulette Goddard. They were international celebrities, loved by millions. The film *Modern Times* had just been released, with Chaplin as the adored Little Tramp and Goddard as the ingenue. Enjoying the sun from their deck chairs, the superstar couple smiled into cameras for some good-natured picture-taking. French creative force Jean Cocteau was also aboard the *President Coolidge* reporting on his round-the-world cruise for the *Paris-Soir* newspaper. Upon realizing who was sharing his journey, he was flabbergasted: "Charlie Chaplin is on board. It is a staggering piece of news.... I was meeting a myth in flesh and blood."[1]

Cocteau was a keen observer of the human condition. There was another figure who caught his eye and moved his pen: "After the figure of Charlie Chaplin, whom I put apart, that of Victor Sassoon stands out in high relief against the panorama of our voyage." Tall, stately, sporting his signature monocle and cane, he seemed a vision from another era. "His considerable personality ... seems animated by some spirit of vengeance," Cocteau wrote. "He handles the country of China as if it were a Rolls Royce and whose stick points out treasures and whose eye, behind its monocle, deserves something better than the mere notes in a fashionable chronicle.... I am now convinced that occult powers, *Kings of the World*, exist."[2] When the *President Coolidge* made port in San Francisco, the local newspaper reported on Sassoon's arrival, "monocled, quietly dressed in blue coat and gray slacks." He was the "no. 1 capitalist in the Far East, notably in Shanghai, where his firm is all-powerful. Real estate, banking, hotels, shipping—you name the business, Sir Victor is in it."[3]

People did not forget Victor Sassoon, no matter how brief the encounter. He was a legendary figure with a personal magnetism as enormous as his wealth. The Singapore newspapers dubbed him "Asia's Richest European."[4] Meeting him in Shanghai at the Cathay Hotel, an American diplomat reminisced, "I can still see Sir Victor with his monocle and a peculiar limp as if he were weighed down by his millions. But limp or no limp a

FIGURE 2. Aboard the *President Coolidge* from Yokohama to San Francisco, 1936. *Front row:* Geoffrey Rootes, William Rootes, Lady Furness, Paulette Goddard, Charlie Chaplin. *Back row:* Jean Cocteau, Alta Goddard, Victor Sassoon, Walter Lang. Charlie Chaplin Image Archives. (Copyright © Roy Export Co. Ltd)

group of young married ladies buzzed and hummed around him, oozing honey all over his shirtfront."[5] On first meeting him, American journalist Emily Hahn tittered, "I thought him unusually quick and witty, *especially for a businessman.*" Baron Robert Rothschild remembered him as amusing, cynical, keen on the ladies. He was a "rather romantic figure" who resembled an Indian prince with his dark eyes. The limp only increased his charm.[6]

Sassoon was a bon vivant with the money to indulge his every desire. He betrayed none of the self-consciousness of great wealth. He was a paragon of graciousness, of privileged worldliness. He was chiefly remembered for "his talent for pleasure, his passion for the turf, his hearty sexual appetite, his taste for expensive ivories and jade."[7] His many love affairs were grist for the gossip mill. But as Jean Cocteau recognized, Sassoon was more than just a playboy photographed in the fashionable chronicles of the day. He was a shrewd businessman, relentlessly ambitious, and worked with the full weight of his influence to protect Western interests and swell his family's fortune. He was known throughout the British Empire as one of the financial wizards of the age. His business decisions were quickly scooped up in the press. He could be brusque and irritable, determined to follow his own instincts. All told, Victor Sassoon was a creature—a legendary one—of the British Empire's opulence and power. He traveled its byways, wheeling and dealing at the heights of imperialism. Newspapers reported his comings and goings across the globe. Yet ironically, he was a figure that epitomized the twilight of this world. As Cocteau remarked in his reflections on the elegant personage with his monocle and ivory-tipped cane aboard the *President Coolidge*, a mysterious force was "playing poker with the men of the old and new world."[8] It was a game that Victor Sassoon would ultimately lose.

The Sassoon Dynasty

Ellice Victor Elias Sassoon, or Mr. Eve, as he was often known, was the scion of the fabled Sassoon family whose influence stretched across a century and spanned the globe. His life floated on a cloud of entitlement. He was the progeny of entrepreneurial wealth and ingenuity built up over generations. The Sassoons were dubbed the Rothschilds of the East, and their business dealings were in every nook and cranny in India, the Middle East, and China. In the early 1830s, when the family's renowned founder, David Sassoon, first arrived in Bombay, the settlement was just a ramshackle outpost with a collection of around two hundred thousand souls. The city directory contained two hundred European names and only a sprinkling of English overseers and traders. The Sassoons joined the thirty or so Sephardic Jewish families that called themselves "Jewish merchants of Arabia, inhabitants and residents of Bombay."[9]

Commerce was already taking place on an expansive global scale when the Sassoons arrived in Bombay. Arab and Asian merchants had a long-established web of "country trade" in the Indian Ocean and China seas, with port towns acting as entry points in the exchange of spices, gold and silver, jewels and cloth.[10] The sea traders were transnational in outlook and adept at fast-changing markets. The British were latecomers, but their arrival gave traders lucrative new prospects in the money-spinning trade in opium. David Sassoon jumped on the opportunity and set up his first opium godown (warehouse). He launched a shrewd trading triangle, exporting Indian opium and raw cotton to China, then loading silver and tea, silk and porcelain onto his clipper ships in exchange. Then the precious Chinese goods were sent to England for sale. Finished products from Britain, especially Lancashire cotton goods, were then sailed back to Bombay, where the profits swelled the Sassoons' coffers. With a dizzying array of connections in the Middle East, Sassoon soon became a middleman for the East India Company. India was the British entry point to all of Asia. Although the company and its armed forces kept a tight grip on trade, they depended on Bombay's local Parsi and Jewish traders. In exchange, East India Company awarded them with local property, with Sassoon shrewdly gobbling up prime real estate. Eventually, David Sassoon was made a naturalized British citizen, an advantage handed down to his sons and their progeny. He was a fixture on the streets of Kala Ghoda and along Bombay's wharves. His charitable patronage bestowed some of the first important public institutions on the shabby city.

Despite its location, Bombay was not an indigenous Indian city. It was a colonial upstart that lived and breathed through its port and maritime connections. For much of its early history, Bombay under "Bloody John," as the East India Company was caustically known, was little more than a trading entrepôt on a sliver of land in the Arabian Sea. It was the only deepwater harbor on India's west coast. The company turned it into a "factory" and a figurative spearhead into the alien subcontinent. The seven rocky islands that eventually comprised Bombay were separated by marshy swamps, through which the jade-green sea roared daily at high tide. It was only in the eighteenth century that the necklace-like islets were fused with reclaimed land. The clear blue sky, the palm trees, the sweep of the Indian Ocean and Deccan hills, gave Bombay a picturesque air. The basic trappings of British life took shape with whitewashed bungalows and paved streets huddled around Fort George and the docks.

Beyond were ramshackle wooden houses interspersed with godowns, bazaars, and street markets; drenching monsoons and fiery infernos regularly swept them away. There were the ever-present threats of plague and cholera, marauding Maratha bands, and the scurrilous behavior of the soldiers and fortune hunters in the East India Company's employ. What sustained Bombay's life were the warehouses, the countinghouses, the bales of opium, raw cotton, silk, and ivory, and the shipyards lining the wharves and quayside. The city was a machine for making money. Maritime trade had built it into a place of some half a million people by 1850. It was a gateway through which a tempest of peoples flowed inland or boarded ships for unknown harbors on the piers at Apollo Bunder. Its rise was meteoric.

The abolition of the East India Company in 1858 threw open the doors to anyone seeking their fortune, and the Sassoons saw their chance. Opium was their treasure trove.[11] The "Milk of Paradise" bound China, India, and England in a vast global trading network. A maze of local agents and go-betweens brokered the transactions. Bombay's piers were heaped with opium and cotton bales, with legal and illicit cargo ready for shipment. The impact of opium on China was devastating: millions became addicted. But opium generated huge trade surpluses for Bombay Parsi and Jewish merchants.[12] The inequities of global capital began early and were endemic. The companies it fostered were instruments of power, money, and faith. It financed businesses, stabilized cash flow, and laundered opium money with extraordinary skill. What distinguished the Sassoon family was the scale of their operations. Known for his unswerving integrity and his shrewd alliances, David Sassoon became the kingpin of a far-flung commercial empire of agents, brokers, shippers, and procurers. His reputation was his greatest asset, that and a web of family connections that spread his influence across the globe. This was how diasporic capitalism was done. Chests of raw opium were carried across the waves on fast-moving clipper ships. On board were the eight sons of David Sassoon. Enmeshed in the family business, they were the intangible resources, the social capital, on which the Sassoons depended. Each of them set out to establish footholds in the treaty ports of the Far East.

The Sassoon base of operations in China was originally Canton and later the rocky island of Hong Kong, which the British acquired in the Treaty of Nanjing (1842) at the end of the Opium Wars. Victoria, as Hong Kong's settlement was known, quickly became a booming colonial entrepôt, with shipping as its lifeblood. Although opium was illegal in China, Hong Kong, as a British territory, was a convenient jumping-off point for smuggling the drug onto the mainland. Makeshift hongs (houses of foreign trade) on the harbor were packed with the contraband. The booty was then dispatched to the tar dens across China by local smugglers as well as by compradors operating as middlemen. There was a volatile, opportunistic profit-grabbing to these dealings. It was a ruthless world filled with intrigue and cruelty, made more treacherous by criminal gangs and pirates. Hong Kong acquired a surly reputation almost as soon as the first British flag had been planted there. But the profit margins were fabulous. The trade in indentured Chinese labor bound for Southeast Asia and the Americas was almost as lucrative as that in opium and probably more criminal. For labor recruiters and people smugglers, Hong Kong was the base to export thousands of men each year while avoiding Chinese immigration restrictions. For some semblance of lawfulness, the British chief magistrate brought in recruits from Bombay's police force along with the red-turbaned, bearded Sikh sepoys who became the archetypal image of Indians in China. Racist stereotypes were threaded through the island's daily life. The sepoys were "red-headed monkeys" to the Chinese. And the British looked down with contempt at the Chinese as uncivilized and barbaric.

The Sassoon hong in Shanghai opened as early as the 1840s, when the city became a treaty port under the stipulations of the Treaty of Nanjing. David Sassoon's second son, Elias David, arrived there to oversee the family's operations. Situated at the mouth of the great Yangtze River, Shanghai was already a bustling regional center, with a commercial camp around its harbor and junk trade. It had a long history of maritime business, traceable back to the tenth century. It was an entrepôt for coastal and maritime shipping, especially for the silk and porcelain produced in the Yangtze River Valley, the cotton textiles, and the silver from China's mines. The city's merchants were joined to the dense trading circuits that coursed through the South China Seas. Shanghai was surrounded by a centuries-old defensive wall conformed to the bend in the Huangpu River, a major tributary of the Yangtze. Its warren of narrow streets was lined with one- and two-story wooden buildings, shrines, and temples. Its wharves were piled high with bales of silk and cotton, paper and tea, and tobacco from China's heartland. This trade was what the Sassoons and other foreign merchants were after, particularly once the Yangtze and Huangpu river systems were opened to steamers.[13] And they had plenty of opium to trade for it. Massive amounts were imported from India to China. The fortunes to be made were dazzling.

The fledgling community of "outer barbarians" was small. In 1843, when foreign trade opened at the port, there were only twenty-five foreigners in Shanghai.[14] The muddy flats along the Huangpu tributary were laid out as settlement plots. The British grabbed an area north of the city walls;

its consulate was one of the first foreign buildings to go up. An informal American settlement was established in Hongkou across Suzhou Creek, a branch of the Huangpu that threaded through Shanghai. The city's first English-language newspaper, the *North China Herald*, rolled off its first edition in 1850. A foreign-controlled Imperial Maritime Customs collected import duties on trade that already surpassed Canton's. Governance over this expanding International Settlement took shape in the form of the Shanghai Municipal Council. The French established their own territorial concession. The Japanese won the same rights as the treaty powers and established themselves in the Hongkou district. Even by the end of the nineteenth century, the number of foreigners still had only reached into the thousands. On the other hand, Chinese escaping political upheavals in the countryside flooded into Shanghai. They settled in the districts haphazardly taking shape under foreign rule. By 1910, the city's population had exploded to half a million people.[15] All the while, the walled Chinese city remained under the nominal control of the Qing government. These fractured divisions kept Shanghai in continual flux. The city was guided more by informal commercial networks and overlapping jurisdictional and diplomatic interests that allowed foreign interests extraordinary independence.

When the American Civil War interrupted the flow of cotton to the Lancashire textile mills in England, David Sassoon swooped into the breach. He expanded his business in Bombay to include exporting Indian cotton and manufacturing cotton yarn to send abroad. It was exactly this kind of flexibility and capacity for innovation that marked members of Bombay's entrepreneurial community. They were aided by surprisingly unimpeded business dealings in their city between Europeans, Jews, Parsis, and Indians.[16] This willingness to bridge the strict racial barriers of the British Empire gave Bombay a remarkable edge in its global reach. Sassoon established seven cotton mills, a woolen mill, and a petroleum enterprise there.[17] Bales of cotton and cotton yarn were stacked up on Bombay's wharves and then loaded onto steamships bound for the insatiable Lancashire looms as well as to the mills in Shanghai and in Yokohama.

It was this market in cotton that became central to the unfolding of global capitalism and modernity in Bombay. The city's explosive growth can be traced to these Civil War years.[18] Demand exploded. Cotton replaced opium as the city's main export and linked it to entirely new global markets. Bombay's merchants and mill owners were awash in cash and indulged in a frenzy of speculative investment. Although the good times of the cotton boom were followed by a staggering crash, the Sassoons weathered the storm. They avoided the bust by investing in mills that could compete with Lancashire's cotton yarn and fabrics. Sassoon company offices were established in Manchester, Liverpool, and London. Even the outbreak of bubonic plague in Bombay in 1897 and the epidemics of cholera and malaria that followed did little to diminish the Sassoon enterprises. The huge Sassoon mills kept churning. What gave them such resilience was their international banking arm,—leverage that few mill owners in Bombay had. Money stuck to the family's hands. Their financial resources were enormous.

Banking in the East

Financial institutions were vital to this expansion of global commerce and to an emerging cosmopolitan capital market. Empire and moneymaking were close allies. They feasted on each other. In a British Empire based largely on private enterprise, banking emerged as the connective tissue. The pound sterling circulated throughout the British domains and knotted imperial authority together. But international transactions were still byzantine and treacherous. The "quid" competed with a profusion of local currencies. Traders bought and sold across the world in a parade of different moneys, many of questionable value. Coins and notes from India's princely states, from the coastal towns of Africa, from the ports along the Persian Gulf and Arabian Peninsula, changed hands dozens of times along the trade routes. Their worth fluttered up and down with every passing breeze. Along with them were Ottoman gold coins, copper coins, the Chinese tael, Mexican silver pesos, Indian cowrie shells, and a range of counterfeits. Although it was the most important piece of commercial information, estimating the value of exchange was an act of prestidigitation. Hindu entrepreneurs in Bombay regularly consulted astrologers on what was a bewildering and frankly nightmarish exchange market.

Whether or not a world market actually exists depends, of course, on the commodity. Gold and silver bullion were historically among the cargoes that sped back and forth across the globe earliest, from the mines, to the mints and the production of ingots and coins, to the marketplace. The importance of silver to the global economy has been largely overlooked. However, historian Jürgen Osterhammel argues that the free silver market was "all in all, the chief globalizing factor from the early modern period down to the late nineteenth century."[19] In China and India, the lust for silver lasted well into the interwar years. Both were bottomless pits for silver bullion. In many areas of the non-Western world, the value of the precious metal was the only real constant in economies that lacked any kind of stable currency. Everything was bought and sold according to the silver standard, even though weights and measures differed radically from place to place. Treasure ships loaded with the stuff docked at the wharves of both Bombay and Shanghai. Unskilled laborers, called coolies in local vulgarism, slung the heavy treasure chests up from the holds of Chinese junks and Indian dhows, from European ships, and scurried up and down the gangplanks. Shuttling bullion—the bulk of it silver—across the seas for deposit in each city's countinghouses earned huge profits for the venerable P&O Steam Navigation Company. The voyage was perilous and could take months to complete.

Beyond bullion, credit was the lubricant that made long-distance transactions possible. It allowed goods to be shipped out while merchants waited for the proceeds from their sales. For historian Fernand Braudel, bills of exchange that guaranteed credit were "the chief weapon in the armory of merchant capitalism in the West."[20] But they were unwieldy and time-consuming elsewhere. Chinese credit bills, or *zhuangpiao*, took weeks, sometimes months, to clear. Funneling money for the opium trade became more efficient when the Hong Kong & Shanghai Bank was established by a consortium of British companies in the China trade along with the P&O Steam Navigation Company; members of the Sassoon family regularly sat on its board of directors. The bank occupied an imposing neoclassical building on Queen's Road right next to Hong Kong's City Hall, and the Chinese shrewdly nicknamed it the "Government of Hong Kong." It became the pivotal financial institution for the trade in opium, coolies, silk, tea, and porcelain.[21] Its ledger entries were calculated by abacus and written out in Chinese brush. But the bank proved its merit in introducing a Western business model and widening the veins of money pouring through the system. The new banking apparatus made capital liquid across a vast geography. Indeed, the shuttles of international commerce flew with such speed that they forced the bank to upgrade its branches in both Bombay and Calcutta. New branches in Yokohama, throughout Southeast Asia, and in Australia made the Hong Kong & Shanghai Bank a global powerhouse. It worked hand in hand with the imperial capital of London, where merchants from across the British Empire went to obtain funds and tap into the trove of credit available there. The exchange bills, or "bills on London," as they were known, could be cashed in any world currency. They embodied the working outward of capitalist energies.

The capacity to handle these liquid assets came together in the City of London—the square mile on the north side of the river Thames and the financial heart of the global economy. The London capital market mobilized credit internationally and financed business far beyond the confines of the British Empire. Investors from countries lacking financial institutions of their own had no choice but to channel their funds through London.[22] British-based exchange banks jumped into the fray and became stewards for these global circuits of capital. They quickly rose to positions of immense power and prestige, offering cheap exchange rates, loans and bills of exchange, and a welcome level of reliability. Through them, the global economy could count on an ever-growing supply of money and accepted payments for trade. The banks smoothed foreign transactions and managed the growing bazaar in currency speculation. They were particularly suited to money swaps in India and China, which were not on the gold standard but instead relied on wildly fluctuating silver-backed currencies. The tentacles of the exchange banks spread across the British Empire and into the Far East, growing into a vast casino-like operation for making money on money. The Sassoons saw their opportunity: they set up the Eastern "exchange" Bank Limited in London to finance trade with the East. It was the financial arm of their expanding ventures. With the London office exercising day-to-day control, the new bank gave them a source of wealth and financial leverage that few other companies could muster.

These innovations in global business took place alongside groundbreaking transport infrastructure. The steamship revolutionized ocean carriage. The cost of shipping plummeted. Cities along major oceanic trunk routes—that is, Bombay and Calcutta, Shanghai and Hong Kong—could gain access to Britain's industrial goods at costs not much higher than those in Britain itself. The opening of the Suez Canal in 1869 was a watershed moment that transformed the economic life of China's coastal cities as well as western India. It saved some 30 percent of the travel distance from London to Shanghai and 40 percent from London to Bombay.[23] At the same time, telegraph cables began snaking underwater and overland, transmitting news and market information between these cities in hours. The archaic vastness of global geography and temporality crumpled. Trade between London, Shanghai, and Bombay skyrocketed. The value of foreign trade passing through Shanghai doubled between 1861 and 1894, and by 1911 it doubled again.[24] Bombay became the most important city "east of Suez." Its foreign trade exploded and surpassed that of Calcutta.

The Imperial Raj

Upon David Sassoon's death, the leadership of the family firm passed to his eldest son, Abdullah, whose name was anglicized to Albert. The Sassoons made their fortune by aligning with the "Britishers," or the "Ducks,"[25] as they were known, as the family swaggered through the Middle East and Asia. Bombay's wealthy Baghdadi Jewish community considered themselves "European" and lobbied fiercely to be recognized by the British as white and loyal.[26] They were given British Protected Person status, a privileged Jewish subset of the "pukka sahib," the code for British white superiority in the racism that governed the Raj. They made a killing in the freewheeling atmosphere of Bombay and the advantages of British hegemony. The rewards of loyalty were many—not just riches but also honors and official patronage as well as British citizenship.

Under Albert's leadership, the Sassoons opened a series of machine-driven cotton mills in Bombay that helped revolutionize India's textile industry. Factory innovation depended on the import of machinery from overseas, primarily Lancashire.[27] The mills made Bombay into an industrial dynamo, Asia's Cottonopolis. What supported this boom was its trade with China and Japan, where the cloth industries used coarse Indian yarn. The chimneys of some sixty new mills shot up into the sky in Bombay's mill districts stretching north of the old Fort area at Byculla, Tarwadi, Mazagaon, Parel, Sewri, Mahim, and Worli. The cotton industry diversified from spinning to weaving, dyeing, and printing cloth. Chemical and engineering workshops opened to service the booming textile sector. Bullock carts piled high with cotton yarn and cloth rumbled from the mills down to the port. Bombay's eastern shoreline became a continuous stretch of docks, moorings, and warehouses jammed with cotton goods ready for export.

The Sassoons owned at least six of the most lucrative mills in the city, profiting from the British Empire in a way that few other families could boast. Their success was a matter of their flexibility and skill in branching out into different spheres of business. They took full advantage of the empire's commercial laws that governed a wide swath of the globe. What counted was loyalty to the firm in a "metaphysical extraterritoriality," in the words of economist Karl Polanyi,[28] that allowed companies such as this to range far and wide. The Sassoons cultivated cotton, opium, tea, rubber, cacao, and coconut on plantations in India and Ceylon. They held majority shares in the African mercantile and the British South African companies, where they specialized in exporting native produce. With their wealth and influence secure, their reach spread out beyond the empire to the frontiers of capitalism. Along with sitting on the board of the Hong Kong & Shanghai Bank, the Sassoons held shares in Hong Kong's Oriental Bank and owned the Bank of China and Japan. Moreover, they were instrumental to the British in establishing the Imperial Bank of Persia. These were striking examples of the growing fluidity of capital and credit on a world-straddling scale. Sitting on multiple boards formed a tight, homogeneous group of bankers and financiers with direct access to the

London money market.[29] The Sassoons secured interest in the imperial German banks and were involved in financing the building of the Berlin–Baghdad railway. They invested in Middle Eastern oil reserves as well as in the Turkish Petroleum Company. There was nothing beyond their reach.

Bombay ballooned to a population of eight hundred thousand to become one of the largest cities in the British Empire. It was the heyday of the British Raj and its "jewel in the Crown," India. The empire seemed secure and unshakable, though it depended on a colonial civic culture divided strictly along racial lines. Despite these barriers, Bombay's native *shetias* continued to wield profound authority over urban life. By virtue of their banking and mercantile interests, the city's leading Parsi, Jewish, and Hindu Banian and Bhatia dynasties formed a remarkably tight-knit oligarchy. Some fifty individuals controlled Bombay's entire mill industry and most of its secondary industries, and they were its major property owners.[30] Much of the city's dynamism was due to the entrepreneurial skills of these Indian businessmen and industrialists. Their power and influence were enormous. That distinguished Bombay from Calcutta, where business and capital were owned and operated mainly by British and Scottish traders. In contrast, Bombay's merchant princes were as important as the Raj to the city's development and certainly more decisive in terms of its educational and social infrastructure. The city's barons financed schools and hospitals; orphanages and rest homes; temples, mosques, and synagogues; museums and science institutes.

Bombay was more Westernized than anywhere else in India, and its mill owners were among the most favored allies of the colonial state. There was a clear logic to this collaboration. The British Empire was largely a private-enterprise affair, and Bombay's elites profited handsomely. But even if the city's wealthy merchant princes rubbed shoulders with their colonial overseers, entry into the exclusive world of the British was obsessively restricted. For the British, the stay in Bombay was only a temporary rite of passage. They built their mansions in the Byculla-Parel districts and on the heights of the Malabar and Cumballa Hills. They remained aloof from Indians and viewed them with acid distain. The privileged members of Britain's imperium inhabited an inner circle around the Byculla Club and the Royal Yacht Club, the social summits of British Bombay. Throughout the empire, the club was a stronghold of British formality and status. It was an exclusive place of rich food and excessive drinking in a social performance as rigid as it was segregated. The overweening sense of self-importance and the snobbery were oppressive.

Opulence and squalor existed side by side in Bombay. To virtually every observer, the city's social extremes were shocking. British journalist

Sidney Low commented that the Island City was "a well into which the races of Asia have poured themselves, or, perhaps one should say, a reservoir out of which they pass as fast as they flow in. It is full of the wealth of the East and the wealth of the West, and of the poverty and vice of both. It has its palaces fit for a prince, and its human kennels unfit for a dog."[31] Western visitors were mesmerized by the brightly painted houses, the temples and mosques. They were fascinated by the crowds thronging the "Black Town" north of the Fort area, dressed in a profusion of colors and costumes, saris and turbans, and flowing tunics and hijabs, with craftsmen and hand-loom weavers in their dhotis, naked to the waist. These images were etched into the Western psyche. The pandemonium, the density, and even the squalor were harbored as a romantic sublime that evoked mystery and the uncanny. The streets were a carnival of "wandering minstrels, dancing women, and jugglers and tumblers trying to catch the eye—and the small change—of the traveler . . . coolies and coolie women passing to and from the quays, bearing their burdens on their heads."[32] The British imagined all this as the exotic lands over which they rightly ruled as a superior race. But these scenes were far more the evidence of Bombay's polyglot global culture and extraordinary diversity.

The Sassoons in London

Through it all, the textile mills and the Sassoon family flourished. In 1872, Albert Sassoon was knighted with the baronetcy of Kensington Gore in recognition of his philanthropy and good works in India. Although he remained a passionate patron of Bombay and kept up the family's generous gifts, the siren call of London echoed loudest for him. He moved permanently to England. The family firm of David Sassoon & Sons was headquartered at 12 Leadenhall Street in the City, at the heart of the British financial empire. It was near East India House and the bevy of warehouses, the banks, and the insurance companies through which global trade flowed. The Sassoons became Englishmen of a Jewish persuasion and paragons of British culture and society. They sprang from their countinghouses into the charmed circle of London's fashionable society. There was an ambivalence to this mimicry by a Baghdadi Jewish family by way of Bombay. They splurged on all the trappings of Englishness but were clearly *not quite*.[33]

Although anti-Semitism was embedded in British society, the old strictures of the aristocratic world were breaking down. The "smart set" in Edwardian London granted the cream of non-English society semi-acceptance, from wealthy Americans to prominent Jewish families from the imperial domains. The brilliant figures of the era were not artists or intellectuals but the fabulously rich. Such cultural politics allied to London's global role. At its height as an imperial power,[34] it was the clearinghouse of the world economy. Success in commerce was the entrance fee, and the Prince of Wales (who later became King Edward VII) welcomed gentlemanly capitalists who shared aristocratic values and loyalty to empire. Glamorous displays of wealth by debonair millionaires and the famously beautiful women by their sides eased the entrance into this exclusive world. The leisured lifestyle was considered quite compatible with the control of trade and other people's money. The Sassoons became known for their lavish entertaining and fabulous art collections, even if stabbing anti-Semitic slurs about the "King's Jews" were a common endurance. Invitations to concerts and fancy-dress balls at the family's mansions were a sought-after commodity. The Sassoons reached an apogee in 1889, when the shah of Persia was their guest. It was the perfect moment to secure concessions for the new Imperial Bank of Persia—a prize the Prince of Wales was particularly set on.

Gaiety and frivolity marked the London social whirl, even as the city suffered the searing social inequalities, the scenes of opulence and destitution that observers found so shocking in Bombay. In his survey *Living London*, journalist George Sims promised that "the diamonds of the West will dazzle our eyes; the rags of the East will bring tears to them."[35] The Sassoons were a world away from the Jewish ghetto in Whitechapel and the "Asiatics" in the slums of Limehouse in London's East End. Patrician Anglo-Jews saw the influx of shtetl Jews from eastern Europe as undesirable and so tried to either remake them into Londoners in their own image or disband them from the slums of the East End. Ships from all over the world were berthed at the East End's great Docklands. Among the crates and sacks piled up on the piers were the cotton goods stamped with the Sassoon seal; these arrived on steamers after the twenty-day voyage from Bombay. But the heavy labor on London's wharves was as remote to the Sassoons as that on the quays of Mazagaon, where the wares had been sent off on their voyage.

The Arrival of E. D. Sassoon & Company

In the meantime, in 1867 Albert's younger brother Elias had resigned from the original David Sassoon firm. The picture of a British businessman and a bold merchant in his own right, Elias had pioneered the Sassoon trade in China. His quarrel with Albert gave him the opportunity to set up his own business, known as E. D. Sassoon & Company, with headquarters in Bombay and offices in Hong Kong and Shanghai. Then, under Elias's eldest son, Jacob, the company expanded operations to Manchester, Glasgow, and continental Europe, the Persian Gulf ports, Baghdad, Calcutta, Karachi, and Rangoon. It branched out along the China coast and to Yokohama and Nagasaki in Japan. The E. D. Sassoon firm emerged from its chrysalis as a modern import and export business, sending massive shipments of Indian cotton goods, wheat and oilseeds, and silver and gold ingots to the Far East. It sold its imported Indian textiles to the best stores on Shanghai's Tianjin and Nanjing Roads. Shanghai was by far the most important city for the entry of Western modernity into China. It was globally connected to a much greater extent than any other Chinese city except for Hong Kong. In the twenty years between 1870 and 1893, when the E. D. Sassoon enterprise was taking shape, the number of ships calling at Shanghai doubled to over six thousand each year. The two most important trading partners importing goods to that city were Britain and India.[36]

The flow of money, goods, and information between Shanghai, London, and Bombay increased exponentially. In response, the new E. D. Sassoon company opened palatial offices on Fenchurch Street in London, close to the commodity exchange for spices, teas, and coffee and not far from the Bank of England and the London Stock Exchange. This was the global epicenter of news and information, of the haggling and dealing of business. Fenchurch Street itself had just been widened in the grand manner of the Edwardian years and lined with stately new buildings. These were signs of the City's commercial glamour in its heyday. The atmosphere was hectic and crowded. Some two hundred banks hovered around the Bank of England on Threadneedle Street and greased the wheels of empire with money and credit. Among them was Eastern Bank, which Jacob Sassoon had founded. It functioned as the banking arm of the Sassoon enterprises and was run out of the E. D. Sassoon offices. It signaled the drift of cotton merchants to London and into banking—that is, from the production and trade in goods to financial speculation on the money market. The London office was run first by Jacob Sassoon himself, and then by his younger brother Edward Elias, who was Victor Sassoon's father.

Yet the heart of the Sassoon enterprises remained in Bombay. After returning there from London and his long Eastern travels, Jacob Sassoon oversaw the E. D. Sassoon cotton mills from offices on Rampart Row in the Kala Ghoda district near the port. In what could be described as gentlemanly competition with the original David Sassoon firm, Jacob bought up poorly performing mills and opened new ones, each named for a family member. The E. D. Sassoon mills were the city's largest, employing some fifteen thousand people. They were designed by an English civil engineer and operated by English managers using the newest equipment imported from Lancashire. Crates labeled with the E. D. Sassoon seal piled up at Cotton Green, were hoisted onto steamers, and then sent out across the seas—to London, Shanghai, and Yokohama. The export of cotton yarn to China alone was massive and contributed mightily to Bombay's wealth. The E. D. Sassoon portfolio became the most prosperous arm of the Sassoon realm, outstripping the "old" David Sassoon company. It was easily worth two to three times as much as the original firm. The London banks looked "upon E. D. Sassoon as quite A1. They are very energetic people ... spending very little money.... They possess very considerable property in Hong Kong and other eastern centres."[37] In recognition of their gentlemanly generosity and civic-mindedness, in 1909 the British government bestowed a second baronetcy on the Sassoons, the Seth baronetcy of Bombay. As head of the E. D. Sassoon firm, Jacob Sassoon assumed the new title.

The Scion of the Family

Victor Sassoon was born into the wealth, culture, and privilege of this Jewish dynasty that bathed in the light of the Raj. The family sashayed between Bombay and London, and their business interests in Hong Kong and Shanghai. Victor's father, Edward Elias Sassoon, had married Leontine Lévy, the cultured daughter of a prominent Cairo merchant who worked with the Sassoon enterprises. The couple settled into London society with a fashionable Mayfair address at 46 Grosvenor Place, near Buckingham Palace. The Mayfair and Belgravia neighborhoods were London's citadel of upper-class elegance and self-assurance. Unimpressed by this sophistication, Edward Elias followed in the Sassoon tradition of international trade and finance, leaving the social whirl to his wife. He spent the bulk of his time in the Far East managing the family's mercantile trade. Somewhat predictably, Victor was born in Naples in 1881 while his parents were traveling. His first years were spent in China, where his father built up the E. D. Sassoon branch of the family holdings.

When in 1886 Edward Sassoon moved his family to London so he could oversee the E. D. Sassoon & Company offices on Fenchurch Street, Victor received an English upper-class upbringing and was expensively educated at Harrow School in London and Trinity College at Cambridge. With the affability and confidence that wealth allows, he was a popular student with an appealing worldliness and wry sense of humor. Tall and slender like his father, Victor's assured manner and charm made him a favorite with the ladies. If the Sassoons were initially pious and observant, the younger generation showed far less attachment to the Jewish faith. There was little to distinguish them from Gentiles of their privileged class. Parties and dancing at undergraduate rags, spirited athletics, and rambunctious diversions at Piccadilly Circus and the horse races made Victor a typical gadabout among what the *Daily Express* newspaper described as the "young bloods" of the new age. Historian Stanley Jackson, who chronicled the Sassoon family, remarked of Victor that with "top hat, morning coat and carnation, with his monocle squeezed into a supercilious eye and the inevitable chorus belle on his arm, he looked a typical 'masher.'"[38] He was a Mayfair playboy, a member of a clubby elite who imbibed pampered lives in London, drinking and dancing until dawn, with weekends spent in Brighton. When Victor's lifestyle raised more than a few eyebrows, however, his parents threatened to cut him off. He was expected to conform to the anticipated arc—university, youthful hijinks, and then settling down with a suitable wife from the Anglo-Jewish families and applying himself to business.

To cure him of his rakish habits, Victor was shuttled off to Bombay to work with Jacob Sassoon in the company's flourishing cotton mills. Childless and suffering from increasing blindness, Jacob immediately took to the handsome and debonair nephew who spent too much time playing polo and carousing at the new Taj Mahal Hotel on Apollo Bunder. But the old tycoon saw in Victor's wry intelligence potential for the future. He made him a junior partner in the company—a strapping young prince of a storied dynasty. Victor boarded a steamer for the four-week journey to Shanghai to further his education and learn the mysteries of finance. Under the tutelage of mastermind Silas Hardoon, who managed the Sassoon holdings, he walked the city's commercial alleyways, talked with the veteran shipping hands, and got to know the merchant insiders.

By that time, the Sassoon enterprises in China had projected a thoroughly anglicized self-image. Victor joined the Paper Hunt Club and the high-status Shanghai Race Club. He listened to Silas Hardoon's lessons on business and perused reports at the E. D. Sassoon offices on Renji Road. With a shrewd business sense, Hardoon had worked for the Sassoons in Baghdad and Hong Kong and quickly rose through the company ranks. In Shanghai, he busily swelled the company's coffers through his positions on the municipal councils of both the British Settlement and the French Concession. The Sassoon assets expanded into insurance, breweries, tramways, and real estate. Shanghai's population reached over one million. E. D. Sassoon & Company poured money into the booming city; buildings were going up everywhere.

Hardoon was known as a dealer of *tu*, a Chinese word that meant both "land" and "opium." He was snatching up some of the city's prime real estate on the fashionable thoroughfares of Nanjing Road and the Bund for both the Sassoons and himself, amassing a fortune in the process. By 1921, E. D. Sassoon & Company already owned twenty-nine prime properties, and the Hardoon Company half the buildings on Nanjing Road. Silas Hardoon was reported to be the richest man east of Suez; his forty-acre estate on Bubbling Well Road was the most sumptuous in Shanghai. He became an indispensable ally of Victor Sassoon's, as would Elly Kadoorie, another Baghdadi Jew who had migrated first to Bombay and then to Hong Kong and Shanghai on behalf of the Sassoon enterprises.[39] The Kadoorie clan struck out on their own under the more reputable business name of Kelly—a common practice in the colonial world. They invested in hotels, land, and utilities in Hong Kong and Shanghai. Jewish businessman Edward Ezra owned the city's largest hotels and was chairman of the Shanghai Opium Combine, which was in charge of the import and distribution of the drug into the city. These were the great Jewish families of Shanghai, with their fingers firmly on the city's pulse. But exclusion was still a reality for the Jewish community around the turn of the century, no matter how wealthy. They could acquire the trappings of Britishness, but its substance remained elusive.

Despite the opportunities in the boom city, his stints at the Shanghai Race Club, and his growing passion for Chinese jade and ivory, Victor insisted on returning to his life in London. He exemplified the youthful generation at the turn of the century, the "generation of 1914." The future seemed theirs for the taking. Well educated, well traveled, secure in a British dominion of wealth and privilege, young people of Sassoon's status embraced newness that soon would seem tragically naive. They were high spirited and self-consciously modern, and they indulged in elaborate hoaxes and daring adventures. They reveled in speed and the new technologies of the age—the cinema, telegraph and telephone, fast cars. To his parents' alarm, Victor careened around London in a flashy roadster. He rode at least three of his own horses in the Grand National steeplechase. But it was above all flight that captured his imagination. He enthusiastically followed the exploits of early aviators and their flying machines. Flying was simply one of a number of pursuits he nurtured his entire life—the others being photography, horse racing, and women. Brighton, where the Sassoons had their seaside estates, was a pioneering hub of aviation and the scene of early flying experiments and air races. With his pilot's license in hand by 1911, Victor was a founding member of the Royal Aero Club. He had all the swagger of a top gun. "Daddy" Sassoon and flying ace Otto Astley owned a two-seater Blériot monoplane they flew in air shows, crashing on more than one occasion. Victor was notorious for reckless landings. He launched the club's magazine the *Aeroplane*, one of the first publications of its kind. With cash in hand, he was behind the Universal Aviation Company, which did much to build and popularize flying machines in the early days.

When war was declared in 1914, thirty-three-year-old Victor failed to pass the stiff medical exam for fighter pilots. Bitterly disappointed, he nonetheless joined up and served as a gunner driver and then as a cockpit navigator in the Royal Flying Corps. Posted at Dover, he was among the most popular and genial figures in the aviation world.[40] But the exploits of these daredevils meant constant risk, and a local newspaper noted that a "Jewish strain" was often found in officers of peculiar daring.[41] In February 1915, Victor and squadron commander John Babington's two-seater Avro 50 biplane went into a spin and crashed during a training flight. Babington was hurt, but it was Victor who suffered the worst injuries, with two broken legs and a shattered hip followed by complications from pneumonia. After he was rushed to London, his mangled bones were painfully set and reset. He remained in a cast for eight months at the family home in Grosvenor Place.[42] At thirty-four years old, he was left permanently disabled, yet another casualty of a long ghastly war. The painful injuries could send him into a sudden fugue state and plagued him for the rest of his life. Confined first to a wheelchair and then to walking sticks, Victor pulled some strings and got a desk job at the Admiralty Office for Test Flying, ready to frustratingly sit out the fighting cooped up in a London office pushing paper. He was assigned to the American Air Service Expeditionary Force as an advisor in France and Italy.

Victor's buoyant hopes for the dashing life of a pilot were ruined. He spent the remainder of the war in London, recuperating and adjusting to his disability. As an antidote, he eventually returned to work in Bombay and Shanghai, and to the E.D. Sassoon enterprises. After a long illness, Jacob Sassoon died in 1916, and the company and barony passed to Victor's father. Victor became the heir apparent. He arrived in Bombay at the war's end, amid the terrible influenza pandemic, strikes, and rioting. As head of the mills department and the dye works, he had his first taste of Bombay's explosive work atmosphere. When five thousand mill hands walked off the job, Victor boorishly assuaged them with a cinema show and sweets during the Diwali festival. His empty gesture belied any responsibility for the poverty and work conditions they endured.[43] It marked the beginning of years of his aggravation with labor strikes in the smoky haze of the mills.

As the old patriarch Jacob had predicted, Victor was keenly ambitious and kept his hand on the E. D. Sassoon & Company tiller. To be a Sassoon was to have a talent for business and banking, and serial directorships in the family enterprises were the Sassoon birthright. Victor's flyboy daring was channeled into the company, and his disability made him even more driven to succeed. Teetering on two canes, he began actively managing the E. D. Sassoon far-flung overseas assets. "Within a few months of taking over in Bombay, few challenged his authority or dared go over his head to the London directors."[44] He moved into the Taj Mahal Hotel and made its Sea Lounge overlooking the harbor into his watering hole. He became a member of the Indian Legislative Assembly, representing the mill owners. An enthusiastic supporter of the exclusive Royal West India Turf Club, he was a familiar figure at Bombay's Mahalaxmi Racecourse. He began assembling his racing stable and vied with the fabulously wealthy Aga Khan for ownership of the best horses.

It was a heady time for Victor, with sojourns in London and Shanghai to manage his family's riches. But it was also a time tinged with family tragedy. In 1923, his younger brother Hector died while undergoing surgery in London. Only thirty-four years old, he had been a commercial force in Hong Kong as director of the E. D. Sassoon enterprises in the Far East. Victor inherited his brother's shares in the E. D. Sassoon company as well as his property and assets in both Hong Kong and Bombay. Family spun his destiny. Upon the death of his father in 1924, Captain E. V. Sassoon assumed the Sassoon barony and became Sir Victor. He inherited his father's company shares, his extensive assets in England, and his properties in China, Hong Kong, and India. Huge portions of the Sassoon fortune were protected from British taxes by an elaborate system of trusts managed out of Bombay and Hong Kong. Sir Victor became, along with his widowed Aunt Mozelle, the main beneficiary of the entire Sassoon empire. Mozelle was content as a society hostess in London and left management of the firm to her offspring, Reginald Sassoon. "Reggie" was a charming figure and a daredevil on the racecourse. But he was far more interested in horses than business. Sir Victor was virtually free to take over the Sassoon holdings. He became chairman of E. D. Sassoon & Company and took on the mantle of the Sassoon legacy. With Bombay the stronghold of the company's realm and himself the city's largest mill owner, he boarded a cruise ship for the voyage to India's jewel city.

✳ 2 ✳
Bombay, Wonder of the World

> Bombay is more cosmopolitan than any other city in the world.
> HARRY JAMES GREENWALL, *Storm over India* (1933)

The trumpet call at the outbreak of the First World War in 1914 was met with jubilation in Bombay and expressions of deep loyalty to the Crown. With its location on the west coast of India, the city was firmly in the war zone, and the British prepared to defend it. Its military compound went into high gear. Nighttime blackouts were mandated, news and radio telegrams censored. The General Post Office was turned into British military headquarters. Freighters and passenger ships lined the wharves at Alexandra Dock and the harbors at Middle Ground, ready to transport waiting soldiers to the battlefields in Europe, Palestine and Egypt, and East Africa. The Indian Expeditionary Force D set sail to secure the Shatt-el-Arab and the Anglo-Persian oil fields at Abadan in modern Iran. Crowds assembled on the quaysides to watch the spectacle of flotillas leaving port and disappearing into the haze. Well over a million Indian troops embarked and disembarked on Bombay's docks. The Bombay Presidency, the administrative subdivision of British India, alone contributed some seventy-five thousand recruits from its twenty million people. Thousands of miles of railway track, thousands of locomotives and railcars, vehicles and river craft were sent out from India for the war effort. Hundreds of thousands of Indian laborers assembled on the Bombay piers for passage to Iraq, where they built roads and railways and manned the port at Basra.

Bombay became India's great military distribution and operations center. Over one hundred thousand dockhands worked the moorings from the Fort district to Mazagaon. The quays were heaped with stockpiles of munitions, food, and equipment for the fighting fronts. The factories squeezed into the Tardeo and Tarwadi districts, and the mills in Girangaon whirred day and night. Railway workers shifted to production of shells, grenades, and military vehicles.[1] The dense urban fabric was militarized. Makeshift barracks were set up on the dockyards and in Colaba and Dadar. The Taj Mahal and Watson's Hotels were jammed with military officers. Twelve military hospitals opened, some for European and others for Indian troops. The newly completed Prince of Wales Museum, the Royal Institute of Science, and the Railway Company Office were requisitioned as infirmaries for the wounded and the disabled who had begun to arrive by the hundreds by the end of 1914. Stanley Reed, the long-serving editor of Bombay's *Times of India*, reported that "a dreadful stream of broken men" poured into the city from the failed British battles in Mesopotamia.[2] Hospital ships bobbed up and down on the quaysides.

The War and Relief Fund was established. At rallies at the Town Hall, Bombay's notables whipped up overflowing crowds against the Prussians and called on the citizenry to subscribe to war loans to help pay India's £100 million contribution to the war effort. The city was swollen with refugees fleeing the conflict. They arrived on the quaysides with nothing but the shock of their ordeal. Toward the war's end, repatriated prisoners of war arrived in the confusion, adding to the numbers in desperate need of medical care and assistance. With all these castaways came influenza. Bombay was the epicenter of the gruesome pandemic of 1918, a vast incubator for what was known as Bombay Fever. The number who died in the Bombay Presidency is inestimable, the vast majority lower-caste Hindus and Muslims penned together in the densely packed slums. Well beyond a million lives were lost. Thousands more succumbed to the ever-present plague, to cholera and smallpox.

The war sent tremors through Britain's imperial colossus. It was a watershed in the tangled bond between Britain and India. The Raj had sacrificed as much money, men, and material to the British war effort as all the other dominion colonies put together. Yet despite their wartime loyalty and sacrifice, Indians gained only a modicum of self-rule. The 1919 Government of India Act provided for an Indian legislature made up of elected and appointed members and gave Indians a role in provincial government and local affairs, but it was not enough. The British retained control over the central administration in Delhi and ultimately in London. The Indian people's frustration and impatience for at least autonomy, if not independence, rose into a fierce rallying cry. Though unclear about their own future, also on the minds of India's elites in Bombay were the breakup of the Ottoman Empire and the uncertainty about its territories along the Arabian Sea.

Even so, Britain hung on to the tried-and-true vision of India as its possession. Bombay's siren call and exotic appeal still stirred the hearts of British civil servants stepping off Apollo Bunder for duty to the Crown. It remained one of the great ports of the world and the portal not just to India but to all of Asia. Nonetheless, the wartime hostilities had made traveling to Bombay on the high seas treacherous, especially from Port Said, Egypt, and down the Suez Canal. Ships were weirdly camouflaged, and passengers were forced to wear life vests for fear of submarine attacks. But once out on the Arabian Sea with Bombay surfacing on the horizon, voyagers were captivated by the myriad ship lights twinkling in the harbor. Their accounts were conditioned by imperial fantasies. Stanley Reed reminisced about his arrival to the "crimson glow of the town lights" and "brightly illuminated tall buildings along the harbor side." Bombay could "match anything the most brilliant foreign city could show." Gleaming white minarets and the chimneys of the cotton mills stood out against the sky. Arriving in 1917, Edwin Montagu, the new secretary of state for India, thought the city "one of the wonders of the world and must produce exuberance, enthusiasm, even to the most prosaic nature."[3]

Bombay laid claim to every dream about the East. But the mysteries of the Orient cherished by Westerners masked the many different Bombays juxtaposed across the sliver of land jutting out into the brine. For the thousands toiling on the docks and in the mills, paltry wages put little dent in inflated wartime prices and scarce food. Many were on the edge of destitution. As it always does, war enriched a few and ruined many. A firestorm of troubles hit Bombay in the war's aftermath: a falloff in trade, financial crises, and currency instability. Unending work stoppages and political protests twisted into riots. The turmoil was symptomatic of the general chaos across the globe in the early postwar years. Panic and public uproar in Bombay followed every rumor, every abrupt shift in the political winds.

At the same time, a new middle class was enjoying the opulence and crazy exuberance of the Roaring Twenties. "Bombay is more cosmopolitan than any other city in the world," writer Harry Greenwall reckoned as he stepped off a steamer and confronted the city.[4] It was a hotbed of modernism, of the swinging rhythms of jazz, of movie stars and the silver screen. It was a cosmopolitan whirl in tune with the cultural spirit that was taking the world by storm. The city was a stew of novelty, of boiling grievances, of passionate loyalties that emboldened the calls for Indian independence. From the heights of the Malabar Hills, the British Raj clung to power and its stilted formalities, seemingly deaf to the upheaval around it.

British Bombay

Victor Sassoon recalled stepping off the ship in Bombay and feeling rather nervous about his new role as boss of the Sassoon enterprises. The Sassoons were the largest mill owners in the city in the 1920s, and Victor Sassoon was reaching the summit of his influence. He ruled over thousands of workers running a maze of machinery. Fourteen factories were under the Sassoon umbrella, with 652,000 spindles and 13,500 looms.[5] The mills worked double shifts supplying uniforms for the armies in Mesopotamia, Palestine, and Africa. As the price of cloth rose 300 to 400 percent,[6] the short-term profits were dizzying. War profiteers, speculators, and mill owners, and above all the Sassoons, amassed a fortune. E. D. Sassoon & Company jumped from an old-style family affair managed by Victor's father and two uncles to a joint-stock company controlled by a syndicate and shareholders anxious to "pocket large profits ... for themselves and their friends." The joint-stock company permitted a scale of investment impossible in the traditional world of family banking.[7] There was no end to the voracious riches to be made.

Alongside the massive Sassoon mills were the Currimbhoys' mills that stretched through Girangaon. They along with the Petit family, the Wadias, and the Readymoney and Thackersey families formed an elite circle of powerful mill owners. The wealth and status of these dynasties were long-standing. They were Bombay's royalty. They had reaped every benefit from the Raj and enjoyed close relations with Crown officialdom. Yet it was an alliance fraught with the convolutions of colonialism. Even though their production was outpacing the venerable Lancashire mills in England, Bombay worked in deference to British interests, which left a lingering and bitter taste. But the gains of bowing to the Raj were too good to deny. The native industrial tycoons could practice an exclusive paternalism over the city and control its future. They were members of the Indian Legislative Assembly and the governor's and viceroy's executive councils. They sat on the Bombay Chamber of Commerce. They were trustees for the all-important Port of Bombay. They mingled with the Raj peerage at the heights of colonial society, at least on social occasions with an official flavor. Nevertheless, no matter how powerful they were or how often they shared toasts with British officials, the racial lines were clear cut. Bombay's moguls were still considered a lesser breed below the mandarins of the imperial service. The patience with this attitude wore thin as the calls for independence grew louder.

But the British continued to float through Bombay in a reverie of past glories. On his voyage to India in 1926, British writer Aldous Huxley remarked, "Everybody in the ship menaces us with the prospect of a very 'good time' in India. A good time means going to the races, playing bridge, drinking cocktails, dancing till four in the morning, and talking about nothing."[8] The institution of the club was a compulsion among Bombay's British upper crust. It was a bastion of snobbery and racial exclusivity. In his memoirs, Humphrey Trevelyan, British diplomat and member of the Indian Civil Service, remarked that it was easy to mock the Englishman in India: "His limitations were obvious, his social prejudices stupid." Trevelyan quoted the London music-hall ditty of the day: "'The men who live in Poona would infinitely sooner play single-handed polo, a sort of solo polo, than play a single chukka with a chap who isn't pukka.'"[9]

The stultifying protocols were relentless. At dinner parties, guests were seated around the table according to their rank. Victor Sassoon regularly pasted the seating charts in his diaries, with himself always near the head of the table. Vivian Stevenson-Hamilton recounted the wardrobe requirements as he entered the machinery of the Raj: "a black formal pin-stripe for luncheon parties and a light formal suit for tea parties, then there would be a morning coat and striped trousers with, of course, a grey top hat and also a black top hat.... A most important item would be a white 'Bombay Bowler' [pith helmet] with a single narrow gold stripe" in the turban.[10] Impeccable social behavior was assumed among chaps at the Bombay Yacht Club on Apollo Bunder. No expense was spared on the comforting inertia the British expected of their white supremacy. Yacht Club members schmoozed at the bar. Rumors were passed and alliances struck on the veranda overlooking the harbor. Indian waiters in sashes and livery scurried between the tables, balancing trays of champagne cocktails and hors d'oeuvres. Accounts of the elegant scenes were scooped up in the English-language press.[11] For the masses of people under British rule, these glowing scenes meant they were unhappily governed, their potential thwarted, and their resources squandered.

The Raj squatted in its past. Lord Willingdon, governor of Bombay and exceedingly popular among the Anglo-Indian community, tried to break down the rigid prejudice and streamline relations between British and Indian elites. Unable to entertain Indian maharajas at the Bombay Yacht Club, where the "color bar" was impregnable, he founded the Willingdon Club as an antidote. It was not far from the Haji Ali Dargah Mosque on the Arabian Sea. There, Indian princes invited British peers for tea. Indian women could join the memsahibs and general company. The Willingdon Club was an instance of the gray social boundaries that often operated between colonizer and colonized in Bombay, at least among social elites. As a sign of openness, the Millowners' Association lushed it up at its gala

FIGURE 3. The Taj Mahal Hotel and Gateway of India on Apollo Bunder, Bombay. (Dinodia Photos / Alamy Stock Photo)

dinners at the Willingdon. Sassoon and members of the city's leading families hosted a sumptuous dinner for Lord Willingdon to acknowledge his broad-mindedness. It was a who's who of Bombay society.

The Sassoon family had breached these racial boundaries thanks to their great wealth and their loyalty to British colonial rule. The alliance between Bombay's Jewish merchants and the Raj was venerable, formed by the pragmatism of global trade and the search for fortune. Despite the ingrained racism of British India, Bombay's upper crust did an unusual amount of mingling. Sir Victor was the heir to this legacy and regularly held court at the Bombay Yacht Club and the Taj Mahal Hotel, where he lived the untrammeled life of a bachelor. The Taj was Bombay's grand hotel—a luxurious Indo-Saracen pile towering over Apollo Bunder. Its sheer mass and iconic red onion domes made it an instant landmark for a city anxious to claim its place on the world stage. The grand hotels were in their heyday in the interwar years. They were glamorous cosmopolitan places and civic showcases, urban monuments to wealth and status. Their lobbies buzzed with the chatter of the well dressed, some heading for the boozy lounges. Chitchat took place over whiskies as the talk turned to horse racing and polo. Those who could only peer over the fence at these goings-on heaped scorn on the snobbery and sarcastically labeled the venues "dens of collaborators." Such scenes only proved the general impression that the English were a selfish, venal people, perfectly indifferent to everyone else. In Louis Bromfield's novel *Night in Bombay*, the hero finds himself outside this charmed circle—the only ones who counted, he sniped, "live on Malabar Hill and go to the Yacht Club, the Willingdon Club, the Taj Mahal and the races."[12]

For all the fogyish pomp and ceremony of the British Raj and its tight grip on the city, Bombay was a freewheeling cosmopolitan hub, especially for South Asia. It had a big-city feel, a modern sensibility, and a mix of global wealth and influence. On Grant Road, urban observer O. U. Krishnan reported, "motor cars whizz along at break-neck speed with their loads of the jewelled, the painted, the silkened, the hatted, the ill-gowned and the well gowned."[13] There was a kinetic energy sparked by Bombay's status as a crossroads of cultures. The visit by the king and queen of Afghanistan in 1927 was a spectacular instance. Amanullah Khan and Soraya Tarzi were the Middle East's power couple, known for their progressive ideas. To the shock of some and the delight of others, the queen wore European dress for the public ceremonies, complemented by a purdah veil. She and her husband were hailed with wild enthusiasm at the Gateway of India. Police held back massive crowds greeting them along their ceremonial parade to Government House. Sassoon reported in his diary that the king was foppish and arrogant at the State Banquet in their honor. But seated alongside the queen, Sassoon chatted about her years in Paris and her work on behalf of women's rights and education. It was this mixing at the summit of global society that provided him the influence he assumed was his for the taking.

The power of Sassoon's elite class depended on their manipulation of social and political circumstance. The Prince's Banquet at the Taj Mahal Hotel in 1928 was an extravagant affair for the toffs. Dressed in their finest, maharajahs, rajahs, and nawabs from around the Bombay Presidency shared tables with British officials in starched tuxedos, medals dangling from their chests. An Old World formality and stuffiness distinguished British colonialism well beyond its worth, as if nothing could damage an imperial world so rich and privileged, so unassailable. But this indifference to the eclectic momentum of the city, its flirtation with modernity and its global crosscurrents, meant the twilight of old colonial Bombay.

In possession of the Sassoon barony along with the family trade and banking fortune, Victor Sassoon spread his wings, engaging in a variety of pursuits. Balancing on his ivory-handled cane, he shuttled between Bombay, Shanghai, and London in a particular strain of cosmopolitan nomadism. Such was the world of globe-trotting bankers and financiers.

They were a homogeneous band in education, tastes, lifestyles, and professional careers. Their lives were steeped in exclusiveness and racism. Sir Victor's network of acquaintances branched across the globe. He used it for both personal and business gain. Sitting at the summit of urban society, he slathered his money across a host of good causes in all three cities he inhabited. As the senior member of the Sassoon family, he was head of both Bombay's and Shanghai's Sephardic communities. But his relationship with his Jewish ancestry was ambiguous. He deftly sidestepped religious observances and was just as likely to work with British, Parsee, or even Chinese associates as he was the Jewish families who had always been close partners of the Sassoons. His ideological glue was the highbrow cosmopolitanism born of empire.

People moved across the oceans with increasing ease and regularity. A fleet of P&O Company steamships delivered mail and passengers to every port in the British Empire. The Suez Canal reshaped the sea lanes and collapsed time and space. The imperial capital of London was more accessible. Global hubs such as Bombay and Shanghai seemed near at hand, and their circuits of contact and exchange deepened. The years after the First World War were the great age of the lustrous ocean liners skimming across global waters. Sassoon was a regular first-class passenger. Steaming out from Apollo Bunder, he sailed to the port of Aden, then up the narrow Suez Canal to Port Said. There, barges heaped with coal sallied up to the hulls of the waiting ships. Swarms of coolies hauled baskets full of the black fuel across swaying gangplanks and hurled the contents into the ship bunkers. The well-heeled passengers leaned over the deck railings to watch the spectacle. From there, the ships sailed westward through the Mediterranean with a stop at Marseille, then through the Straits of Gibraltar and on to London.

Sir Victor sailed in extravagant luxury on liners such as the fabled P&O *Viceroy of India*. Outfitted in mahogany, floors swathed in Persian rugs, the ersatz staterooms mimicked the baronial atmosphere of the British club down to their fireplaces. A special locker on board stored a thousand quarts of ice cream in five flavors while the Iron Cow machine produced milk and fresh butter for the voyage. A two-week journey punctuated by feasting, lawn tennis, and swimming in the pool: such was life on the high seas. Sir Victor hobnobbed with the maharaja of Kapurthala and Sayajirao Caekwar III of Baroda. He shared drinks with British bankers Sir Henry Strakosch and Sir Reginald Mant, who along with Sir Cecil Kisch were the "trinity of British finance" in India.[14] The ship was a floating sanctuary for the world's moneymen to get away from it all, sharing gossip and nonchalant conversation about India's currency and its future.

Beyond his conversational virtuosity in business, Victor Sassoon's most passionate topic was horse racing. Horse racing was huge in the years between the wars. The turf was a massively popular spectator sport and one of the foremost urban spectacles. It drew enormous crowds, far more than cricket or football. If betting is included, then horse racing was the supreme sport of the 1920s and 1930s. Indeed, it was racing that sold newspapers across Britain. Horse racing was also one of the first sporting events to be heavily covered on the radio and in newsreels. The enthusiasm for its visual imagery and linguistic zing made it omnipresent in the public sphere.[15] In Britain, the Grand National, the Epsom Derby, and the Royal Ascot drew hundreds of thousands of fans, who strained their necks in the grandstands and lined the railing as the horses thundered past. The races were a celebration of collective urban life. The highest and the lowest in the social pecking order flocked to the track for the thrill of the action, the pomp and pageantry. The gulf between the classes vanished for a moment of shared passion. The mix of people cheek by jowl, the alcohol and gambling, the excitement fizzing through the air as the muzzles thrust across the finish line, made the races into extravaganzas. The sport was quintessentially British and spread to the colonies, where it became the premier event in Bombay, Hong Kong, and Shanghai.

The crowds in the stands could cheer on their favorite steeds, but only the wealthiest could indulge fantasies about ownership. Thoroughbred horses were a privilege of a global oligarchy, and the prestige of possessing the high-strung animals was enormous. The turf promoted the qualities of the gentlemanly class—male bonding, fierceness, the kind of leadership willing to take risks. Sassoon's peacock blue and gold hoop racing colors stretched first across the finish line in a bevy of high-octane contests that made him into a champion international horse breeder. He was snapped by paparazzi at the racetrack and interviewed for newsreels. The races made Sassoon and his clubby set into well-known celebrities in the media. Their public image was of achievement, fascination with their wealth and prestige. Great deference was given to this global cadre and their ceremonial trappings. Dressed in top hat and tails, Sassoon schmoozed over champagne and canapés in the exclusive spectator boxes reserved for blue bloods. The cameras flashed as Sir Victor held the reins of his winning horses. His dazzling colt Hot Night was named one of the outstanding thoroughbreds of 1927 and became a star with a full-page photo in the *Illustrated Sporting and Dramatic News*. The steed received yet another accolade as winner among horses with the "most beautiful heads," and he was an equine idol on the cover of the London *Bystander*.[16]

Sir Victor's name in horse racing became legendary with his lavish spending on his Eve Bloodstock stable in Poona in conjunction with the Royal Western Indian Turf Club. The stable was near the Sassoon villa that had long been an oasis from the stifling heat in Bombay, and where he served his famous curry lunches during the Season. With its private training facility and racetrack, it was state of the art and a major source for Indian thoroughbreds, designed along the lines of the famed thoroughbred center at Newmarket in England. The lavishness of the Poona grounds drew the ire of sermonizers. Sassoon was roundly condemned in the Indian press for his personal indulgences. "We cannot too strongly condemn such an extravagant luxury," the *Bombay Times* raged. "How can one reconcile the cry of the millowners that they are down and out with Sir Victor's ambitious project?" The *Times of India* fumed, "True, the money is private wealth, but it is enough to pay the Bombay mill workers for several months the amount proposed as a reduction in wages. . . . There is enough in the world for rich men to spend money on without indulging in idle vanities and luxurious and extravagant tastes."[17] The searing social inequalities of the British imperium were obvious to all. But it did little to dim Sassoon's infatuation with the horse-racing world.

In 1925, the opening of the Mahalaxmi Racecourse in Bombay was a gala event, with the jet set of the Middle Eastern racing world in attendance. It was immediately rated as the finest racetrack east of the Suez. Its lavish grounds were near the Byculla district and emblematic of Bombay's colonial scenography. The racecourse was part of city life and an urban space loaded with symbolic weight. It was also a hybrid meeting place for British and Indian elites outside the racial strictures of British rule. On display at Mahalaxmi was the long-standing cordiality between English and Indian specific to Bombay.[18] Maharajahs and millionaires, Arab horse dealers, British officials and Bombay high society, watched the parade of dignitaries and mingled in the turf club enclosure. Dressed in high style with champagne flute in hand, they surveyed the horses and jockeys as they sauntered onto the track. There was an aura of triumphalism at Mahalaxmi; it was grand social performance. The double-decker grandstand was jammed with thousands of racing enthusiasts electrified by the thoroughbreds flying down the track. Mr. Eve's Some Surprise streaked across the finish line to take the Kabul Cup. Natty in white suit and fedora, Sassoon collected his trophy from Queen Soraya Tarzi to a rousing ovation by the crowd.

The unveiling of the new Mahalaxmi was an opportunity for elaborate party-going by Bombay's wealthy and well connected, who reveled in the Roaring Twenties hedonism of jazz, raucous drinking, and dancing. At the Advertisement Ball held on the grounds, they turned out to promote the city's industries. Fancy-dress balls were all the rage in the Twenties. The taste for wild costumes found the cream of Bombay society with stylized cigarettes, watches, cameras, and tires decorating their getups. They strutted their stuff amid billboards for Shell Motor Spirits, Wakefield Oil, Rover Cars, and Exide Batteries. It was a fitting revelry for a city dedicated to making money.

Mahalaxmi hosted Bombay's "first Cabaret" the next night, the racecourse transformed into a magic theater of entertainment. The Race Burlesque comedy show written for the event by Victor Sassoon and Major P. C. Saunders kept the audience in stitches. It was the men's star turn and just one of many cabaret shows and costume parties that Sassoon thrived on. He abandoned himself often to the theatrical dandyism shared by the British upper crust in the 1920s. The evening's finale featured a streamer battle with the audience in a "riot of fun."[19] In all, the cabaret night was a zany Roaring Twenties affair for those in the money. The frivolity and stylishness of the era were the privilege of their social standing.

Bombay Byways

Despite Sassoon's jollity, his arrival in Bombay coincided with fierce social clashes there, making his rich-man excesses all the more glaring. Bombay was a space of parallel cities. Its social heights were gilded, but its lowest classes bore that weight. The inequality was staggering, as in global cities in other parts of the world. A massive influx of migrants pushed Bombay's population to well over one million. Floods of desperate people converged on the city. The docks were jammed with those shipping out for back-breaking labor somewhere in the British colonies. Or they searched for jobs in the city's mills and factories. Some 240,000 people depended on the cotton factories for their livelihood. Another 18,000 worked in the railway workshops, 10,000 in the dockyards, and an additional 7 to 10,000 on the docks themselves. Added to this were 9,000 laborers in the building industry.[20] Destitute women fell into the sex trade in the alleyways of Kamathipura. The merriment at Mahalaxmi was a far cry from the thousands of peddlers, street mendicants, and beggars swarming the city's streets. It was this juxtaposition of showy wealth to destitution that marked the global cityscape.

Masses of people found lodging in Bombay's warren of creaking, tenement-like *chawls* and wretched slum districts that threaded through the warehouses and factories of Parel and Worli. High-minded slum clearance projects did little to improve this landscape of survival.[21] *Zavli* sheds made of dried palm and date leaves and pavement dwellings clung along the alleyways. Daily life spilled onto the dirt lanes and narrow gullies. These scenes of poverty were ignored by British officialdom as endemic to India. In a viewpoint filled with snooty absurdities, the British saw their resource-rich jewel colony as a repository of squalor, beggars, and skeletal cows. Sir Frederick Sykes, the governor of Bombay, took the obligatory tour of the chawls upon his arrival in the city. He found that "nearly all the families were living in one-room tenements.... Here father, mother, and children, and one or more relatives lived, slept, dressed, and cooked their food, surrounded by chickens, goats, and dogs. The windows were usually stuffed up with rags, and the darkness made it difficult to see one's hand before one's face."[22]

This archipelago of disregarded slum districts was a dismal foothold for waves of immigrants setting up lives in the city. The newcomers were part of the vast global labor pool that drew the willing into the urban vortex far from their place of birth. Bombay depended on this restless movement and human energy to keep the city's economy rolling despite the crises in the surrounding hinterland of the Gujarat. Internal migration was the lifeblood of the laboring swirl. Every rural off-season, every drought and famine in India brought waves of desperate and needy people to Bombay. The city was for bettering their lot and scraping a few rupees together to send back home, even if these dreams were hedged in by ethnic and religious rifts. Byayyas from central India and Kamtis from the south lived alongside migrants from Konkan, Deccan, and Gujarat. Many of the mill hands came by sea from Rhatnagiri, a port town in Maharashtra. British social anthropologist Margaret Read watched their vessels arrive at the dock "crowded with passengers from Rhatnagiri, mostly men, hollow cheeked and thin legged.... The gang planks down, they trooped off, each shouldering a bedding bundle and carrying a small tin box. In silent small groups they threaded their way through the shouting and hustling of the docks, and boarded a tram for the mill section of the city."[23] Bombay's population ebbed and flowed with the seasons, with the influx of strangers and fortune seekers, with migrants escaping famine, war, and the indignities of ethnic and caste violence.

The multitude of castes and subcastes, tribes, religions, and ethnicities composed a social pyramid of extraordinary intricacy. But in Bombay, somehow there was an escape from the ties that bound. Everyone was from somewhere else. Men congregated at the liquor shops after hours or visited the playhouses in Kamathipura, Bombay's red-light district off Falkland Road. It was the seedy underbelly of the global city. With some thirty to forty thousand prostitutes of every ethnicity, the sex trade in Bombay was unlike anywhere else in India.[24] Rural migrants were the great reservoir from which the brothels drew their recruits. The city's circuits of migration spanned Asia and Africa as well. Freed slaves, laborers, and seafarers from Zanzibar and East Africa[25] found cheap lodging in Kamathipura. Some found work in the sweltering engine rooms of steamships. They were thrown together with Chinese migrants grinding out work on the docks for shipping companies. Kamathipura was the city's Chinatown; Shuklaji Street was a kaleidoscope of Chinese bakeries, laundries, food stalls, and silk peddlers. The Chinese Temple on Nawab Tank Road in Mazagaon provided a community space for clans speaking different dialects. Smoke-begotten dreams awaited in the opium dens down dark alleys. The imagery of scheming moneylenders and gamblers mingling with the hypnotic vapors of the opium sanctums followed the Chinese wherever they settled.

Bombay was a magnet, yet it was a rootless place. It was for making money. But there were no guarantees: a toiler's life was a constant struggle with indigence and insecurity. Social reformers churned out vivid accounts on the plight of the *mazdoors*, or workers, and their families. Their muted lives ground on with little of the city's magic. Survival depended on the social bonds of ethnicity and faith. The maze of footpaths through the chawls were where workers were recruited by *jobbers* or *sirdars*, where they bargained with moneylenders, and where they met with the neighborhood boss, or *dada*. The *dada* knew everything about his people and was expected to protect them. The gymnasiums were the haunts of local gangs ready for their next street fight that turned religious processions into violent clashes between Hindus and Muslims. The sectarian antagonisms were irreconcilable. The area of Pydhoni with its startlingly white Minar Mosque was a tense dividing line between the city's Hindu and Muslim quarters. Muslim Pathans, known as fearsome moneylenders and mill henchmen, were despised by Hindus and targets for vicious reprisals. Ethnic and religious jealousies, always just beneath the surface, were instantly ignited by wild rumors and ruffians spoiling for a fight and fast looting. In 1929, rumors spread that Pathans were ritually sacrificing Hindu children, just as they were also accused of breaking a strike at the city's oil facilities. Some 150 people were killed in the murderous rioting that followed.[26]

"In every city in Asia where the factory chimneys are smoking and the factory whistles calling, comes a stream of migrants from the countryside," Margaret Read wrote. "Narayan arrived in his mill in Bombay on the same day as Ming Wong in his mill in Shanghai, and Yuki in her mill in Osaka. None of them was known to the other. Yet each ... was known to the captains and financiers of the cotton industry throughout the world."[27] All of them were ensnared in the web of global capitalism. Infiltration by political agitators, especially those of the communist persuasion, put each mill on a knife's edge. The Russian Revolution transfixed both Indian and Chinese labor activists in their hope for seizing social and political power. In 1920, the First Congress of the Peoples of the East in Baku, Azerbaijan, was sponsored by the Comintern, the international organization advocating world communism. Delegates from India, China, Turkey, and Korea debated the global anticolonial struggle.

Vladimir Lenin's goals for staging the worldwide communist revolution laid out the road to London through Afghanistan and India. The oppressed peoples of Asia were the rallying point against capitalism and imperialism. Communist propagandists traveled from Moscow, through Tashkent and Kabul, to Bombay and were deeply entrenched in trade union struggles. Followers of communist luminary and Comintern member M. N. Roy (Manabendra Nath Roy) formed the Bombay Provincial Working Class Party. By 1927, China had replaced Afghanistan as the stepping-stone to a communist uprising in Asia. The Girni Kamgar, the Millworkers' or Red Flag Union, and its communist leaders railed against slave labor in the mills of Bombay, Osaka, and Shanghai. They urged Bombay's unions to follow the example of the Kuomintang (Nationalist Party) in China. Their call for a united front against imperialist exploitation found a robust following. By 1928, communist support among Bombay's mill workers had grown large enough to call a general strike that lasted six months. But beyond overthrowing the capitalist world order, workers, according to factory reports, were simply "well aware of the immense profits being made by the mills" and "not unnaturally" wanted their share.[28]

Rage at the hardship and poverty of many workers amid the opulence of elites broke out in unending protests across the global urban world, especially in the early 1920s. It turned the streets of London, Shanghai, and Bombay into a whirlwind of social protest. In January 1919, thousands gathered at Bombay's mill gates and succeeded in blocking the entrance over wage disputes and demands for bonuses. The strike action spread like wildfire to seventy-five of Girangaon's eighty-five mills. An estimated 120,000 mill hands walked out; bus and tram workers and postal and municipal workers followed. Unwilling to admit his company's part in the vicious cycles of poverty, Victor Sassoon consistently blamed the walkouts on communist moles. But the strikes were being supported by Benjamin Horniman, the founding editor of the *Bombay Chronicle*. The newspaper became the mouthpiece backing labor and opposing colonial exploitation. By April, Parsis and Muslims were at each other's throats: three days of rioting ended in ethnic murders. Another general strike was called in 1920, this time beginning in the Jacob Sassoon mill and spreading throughout

Girangaon. Mass rallies that spiraled into violence such as stone-throwing at the mills and passing trams ended with police firing into the crowd, killing five workers during the 1919 strike and others during the 1920 walkout.[29] With skilled mill hands in high demand and production shut down by the strikes, the mill owners grudgingly succumbed, agreeing to substantial concessions.

In the early years after the First World War, the textile boom and the gnarly excesses of profiteering reached a crescendo, with mills sold at fabulous prices and huge capital investments laid out. The gains reached their zenith in 1921 and then broke, resulting in shocking losses by shareholders and layoffs of mill hands. The prolonged recession that followed was made worse by mismanagement and corruption by the mills' managing agents. Run by British expatriate businessmen, the managing agency system was the classic colonial swindle and a relentless target of Indian rage. Between 1921 and 1924, some four hundred strikes took place in Bombay.[30] The voiceless "colored people" who were subjects of an arbitrary imperial capitalism had their say in the battle for workers' rights. Their frustration reached an early boiling point during the visit of the Prince of Wales to Bombay in 1921. His visit was the first leg of a grand royal procession to the Coronation Durbar in Delhi. The arrival of the sensationally popular heir to the throne was hailed with the full measure of British pageantry and a "blaze of Oriental splendor."[31] Press photographers followed his every move; cameras rolled for cinema newsreels. British officers in their white starched drill uniforms saluted him at Apollo Bunder as he stepped off the ship, their Bombay Bowler pith helmets gleaming in the sun. The royal's time in the city was spent carrying out ceremonial functions, playing cricket and polo, and greeting local dignitaries at the surfeit of nightly balls. Yet all this was a vainglorious defense against the flood tide of Indian independence. Indian officials and British intelligence warned against possible violence. As the prince arrived in Bombay, Mohandas Gandhi, leader of the Indian National Congress, gave notice of a civil disobedience campaign that would begin in Gujarat.

Gandhi had left London in 1915 and arrived in India to a rapturous welcome on the pier at Apollo Bunder. He had a deep aversion to India's industrial cities and so did little to support the strikes rumbling in the streets of Bombay. The home rulers were led mainly by Gujaratis who had little in common with Bombay's Marathi laborers. For Gandhi and his supporters, the soul of India lay elsewhere, in its villages. For the mill workers, the communist firebrand Shapurji Saklatvala, known for his defense of their plight, was a far more important figure (see chapter 5). Although Gandhi disliked Bombay, an old mansion on tree-lined Laburnum Road became the headquarters for his campaign. It was from there that he launched the Non-Cooperation Movement and his *swadeshi* ("of our own country") politics for the boycott of British cloth. These were stirring times. But rather than support Bombay's strikers, Gandhi chose for a more self-reflective *satyagraha*, or passive resistance. On National Humiliation Day in April 1919, he led massive crowds with National Congress flags unfurled to Chowpatty Beach, Bombay's traditional place for gatherings and ritual cleansing. Later that month, widespread rioting and looting in the city was provoked by news of British troops massacring nearly four hundred Indians protesting the suspension of civil liberties in Amritsar. Gandhi's movement elbowed out the more moderate, liberal elite led by Parsis. Bombay's Parsi leadership walked a fine line between affinity with the Raj and Indian nationalism, so it was wary of mass politics and confrontationist tactics. At the Excelsior Theater in the Fort district in early 1921, Gandhi reproached a large crowd of Parsis, declaring that "by wearing these foreign clothes they were starving millions of their own countrymen."[32]

Amid the tensions, the visit by the Prince of Wales was greeted by boycotts and marches, including a grand procession of women to Madhava Bagh to offer prayers for *swaraj*—freedom of the motherland. The campaign to "Be Indian and Buy Indian" fueled nationalist passions. A mass meeting of some fifty thousand to protest the prince's visit was held at the Elphinstone Mills in Bombay's Dadar district, where Gandhi pressed the swadeshi cause and ignited a pile of foreign cloth. Newly made saris rippled through the air as they were thrown from the mill windows. Nationalist sentiment combined with anger and agony over grueling poverty to make the moment explosive. Bonfires of British cloth lit up the city. To disrupt the royal processional route, tram cars were burned and Europeans were stoned—one was beaten to death on Marine Lines and Charni Road. The Byculla Club was attacked. Anyone not wearing an Indian cap made of khadi (homespun cotton cloth) was assaulted. Rioters struck at Parsi Zoroastrian temples. Parsis, Jews, and Christians were beaten in what had become a sectarian battlefield. A mob of Parsis gathered on Princess Street to defend the Atash Behram, one of the most sacred sites of Parsi worship, and attacked Hindu and Muslim passersby. Government troops and police killed fifty-three demonstrators in the mayhem. But spilling blood only intensified the wrongs.

Bombay Modern

The social and political troubles in Bombay were staggering. Nevertheless, the 1920s were also a time of remarkable urban transformation. The decade accentuated the city's intense vitality and mesmerizing possibilities, not just its crushing awfulness. The contradictions of life were a feature of global cities, but Bombay seemed to embrace the incongruities in monstrous measure. It had a frenetic, bitchy nature. The *chawks*—junctions of multiple streets—were a frenzy of people and vehicles in unbearable congestion. On a tour of Bombay in 1927, a bewildered traveler witnessed the traffic on Kalbadevi Road "when countless trams pass through it, and all sorts of vehicles thread their way through a sea of human beings of all creeds and castes. . . . The noise is deafening. The incessant clanging of the tram gongs, the ringing of hundreds of bells and the noise of drums from the temples, the raucous voices of the oxcart drivers, the penetrating shouts of the hack drivers . . ."[33] The city's food markets and bazaars were packed with shoppers haggling with vendors from the world over. The odors were oppressive, the air heavy with the smell of spices, dust, and cow dung. Huge kites and crows soared over the city and perched on seemingly every tree, roof, and windowsill. Worshippers filed in and out of Hindu shrines, Parsi temples, mosques, and churches. During the monsoon season in June and July, torrential rains turned the roadways into muddy streams. Floods of watery muck and rubbish inundated the slums.

The intensity of its public life made Bombay into urban spectacle. The mixing of class and culture, of ethnic and racial groups defined modernity in global cities, with Bombay's social prism bending into a wide spectrum. Alongside the agonizing poverty, these were prosperous years when an upward-bound middle class emerged. Its members were a product of the links between global commerce, colonialism, and new forms of communication. At their core were merchants, businessmen, and bankers. They were multiethnic, well-educated managers and bureaucrats, clerks and secretaries, lawyers and intelligentsia. Their jobs were as much tied to the rhythms of Bombay's global connectivity as those of the mill workers. A phalanx of office workers kept the city's elaborate mercantile apparatus humming. Education at the University of Bombay or Elphinstone College was the stepping-stone to an urbane lifestyle and a white-collar job. It was a path to power and glory, although the color bar denied talented Indian clerks and civil servants access to senior positions in *babudom*, or administrative bureaucracy.

Nonetheless, this new salaried class toiling in their offices occupied a singular place in Bombay's public discourse about the significance of the middle classes. They were far more than just middlemen minorities toiling in colonial trade. They did not fit into any traditional category. But it was precisely this social group that was ascendent in the interwar years. It was their ability to invent their identities within the context of global business

FIGURE 4. Bara Bazaar Street, Bombay. (Dinodia Photos / Alamy Stock Photo)

that made the middle classes omnipresent even in the colonial world.[34] Young people entered the bliss of jobs in the major banks and trading houses, in the offices of wholesale importers, in newspaper offices, in the insurance companies and advertising agencies that made Bombay a hub of high-end services attached to its global economy. They were trained as Western-style office managers, salesmen, and clerks that worked with international supply chains. They skipped back and forth between their own dialect, Bombay Hindi, and the English requisite for professional ambitions. Keeping up with news in the *Bombay Chronicle* and the *Times of India* was part of the ascent. They did not simply mimic Europeans. They had agendas of their own, including forming the Bombay Clerks Union, which estimated that some fifty thousand clerks were living in the city.[35] For the wealthiest of Bombay's bourgeoisie, taste was inspired by self-indulgent voyages to London and Paris, where fortunes were spent shopping for exotic Western fashions and furnishings. As if in a vise, Bombay was caught between admiration for the West and the reality of colonial domination.

The city ballooned past its old districts as the population soared by 40 percent to well over a million inhabitants. The sheer scale of this growth triggered radical changes. On his visit to Bombay, author Aldous Huxley drove out along the "long tentacles of suburban squalor.... Mills and huge grey tenements, low huts among the palm-trees flank the outgoing roads for miles, and the roads themselves are thronged with the coming and going of innumerable passengers."[36] The housing shortage was acute. Scores of working- and middle-class people hunted endlessly for lodgings. Development was at best piecemeal and divided between the Bombay Municipal Corporation, the Bombay Improvement Trust, and the Bombay Port Trust, all controlled by British overseers. The British government's Development Department promised a vast construction scheme for middle-class housing and fifty thousand concrete chawls to replace the dense labyrinths of shanties. "Concrete has great potentialities," British authorities argued. "Good, dry, sanitary cottages, architecturally correct and pleasing to the eye, can be built with concrete blocks both cheaply and quickly."[37] The slum clearance did little but create even more miserable tenements while the housing programs sent land speculation into a frenzy.

Except when land values momentarily dropped during the Great Depression, the real estate market kept up a feverish pace right through the 1930s and 1940s. The property business exploded into a boom of speculative development. It was fueled by the profits from global trade, which was quickly reinvested in land and trophy buildings as fixed assets. Quick profits were made on the rents. Urban property and the built fabric became a form of trade themselves, tied to the accumulation of capital on the world markets. The streamlined art deco style taking the world by storm adorned spanking-new office buildings in the Fort district and along the new Hornby Road carved out to Ballard Estate (see chapter 3). Art deco was the aesthetic link between art, commerce, and industry. It was modernist imagery adapted to the realities of business.[38] The new East India Cotton Association building dominated the busy Kalbadevi area and was the tallest building in Bombay. The story of cotton was emblazoned on its facade in swank art deco relief as a tribute to the city's main export. Apartment buildings dressed in art deco sprung up in the old districts, on the Malabar and Cumballa Hills, and along the sinuous curve of Marine Drive as speculators poured money into real estate.

Affluent Indian home seekers drove their new motorcars northward to the town-planning schemes and garden suburbs set out by the Bombay Improvement Trust. Automobile ownership was a prime symbol of upper-class wealth. Families snapped up bungalows in the new areas of Parel, and Worli with its terraced promenade facing the sea, and further out past the coconut palms and mango groves to Bandra, with its garden bungalows, where many Europeans were settling. Farther north at Salsette Island, developers were buying up lots to sell for a killing.[39] Neat holiday villas appeared on the beaches at Juhu and Versova. These privileged places, where home owners enjoyed the evening breeze on the western shoreline, meant an increasing West–East class divide in the city. Further to the north, the poor found shelter in the neglected areas of Santa Cruz, Kurla, and Andheri. These were described as hideous slums.

Construction took a variety of turns, but the Western-style flat opened an entirely new lifestyle for middle-class Indian families, who could now switch on electric lights and electric fans humming in the hot air. The global spread of European bourgeois cultural standards was hardly smooth, however. The Indian National Congress debated the merits of a modern Hindu household. Indian elites found their own path through the thicket of global cultural forms. But in this search for distinctions between desirable and undesirable modernity, consumption became a marker of status despite caste and family tradition. It produced what architectural historian Swati Chattopadhyay has called a "conventional cosmopolitanism."[40] British and US imports of electric gadgetry skyrocketed.[41] Advertisements marketing a Western modernist aesthetic filled the pages of daily newspapers and magazines. Living rooms, modern kitchens and bathrooms, and for the most trendsetting, sewing machines, radios, and telephones were trappings of modern bourgeois life copied from the West. Bombay was synonymous with this imported consumerism. The American way of life paraded in Hollywood movies added further fantasy. The business magazine *Capital* reported that in the new apartment buildings, "Europeans and Indians live together, and you might walk into the drawing room of a Parsi or Khoja and not perceive any radical difference of furniture or arrangement from the drawing room of the European next door."[42] It was a modern atmosphere that would have perplexed older residents used to the dignified seclusion of the traditional Indian dwelling with multiple families.

The Ideal Homes Exhibition held at Bombay's Town Hall in 1937 was meant to push Indian industries and arts in the direction of these Western motifs. The essence of swadeshi encouraged indigenous crafts and an Indian style in interiors. Although Indian design production had its appeal, the glamour of symbolic Western capital for bourgeois sensibilities was just as enticing. The public wandered through European-style living and dining rooms, bathrooms and nurseries. Western influence was a long-standing conundrum for colonial India. Cosmopolitan upper-class families embraced Western styles at the same time they supported calls for national independence. The modern home was a sign that its owners were open to global influences. But "a 'zenana' [women's quarters] and a bathroom with chromium-plated hardware cannot be reconciled so easily," the writer of a review article ruminated in the *Times of India*. Was it too much to hope that "India's architects can synthetise these two in one happy stroke"? It was a valiant question. However, a photo of a Hollywood movie star posing alongside her dining-room table groaning with gleaming china and crystal graced the newspaper coverage of the exhibit.[43] These luxe trimmings were available at the Army & Navy Stores, at Whiteaways, and at the Evans & Fraser department stores on Hornby Road that catered exclusively to British tastes and to Bombay's Indian bourgeois with Anglophile sensitivities.

The Arabian Sea lapped along the edges of the city. Creating new land from its watery depths was an ongoing tactic for urban expansion and growing the real estate market. Huge reclamation schemes extended Bombay's tongue of land vertically to the north and horizontally in both the east and the west. How to pay for these projects was one of the most contentious political issues furrowing the brows of city leaders. The long-simmering Back Bay Reclamation project finally started after the First World War. The lithe curve of Marine Lines and the promenade along Marine Drive took shape along the bay, which emptied into the Arabian Sea. The monsoon surf broke over huge mechanical dredges and rubble mounds. Gigantic cranes installed the massive seawall that slithered for four miles along the shoreline. It was prosperous businesspeople with a Western sensibility who campaigned for the development of Bombay as a modern city. Leading mill owners, including David Sassoon, had formed a syndicate to finance the project. Although it was billed as the promised land that would make Bombay the "Urbs Prima of India,"[44] the Back Bay project was marred by construction delays, mismanagement, and corruption.

Nevertheless, it turned the muddy flats into land ripe for investment. As the project neared completion, the city's Parsi industrialists and deep-pocketed entrepreneurs, the maharajas and *nawahs* who frequented Bombay, began scooping up tracts of land and building luxury apartment buildings and mansions in art deco style. They poured money into real estate. Art deco was cosmopolitan performance. It was a global cultural form eagerly adopted by Bombay's educated bourgeoisie, who had grown wealthy on the city's commerce. The visual aesthetic was the signature of the "ocean voyaging, jet-setting international Indian." Even the princes investing in Bombay's real estate adapted themselves to a Western lifestyle and art deco as an attempt to swim with the political tide.[45] Marine Drive (originally called Ocean Way) became an iconic symbol of the city's global predilections, especially its buildings designed by architect Gajanan Mhatre, who translated art deco modern style into an Indian genre.

Bombay was India's cosmopolitan beacon for every media and entertainment craze. It was a global helm, attached to international rhythms more than to the subcontinent. The saying "What Bombay thinks today

India will think tomorrow" swelled into an infectious boogie-woogie beat in the Roaring Twenties. Especially for the younger generation arriving at adulthood after the war, the British clubs and their stuffy protocols held only slight attraction. Showing up there was no more than a professional necessity. Instead, for their leisure time they succumbed to the syncopated rhythms of jazz and the tango in the cabarets. They were eager to spend money on clothes and gadgets, on wild-oats expeditions. They merged into the global cultural whirlwinds. Bombay's grand hotels were scenes of this shared cosmopolitanism. Their lobbies and bars were places where tourism, mass media, and urban spectacle converged. They were where "things happened"[46] in the crazy years of the Twenties. The Harbour Bar in the Taj Mahal Hotel was the chicest place to meet for drinks and chatter with British officialdom, Indian princes, and the city's millionaires. Green's Hotel was the canteen of seafarers, racing fanatics, and get-rich-quick operators. The atmosphere was more rakish than the imperial Taj, and its terrace overlooking the harbor was one of the most popular places in the city.

The hotel ballrooms echoed with the lively music of jazz and swing orchestras. Jovial crowds cavorted, forming lines for the rhumba and dancing the Charleston, the turkey trot, and the Brazilian maxixe. Swing and jazz musicians from the ocean liners docked at the port were invited to beat out their rhythms at the fashionable hotels. The global exchange in the new cultural forms was exciting. Hot music took Bombay by storm, with scores of American and Indian musicians mounting its stages to show off their talent. At some points, some sixty bands were pounding out their beat in the city's venues. Their siren dance rhythms could be heard on regular radio broadcasts from Radio House on Apollo Bunder Road.[47]

Upper-class families and the city's business and intellectual elites shed the traditional custom of women's domestic seclusion. Strict Muslim observance of the veil was anemic in Bombay, hence barely visible. Chic young women were out and about on the city streets and in the cabarets, flaunting the flapper's bobbed hair and slim figure that were all the rage. Cheeky and coquettish, they ignored old-style taboos. Harry Greenwall walked into a hotel ballroom to find "a Parsee girl in a lovely 'sari' foxtrot[ting] with a Swedish officer off the cruiser lying out in the bay . . . women in frocks that were created in Paris; Hindu ladies in flame-coloured Indian costumes, dancing the dances of the West to music that has come to Bombay from America via Vienna."[48] By day, these women worked as typists and telephone operators and in department stores, radio, and motion pictures. The emergence of these socially emancipated New Women was a worldwide phenomenon. They were a vision of cosmopolitan modernity, of freedom and fashion, as discernible on the streets of Shanghai and London as they were in Bombay. Care-free Twenties glamour was spun by advertising, the motion picture industry, and magazines. It crisscrossed the globe. This classy urban chic was an altogether different image from the women freedom fighters wrapped in modest Indian-made saris while boycotting British textiles and protesting on the streets. In whatever their guise, the women of Bombay, of Shanghai and London, embodied the anxieties about the modern age and the social tensions it wrought.

The public craved the novelties carried on the waves of the global culture market. City life in the Jazz Age was about foreign imports and the commercialization of entertainment. Becoming self-consciously modern meant becoming aware of the wider world of mass culture. Bombay was a regular stop on the entertainment circuit traveled by the steamers and ocean liners. A steady stream of European and American theatrical and music troupes descended on the city in the 1920s and 1930s. They were a pathway of global exchange. At the Excelsior Theater, the Hawaiian Troubadours serenaded the crowds with A Night in Honolulu featuring steel guitars and hula dancers, while the Louisiana Quartet offered "negro melodies and quaint old plantation harmonies." The Forbes Russell Comedy Company decamped from the Strand Theatre in London to the Excelsior for a successful run. It was followed by a "saucy and spicy" Our Cabaret show from London that produced "hysterics among the audience and very few really blushed!"[49] The Roman Singers graced Bombay with Neapolitan and Venetian folk songs along with operatic selections. For social butterflies, even charity balls badgering the wealthy for donations became an excuse for hijinks and a chance to show off dance moves. The Grand Zoo Ball at the Gymkhana Cooperage was the highlight of the 1926 charity season, with revelers cutting a rug in animal and flower costumes under a canopy of balloons.

By the mid-1920s, Bombay was already the motion picture capital of India. Only Shanghai could compete with it as Asia's entertainment and media hub. Its turn at the seventh art was tied to investments by its industrial tycoons. The cotton kings used film as a commodity on the derivatives market, funneling unreported income in and out of the motion picture studios under the noses of tax collectors.[50] It tied the film industry directly to the city's global economy. One of Bombay's oldest studios, the Kohinoor Film Company, was started by local mill owner Dwarkadas Sampat. The Prabhat Film Company and Bombay Talkies made names for themselves with hit movies, especially those starring India's first superstar, Devika Rani. Mill owner F. E. Dinshaw offered his estate to Bombay Talkies for use as its studio. The Tata family financed National Studios.

Movie theaters dripping in art deco splendor graced the old districts of south Bombay. The Regal on the Colaba Causeway was owned by Parsi businessman Framji Sidhwa, who had direct contact with Hollywood's Metro-Goldwyn-Mayer Studios. It was one of the finest cinemas in the city, equipped with elevators, air-conditioning, soda fountains, and an underground parking lot. In a first for Bombay, its stunning art deco facade was outlined with neon lighting. The Plaza Central cinema, the Empire Theater, and the Broadway, Eros, and Metro all opened as well. The sleek Eros building housed a European-style ballroom and restaurant along with luxury offices. It was a speculative ensemble joined to Bombay's golden era in the Jazz Age. All these luxurious venues situated in the upscale areas of Colaba and the Oval Maidan catered to European and Anglo-Indian tastes and featured Western fare, especially British and Hollywood films. By the 1930s, seventy-seven movie theaters were offering fans a mesmerizing choice on the silver screen. The audiences were a mix of men and women of all ethnicities. The more mundane cinemas spread out into the quotidian districts with a distinctly Indian middle- and working-class clientele. These moviegoers watched Hindi films and followed the exploits of their favorite movie idols. Bombay's eight large film studios turned out twelve to fifteen motion pictures a month, mostly in Hindi-Urdu. But for all this, Dennis Kincaid, a British civil servant and "exile in postwar Bombay," snootily bemoaned that "too many things seemed to be inferior, yet nostalgia-inducing, imitations of London."[51]

Examples of Bombay's global role that were just as conspicuous were the reclamation projects on its eastern shoreline. The most prestigious among them was the Gateway of India on the tip of Apollo Bunder. The monumental triumphal arch was designed by George Wittet, Bombay's foremost colonial architect. There was no doubt that it paid for young British, in this case Scottish, architects to work in the colonies. While his contemporaries in England, the London *Daily Mail* reported, "were . . . lucky to have the job of designing small cottages or doing even humbler work," Wittet oversaw construction of some of the most notable buildings in India.[52] He executed an astonishing number of projects for the government of Bombay, all of them in the historicist pastiche favored by the Raj. The same can be said for John Gammon, a British civil engineer who worked for the Public Works Department and designed the precast concrete foundations and domes for the Gateway.

The stupendous entry into the city commemorated the first visit by a British monarch to India—the 1911 stay of King George V and Queen Mary. It was a "symbol in stone of this city's proud and well-deserved title, the Gateway of India."[53] The Jijibhoy and Sassoon families donated lavishly to its construction. They also led the festivities surrounding its inauguration, which took place on December 4, 1924, in full military splendor. British and Indian cavalry regiments and soldiers perspired in starched uniform, with the sweeping view of the bay behind them. It was a grandiose celebration of the British Raj. But the Gateway was almost instantly passé. The city's art deco marvels had already surpassed the Indo-Saracen bravura that had marked colonialism. The streamlined moderne aesthetic was the visual signature of a new kind of cosmopolitanism. Bombay followed the latest cultural gestures sweeping the globe and shaped them into its own brand of modern style.

✵ 3 ✵
Bombay, Global Helm

> On the pier and the pier-shed roof hundreds of faces peered up
> at the splendor of the ship, each face bright with a look of
> wonder and expectancy.
>
> LOUIS BROMFIELD, *Night in Bombay* (1939)

The Gateway of India was not the only symbol of Bombay's status as a global helm under British dominion. Thousands of acres of land were dredged up from Bombay Harbor on the eastern shore. The reclamation projects were financed with the riches earned from global trade. From Colaba and the old Sassoon docks in the south to Mazagaon-Sewri in the north, a system of wet docks, dry docks, and bunders (piers) were constructed by the Bombay Port Trust. It was a vast urban space dedicated to the routine work of global business.

The physical expansion of the city worked in tandem with its maritime trade. Some ten thousand men worked the docks in Bombay.[1] At the new Alexandra Dock, powerful cranes clawed up heavy cargo and swung it on and off the ships. Goods were registered and stored in closely guarded warehouses or confiscated by customs officials. Ballard Pier was the landing place for ships from Europe, where customs agents policed the influx of passengers and rifled through their luggage before it was taken ashore. The boundary between port and city was open and porous. The pageant on the wharves was captured in Louis Bromfield's novel *Night in Bombay* as a "great ship" moored at the pier: "Seven hundred passengers of all colors and races and creeds and nationalities were jammed together waiting to pour down the gangplank into the dusty, sunbaked city. On the pier and the pier-shed roof hundreds of faces peered up at the splendor of the ship, each face bright with a look of wonder and expectancy."[2] The railway terminus and telegraph office stood adjacent for the convenience of travelers. Moreover, Bombay was the first port of call for news and newspapers into the subcontinent. Thirty-thousand-ton mail steamers berthed alongside massive hydraulic cranes that off-loaded the five to six thousand mailbags arriving with each voyage. The sacks were hoisted by elevators to the first floor of the new Mail Depot, where an army of sorters threw them into bins to be whisked by train to all parts of India within three hours of their arrival.

The old mango trees at Mazagaon-Sewri were pulled down, the Koli villages removed. The swampy east of Bombay became a landscape of quaysides, depots, and railway sidings. This expansion of port facilities to handle the swelling commercial and passenger traffic took place in all the port cities servicing the major maritime trunk lines. Along with Bombay, Karachi, Madras, Colombo, and Calcutta were the behemoths of trade in South Asia.[3] The flow of commodities through the Port of Bombay was staggering—some five to six million tons annually. By the 1920s, Bombay was handling two-fifths of the total value of India's foreign commerce, 70 percent of its coastal trade, and the bulk of the re-export trade to the Persian Gulf and the Arab and East African ports. Its foreign trade surpassed that of Calcutta and Karachi and remained robust even as the world slid into the Great Depression. The flags of Britain, Japan, China, and the United States as well as those of European nations fluttered in the sea breezes as the ships made their way past the lighthouses and waited for anchorage. They were laden with imports of textiles, metals and ores, machinery, railway plant, and rolling stock. Even in the economic slump of the 1930s, the foreign automobiles and consumer goods arrived with increasing regularity. Sought-after luxuries packed in crates awaited opening. Once the ships berthed at the piers, coolies and cranes hauled their cargo onto the quayside. Millions of rupees in gold and silver were brought in on the ships as well. Over one-third of this foreign trading bonanza took place with Britain and the British colonies. Frozen fish from Britain arrived each month along with drugs and medicines. Gigantic bags of rice from Java piled up on the piers. Beer was imported from Germany and the Netherlands, whiskey and wines from across Europe. Jowar and dates arrived from Iraq, green tea from China.[4]

The waterfront was lined with industries tied to the city's global trade. Here were coal and manganese depots and the British Imperial Chemical Industries facility that was managed from the company's headquarters in London. Britain's Unilever conglomerate established the Hindustan Vanaspati Manufacturing Company in Bombay, its first Indian subsidiary, to produce edible oil and then continued with the manufacture of soaps and personal products. The E. D. Sassoon enterprise was behind the Eastern

Chemical Company, which specialized in acids, sodas, and heavy chemicals for industry. The impact of the automobile on the city's economy was just being felt. Spanking-new motorcars and motorcycles from Britain and the United States rolled off the ships in increasing numbers—nearly nine thousand in 1930. The partiality for American Fords and Buicks began to undermine the British models.[5] Global car companies launched. In 1928, General Motors constructed an assembly plant in the old grain depot at Sewri and a month after its opening was manufacturing one hundred cars a day. The Firestone Tyre and Rubber Company and Dunlop Tyre followed along and began small operations as Indian subsidiaries.

The automobile was shifting the demand for fuel to refined oil. Some 125 million gallons of petroleum were imported into India through the Port of Bombay each year, more than double that of the prewar years. About 40 million gallons of the fuel came annually from British Burma, and another 60 million gallons a year imported from outside the imperial domains, especially from Persia.[6] Looking for a fresh source of supply, British Burmah Oil began to work Burma's Yenangyaung oil fields. The Yenangyaung Oilfield Southern Extension Company was formed to test the area. Its main investor was Sir Victor Sassoon, "whose name and distinguished career and position are a guarantee of the seriousness and character of the enterprise."[7] With their rival Standard Oil also eyeing the Indian market, Royal Dutch Shell and the Rothschilds banded together with Burmah Oil to form Burmah-Shell Oil Distribution and Storage, with facilities at Bombay's port. The city's waterfront infrastructure adapted in parallel with global commerce. The ships lined up at Pir Pau Pier and pumped the fuel through pipelines to tanks at Wadala, north of Sewri, where the marshlands were transmuting into an oil storage and refinery landscape.

The export of Indian produce through Bombay increased steadily year by year. Even in the dour 1930s, export trade out of the port was still booming. Between 1930 and 1932, it jumped by some 80 percent, and then it remained high afterward.[8] A myriad of Indian products was stored in the warehouses at Mazagaon-Sewri to await shipment overseas. But cotton was king. The 178 concrete warehouses at Sewri were daringly conceived by engineer John Gammon based on pioneering structural design. They covered twenty blocks, each jammed with 7,500 bales of cotton stacked eighteen bales high. The availability of cotton relied on the monsoons in India and imported cotton from East Africa. Practically all the fine East African cotton was then re-exported to the United States and Japan. Cotton textiles from the United Kingdom were turned around and re-exported to Persia, Arabia, and East Africa.[9] Bombay was a central hub in this vast cotton trading network. During the busy season from November to June, railcars were crammed with upward of three million bales of cotton at the Cotton Depot.

The cotton trade was imbued with its own urban aesthetics and design. The plant was inscribed on the map of Sewri, with alleyways dubbed Cotton Green and Cotton Avenue. The new Cotton Exchange was a striking modernist building in minty green, with a vast trading hall akin to that in New York and London. Importers and exporters, commission agents and brokers awaited global prices and haggled over the shipments. The cotton market in Bombay was the largest in Asia.[10] Hundreds of thousands of people across the globe—cotton growers, traders and their clerks, mill workers, cotton textile manufacturers—depended on these dealings. Together they formed one of the densest and most far-reaching webs of global trade. This required a logistics chain that ran from plantations to department stores, crisscrossed territorial boundaries, and reacted to the transactions in Bombay's Cotton Exchange with lightning speed. Speculation on cotton futures could reach frenzied levels.

India's vast exports flowing through Sewri were controlled by the imperial capital of London. The system of payment for India's goods was a case study in colonial domination. Special "council bills" of sale were paid in pounds sterling and other currencies through the exchange banks lodged along the maze of streets in London's City. In other words, the money held in escrow from selling India's production abroad piled up in the London vaults of the Hong Kong & Shanghai Bank, the Chartered Bank of India, Australia, and China, and the Sassoons' Eastern Bank. The funds were a liquid asset available to the banks for any purpose. Once the goods were received by the purchaser, the money was then released and sent by telegraph to be cashed in rupees through the exchange banks in Bombay, or it was sent by ship as gold and silver bullion. The piece of the action on these currency exchanges went entirely to the banks.[11] An astounding ten *pukka* (British-based) exchange banks had branch offices in Bombay ready to make a tidy profit off this colonial system. They were nestled around the stock exchange in the Fort district including the Hong Kong & Shanghai's imposing neoclassical edifice on the corner of Churchgate Street. Even the National City Bank of New York settled into Bombay for its cut. This distorted operation worked against India's producers. Despite the spectacle of the cotton market at Sewri and the commodities hauled onto ships at Alexandra Dock for export, turning the massive amount of Indian goods sold abroad into local profit was grueling at best. Even worse, these rupees were paid by the Indian government and earmarked as expenditures. The system drained the Indian government's budget on top of the tribute remittances required by Britain. The Raj arrogantly took a huge cut from India's exports entirely for its own purposes.

The massive port facilities at Bombay were a nexus in the corridors of both goods and people that stretched across the globe. The rivers of exchange carried along the souls who were largely invisible just as often as they ferried extroverts like Victor Sassoon who craved the limelight. Steamers were the means of transport for all social strata. Four steamship companies plied the coast from Karachi to Burma laden with thousands of tons of Indian goods along with mail, bullion, and passengers. Movement and migration became a defining aspect of social identity. Pilgrims from all parts of India and beyond assembled on the Bombay quaysides and pushed their way onto the gangplanks of ships bound for the Holy Land. The number of Indian pilgrims to the Hajj in Mecca reached thirty-six thousand in 1927 alone. Most of these faithful went through Bombay rather than Calcutta.[12] Chinese Muslims from as far away as Turkestan traveled the caravan routes to northern India and then boarded trains for Bombay. They hid their life savings in silver stuffed in their belongings. Such tides of humanity defined the global city. Bombay was a visual theater of people passing through, holed up in hostels, boardinghouses, and makeshift camps, then awaiting passage on the quaysides. The waterside was a transitory public sphere that shifted incessantly with the ebb and flow of people and ship schedules.

Seasonal and casual workers from across the Indian subcontinent assembled at the Port of Bombay in search of jobs overseas. From there, millions of Indians spread out across the British Empire. The migrant laborers were corralled by middlemen with extensive networks throughout the Middle East and Southeast Asia and then channeled to Burma, Malaya, and Ceylon.[13] This vast outflow of humanity was the fluid workforce the global economy depended on. Many thousands of Indian coolies bound for work in the Persian and Arab oil fields as well as in Africa passed through Bombay. They shared steerage on the tramp steamers with traders from Kuwait, Bahrain, and Dubai, many of them carrying contraband. Young women were smuggled in as prostitutes to service British Tommies and Indians. The human cargo was plentiful. Poverty drove the restless across the seas to find a living. Criminal networks thrived on their fragile hopes, offering little beyond servitude and dislocation.

Thus, there was more going on at the port than dockworkers heaving cotton and commodities onto ships. Sailors and dockworkers suffered agonizing poverty and operated on the margins of legality. Bombay's wharves were a stark demonstration of the social disparities that marked global cities. The dhows bobbing up and down in port were a murky space of illicit contraband. Bribery and corruption were rampant. Racketeering was a way of life, especially for the Maratha and Mahar laborers who were pressed into gangs by *toliwallas* (labor contractors) to handle cargo and were paid pathetic day wages. Traffickers offered every conceivable contraband from the souks and markets across South Asia and the Arabian Peninsula. Huge quantities of gold and silver were smuggled across the Arabian Sea to Bombay in clandestine operations that exploited the byzantine money trade. Although they were strictly controlled, weapons, opium and hashish, and jewels regularly changed hands on the quaysides and jetties behind the backs of customs officers. Indian sailors developed a well-honed global network of illegal gunrunning and drug trafficking between Kobe in Japan, the Port of Bombay, and Hong Kong and Shanghai.[14] Criminal rings reaped tidy profits by illegally exporting Indian opium through Bombay, then across the Arabian Sea to ports along the east coast of Africa, especially Durban in South Africa. Bombay's corruption and illicit trade oiled the wheels of global commerce, relying on deft maneuvers by the disenfranchised and lax customs regulations.

Alongside the smuggling and gunrunning on an epic scale was the flow

FIGURE 5. Dockworkers at the Port of Bombay. (Dinodia Photos / Alamy Stock Photo)

of information and gossip. In 1930, some seventy thousand Indian sailors, or *lascars*, pivoted around Bombay's port.[15] They came from across the subcontinent and formed a dense communication network with antennae everywhere they sailed. From a global perspective, dockworkers were at the forefront of labor struggles against capitalism and colonialism, as true in London and Shanghai as in Bombay. In 1931, the number of unemployed seamen in Bombay was estimated to exceed ten thousand, many of them trapped in the city's miserable lodging houses in the districts of Mazagaon and Dhobi Talao. The utter destitution and indebtedness of the sailors desperate for work along Bombay's waterfront made them ripe for rebellion. The local Indian Seamen's Union regularly organized strikes for better pay. The communist International of Seamen and Harbour Workers used the *lascars* to traffic material and propaganda leaflets from Europe through Port Said, Egypt, and then into Bombay to distribute among the *mazdoors* (workers) and unions. It promised an international brotherhood and called for global strikes and boycotts against imperialism.[16] Officialdom railed against foreign communist agitators stirring up mill hands, railroad workers, and dockworkers. However, the geopolitics of the 1930s was a complicated terrain in which Bombay played a fluid role. Consignments of silver bullion, arms, and ammunition were sent surreptitiously by the British through Bombay, then by train up to Burma, and on to nationalists in China fighting both the communist insurgency and the Japanese invasion. The traffic was handled by private contractors, among which Arnhold & Company (a Sassoon holding), with its deep links to both London and Shanghai, played a prominent role.[17]

The Apollo Reclamation north of the Gateway of India fanned out into the Ballard Estate, Bombay's European-style business district owned by the Bombay Port Trust. The project was an indication of the power wielded by global capital over the urban fabric. It was one of the few planned districts in a city of thousands of buildings scattered in confusion. The Ballard area had been created from material dredged up from the salty brine in the construction of Alexandra Dock. Indian-made concrete piles were driven into the mud and then a matting of concrete spread over the area. Forty-three blocks of handsome buildings were then constructed along tree-lined boulevards in what quickly became a thriving hub of commercial activity and a windfall for the Port Trust. The Anglo-Indian-style buildings were designed by architect George Wittet in brick and stone masonry. Bombay's status as a global helm was inscribed in the design aesthetics. In the new Customs House, Seamen's Society, and Bombay Port Trust buildings, Wittet attempted "to introduce a feeling of the sea."[18] Decorative facades featured sculpted ships in yellow Kurla stone, while street names such as Cochin and Calicut honored Bombay's maritime influence. The entire urban development scheme was paid for by international trade and meant to bolster the city's global reach.

Everything that happened in Ballard Estate was news. The leading commercial and shipping firms moved into the new buildings, among them Burmah-Shell, the Asiatic Petroleum Company, and the shipping giants British India Steam Navigation Company, the Scindia Steam Navigation Company, and the venerable P&O line. They were followed by foreign consulates, news publishing houses, and the Paris-based Pathé Frères film production company. Responding to Bombay's booming motion picture industry, the Pathé building featured special storage vaults for celluloid and a specially built screening room. It was the only building of its kind in the East. Among the tenants in the Ballard Estate was the head office of E. D. Sassoon & Company. The firm left behind the old offices on Rampart Row and set up shop in its new building on Dougall Road. It was here that Victor Sassoon and the company's board members and mill managers plotted out their business strategies.

Bombay Business

Bombay emerged as a modern helm in a far-flung global arena. The First World War had opened the door to the city's boom years of the 1920s. The Depression that followed in the 1930s certainly impacted India but scarcely affected Bombay's robust economy. Its consequences struck India's vast rural areas far worse. In Bombay, any falloff in foreign trade gave the opportunity for homegrown industries to thrive.[19] The clubby, closed circle of the Raj meant little competition from British firms. British businessmen had a rather gloomy view of their prospects in India, so they stuck to recycling profits in the tried-and-true textile industry. Hence, the opening was there for Bombay's native entrepreneurs. But notions about the marvels of Western technologies were caught in the net of Swadeshi nationalism and independence from colonial rule. On the one hand, Western ideas of progress were often criticized as alien to India's traditions. At the same time, new industries were symbols of India's confidence in its own future. Members of Bombay's monied class were torn between the colonial system they had profited from and the nationalist movement they dreamed about. The Raj was a tool of the city's financiers and industrialists, who had attained their success securely within the expansive overseas markets of the British Empire and remained loyal. They were deeply entrenched in British trade, with some of the city's capitalists also working as middlemen brokers for Lancashire cotton companies. Yet they understood themselves as far more than just compradors. They were a long-standing oligarchy of urban elites. Their hearts belonged to India's self-determination. At the very least, Bombay's industrialists had to negotiate a new kind of capitalist patriotism embedded in the Swadeshi movement.[20] This was particularly true of the Parsi families, who had always been the city's power brokers. They were avid supporters of the nationalist cause, especially during its moderate phase. But this support also meant dismantling the lucrative commercial web spun by empire.

The upshot was that Bombay's merchant financiers worked both within and against colonial power.[21] Their strategy was to invest in a forward-looking vision by underwriting industry at a time when the British themselves had grown blasé about economic investment in India. The "irresistible wave of Swadeshism" would ensure the industrial future of India and of Bombay, according to industrialist and financial titan Ardeshir Darabshaw Shroff. Even during the Depression years, Bombay's banks boomed.[22] Thirteen major financial institutions there served wealthy Indian investors who had large stakes in private companies, from steel plants to shipping lines. Brokers discreetly funneled money into speculative ventures. All sorts of open-ended financial arrangements were carried out by banks and insurance companies for investment schemes. Stanley Reed remarked that "Bombay had long been the money and bullion hive of India, and the honey poured forth from the profits" was now retained for industrial development. "Bombay became the rentier of India . . . it was reasonable to assume that three or four million pounds came into the city every year from investment in enterprises in other parts of India. What money-spinners they were!"[23]

Strict separation of the races was a central feature of British rule in India. But as a global city, Bombay was an intense pocket of dynamic wealth creation and multiculturalism. The city's homegrown gentlemanly capitalists sat on innumerable boards and were investors in one another's companies. That is how business was conducted. They were knitted together by blood and marriage. They held the most important positions in Bombay's Chamber of Commerce and its banks. They controlled the media. And they were the city's main property owners. A thin slice of Bombay's native upper crust owned virtually all the wealth, all the land and real estate. This conservative family-firm model was a peculiar feature of Indian capitalism.[24] But in Bombay, it was neither conventional nor risk adverse. The city's magnates were passionate modernizers and reshaped Western ideals into an Indian expression. They sat at the commanding heights of the world economy in Southeast Asia. They had long operated in international business.

The board members of E. D. Sassoon & Company provide a closer look at this urban oligarchy and the expansiveness of their global reach and power. They included Sir Fazulbhoy Currimbhoy, from one of the most esteemed Khoja cotton merchant and philanthropic families in Bombay. The Currimbhoys' trading interests stretched to the Arabian Peninsula, the African coast, and Canton and Hong Kong in the China trade. They controlled twelve of Bombay's largest cotton mills. Gujarati businessman and board member Narottam Morarjee was one of the great shipping and textile magnates. In 1919, he founded the Scindia Steam Navigation Company that sailed from Bombay to London and unfurled the Indian flag in shipping in international waters. It was the first shipping line to challenge British domination of Southeast Asian coastal waters. S. R. Bomanji was a powerful Bombay politician involved in the cotton, banking, and shipping industries and vice president of the Indian Chamber of Commerce. He lived partly in Hong Kong and Shanghai and, like Victor Sassoon, shuttled back and forth between Bombay, the Far East, and London to oversee his chain of businesses. Bomanji became a pillar of British society and acted as political broker between Indian nationalists and the British. The Parsi Dinshaw-Petit family were bankers, shipowners, and managing agents for mills and steamship companies, and they traded across the Arabian Peninsula and East Africa. Board member Framroze Edulji Dinshaw was Bombay's legal luminary and a devoted Indian patriot and nationalist. Dinshaw made his mark by his sheer presence on the scene. He sat on the boards of some sixty-five of the city's companies, including the Tata Iron and Steel Company. He was a pioneer in both the cement and the motion picture industries, and he played a key role in the start of the Bombay Talkies film studio. The Dinshaw family owned half of Karachi as well as vast assets in Bombay.[25] Altogether, Bombay's native *shetias* were among the most illustrious commercial families in India and Southeast Asia, with extensive land and business holdings. Their names attached to any business scheme assured it would find investors and get off the ground. They controlled the future of Bombay to a far greater extent than the British perched in the Malabar Hills, detached from the city unless it directly served the Raj's interests.

In January 1924, the city's magnates were invited to a private showing of the film *The Building of the British Empire Exhibition* at the Empire Theater near the Maidan. The event was meant to generate Indian backing for an extravaganza to be held in London: the celebration of the British Empire and its imperial ties. An array of marvels from the "family of nations" were to be spread out across two hundred acres in the London suburb of Wembley. The spectacular pavilions and the amusement park would welcome twenty-five million visitors in what was part trade fair and part theme park. Indian supporters of the exhibition argued that participation "gave India a splendid opportunity of advertising its wares among the other nations of the world and it would be unwise to throw it away."[26] But the Swarajists (advocates of Indian independence) who won a majority of non-Muslim seats in the Legislative Council of Bombay agreed to donating only a pittance of money for the city's exhibits, on the grounds that it meant further exploitation from the British overseers. They attempted to cancel the project altogether.

The compromise was an India Pavilion shaped as a replica of the Taj Mahal. The Indo-Saracen fantasy was the most spectacular of the exhibition's pavilions, thrilling visitors, including the Queen. The political wrangling over expenditures meant that the Bombay Court was compressed into the smallest floor space in the pavilion. Neither the cotton mill industry nor the Tata iron and steel conglomerate were present. They "saw no practical benefit to themselves in setting up an exhibit at Wembley."[27] Instead, the Bombay Court was graced with a model of the Gateway of India and development projects such as the port extension and the Back Bay scheme. The Press Exhibit and Bombay School of Arts showcased the city's progress under British rule. To a large extent, the exhibits stayed true to an exotic colonial dreamscape of Bombay's famed bazaars and Indian arts and crafts—carpets from Samarkand, silks from Kashmir, carvings in ivory and jade, and replicas of the Hindu gods. Visitors could see "Bombay jugglers and snake charmers."[28] There was little notice of how much the city's economy had advanced. Since its commercial and industrial concerns participated halfheartedly, whether their exhibits gained any advantage to Bombay was a matter of conjecture. The incongruity of colonial rule in a country ripe for independence was as much on display at the British Empire Exhibition as the artifacts themselves.

In actuality, the Indian business class was behind construction companies, telecommunications and the media industry, transportation and aviation. Finance, insurance, and real estate—what would eventually be called FIRE industries—were at the top of its agenda. This global capitalist frontier emerged early and not just in Western cities. It was connected directly to Bombay's global trade. Information was at the core of these ventures. The global telecommunications infrastructure put in place by the 1930s lessened investment risks and made the control of assets over long distances more feasible. Access to data on price fluctuations, shipping, credit availability, and market trends privileged specific global cities such as Bombay as well as Shanghai and London. The mix of expert services and novel communication technologies made these cities into dense hubs of information and investment that connected them across oceans and continents.

Along with the Suez Canal, the telegraph reshaped commerce and communication at a global level. The new medium was predominantly British and was meant to solidify hegemonic control over the colonial domains. The all-English or "all red" telegraph system was an aggressive imperial strategy. Early on, Bombay was linked to Calcutta, Agra, and Madras through overland telegraphic connection that was expanded to a twelve-thousand-mile web across India. The city was in touch with Europe by cables that snaked overland through Ottoman lands. Once the British-Indian Submarine Telegraph Company laid the first underwater telegraph cables through the Suez Canal, messages sped to London in a budding global telecommunications system. The wired networks created a new consciousness of speed and tempo. The impact on global commerce was immediate. The pace of trading accelerated once buyers and sellers of commodities were in direct contact. Shipping was managed and cargo brokered at a new speed. The mammoth British-led Eastern Telegraph Company stretched lines from India across the Bay of Bengal and the Strait of Malacca to Singapore, and then to Hong Kong and Shanghai.

By the late 1920s, the newer technology of the wireless telegraph was zipping messages between Bombay and London through radio transmitters. Wireless communication was a modern miracle. The Imperial Wireless Chain created by the British government was set up to strengthen the communication network winding across the empire. The King himself inaugurated the service between London and Bombay in 1927 with a message to the viceroy. Expansion of the service was then taken over by the Indian Radio & Cable Communications Company. Telecommunications fused India to global trade in ways that were unimaginable just a generation before. News wires shot information across the globe. Companies gleaned the latest business figures as the data came across minute by minute. Before dawn, the E. D. Sassoon & Company office in Ballard Estate would check the price of raw cotton on the New York Stock Exchange and futures market via wireless to buy the product at the best price. Companies ready to ship cotton wired bids. If buyers were not fast enough, they missed out. E. D. Sassoon's Manchester office, which was in daily touch with management in Bombay, exhorted one shipper to send its offers before 9:00 a.m. "You must keep in mind that we, in this market, have to compete against people, who are all cabling direct to Bombay ... we cannot run the risk to lose our clients."[29] The new technologies increased the mobility and liquidity of assets. They collapsed the temporal plane of global capitalism and made it intensely competitive. Urban helms such as Bombay, Shanghai, and London were yoked in a web of electronic communication.

The electronic infrastructure girdling the planet was an exhilarating investment arena for Bombay's capitalists. Electric impulses along cables and wireless transmissions between Bombay, London, and Shanghai carried the information on which capitalism thrived. Conveying speech through radio waves was a new investment arena. Indian investors formed radio clubs to pay for transmitters and receivers. In Bombay, they initially met at the Taj Mahal Hotel before settling on the old Sailors' Home on Apollo Bunder Road as a permanent location, where hundreds of prominent citizens vied for membership. In 1927, the various clubs joined together as the Indian Radio and Communications Company under the leadership of Ness Wadia of Bombay's celebrated Wadia shipbuilding and cotton dynasty. The colonial government then took over the enterprise and introduced All India Radio with its BBC Empire Service broadcasts from London. Each year, programming on Empire Day in May was devoted to imperial topics and broadcasts.[30] The number of subscribers skyrocketed.

But it was telephony, as it was then known, that was the most exciting piece of new communication equipment. From its headquarters in Bombay, Chicago Telephone & Radio Company imported telephone equipment from the United States and then sold it to the mills and factories. By the 1920s, the chairman and part shareholder of the Bombay Telephone Company was none other than Victor Sassoon, who reported to the board that the new automatic telephones were in high demand. Local investors put together the densest automatic phone system in the British Empire. Direct telephone service to London was opened in 1933. Business publications reported that telephones were widely used during periods of wild fluctuations in bullion prices. Technological speed determined the value of money. A spike in the price of gold meant millions of pounds sterling were negotiated over the phone between India, Europe, and the United States. The newest strategy was the "conference call," in which "executives of big firms . . . could discuss matters as if though seated around a common table."[31]

Over 170 insurance companies were founded in India between 1929 and 1939—an entirely new market that smoothed the path for business and real estate investments. Firms such as New India Assurance, United India Assurance, and the Hindustan Cooperative Insurance Company were homegrown Bombay entities that provided Indian businesses with the services denied by British firms. They poured surplus funds into sumptuous headquarters as property-based wealth creation.[32] Real estate was a signature of global finance and its increasing hold on urban development.

The insurance buildings graced the newly opened Sir Pherozeshah Mehta Road, dug out in 1928 as a connective artery between the old Fort area and the new Ballard Estate business district. These were urban assets that tied Bombay's development into the global circulation of capital. In fact, the city's banks and insurance companies championed the Indian version of art deco that took the world by storm in the 1920s and 1930s. It was pure architectural spectacle, and it was nakedly commercial. The streamlined aesthetic harnessed the rhetoric and power of the Swadeshi movement. It was associated with cosmopolitanism and at the same time signaled national identity. It was a new kind of civic nationalism that translated as an eclectic moderne of Bombay invention by architecture firms such as Master, Sathe and Bhuta; Iyengar & Menzies; and Kora & Bhat.

Trained in Bombay, the architects of the new buildings developed a global worldview and an enthusiastic adaptation of the new materials and building technologies. The lavish ornamentalism of art deco made the buildings charmed symbols of Bombay's modernity. Bold modernist sculptural applications marked the Bombay Mutual Life building and the People's Insurance building. The bas-reliefs on the New India Assurance building depicted workers welding gears and cogs, along with a woman at a spinning wheel in an ode to the swadeshi cause. Global art deco often referred to the distant past and exotic elements both Western and non-Western. Streamlined scenes from Hindu and Mughal mythology as well as classical and Egyptian motifs made the buildings into civic marvels. The Lakshmi Insurance Company building was embellished with an elephant motif in red sandstone and crowned by a bronze statue of the Hindu goddess of wealth and good fortune. Around the Oval Maidan, Marine Drive, Malabar Hill, and Altamount Road, art deco was the aesthetic language that dramatized Bombay's vibrant commercial culture and cosmopolitan sensibilities.

Cement was applauded as a "made in India" material, symbolic of the emancipatory dream of modernity. The traditional building materials of stone or of brick and timber were exchanged for reinforced concrete. The city newspaper *Times of India* lauded concrete for its efficiency and malleability, its color and design qualities.[33] Bombay's art deco buildings showcased the possibilities of concrete structures graced with flamboyant design. Some thirty-three contractors in the city specialized in reinforced concrete construction, far more than either Calcutta or New Delhi. Bombay's venerable Katni Cement Company was financially backed by Sir Cowasji Jehangir, one of the most prominent members of the city's Parsi community and a captain of industry. Jehangir was a member of Bombay's Readymoney family and a force to be reckoned with in the fight for India's independence. Katni Cement was joined in the 1920s–1930s by a proliferation of cement companies privately owned and run by Indians, among which were new Tata and F. E. Dinshaw enterprises. The Wadia family firm constructed the first concrete road in India. The Ferro Concrete Company built Bombay's Central Railway Station. In 1936, ten of these start-up ventures merged to form Associated Cement Companies Limited, one of the largest producers of cement in India.[34] Showcasing Indian-made cement in construction projects such as the new godowns (warehouses) at Sewri or the fabulous art deco buildings on Marine Drive became a swadeshi statement about India's ability to independently industrialize. When Bombay imagined India's modernization in the 1930s, its vision was based on these novel private companies backed by global money from Bombay's mercantile and industrial elites.

The winds of independence blew through the streets and into the skies over Bombay during its first steps toward aviation. Air travel was on the cusp of revolutionizing global connectivity. The British pursued the dream of Icarus with missionary zeal. Aviation would tie together the four corners of its empire. Campaigners for flight jumped on establishing air routes to India as a sign of British dominance in the field. Trials in intercontinental flights between London and India took place in the early 1920s. By 1926, the new Imperial Airways made Bombay and Delhi a journey within five days of London. Airmail service between London and Bombay was launched. Global space was shrinking. The first air routes were networking cities in undreamed-of ways. Aerodromes were established. Flying demonstrations and joyrides introduced the Indian public to the thrill of air travel. They were spectacular urban events. In a breathtaking aerial display in 1920, a Handley-Page 9 plane took off from the makeshift airfield at Bombay's Juhu Beach and flew over the city to welcome the viceroy as the ceremonial gun salute was fired. The giant aircraft carried passengers aloft in the comfort of a silk-lined cabin equipped with writing desk and electric lighting. For thirty minutes, they experienced breathtaking bird's-eye views of the city; nighttime flights meant aeronauts could enjoy the famous twinkling lights of Bombay.

Victor Sassoon had been enthralled with flight since his early days in Brighton. He was a founding member of Britain's Royal Aero Club and flew in air shows before the 1915 crash that ended his flying days (see chapter 1). He remained an enthusiast and active patron of aviation throughout his life and continued to practice his landings with pilots willing to risk their lives. To a certain degree, his love of aviation was in the family bones. Victor shared a temperamental kinship with his cousin Sir Philip Sassoon, who devoted his career in Parliament to the development of British aviation. As undersecretary for the British Air Ministry, he promoted civilian air travel and led the so-called Millionaire's Squadron. Sir Philip flew to India in 1928 to promote routes between England, the Middle East, and India. During his rugged trip in an Iris II flying boat and then a Royal Air Force bomber, he made stops in Cairo, Baghdad, Basra, Karachi, and Delhi. He toured the RAF's northwest frontier air stations that were already being used for bombing raids against intractable tribesmen.[35] By 1933, British aviation enthusiasts had concocted the idea of flying over Mount Everest to "increase our prestige in India and the East generally." One of the pilots was the Marquess of Clydesdale, the youngest squadron leader in the RAF, who claimed the adventure would "show India that we are not the Degenerate Race that its Leaders represent Britain to be." In a dramatic display of aeronautical daring, the group cleared the summit by five hundred feet, snapping photographs of the panorama.[36] They returned to London in triumph.

Victor Sassoon's contribution to Indian aviation lay in the domain of flying clubs. He threw his unrealized ambitions as an aviator into founding them. Flying clubs were considered instrumental in training pilots and garnering public support for air travel. Inspired by his ardent speech on aviation in 1927, the Indian legislature established the Aero Club of India and Burma to encourage new clubs throughout the subcontinent. These organizations were vital to creating air-mindedness and providing would-be pilots with their first skyward forays. It was assumed that good horsemen and sportsmen would make first-rate pilots, and since India's "horsemen [had] taught the world how to play polo, [it] will produce some of the finest pilots the world has seen."[37] Chaired and financed by Sassoon, the Aero Club was quickly affiliated with the Royal Aero Club in Britain, which he had established in his youth. Sir Victor's grand gesture of one hundred thousand rupees to establish the Irwin Flying Fund made him, according to the British viceroy, "the father of Indian aviation."[38] Sassoon joined with local enthusiasts at the Taj Mahal Hotel to officially inaugurate Bombay's local flying club. The organizing committee was filled with members of the city's ruling families: Tata, Fazalbhoy, Currimbhoy, Mehta, Petit. Soon the club was flooded with over two hundred applications. Sassoon immediately put in orders with the De Haviland Company for eight Gypsy Moth biplanes.

The shed on Juhu Beach that served as an early aircraft hangar was retrofitted and improved with workshops and a wireless station. J. R. D. (Jehangir Ratanji Dadabhoy) Tata, considered the visionary founder of Indian commercial aviation, received the first pilot's license in February

1929 and took off in a Gypsy Moth from Juhu airfield. His license number 1 was signed by Victor Sassoon. Sassoon also signed the license for the first woman pilot in India—Tata's sister Sylla. She was the epitome of the Twenties New Woman and had married into Bombay's illustrious Petit family. With aplomb, Lady Sylla climbed aboard her planes in aviator helmet and goggles. Her boldness at a time when the risks were serious did much to promote aviation. In the 1929 gala at Juhu Beach to commemorate the gift of a Gypsy Moth, Lady Sylla led an aerobatic display in the new aircraft and the "bombing of cars with bags of flour."[39] But Sassoon had grander ideas for Bombay and hoped it "would beat all other cities in India in civil aviation" with an aerodrome in the Back Bay and a seaplane base.[40] In the meantime, those out for a dip at Juhu Beach watched the Gypsy Moths and DH.9s circle the palms, "descending low over the beach and frightening the horses and the lovers, then soaring high up into the blue to make a banking turn and descend over the trees."[41] Carloads of enthusiasts assembled at Juhu and lined up to make the skyward journey.

Bombay, Cottonopolis

Ultimately, Sassoon had a mercantile way of seeing the world: he was every inch a cotton capitalist. For global entrepreneurs such as he, the British Empire meant making huge amounts of money. The owners and managing agents of the cotton industry were pilloried for handing down decisions from far-off offices in London with little notion of their consequences on the factory floors. Sir Victor was sneered at by many as a fabulously rich tycoon and a gourmand of life's pleasures. He reveled in flaunting his luxurious tastes, true enough. But he was more than just a figurehead for E. D. Sassoon & Company. As a venture capitalist, he actively embraced the new technologies of the modern age. He trudged through his mills, snapping photographs of the spindles and machinery in action, then cabled his ideas for updating production to the firm's Manchester office at India House.

The chimneys over Girangaon no longer belched coal pollution into the air. The mills were largely driven by hydroelectric power generated by the Tata Power Supply Company, with the Sassoon mills purchasing the majority of the current. The Sassoons as well as the Wadia family were considered the most forward-thinking mill owners in Bombay. They introduced efficiency measures early, including double-frame production, and carried them furthest. That the laborers bore the brunt of these innovations was, in their minds, the price to pay to remain competitive. Many of the mills organized recreational and welfare programs for their mill hands as a way to assuage the workload. The programs were also a foil to avert the strike waves and prevent inroads by the labor unions.

The Sassoon family had put this kind of paternalism to work for generations. In 1926, Sir Victor addressed a packed audience of mill hands at the Laxmi Cinema in Parel for a meeting of the E. D. Sassoon Welfare Institute. Nineteen cooperative societies had agreed to join the endeavor to rid themselves of the pernicious Marwari and Pathan moneylenders that preyed on workers like vultures. The Welfare Institute's members would put away small amounts of money each month that would be saved for future needs. In a speech loaded with uplift for the ignorant masses, Sassoon impressed on his audience the rewards of "saving a little each month and making deposits in the society. You will earn interest on these savings and ... you will have your own money to draw upon in the event of an emergency at any time." The mill hands asked for cooperative canteens in the mills, and night schools and reading rooms for themselves and their children. These were reforms the Sassoon mills put into operation in the following years. In addition, day nurseries for infants and young children were opened. By the 1930s, Bombay's Manchester mills owned by E. D. Sassoon & Company were regularly sponsoring train trips for mill hands to the Dussehra festival in Ahmedabad.[42] But these improvements did little to stop the industrial actions that defined the ongoing conflicts between cotton capitalists attuned to global markets and textile laborers stuck with low pay and long hours. Nor did they prevent Bombay's street protests and populist civic activism.

Like many of Bombay's mills, directors and managers of the Sassoon enterprise were a cabal of familiar associates who had been involved with the family for decades. The Sassoons recruited their firm's leadership from the inside. E. D. Sassoon & Company was a combination of family proprietorship and corporate entity. It was the consummate old-boy network that operated successfully within the framework of empire. Ultimately, gentlemanly capitalism was a device for skimming the profits off every aspect of production and slipping it into the pockets of these wealthy mill-owner families. Bombay's managing agent system came under withering criticism, especially as global competition hacked away at the city's cotton textile industry. Critics blamed the backslapping boards of directors for knowing little and caring less about cotton manufacturing and for lacking the technical know-how to keep the mills successful. Shareholder profits carried far more weight than production goals.

Global connectivity was carried out by specific individuals. Once again, the E. D. Sassoon board of directors provides a glimpse into the privileged anglicized magnates who ranged worldwide. Sitting in the company offices at Ballard Estate were board members Abraham Jacob Raymond and his nephew Albert Raymond. They were also major shareholders in the company as well as trustees of the Sassoon Charity Trusts. Born in India, Abraham Raymond was a shrewd businessman and an intractable personality who had been with the Sassoons since their early days in Hong Kong. He was an influential voice not only in Bombay, where he was involved with the Bombay Zionist Association, but also among Hong Kong's British oligarchy, with a director's seat at the Hong Kong & Shanghai Bank and appointments to the Diamond Jubilee and Coronation Committees. Albert Raymond was also a well-known Hong Kong businessman who was behind the development of the China Light and Power Company (see chapter 7). The Sassoons preferred British managers for their mills, the most important of whom was Fred Stones. He was a big, burly Lancashire man over six feet tall—a "plump laddie," as Victor called him.[43] Stones was blunt and bluff, a wielder of Sassoon authority in both Bombay and London. The global titans in the Sassoon head offices had little to do with the migrant laborers running the textile machinery. Only at the level of the factory floor were Gujarati managers brought in under contract.

The Bombay Millowners' Association was one of the most powerful forces in the city. After 1919, it held seats on the Bombay Municipal Corporation, the Port Trust, the Bombay City Improvement Trust, and the Bombay Legislative Council. Victor Sassoon represented the mill owners in the Indian Legislative Assembly. He was a magnetic figure among the generally dour politicians—wealthy, debonair, quick witted. He was not above grandstanding with extravagant orations laced with ridicule. On the government's rule allowing bachelors to retire earlier than married men, Sassoon (himself a bachelor) joked to general laughter, "Does Government think that bachelors deteriorate earlier than married men?" To dramatize a political point, he showed up at the assembly wearing a gray top hat at a rakish angle. "No European had ever before entered the Assembly with his hat on," a Singapore newspaper reported. That Sassoon's stunt made the news was an indication of how far and wide his parade of wit could reach. The assembly president tried to ignore the entreaties of Muslim members until Sir Victor saved him by finally removing his hat in a sweeping gesture.[44]

Despite the chicanery, he walked a fine line between allegiance to British interests and the reality of colonial domination. The nature of empire was never simply black and white. The Raj and India's global magnates used each other when it was expedient. On the one hand, Sir Victor was a member of the exclusive European Group in the Legislative Assembly. It was the ultimate lobbying clique on behalf of the British imperium, both admired and distained for its power over Indian affairs. Indian government officials complained that this privileged network of good fellows with direct connections to the City in London obstructed their freedom of action. An aggravated member of the Legislative Assembly grumbled that the "masters of the Government of India are the European Group in this House and the Government of India is a mere tool and a slave of that Group."[45] The group's swank gatherings at Bombay's Taj Mahal Hotel were the envy of Raj officialdom. Chumming among the guests was the venerable Sir Frederick Sykes, governor of Bombay. As the city's largest mill owner, Sassoon worked in close association with Sykes, especially on trade policy and currency issues. Sykes had served as controller of civil aviation before taking up his post in Bombay. The men's shared interest in the Royal Air Force and the development of aviation made their rapport an easy one.

Yet it was impossible to ignore the city's Indian business titans, who were steadily aligning with the nationalist cause. The European Group entertained Bombay's Purshotamdas Thakurdas and C. V. Mehta of India's premier intelligentsia; both men were closely associated with British business circles, yet they openly espoused the emergent nationalism of the Congress Party. The group met with Indian freedom fighter Lala Lajpat Rai and offered talks with his independence movement. Gandhi himself treated Bombay mainly as a commercial center. But he met with the mill owners to discourage the import of Lancashire cloth in favor of homegrown Indian textiles. When the Chamber of Commerce in Manchester got wind of Sassoon's having taken a leading part in these conversations, they were livid. C. D. Silas, one of Sassoon's merchants in the Manchester Chamber, was labeled "the enemy" and nearly forced to resign.[46] Extending his hand to both sides in an increasingly raucous colonial relationship could shake Sir Victor's normally impervious position. It was over cocktails and dinner that he talked currency and economic policy with British and Indian corporate barons, Raj socialites, and Arthur Moore, the editor of the Calcutta *Statesman* newspaper. He was a confident and frequent guest of the viceroy, Lord Reading. The bond was helped along by his gift of £37,500 for Bombay's needy and destitute in memory of his father, Edward. Sassoon backed Lord Reading's Factory Acts, which attempted to alleviate working conditions. These limited the workweek for textile laborers to sixty hours and raised the minimum age for child workers to twelve. Sassoon begrudgingly lent his support to India's first Workmen's Compensation Act, although he was skeptical about how it would be applied and demanded that the mill owners be protected from fraud.

The Currency and Tax Revolt

Despite these clubby alliances, Sassoon frequently found himself at loggerheads with British officialdom, which expected his unqualified support. His line in the sand was drawn over currency and taxation. These battles were evocative of the twisted colonial policies that crossed with and impeded global business. Global capitalism worked within a geopolitical system set to safeguard British imperial interests. Particularly in the 1930s, the Great Depression pushed the British government into protectionist policies and squeezing all it could out of India. The impact on Bombay's cotton industry was crushing. The cotton industrialists who had profited so handsomely under British rule found themselves battling against the colonial state that fed them.[47] Sir Victor's fraught position was also emblematic of how Bombay's industrial elite attempted to salvage the textile sector and its global competitiveness while facing the wrath of mill workers trying to save their jobs. It was an unnerving situation that spoke volumes about the vagaries of globalization and the social disparities inherent in cities that had reached these global heights. Currency and taxation reveal globalization from below, at the level of the city, as well as the on-the-ground controversies and disputes that characterized global processes.

The Meston Settlement that formed part of the Government of India Act provided for the transfer of public funds from the provinces to the central government in Delhi and limited the local power of taxation. It put Bombay under far more stringent circumstances than in the past, just as the city was facing the pressures of a swelling population and the need for expensive social reforms and development schemes, especially the costly Back Bay project. Huge sums now had to be handed over to Delhi without local leaders having any real power over their own coffers. The Bombay Presidency was starved for cash and waged a bitter campaign against the Meston Settlement, claiming that "the Government of Bombay is left with the administration of all the expanding services, but every form of expanding revenue is taken away from it."[48] Bombay's government initially resorted to new taxes to cover the shortfalls. But a levy on electrical use and on tobacco sparked immediate resistance. The gap was then made up by borrowing, with the result that the burden of debt hung a millstone around the neck of the city's administration.

The revenue obligations imposed by the Raj were also roundly condemned by Bombay's businessmen as a boldface shot at suppressing the city's industrial renaissance. Colonial dependency was a cruel yoke. The less Britain invested in India, the more it tried to extract revenue through taxes, currency manipulation, and simply appropriating India's earnings.

With the First World War's end, London had reemerged as the financial center of the world, with the pound sterling as its foundation. But it could only maintain that position with the help of India by manipulating the Crown colony's financial policy. London held the purse strings. The idea that fiscal policy was dictated from Whitehall entirely for the benefit of Britain stuck in the craws of Bombay's capitalists. The British were riding roughshod over Indian needs and robbing the country for their own benefit. The injustices broke out into fierce political battles. Sassoon used his bully pulpit in the Legislative Assembly to denounce the servitude demanded by British overseers: "It might be advisable and suitable for us to send the peons from our offices to take our places with instructions to cry 'aye, aye' to every demand of the Government." India, he fumed, should look after its own public services rather than going through London. He argued against state management of the Indian railway and instead insisted, "I want the Bombay railways managed in Bombay. . . . No, not by the State . . . by company management."[49]

Stanley Reed of the *Times of India* groaned, "Unfortunately two measures were taken which weakened the confidence of the industrial classes in the good faith of Britain . . . the cotton excise duties and the management of the currency."[50] The Bombay mills produced low-grade yarns and cloth destined for the home market and for Asia, while the lucrative British and European markets were left to Manchester and its better fabrics. Unwilling to tolerate any competition, the British imposed heavy import and excise taxes on Indian cotton textiles. Imperial policy staunchly defended the Lancashire cotton barons, who worked in tandem with the India Office in London and lobbied Whitehall fiercely. Lancashire exercised a notorious degree of influence over British policy in India. It was losing market share in India and did everything it could to defend what interests remained.

The excise taxes hamstrung Bombay just when its mills were facing severe competition from Japanese cotton textiles. Colonialism both reinforced globalization and impeded it. The torturous junctures played out in global cities with striking intensity. Japan had already muscled in on Bombay's yarn trade with China. Trade between India and China had become more modest once the sale of opium fell off. But cotton yarn replaced the poppy as India's major export to Hong Kong and Shanghai.[51] P&O steamships loaded with the yarn still sailed regular routes between Bombay and Shanghai. While colonial policy hobbled Bombay, Osaka was free to respond to global demand and steam into the Huangpu River loaded with cheaper yarn for Shanghai's mills. Japan was also importing both coarse and better-quality fabrics into India in direct competition with Bombay's textiles. Mill owners could point to the surge in imported cotton textiles at the port as clear evidence of this activity, while bales of unsold local cotton cloth and yarn at Bombay's mills piled up in the Sewri warehouses. Even more galling, the leading Japanese textile company, Mitsui, was purchasing defunct cotton mills in the city and turning them into profitable businesses.

The cotton duties drew the wrath of Bombay's mill owners. They besieged the governor of Bombay in protest and threatened to reduce the wages of their workers as their only recourse. It was a risky strategy that threatened the city with more strikes. Sir Victor raged in the press against the injustices of British Finance Minister Basil Blackett's excise tax, which gave the Japanese cotton industry a 17.5 percent advantage over Indian-produced articles: "It would be inconceivable in any country but India that a Finance Minister should view with such nonchalance the handicapping of a home industry."[52] Blackett presented the fait accompli to the Legislative Assembly, where Sassoon shot back that Blackett "had the face of a cherub and the methods of a tank."[53] It was these injustices Bombay was forced to swallow that aligned its businessmen ever more closely with the nationalist rebels against British interests. Added to the attraction of the swadeshi cause was the growing demand for homespun Indian-made cloth, which helped keep the cotton trade alive. Patriotic "Buy Indian" campaigns were a foil to the injustices of imperial rule.

The eventual suspension of the excise tax was hailed as a momentous nationalist victory, as were tariffs slapped on yarn imported into Bombay. The debates in the Legislative Assembly over tariffs on Japanese imports were intense. The mill owners claimed that Japan's use of women as cheap labor working night shifts in the Osaka mills made the competition insufferable. By comparison, the cost for Bombay's labor was steep. Sassoon likened the Indian mill industry to a "wounded man lying in the road." In a fiery defense of Bombay's cotton mills, he insisted that local industry be saved, if for no other reason than to employ the surplus rural population that flooded into the city: "A prosperous textile industry was essential to the well-being of India."[54] But his speech mostly fell on deaf ears. A cauldron of antagonism fueled attacks against the "multi-millionaire millowners." Indian nationalists were incredulous to their cries for help. The Bombay mill owners were bitter enemies, blamed for mismanagement and overcapitalizing their businesses. Labor unions pilloried management for pocketing profits and doing "precious little" by way of innovation, then blaming their fiasco on Japanese imports.[55]

British colonialism was the problem. The trade unions called for nationalization of an industry "still in the hands of European managers and officers." They demanded that Indian mill workers be protected from the kind of abuse their Japanese counterparts endured. They chastised the government for being intimidated by millionaires. In addition, they groused that mill owners were backed by Indian politicians and the press, "even though they badly treat their employees."[56] Sassoon was accused of not taking these populist attacks seriously and instead relying on the backroom politics of a select committee to push through higher tariffs on imported yarns and piece goods. What the mill owners thought was a matter of trade policy negotiated among gentlemen degenerated into a furious political battle. Quite capable of wielding their power, they launched a public crusade, calling an All India Conference of mill owners and alerting the press to generate popular support.

Nothing drew ire as quickly as the currency ratio. In the minds of Indian nationalists and industrialists alike, it came to represent every aspect of India's economic backwardness. The instability of the rupee was a chronic problem. Every few years, the British would call a currency commission to address the situation. Maintaining some fragile confidence in the rupee was a matter of their self-interest. It made certain that India could pay its loans and home charge remittances to London, which offset Britain's deficit in other parts of the world. This became a centerpiece of British economic policy. London restricted the amount of silver coinage minted and the flow of paper money in India to keep the value of the rupee high. India was then more likely to pay its obligations without resorting to more borrowing. But many Indian businessmen and politicians were convinced that the rupee was overvalued, making Indian goods too expensive on the global market and strangling India's trade. A storm of protest broke out any time the exchange rate was pegged at a higher level, because it penalized India's commercial and financial interests. If the rupee was depreciated in value, it lowered prices but put a tremendous strain on the Indian government.

All this made monetary policy in India a high-wire act made worse by its antediluvian banking system. When it came to India's banks and capital flows, even the venerable John Maynard Keynes admitted, "I am not clear."[57] Exchange and interest rates bounced like pinballs between Bombay's presidency banks, exchange banks, joint-stock banks, and private banks owned by shroffs, Marwaris, and money changers. The rupee's volatility was not just a headache internal to India. Indian mercantile interests reigned supreme throughout the western Indian Ocean basin and down the east coast of Africa. The exchange banks that financed all of India's global trade controlled the council bills that paid businesses in rupees for their exports. They received deposits in rupees and provided short-term loans and letters of credit in rupees. Rupees were stashed in pockets throughout the Arabian Sea and Indian Ocean trading networks. British banks along the Arabian littoral operated only in rupees. Customs fees were paid in rupees. Without some stable notion of the rupee's value, business was reduced "to the uncertainties of gambling," wrote Indian economist and political reformist B. R. (Bhimrao Ramji) Ambedkar.[58]

The twisted maneuvers around currency policy were tied directly to the global market in silver and gold bullion. Silver and gold had two interrelated meanings. They were commodities, bought and sold as a form of wealth. They were also the mechanism for measuring the value of currency. In both senses, they were essential to the economic life of London, Bombay, and Shanghai and were a vital connective tissue between them. The gold standard did not function worldwide. As a prime example, the Indian rupee was a silver-based currency. India was long known as a bottomless pit of the precious metal. Its appetite for both silver and gold was legendary, and it imported vast quantities of both. Gold came from South Africa, silver from the Americas. In the 1920s, India was importing countless millions of ounces of silver each year. Its value was stunning.[59]

The metals were filtered through Bombay, which possessed the largest bullion market in India. The flow of silver bullion had long irrigated the city's prodigious money markets and banking networks. For instance, the city's illustrious Mehta family that drafted the Bombay Municipal Act and founded the *Bombay Chronicle* newspaper had risen to prominence as bullion brokers. Even more than paper currency, bullion greased the urban economy at every level. Traders started each morning reviewing cable messages concerning silver prices that had accumulated overnight from Shanghai. By the afternoon, Bombay's prices were cabled back to Shanghai and to London and New York. Silver was a visible possession from the banks down to the chawls. "Everybody buys silver," one of the city's eminent Parsi businessmen reported. "Silver is the poor man's gold. . . . Any silver money which the peasants get when they sell their crops, or things of that kind, they go to the silver merchant."[60] The only property women could own was personal ornaments, always of silver. Indian families hoarded silver jewelry, coins, and ingots as a hedge against the untrustworthy rupee and times of crisis. It was their store of wealth against the uncertainty of the global financial markets.

Ultimately, the value of the rupee and Bombay's economic stability depended on this silver hoard. It did the sorting between extreme wealth and extreme poverty. But the First World War had put tremendous pressure on the fragile rupee. The Indian financial tribute sent to London for the war effort was enormous. While the circulation of rupee notes rose to unprecedented levels during the war, the proportion of overpriced silver bullion held in Indian government reserves in Bombay plummeted to just 10 percent. There was little to nothing backing the quantities of paper currency floating through India. Panic mounted about a collapse of the rupee and a run on the banks. It risked snowballing into a backlash against British rule and civil unrest.[61] The impact of these gyrations in the value of money and bullion was immediate on the streets of Bombay because everyone was subject to the spins on the freewheeling currency markets. In 1918, wild rumors about the worthlessness of the paper rupee note traveled through Bombay's bazaars. The popular Postal Savings Bank and the Bombay currency office were besieged by frenzied mobs demanding to exchange rupee notes for silver coin. The nightmare scenario seemed to be playing out. The situation was saved only by a cargo of two hundred million ounces of silver bullion—melted down from silver coins—from the United States. Violent fluctuations of the rupee continued from 1921 through 1924 and did nothing but agitate Bombay's already sulfurous social atmosphere.

Global cities were where capital concentrated and accumulated. Their banking and capital markets, and the steady growth in financialization, greased the global economy. At the same time, however, Bombay was also a colonial dependency. In the absurdities of empire, India's silver rupee was actually a gold-backed currency. Its value depended on the gold price of silver. This Manichaean system of exchange bound the rupee to the quid. India purchased silver in London with its gold assets, which propped up the liquidity of the pound sterling. These gold reserves from India were then held in the City of London by fiat and freely used for Britain's own interests (see chapter 5).[62] It was an untenable system that kept Indian currency and wealth in a British stranglehold.

The criticism of British currency policy came directly from the business world of Bombay, where India's full conversion to a gold standard was held as canonical belief. It was seen as the panacea for all India's ills. The gold standard was directly related to the balance of trade and the notion that based on gold, the currency would be solid and fixed on the global marketplace. Essentially, the supply of money would become automatic, and most important, it would be out of the hands of London and the Lancashire lobby that manipulated India's currency for its own benefit. Bombay cotton trader Purshotamdas Thakurdas, who got his start selling cotton to the Sassoon mills and became one of the city's legendary industrial barons and politicians, led the celebrated battle over the rupee exchange ratio. Known as "King Cotton," Thakurdas's gaze was penetrating behind his spectacles as he argued that the "Gold Standard and gold currency are after all India's birthright."[63] It was the only way to stabilize the currency and provide faith in India's finances.

Bombay's industrialists battled fiercely against a rupee tied to silver and a currency ratio raised to one shilling sixpence (1s. 6d.) against the pound sterling. The decision was announced in London in 1924 and then cabled to India without recourse. The whole of the viceroy's Executive Committee threatened to resign. The exchange standard still tied India to the apron strings of sterling. The currency ratio represented over a 12 percent bounty for imports at the expense of the Indian producer. All the Indian Chambers of Commerce were against it. For the Bombay textile industry already damaged by global competition, this was an assault on India's home industries with dire repercussions. It made competing with cheap Japanese cotton imports nearly impossible. Representing the Millowners' Association, Victor Sassoon was a singular figure on behalf of Bombay's cotton mills. He stood before the Royal Commission on Indian Currency and Finance at the Imperial Secretariat in Delhi and gave exhaustive oral evidence of the harmful impact the high exchange ratio had on Bombay's textile exports and even on its home market. In an interview with the *Times of India*, he accused the Currency Commission of a "deliberate distortion of facts" based on "unproved and apparently unprovable assumptions."[64] Bombay's business elites fought the government in Delhi and the India Office tooth and nail over the currency exchange rate and demanded it be reduced to one shilling fourpence. Sassoon recounted the behind-the-scenes intrigue, the skulduggery and the under-the-table bribes, in his diary. It was treacherous political terrain.

To bolster the cause, Bombay's global magnates launched a campaign to mobilize public opinion in favor of the gold standard and the 1s. 4d. currency ratio. The Indian Currency League was organized at one of the city's legendary garden parties at the Willingdon Club. Sassoon served as the initial chairman, although the position was taken over by the preeminent nationalist reformer Srinivasa Sastri. In October 1926, the league called its first meeting, where Sassoon addressed the crowd. In a rousing speech, his verdict on the "national disaster" of the elevated currency ratio brought cheers from the crowd.[65] The league was Bombay's propaganda tool, with branches set up throughout India. Sassoon traveled from town to town, campaigning for reform. He and Purshotamdas Thakurdas kept up the pressure by hosting a party for five hundred guests at the Willingdon Club to honor the governor of the Imperial Bank of India. League advocates chatted up the cream of Bombay society as they wandered the grounds, drinks in hand. The Indian Currency League was pro-Bombay and pro-capitalist. It also helped move the city's merchants and mill owners closer to the Swaraj nationalist cause.

The *Bombay Chronicle* and the *Times of India* published a cascade of partisan articles that pounded out the currency ratio message. The *Bombay Chronicle* was a powerful voice for the nationalist movement and even offered cash prizes for the best essay on the topic "Why 1s 6d Ratio is Ruinous to India." Money bought influence in the press. Other major newspapers were owned by the city's tycoons—the *Indian Daily Mail* by the Petit family, while the *Prajamitra* was owned by the Tatas and could be counted on in the campaign. Sassoon himself proposed publishing a newspaper to boost grassroots support. Named the *Morning Post of India*, it was to publish editions in Bombay, Calcutta, and Delhi, but it never got off the ground. Sassoon was also motivated in this regard by ongoing personal criticism in the press. In a stormy dispute over his company's capital reserves, the *Bombay Chronicle* accused him of posing "as a guardian of the poor in the Currency question" but "out to crush the poor shareholders of the Company that bore the name of the Sassoons."[66] The shareholders were used to raking in the dividends of the boom years. This negative press hinted at the thorny role Bombay's capitalists played as both hard-headed factory owners competing on global markets and would-be local politicians. The nationalist Free Press of India, the country's first Indian-run news agency, was controlled by Bombay's business titans and became a mouthpiece for the Currency League. The league collected petitions containing thousands of signatures, especially by businessmen associated with the Bombay banks and stock exchange. Sassoon took on Finance Minister Basil Blackett in the press, accusing him of perpetrating an injustice to India with the 1s. 6d. currency ratio and "conjuring up bogeys" about any reform.[67] Despite the league's Herculean efforts, in 1927 the government pushed the currency bill through by only three votes and pegged the value of the rupee at 1s. 6d.

The fierceness of these currency exchange battles was tied directly to the Bombay cotton industry. It was clear that its celebrated production was in dire straits. The combination of a fading species of colonial capitalism and the tightening global competition was its undoing. The financial losses were staggering, as was the declining value of cotton shares on Bombay's stock market. The downturn meant reducing the costs of production by rapidly optimizing equipment and reducing the bonuses and salaries workers had come to depend on. The Sassoon mills introduced yet another efficiency scheme, with spinners operating more spindles and weavers handling three looms instead of two. Over five thousand of its twenty-seven thousand workers were dismissed. In the minds of mill owners, it was the only way to save their industry from ruin.[68] Fred Stones, an E. D. Sassoon & Company mill manager, remarked, "Labour must be educated to realize that the whole question of success or failure is the ability to meet foreign competition, which in effect means lower costs of production."[69] The impact on Bombay was immediate.

The 1924 mill workers' strikes hit with tremendous brutality. For mill hands, the malign forces of the global cotton nexus were stacked against them. They blamed European managers for blatant racism and callous disregard for Indian laborers. Over eighty mills were completely paralyzed by the first walkout. During a long three months of "unrest, discontent and despair"[70] and then another three-month walkout in 1925, well over sixty thousand mill operators were idle. They commandeered the streets and hurled stones at the mills, passing motorcars, and trains. Thousands fled Bombay for their villages, while thousands of others stuck in the city were near indigence. Then the oilmen at Sewri joined the strike. Rumors spread like wildfire that the walkouts were instigated by Bolshevik agents. In 1926, the government passed the Trade Unions Act that monitored trade unions and attempted to quell industrial unrest. The furor over the 1929 Public Safety Bill to keep foreign communists out of India and restrict strike action made clear the government's dread of the "Red Poison" and Bolshevik conspiracies. Sassoon plunged into the debate in the Indian Legislative Assembly, warning that communists were being sent to India as trained propagandists. He gave a graphic account of his personal experience of the dangers of communism in China. In an interview with the *Times of India*, he recoiled in horror at "'Red' intriguers from Moscow. The grievances of Indian labourers . . . are being assiduously utilized as tools for spreading Communist doctrines." The Swarajists who opposed the "Anti-Red" bill played down the communist danger and alleged that Lancashire was financing the strikes. But the real problem of Indian workers "was that they were hungry. Mud houses were no sign of prosperity. The soil for Communism was there in hungry stomachs and mud houses."[71]

The Royal Commission on Labour, set up in 1929 to examine labor conditions in India, agreed precisely with this view. The Whitley Commission, as it was known, was to recommend measures for improving labor relations in India. As the principal mill owner in Bombay and a member of the Legislative Assembly, Sassoon was immediately named among the 12 members, 6 of whom were Indian and 5 English, including the 1 woman. Stung by the attempt to sabotage their movement through the Public Safety Bill, most workers' organizations boycotted the commission as a ploy. The *Labour Monthly* reported, "This Commission, dominated by capitalists like the Bombay millowner Sir Victor Sassoon, who, by starvation plus brutal force, temporarily defeated the textile workers of Bombay," had no chance of support. It was a struggle between Indian rights and global capital. Sassoon predicted that "Bombay appears to be heading towards economic suicide."[72]

Undaunted, the commission set off on two tours of India totaling sixteen thousand miles. It conducted hundreds of interviews, investigated labor conditions in textile mills, steel factories, and small-scale manufacturing, and witnessed some of the most impoverished conditions in the country. In between leisurely meals at various Government Houses, Sassoon and the rest of the commission inspected slums and health offices in addition to "mills with 15-hour shifts," and they descended into "one of the worst" of India's mines.[73] Although the commission was clearly meant to shore up the Raj's hold on India, there was simply no denying the obvious. It reported that grinding poverty was the main cause of India's unrest and despair. Employers contributed to the hardship through pitiful wages and often appalling working conditions. Most workers were in debt to unscrupulous moneylenders. The commission recommended ending the jobber system and cleaning up factories. It endorsed cutting back mill work to fifty-four hours per week.

Interviewed by the commission in Bombay, E. D. Sassoon manager Stones claimed that it was impossible for the company to pay for health and unemployment benefits for workers along with higher wages. Given the competition the mills faced from Japanese textiles, it would "kill the goose that lays the golden eggs." Instead, he defended the Sassoon company record for twenty-three blocks of decent chawls, night school classes, and the E. D. Sassoon Welfare Institute that assisted the mill hands' cooperative societies. The company was the only one in Bombay that provided cheap grain and tea shops at its mills for the mill hands. Stones later earned a knighthood for his services to India in enacting these welfare reforms at the E. D. Sassoon mills.[74] But the company sidestepped the underlying motivation. Although these measures responded to worker demand, they were also meant to control cooperative efforts and counteract the organization of textile trade unions along the lines of those in England. The gulf between workers stuck in a local downward spiral and capitalists dealing on the global market was just too wide to close.

In 1928, the mills were shut down again for six months by a general strike directed by the communist-led labor movement. The disturbances continued into 1929. Bombay came to a standstill. Shops were looted. The mill gates were scenes of violent protests and picket lines. Bales of cloth were set aflame. Fueling the turmoil were the crusade for independence and full-scale agitation against British rule. Congress leaders urged the boycott of the city's foreign-owned mills. Panicked by the instability and by the Depression, capital poured out of the country. The hemorrhaging worsened the already dire economic situation. The value of the rupee plummeted. Silver hoards were sold off as families looked for a way out of destitution. They were forced to sell what little they had. The smoldering fury broke out into devastating riots and general strikes again in 1932 and 1934. The storm continued to rage over the arrest of Gandhi and Swarajist leaders. During "Red Week," the city was beset by arson. Vendettas between Muslims and Hindus ended with fierce street fighting. Temples and mosques were vandalized.

Meanwhile, cotton piece goods piled up in the Sewri warehouses. In 1930, commodity prices collapsed, and the Bombay cotton market was in a state of panic. The high exchange rate did nothing but aggravate the crisis, which was why the mill owners fought the currency ratio with such ferocity. Victor Sassoon was pessimistic that the calamity in the mills could be resolved: "The outlook, strike or no strike is, in my opinion, very gloomy."[75] Between foreign competition and the worker demands for higher wages and opposition to efficiency measures, Bombay's mills had little chance at solvency. To save themselves, the mill owners negotiated the Ottawa Agreements of 1932 and the Lees-Moody Pact that followed. The Bombay and Lancashire cotton producers momentarily allied and slapped quotas on Japanese textile imports. It was a devil's agreement made entirely within the structure of British imperialism and the close contacts Bombay's industrialists enjoyed with Raj officialdom. It guaranteed British preferential access to the Indian market for some 160 industrial goods. In return, only ten types of Indian goods, mostly raw materials, were granted free access to the British market. And they were goods the British would have purchased regardless. The agreements poured gasoline on the fire of discord and sent India's small homegrown traders and nationalists into a fury.

Sir Victor instructed Stones to meet with "the devil himself" if he could find a way out of the strikes and the boycott. Despite intense negotiations with workers' unions, the beleaguered manager could "not deliver the goods."[76] By 1932, eleven mills in Bombay had temporarily closed. Another nineteen had been liquidated, including fabled mills owned by the Currimbhoy and Petit families.[77] Other mills on the brink of folding were quickly gobbled up by the competition. E. D. Sassoon & Company took over the David Sassoon Mill, the Apollo Mill, the Elphinstone Mill, and the Manchester Mill. But this did little good. Stones remarked, "Entering the harbor some months ago in the late evening, the city stood out like a chain of fairy lights and I could not help but wonder with the deepest anxiety what the future had in store for such a cosmopolitan city, knowing as I did, the long depression it had been called upon to face."[78]

In March 1928, the European Group gave a going-away dinner in New Delhi for Sir Basil Blackett upon his retirement and return to England. Amid the speeches and boozy toasts by members of the Indian Legislative Assembly and Britain's ruling elites, Blackett took an optimistic tone in his remarks about the future of India. He had won his finance bill against the opposition of Sassoon and the Bombay titans who opposed the tightening noose of British policy. In contrast, Sassoon maintained a frosty cordiality but was not done lobbying his cause. He demanded more representation by provincial leadership in the legislature against the cabal in New Delhi, and in fact helped organize the Country League of India to lobby for more open rule. For his part, Purshotamdas Thakurdas predicted that the government's policies would drive more political parties into the Swarajist camp.[79] Nonetheless, Blackett attempted largesse and declared his faith in the immense possibilities of India and the crucial role its capitalists would play. He thanked Sassoon and his allies for taking a defeat over the exchange ratio in a sportsmanlike spirit. Whatever might have been the rights or wrongs of a particular figure to stabilize the rupee, he said, "I am inclined to say what I once told a very distinguished Cabinet Minister: 'It does not much matter what you decide, but for God's sake decide it now and do not put it off till to-morrow.'" The distinguished audience erupted in laughter and cheers.[80]

For the Sassoon cotton empire, the writing was on the wall. Sir Victor spent much of 1929 and 1930 touring India with the Labour Commission or relaxing in London, relishing the social season and thoroughbred racing. By 1931, he was already moving his assets to Shanghai. "The political situation does not encourage one to launch out in big schemes in India for the time being," he lamented to a Reuters reporter. "It looks as if India under Swaraj will have a great deal of internal trouble . . . there is a general feel in India against the foreigner's developing the country, which they call 'exploiting' it."[81] Casting himself as a foreigner simply alluded to the long-standing view of the Sassoons as Europeans who profited splendidly from the British Raj. Yet his stance against British financial policies in India made this alliance tenuous at best. He had seen enough and had had enough. His decision to "quit India" flashed around the world and made the front pages of the business news in India and China, in Europe and the United States for what it might mean. There were few sympathies for capitalist mill owners like Sassoon among those eager for India's independence. But it was queer to think of Bombay without the Sassoons.

There was also fear that Sir Victor's example might be taken up by other industrialists, damaging any hope for the country's future. "There would be heart-searching and great renunciations should Sir Victor completely abandon India, and it is obvious that he never will," a London paper reported. "Bombay is a proud and glittering city and much of its pride and splendor are connected with the house of Sassoon."[82]

The paper's optimism was wistful. Interviewed by the *Times of India* before his departure for China, Sassoon was asked about the textile industry in Bombay. "Is it still in existence?" he quipped. "Bombay is worse than Shanghai so far as trade is concerned."[83] Sailing away in grand style with reporters at his heels appealed to his sense of the theatrical. But he carried with him a sense of both nostalgia and fatalism. What was left of the Sassoon cotton textile empire limped on. But Sassoon had abandoned Bombay. It was time to pull out of trade and into finance. His decision followed the shifts taking place within the British world system itself. Britain was still in a commanding position over long-distance commerce and high finance, even if it was in the autumn of its empire. Only in London could the complex commercial choreography of transferring the Sassoon fortune from one global city to another take place. London's City was where the intermediaries and the regulators of the supply and demand for money were located. It was the headquarters of global banks, among which was the E. D. Sassoon financial enterprise. In the ironies made from his alliance with the British Empire, Sir Victor headed for the imperial capital and the E. D. Sassoon offices on Fenchurch Street, the control center for his wealth. From there, he plotted out the financial maneuvering that freed him from Bombay and opened tempting prospects for investments elsewhere.

* 4 *
London, Magnet of the World

> We have only to open our eyes and on every hand is a touch of
> something that stirs the sense of wonder within us.
>
> ARTHUR MEE, *London* (1937)

The imperial capital of London was the "magnet of the world." Agog at its cityscape, journalist Arthur Mee wrote, "We have only to open our eyes and on every hand is a touch of something that stirs the sense of wonder within us."[1] Novelist and playwright J. B. Priestley captured the changes that had taken place in England, and principally in London, since the First World War: "This is the England of arterial and by-pass roads, of filling stations and factories that look like exhibition buildings, of giant cinemas and dance-halls and cafés, bungalows with tiny garages, cocktail bars, Woolworths, motor-coaches, wireless, hiking, factory girls that look like actresses, grey-hound racing and dirt tracks, swimming pools, and everything given away for cigarette coupons."[2]

With a population exceeding eight million by the mid-1930s, Greater London was leviathan. It spread out like a vast octopus, gobbling up villages and hamlets across the surrounding Home Counties to reach over eleven million people. Railroads and roadways stretched out their arms across the farthest terrain, pumping hundreds of thousands of people and vehicles back and forth, to and fro, in the rhythms of a global city. The old districts in the center of London were chronically jammed with motorized vehicles of every size and kind—motortrucks and vans, motor coaches, motorcycles, cars and taxis. They skirted the horse-drawn carriages and wagons that still lugged along the roads. Daily, hundreds of thousands of people clambered onto buses, trams, and railcars, and into the Tube. Irish novelist Shaw Desmond attempted to cross Piccadilly and "saw the Baby Austins run in and out of the inextricable traffic seemingly to run under the motor-buses and out on the other side.... Taxi on taxi. Bus on bus. Car on car. Life tearing past at thirty miles an hour, and death treading on life's heels. That is the London of 1929."[3]

The forces propelling its growth and their impact on daily life were topics of passionate debate among urban observers. A point of contention was London's mix of ethnic neighborhoods that made up one of the capital's most celebrated or most disturbing qualities, depending on the point of view. The two sides were in constant, chattering dialogue. As author Robert Sinclair quipped, "London... is no longer a town, it is a nation."[4] Any urban explorer could easily come upon the cultural diversity that had long marked London as a cosmopolitan global city. It was an immense seaport through which cargo and people from across the world flowed. It was a mirror of the British Empire. Its ethnic mix and babble of languages tied the capital directly to its colonial domains. Tens of thousands of Indians and Southeast Asians, Chinese, Africans, West Indians, Irish, Italians, and Jews made up its global canvas. London was described as a "huge patchwork quilt."[5] These traits were just as true of Bombay and Shanghai, for all three cities were global helms. But while the profusion of peoples in Bombay and Shanghai was seen by Westerners as exotic oriental allure, the sight of "Hindoos" and "Chinamen" on the streets of London was shocking. The multiethnic neighborhoods of the imperial capital were at best disturbing, or at worst stigmatized as suspiciously foreign and threatening.

London's global reach was marked by thousands of ethnic eateries and cafés, where foreigners found jobs cooking or serving food or washing dishes. Immigrants became tradesmen of one type or another. Street markets spilled over with trinkets and goods from across the world pushed by small-time vendors. "They have to live in London," journalist James A. Jones sniped, "because it is a necessity of the most regrettable; but to alter their life—ah! Some of them do not know one word of English after forty years; and why should they, when they can do all their shopping in their own tongue."[6] London relied on its immigrant workers. They toiled in sweatshops and factories and on the docks, as they did in Bombay and Shanghai. They were the itinerant workforce of the global economy. They did the dirty work few others would touch.

People from all walks of life traveled the seas to escape poverty and persecution, searching for opportunity. Streams of exiles and refugees sought a haven in London and somehow found a foothold amid the city's immensity. London's Russian Refugees Relief Association raised money and collected food and clothing for the thousands fleeing the Russian Civil War. As the Nazi Party came to power, Jews from across Germany and eastern Europe fled to London to escape persecution. Many of these refugees were highly educated but stuck working in the low-level jobs that were the migrant's plight. London's growing community of Muslims donated to the London Mosque Fund for a place of worship. Intellectuals and reformers from across the British Empire traveled to London to challenge the colonial order and organize their nationalist causes. Mohandas Gandhi and Jawaharlal Nehru were both educated there. The city was long a crucible for revolutionary ideas. Its ten-thousand-strong African population was a hotbed of radical Pan-Africanism. Students arrived for university training. The Chinese Christian Students' Union gathered its charges at the Hall of Good News, while the Chinese Girl Students' Aid Committee found homes for young women.[7] All this signaled the ethnic diversity deep within the global urban realm.

But even grudging acceptance of the capital's multiculturalism ran up against outright hostility to strangers. London's cosmopolitan qualities dissolved in the face of a ferocious backlash against foreigners. The Aliens Registration Act of 1919 and the Aliens Order of 1920 restricted immigration by requiring migrants to be in possession of prearranged work permits issued by the Ministry of Labour. Immigrants were compelled to register with the police. The ethnic enclaves tucked into the muddle of streets, especially in the East End, were chided for being an impenetrable thicket of poverty and communist plotting. The alien acts were used against Jews as bogeys and against pro-independence activists from India and Africa deemed a public threat. Racism and xenophobia ramped up. As unemployment rose during the economic slump of the 1930s, foreigners became easy scapegoats. Popular opinion accused them of threatening the jobs and homes of Englishmen, just as it pointed the finger at the mill hands of Bombay and Shanghai for ruining England's reliable textile industry. Blame spread in every direction. But migrants continued to flood in.

London Modern

London's Thames Embankment was a visual theater of the global companies and infrastructure of the twentieth century. The colossal, curved Unilever House opened on that site as the control center for the consumer goods enterprise, with operations outsourced across a breathtaking worldwide geography. Some three thousand people rode up a dozen elevators to offices in what was dubbed the "wonder building of modern commerce."[8] The massive headquarters of newly formed Imperial Chemical Industries towered over the north bank of the Thames at Millbank. It employed tens of thousands of people across the globe, including at its facilities in Bombay and Shanghai. Multinational corporations tied their identity to art deco as the image of the future. It had a big-city feel. The sprawling global operations of Shell-Mex & British Petroleum were headquartered at Shell Mex House on the Thames Embankment. One of the largest buildings in London, its bold moderne design was topped by an imposing ziggurat clock tower. The massive brick Battersea Power Station with its giant chimneys dominated the south bank of the Thames, as did the Deptford Electric Supply Station that was among the largest in the world. The control rooms for these dynamos were showcases of art deco splendor. Their generators powered the electrification of London's railway, tram, and Tube networks as well as the city's new industries.

Already the hub of newspapers and publishing, London was the command center for the swelling quantity and increasing transmission speed of information vital to global transactions. Newspapers and periodicals, specialized publications and professional organizations collected and distributed bulletins, data, and reports from across the world. New Carmelite House was the enlarged art deco headquarters of the *Daily Mail* and could "turn out half a million papers in an hour." The Daily Express building on Fleet Street was a sleek moderne masterpiece with a glass frontage framed in gleaming chromium. "Fleet Street never sleeps, and cannot afford to yawn," wrote journalist H. V. Morton, adding that the world flings "news at it by wireless, cable, telegraph, telephone, and luncheon tables."[9]

Telecommunications was a high-tech industry with its own built form. The BBC, originally known as the British Broadcasting Company, became a public corporation in 1927. Its Broadcasting House in Portland Place was an art deco icon for on-air media, replete with the sculptural reliefs — in this case Prospero and Ariel from Shakespeare's *The Tempest* — akin to the moderne corporate buildings in Bombay. Its studios and control rooms were designed as acoustic platforms. The BBC Empire Service beamed out short-wave radio programs in a new high-tech fusion of British domains, with broadcasts directly to Bombay. By the 1930s, the south end of the Crystal Palace in Sydenham had become the home of the Baird Television broadcasting station. It beamed out early programming with the most powerful television transmitter in Europe.

In the early years after the First World War, London's economy roared into recovery. A backlog of investments in factories and industries coupled with pent-up consumer demand sent machinery whirring and people back to work. Money seemed easy. Speculation ran rampant and fortunes were made overnight. But the good times were hardly shared by all. London's working classes faced soaring prices, overcrowding in miserable slums, and fruitless hunts for decent housing. The burdens of everyday life fueled anger and frustration, especially after the sacrifices of the war. The worker uprisings in Europe at the end of the First World War, especially the Russian Revolution, radicalized labor activists worldwide. The moment was filled with electrifying fervor and potential. Support for the Labour Party surged in London. Strikes and protests seemed unending in 1919 and 1920. They matched the turmoil in Bombay and Shanghai, and so many other cities worldwide. There were rent strikes, hunger strikes, police strikes, prisoner strikes, strikes at Shakespeare's Globe Theatre, trawler strikes, tramway strikes, strikes by law clerks and by waitresses, by sales clerks at department stores. Masons stopped making tombstones, and craftsmen stopped making pianos. Drapers in the city's textile warehouses walked out. Some five to six thousand bakers joined them. Early morning queues formed around bakeries in the hope of grabbing daily bread. Soldiers awaiting discharge and short of job prospects rioted. In the hot summer months, young men waged pitched battles with police. In "a blow against the public," motormen shut down the Tube. Stoppages by electricians threatened to "plunge London into darkness."[10] Engineers walked out at London's aircraft factories. The shipyards stood still. Stevedores shut down the docks.

Protest marches became the routine of daily life. Massive peace demonstrations occurred at Buckingham Palace in 1919. Tens of thousands marched from the East India Docks and Battersea, from St. Pancras to Hyde Park to protest food prices and profiteering and "an apathetic government" immune to the plight of the working classes. The India League organized mass meetings for home rule. Protests took place in Trafalgar Square against the war in Russia. There were marches by Sinn Féin for Irish independence. Trade union demonstrations were massive events. Thousands of women in "gala frocks and carrying flowers and banners" marched from Hyde Park to Kingsway Hall to hear speeches for equality in public services. The protracted railway strike in the fall of 1919 threatened to cut off London's food supply and "light the flaming torch of unrest." At a public meeting against a fare hike, the audience cheered as rail travel in London was condemned as "one of the greatest scandals that ever existed in this or any other city."[11]

At the end of 1920, the boom times stumbled into a collapse that was as brutal in London as it would be in Bombay just a year later. Unemployment was punishing. The number of citizens seeking some sort of relief payment shot up from 23,000 in 1920 to 196,000 by 1923.[12] Out of work ex-servicemen set up market stalls. Legal and illegal street vending popped up everywhere. The unemployed were well organized, with their own militant organizations and communist leaders. Labor Day 1920 brought thousands out in a sea of red flags from the Embankment to Hyde Park for "a pageant

FIGURE 6. Mounted police and marchers, Means Test protests, Hyde Park, London, 1932. The National Hunger March of September to October 1932 was the largest of a series of such demonstrations in Britain. (The Print Collector / Alamy Stock Photo)

of gaiety and defiance."[13] In October of that year, a massive demonstration by some 20,000 unemployed at Whitehall ended tragically. The packed crowds were run down by mounted police using "Cossack tactics" and baton charges in an indiscriminate attack on the marchers. "Screaming women and children were trampled underfoot, or pushed in front of passing vehicles."[14] Despite the casualties, the Tory press railed against the "rioters" and "communist plots." The protests continued in 1922, when some 50,000 unemployed wound their way to Hyde Park in a Hunger March.

The incongruities between this intense populist turmoil and the just as impassioned enthusiasm for sports and recreation were among the most startling characteristics of the age. Waves of both enraged and enthusiastic release were played out in the public spaces of the city. It was the texture and feel of modern life. One way or another, people were out in the streets, in the public domain. Alongside the inflamed social unrest was an obsession with spectator sports. Masses of fans watched with strained necks as race cars and cyclists whizzed by in contests on London's thoroughfares and in its stadiums. Football (known as soccer in the United States), cricket, and rugby all claimed thousands of devoted followers.

But among the myriad of options open to Londoners avid to get a glimpse of their sporting heroes, horse racing claimed first place. The turf drew giant crowds with their bets in hand. Winning horses and their jockeys were celebrities idolized by millions. People packed the racecourse stands and listened raptly to BBC Radio's transmission of legendary racing jubilees. For the BBC, it was "a new and thrilling kind of broadcasting entertainment."[15] The Grand National, the Royal Ascot, and the Epsom Derby were mega-events captured on flickering newsreels by Pathé News and shown in movie theaters. The racing festivals were steeped in tradition and treated like national holidays. The high-society whirl around the horses reveled in its own special glamour, spurred on by the radio, the press, and cinematic news bulletins that captured the excitement.

Britain's famed turf personalities gathered at the London Press Club for the Derby Lunch the Monday before the Epsom Derby in June 1927. It was instituted by journalist and crime writer Edgar Wallace and a social ritual for gentlemanly sportsmen and good mixers. Racing sold newspapers across Britain, and the Derby Lunch was a celebrity event eagerly captured in the sporting press with photos and caricatures of the debonair attendees. Victor Sassoon joined the who's who of the racing world for Wallace's jokey welcoming speech, the backslapping and high-spirited banter, and the paddock gossip. He even offered tips on his colt Hot Night, a race favorite of "devastating speed."[16] And later, for King George's pre-race dinner at Buckingham Palace, he was seated at the table with members of the Jockey Club. Sassoon also joined the derby parties and the thousands assembled in the stands, and shared in the excitement at the arrival of the King and Queen. The throng watched a prancing Hot Night led out onto the track. It was a thrilling race covered on the radio and film newsreels. Hot Night was a nose in front, but Call Boy shot ahead and won the race by three lengths.

Sassoon spent only a month or two in London during the Season in spring and early summer, dutifully visiting his mother and sisters Isabelle and Lydia. As newspapers reported, "He comes to London to visit members of his far-flung family, to watch a race or two . . . and to attend various social functions with a detached and inscrutable air."[17] Even so, for many the Season was a relentless pursuit of social and political influence. Friends of friends of his friends came tumbling in Sir Victor's direction. When not at the racecourse, he was seen at galas with London's glitterati and among the haut monde on the charity circuit. High society was an institution. Businessmen at the pinnacle of global finance managed through education and social connections to enter the charmed circle of British elites. But it paid not to be overconfident in a social whirl where class still fixed one's pedigree. Peerage was a supreme caste steeped in snobbery. Despite Sassoon's influence, a casual bigotry was whispered about the exotic traits of Jews from India. British blue bloods instinctively looked down on them. Nonetheless, in public Sir Victor remained serenely among the elect, above the trivial chatter. He was a celebrity figure, a connoisseur, and an adroit social tactician. His family,[18] after all, were tantalizing personalities and staggeringly rich. Money talks, and the Sassoons could speak the language with certainty.

The tabloids played off the popular obsession with wealth and high society. An explosion of print newspapers was produced in interwar London and enjoyed a devoted following. Newspapers were the dominant mass medium in Britain. Dailies sold millions of copies. They heavily influenced the public imagination and constructed a common popular culture associated with urban life. They also normalized certain modes of celebrity.[19] The *Sketch*, the *Bystander*, and the *Tatler* were London's premier personality rags. Their front pages and famous photographic spreads featured a combination of old money and new faces drawn from entertainers, politicians, and the global elites who traipsed around the world.[20] The details of their personal lives—however vacuous—sold newspapers. That London supported three highly successful celebrity tabloids was evidence enough of their popularity and sway. They were everywhere, available "in the doctors' and dentists' waiting-rooms," remarked satirist Malcolm Muggeridge, "to display the activities of the rich and fashionable mostly for the edification of the poor and unfashionable."[21]

London's West End nightlife was a constant draw for the fashionable set and for the "Bright Young People"[22] who flitted around the edges of acceptable behavior. It was a Roaring Twenties parade of easy money, outlandish display, and moral scandal. Youthful cavorting was an experience Sir Victor knew well from his earlier days in London. Now in his forties, he was well beyond any repetition of juvenile antics. He watched as hedonism reached new heights among the well-bred men and women in their twenties with fabulous sums at their disposal. They gambled for high stakes at the racecourse and flung chips at the baccarat table. Journalist Beverley Nichols recounted the dawn-to-dusk parties that dictated their lives: "There were Mozart parties in which, powdered and peruked, we danced by candlelight and then—suddenly bored, rushed out into the street to join a gang excavating the gas mains at Hyde Park. There were swimming parties where, at midnight, we descended on some municipal baths . . . and disported ourselves with abandon that was all the fiercer because we knew the press was watching."[23] Young rakes in their sports cars screamed through the night on the London streets to the consternation of neighbors and the police. There was a boundless vanity in all this. The libertinism was strangely oblivious to the protests and riots in the streets. For a press eager for scandal, however, the wild Mayfair parties and self-stoking eccentricities were fodder.

Yet the definition of Bright Young People was murky enough to include the older denizens of London's entertainments. The wealthy in evening dress descended into Soho's sleazy nightclubs to rub elbows with the city's rogues and take in the jazz scene. The clubs played cat and mouse with municipal drinking and gambling laws. Pretty female dope sellers slipped quietly through the thicket of tables, whispering about the white packets of cocaine hidden in their purses. Drugs and sex were openly peddled. Frequent police raids made the escapades all the more wicked.[24] Daily newspapers feasted on the glamorous goings-on in the West End's clubs and restaurants. The cultural phenomena of London's nightlife fascinated readers. With their dancing and floor shows, Ciro's Club and the Kit Kat Club were the haunts of the fashionable demimonde. As the writer of a probe of London's underworld noted, "Swagger lunches and elegant dinners, dances, and high-class music, Ciro's provides it all. You have to pay for it, of course; exclusiveness was ever expensive."[25]

Urban life was saturated with the surface glamour of film stars and meteoric celebrities, the silver screen and spectacular musical revues. They formed a sequence of intense sensory impressions, whether in person or described in the tabloids. The cabaret revue, especially at midnight, was a trendy destination for partying night owls. One night, Sir Victor was at the Hippodrome with London financier Carl Bendix. Another night, he was in a fashionable box just above the royal family for the Midnight Revue at the London Pavilion. And his photographs of the Winter Garden's Rhyme and Rhythm song-and-dance cabaret made full-page coverage in the *Sketch* tabloid with the headline "Sir Victor Sassoon Amuses Himself with His Camera."[26] In addition, the privileged Upper Four Hundred had taken up the habit of dining out, making London into a scene of first-class restaurants rivaling those of Paris, according to journalist Charles Graves.[27] Quaglino's, with its hundred waiters at attention in starched white aprons, was the height of civilization. The chef made certain that oysters and blue trout were always on call for the Prince of Wales. Any appearance by the Little Man, as the newspapers christened him, was an immediate sensation. Celebrity sightings were frequent at the Ritz before lunch and at the Savoy Grill every day of the week. The Savoy, where Sir Victor regularly met acquaintants, "no matter how unseasonable the season, is always a hive of interesting bees," the *Tatler* oozed.[28]

London, Imperial Capital

In July 1930, Sassoon attended the opening of India House in the Aldwych district of the West End. The lavish new London headquarters of the government of India, it came into existence as a result of the 1919 Government of India Act, which gave the country greater control over its own destiny. The high commissioner for India, with responsibilities independent of the old India Office in Whitehall, settled in and welcomed a cadre of Indian civil servants.

Designed by architect Herbert Baker, Britain's most prolific imperial architect, India House was an orientalist palace, with entrance gates guarded by imposing lion and elephant pillars. The interior was a "fairyland of the East," remarked journalist Arthur Mee, who was spellbound by the delicacy of its Indian arts and crafts.[29] After a celebratory carriage procession through London, King George officially opened the door with a gold key and unveiled the building to the applause of a host of Indian princes and British officials. India House symbolized how progress was possible "within the unity of the Commonwealth." The King delivered an address soaked in empire that was broadcast to the colonies and dominions over the BBC. It was a "Great Day for India," exclaimed the viceroy.[30] The building was a vital meeting ground for Victor Sassoon and the elite coterie who rambled between Bombay and London. They were masters at this kind of politicking. Invitations to the exclusive "at homes" of the high commissioner were the occasion for chats with Raj officialdom and Indian high society, with the Japanese ambassador and Chinese ministers, and with the English peers who inevitably circled round.

The opening of India House was one in a series of spectacular celebrations of imperialism held in London. The British Empire Exhibition of 1925–1926 at Wembley was perhaps the most grandiose "family party of nations." When it was held, the British Empire was at its height, with fifty-eight countries covering 20 percent of the world's landmass. London clung tenaciously to its identity as the imperial capital of this vast domain. The spectacle of empire fused with the city's built fabric, its public routines and private affairs.[31] Undeniably, London was a theater of pomp and pageantry. Wandering through Whitehall, H. V. Morton looked, "but not with my eyes, and I see that the Empire is here: England, Canada, Australia, New Zealand, South Africa, India . . . here—springing in glory from our London soil."[32]

The city was awash in private gentlemen's clubs dedicated to empire, all of them around Pall Mall and St. James Street, within line sight of Whitehall. This was clubland. There was the East India Club for officers of the Indian civil service, the Oriental Club for men who had made their fortunes in India, the Imperial Colonial Club along with the United Empire for landed gentry, and the Overseas League. The clubs were passports of entry into the ruling class and practiced a cult of self-satisfied exclusiveness. Their lavish headquarters were ceremonial scenes for the proprietary hauteur that governed Britain's treatment of its colonies. This same imperial "clubbability" was transported to Bombay and Shanghai in its most zealous form. London's Royal Empire Society and the Royal Asiatic Society busied themselves collecting vast libraries dedicated to the colonial domains and setting up branches in Bombay and Shanghai. An armada of institutions and professional and scientific societies sprang up on the streets of Westminster, where they cataloged and oversaw the treasure trove of information and material brazenly seized from the imperial domains.

The showpiece Wembley Stadium and park in northeastern London was inaugurated by King George V in 1923, in time for the British Empire Exhibition. The event covered 216 acres, cost £12 million, and was the largest exhibition ever staged anywhere in the world. It attracted twenty-five million visitors over two seasons. At night, the grounds were lit by floodlights that transformed the white buildings into a magic city. A highlight was the Pageant of Empire. A cast of fifteen thousand volunteers performed the saga over three days, with each episode portraying the history and inevitability of British imperialism. Londoners saw their city as constitutive of empire. At the exhibition's heart were the sixteen pavilions representing the empire countries, with the replica of India's Taj Mahal and its lakeside gardens the most spectacular. A monumental Chinese gateway led to the Hong Kong exhibit and a complete Chinese street, where "Chinese merchants and workmen go about their daily tasks just as they would if they were in Hong Kong."[33] Fairgoers watched Chinese "girls" spinning silk and artisans carving ivory, and they enjoyed a restaurant where birds' nest soup and sharks' fins were served by Chinese "boys."

For many Indians, the British Empire Exhibition was at the very least a public embarrassment, at worst just plain insulting. Bombay's hostile reaction to Indian participation in the event was clearly a case in point (see chapter 3). For most British, the idea of empire was endlessly seductive. For others, the pageantry of empire had worn thin. And for still others, anti-imperialism was a full-blown discourse. The working classes protesting on the streets of London could see little to be gained by colonialism, even if a popular jingoism had its appeal.[34] The exotic Orient as mass entertainment had little to do with the imperial atrocities still carried out, or the grinding poverty in Bombay, or the coolie trade and prostitution rings run out of Hong Kong. Ending the traffic in human beings was an ongoing campaign by British reformers and was raised to the level of Parliament. But these sins did little to mar the glorious imagery of empire shaped by official propaganda. In 1934, some fifty thousand spectators jammed the White City Stadium to watch the opening ceremonies and parade of athletes at the British Empire Games. In a celebration of the bond between sport and empire, sixteen nations sent five hundred athletes. They marched smartly past the royal reviewing stand and around the stadium with their national flags held high, then took the oath to compete "for the Honour of our Empire and for the glory of sport." This was an exercise in imperial ritual heavily covered in newsreels and the press. It was the first Empire Games in which women were allowed to participate, and the first appearance by Indian and Hong Kong competitors, although the Indian cricket team had played matches in London two years before. The athletic events were broadcast live on the radio.

By the 1920s, the tourism industry had made it possible for the more comfortable of the middle classes to visit the empire and revel in Britain's achievements. Colonial traffic ceased to be the preserve of military and colonial officialdom, or of global magnates like Victor Sassoon. Global travel corridors opened up. Millions of people were crisscrossing the seas in fleets of steamships. Well-heeled travelers in first class, anxious immigrants in steerage found themselves on board with enthusiastic members of the middle classes aching for a pleasure cruise. Visiting the empire was being cosmopolitan—aware of other cultures yet superimposing British values over a vast geography and feeling supreme. Cruise lines and tourist agencies such as the celebrated Thomas Cook & Sons were charting entirely new global networks. Tilbury Dock down the Thames was expanded to handle the increasing number of passenger ships in the 1920s. Tickets on the P&O and British India Steam Navigation ships were within range of middle-class sightseers. The Ellerman Line offered an all-sunshine Round Africa to India tour with ten days of sightseeing in India for a low fare of £150. The White Star and Red Star Lines offered cruises to Asia with stops in Hong Kong and Shanghai. The three-smokestack *Belgenland*, the largest ocean liner in the world, was docked in London, ready to set sail on a 133-day world cruise with stops in Bombay, Singapore, Hong Kong, and Shanghai. European passengers were carefully segregated from Chinese passengers in Chinese waters.[35] Despite the excitement of touristic cruises, the briny deep could be treacherous. Typhoons in the China Sea regularly forced ships ashore.

Those with the cash and courage could opt for air travel. Initially, it was the wealthier middle classes, British officials, and journalists along for the thrill. British Imperial Airways established weekly flights to the European capitals in the late 1920s. Weekly service between London and Karachi began in 1929 and then was extended to Delhi, Bombay, and Calcutta. Commercial flights still required nail-biting fortitude on the seven-passenger

Hercules biplane and later the nine-passenger Atalanta for Imperial Airways' eastern routes. Travelers endured deafening noise and jolting turbulence. Nonetheless, by the late 1930s, the number of Imperial passengers lifting skyward had jumped to over sixty thousand. The airport terminal was created to service these new aeronauts. It was an entirely new building type. In 1939, Imperial opened its art deco Empire Terminal next to London's Victoria Station, with its dramatic *Wings over the World* sculpture symbolizing the new era of flight. First-class passengers dined on the train ride to Croydon Airport for flights to Europe, or took services to Africa, India, the Far East, and Australia. Like the British Empire Exhibition, the BBC Empire Service, and the Colonial Empire Marketing Board (see chapter 5), Imperial Airways was an ongoing source of information about Britain's imperial domain. It molded popular images of empire through its advertisements and through the tabloids. Accounts by reporters in magazines and newspapers rhapsodized about soaring over strange and mythic lands.[36] The widespread touristic global perspective emerged from this chrysalis of empire.

Most travelers, however, were satisfied enough with third-class tickets aboard passenger ships. Upon their arrival in Bombay, tourist itineraries began with excursions to the British city with its imperial monuments, and then on to scintillating forays into the native "black" town. There was the Taj Mahal tour by moonlight and visits to Elephanta Caves. With guidebooks in hand, tourists indulged in the exotic cultures of India that were familiar from world's fairs and the British Empire Exhibitions. Their perspectives were already well trained. They explored the sites evocative of the relentless march of British imperialism. They basked in the glow of British civility and taste, the modern infrastructure and engineering feats conjured by Raj officialdom. The imperial ethos rang through John Murray's veritable *Handbook for Travellers*, which laid out the modernization of Bombay with the Back Bay and Salsette schemes and the tenement housing that was "mainly due to the energy of Sir George Lloyd, the late Governor of Bombay." Well-worn imagery reiterated imperial perspectives. Travelers, the *Handbook* went on, "will be struck by the exotic scene on landing in Bombay. The quaint native craft in the harbour; the crowds of people dressed in the most brilliant and varied costumes; the Hindus of different castes; the Muhammadans, Jews, and Parsis." Descriptions zeroed in on the "narrow and tortuous" streets and bazaars of the native town, with its "gaudily painted temples" and the "streets teeming with life."[37]

It was symptomatic of the moment that these excessive displays of loyalty to the British Empire took place amid the growing call for *purna swaraj*, or Indian self-rule. Britain paraded a global supremacy it was already beginning to lose. Time was running out. The Indian merchant community in London centered on the neighborhoods of Aldgate, Spitalfields, and Poplar in the East End. Although it numbered only seven or eight thousand, it was well organized and articulate. An Indian Social Club and Chamber of Commerce were founded. Gujarati and Punjabi entrepreneurs, who often came to London by way of years in South Africa, set up family-run businesses, the earliest tapping into the growing demand for Indian cuisine. By 1931, the Bombay Emporium off Tottenham Court Road was importing Indian groceries and spices. A flurry of Indian restaurants hosted political activists, intellectuals, and students, many of whom were preparing for the Indian colonial service.

A landmark cultural scene took place around the Gower Street Indian Student Union and Hostel in Bloomsbury. It was a hub of lectures by Indian personalities and the headquarters of the *Indian Student* journal. Anyone taking part was suspected by the British government of harboring communist sympathies. Indian intellectuals joined London's Bloomsbury circle and were involved with the Theosophical Society. Progressive Indian writers assembled at Sasadhar Sinha's Bibliophile bookshop near the British Museum, which published the magazine *Indian Writing*. But the racism was scathing, and Indians faced constant antagonism. An Indian student wrote that "the prejudices resulting from an imagined consciousness of superiority of race, culture, and history over the supposedly backward, inferior, uncivilized races of the East, seem to be so rooted in their minds that they are not easily dislodged." His experience of being let go from his job as an assistant teacher in a suburban London school on racial grounds was typical. "Fancy, sons of officers, learning under a black man!" the parents had complained.[38]

Lawyer and activist V. K. Krishna Menon (Vengalil Krishnan) almost single-handedly made London's India League into one of the most powerful lobbying voices in the fight for independence. Editor of the *India News*, Menon was an internationalist and lifelong socialist who believed in justice for the toiling masses of India as well as those in South Africa and China, who all suffered the same ignoble oppression at the hands of global capitalism. The India League's membership included British elites as well as Indian students and intellectuals. Backed by Labour MPs, it gained considerable weight in Parliament. In addition, it was the official voice of the Congress Party in London. The league sponsored fiery public meetings, with speakers bitterly criticizing the betrayals of empire. It organized cultural events to re-educate average Englishmen raised on Rudyard Kipling about the reality of their Crown possession. It waged an ongoing information campaign to counter British government puffery on the "family of nations." Menon's impassioned speeches at Hyde Park's Speaker's Corner fired up Indians across London in support of self-rule. He was a celebrity Indian nationalist with a following across the city and was elected a Labour councilor for the St. Pancras ward. Eventually, he was made India's first high commissioner in London.

In 1932, the India League launched a fact-finding mission to India. It was just two years after the British government's Whitley Commission had set off on its own tour of the country, with Victor Sassoon a keen participant. The Whitley group offered absurdly tepid labor reforms to help shore up British control over what was a dire situation. In contrast, on the league's journey across the subcontinent, Menon and three Labour MPs found that "tyranny and terrorism stalked the land." Their report accused the British Raj of utter ruthlessness and exploitation. The empire was built not by enlightened Britons but by people who did not care a whit about the condition of the 319 million people they governed badly, and then used the cruelty of police and prisons to suppress them. The European group that was Sassoon's linchpin in the Indian Legislative Assembly did nothing but defend privileges for themselves and British companies. In particular, the league's report pointed to the Bombay Europeans, who claimed that any conciliation with the "revolutionary movement" for home rule was "suicidal" and that repression "must be prompt, vigorous and even ruthless."[39]

The Society Racket

Indeed, protecting his business interests was Sassoon's priority. His stays in London were more than mindless frivolity. There was nothing serendipitous about his social calendar. For one thing, the head office of E. D. Sassoon & Company banking was in London. And Sassoon's celebrity life was about the personal connections that were the pillar of his wealth and power. Commerce and high society were acknowledged bedfellows, and knowing the right people was cardinal: these connections formed the glue of the British world. Sir Victor's companions had their fingers on the pulse of all three cities they inhabited. The cosmopolitanism of empire was inscribed into how business was done. Billie and Jack Liddell were regulars at Sassoon's cabaret tables and moved easily in high society across the waves. John (Jack) Hellyer Liddell was manager of the Hong Kong & Shanghai Bank on Shanghai's Bund. He had been born in Shanghai to a family with deep roots in the International Settlement. After his education in London, he returned to run his family's import-export business. Liddell was well educated, well dressed, the product of the sophisticated cosmopolitanism of these years. And he was eventually the last British chairman of the Shanghai Municipal Council. His wife, Billie Coutts Liddell, was an avid horse enthusiast and co-owned the We Two Stable in Shanghai, where she trained the rugged Mongolian ponies herself. Billie's celebrity as a horsewoman caught the eye of London's tabloid the *Tatler*, which often featured her in its tidbits on Shanghai personalities. This kind of celebrity and global power was the hallmark of well-connected insiders entrenched in the summits of urban life. Billie Liddell was a supreme public figure, known in London and Shanghai as a "slim, svelte creature, with a mind like a rapier, who ordered men about all her life, never did a day's work, shopped annually in Paris and was about the best-dressed woman on the China coast."[40]

In a real sense, "the British world was a species of global networking"[41] held together as much by the kind of personal contacts Sassoon cultivated as by official policy. He and his cohorts shared a common global way of life. Their web of financial relationships was spun from a social thread. Sir Victor's troupe of players in London included Peggy and Jack Reed. Reed was the National City Bank of New York's man in Asia. National City Bank had antennae in twenty-three countries, with head offices in Shanghai and Bombay. It was blamed for manipulating Wall Street's stock market and partially causing the crash of October 1929. But it had muscled in on the joint-stock banks that commanded international trade[42] and become one of the largest and most profitable banks in Asia, with deposits at the Hong Kong & Shanghai Bank and dozens of other institutions. Reed regularly trundled between New York and Shanghai and across the Atlantic to London to keep an eye on the silver markets that were the backbone of the Eastern currency trade. He was a legendary currency dealer and made the bank a fortune purchasing gold in Tokyo and silver in Shanghai and selling them on the London and New York financial exchanges.

Individuals like Liddell and Reed have dissolved into the ether of history and have long been forgotten. But in the 1920s and 1930s they controlled global finance. They were the world's moneymen, with pedigrees from the City of London (see chapter 5). They possessed the knowledge and information, the status, and the networks to rig the odds in their favor. They pulled the levers on the machinery of profit and tied London, Bombay, and Shanghai together in unseen ways. Their impact on these cities was profound. This infusion of global money was behind the real estate speculation as well as the investments in infrastructure and industry that made these cities modern.

London financier Carl Bendix and his society-hostess wife, Daisy, were also regulars on the Sassoon circuit. Carl Bendix was the chairman of the board of both the India Iron & Steel Company and the Steel Corporation of Bengal. When he wasn't hosting parties at the Savoy, he was "busy with many financial undertakings in the City." He and Daisy Bendix were a celebrity couple who made regular appearances at charity pageants and the lavish balls of the London Season. Their family had a "delightful house in New Cavendish Street" and "the most wonderful period home" in Sussex, according to full-page coverage in the *Tatler*.[43]

Daisy Bendix was among the socialites whose lives were gauzily chronicled in the *Bystander* and *Tatler* celebrity rags that Londoners were addicted to. She began her short theatrical career as a chorus girl in London revues. By the time she married Carl Bendix, she was shaping her public image with the skill of a diva. She appeared on the cover of the *Bystander* in 1931 as "one of London's most popular hostesses."[44] With her bobbed haircut and schoolgirl shape, Daisy was every inch the picture of a Roaring Twenties flapper. She was a media darling in an age when the imagery of the modern woman was a global phenomenon. She made her entries at charity events in flamboyant costumes that were all the rage among society beauties. The Roaring Twenties were an age of showiness. London's high society reveled in brilliant hijinks and parading their eccentricities. Their appearances in attention-grabbing regalia were a form of celebrity branding. Daisy Bendix wore a colossal crinoline as Madame Pompadour for the 1929 Galaxy Ball, then was adorned as Botticelli's nymph for a Maternity Hospital charity ball at the Prince of Wales Theater. She made an iridescent entrance as Crystal Gazer for the One Thousand and One Lights Ball at the Park Land Hotel. These were hedonistic, glamorous masquerades produced by the wives of some of the wealthiest, most influential financiers of the era. Such frivolity was something the unwashed rest of the world could only stare at. Celebrity sightings of the rich and famous along with the social disparities disregarded by media magpies stamped the social panorama of the global city.

These men and women, then, formed the clique whose names appeared again and again in Sir Victor's meticulously kept diaries. Sleuthing through the pages unveils the apex of urban society. The men were members of the global financial oligarchy, their wives society queens. They boarded luxury liners and flitted between the world's most cosmopolitan capitals. If their financial deals took place in the back rooms of gentlemanly capitalism, they were expert at managing their public celebrity and made certain they were in the society pages. Sassoon reported on their marriages and divorces, their love affairs. He glued photos in his diaries of their smiling faces over cocktails at exclusive clubs in London, then in Shanghai, and then in Bombay. His journaling was a memory board of the social metabolism that kept global business thriving.

Daisy Bendix was joined by a host of glamorous, high-profile women who made up Victor Sassoon's globe-trotting entourage. Specific individuals served as conduits for exchange and shaped global networks. Although they have been entirely overlooked in this history, the women around Sassoon claimed the limelight in their own right. In the 1930s, Sassoon purchased West Green House, a stately country estate in Hampshire. It allowed him to play the English baronet from time to time. The Duchess of Wellington along with her companion Yvonne Fitzroy occupied the house for many years. Fitzroy was a privileged socialite and budding actress, a progressive, cultivated New Woman of the early twentieth century. She had served on the battlefields of Russia and Romania as a nursing orderly with the Scottish Women's Hospitals and penned her experiences in *With the Scottish Nurses in Roumania* (1918). Sassoon had met Fitzroy in India, where she worked as the private secretary to the imperious Lady Reading, the wife of the viceroy. With her inquiring mind and writerly gift, Fitzroy chronicled her travels across the subcontinent in *Courts and Camps in India*. Her tales of colonial India reflected the high-handed elitism of a white British woman, and her encounters marked the cosmopolitanism born of empire. Fitzroy returned to London, where she was a regular feature in the tabloid society pages and on the lecture circuit. Sir Victor wrote regularly to her during his travels. His letters were filled with reports on the political situation in China and his sense that he was "walking a tight rope." He complained about troubles in the Sassoon & Company Manchester office and the boomerangs in the global financial market that "kept me hard at it."[45]

Sassoon's photos of glamorous paramours and companions, along with the social whirl that filled his days in London, Bombay, and Shanghai, were all carefully curated in his diaries. His favorite subject was the women who fluttered around him. He had a long-standing reputation as a lady chaser, although his affairs were brief and his nose sharp for those on the make. Among his conquests was the alluring Aimée Lopes, a Brazilian femme fatale who was rumored to be the mistress of Brazil's President Getulio Vargas and eventually married Rodman de Heeren, heir to the American Wanamaker fortune. She was first sent to France in 1938 by President Vargas as a secret agent. Operating undercover as a fashion celebrity residing in luxury at the Hotel Plaza Athenée, Lopes mingled easily in French and British high society. She appeared at the races in England on the arms of wealthy male patrons of the horse world. In Paris, she was friends with Coco Chanel and *Vogue* editor Bettina Ballard, and she was showered with jewels by the Duke of Westminster, who was besotted with her. Dripping in gleaming diamonds, she "was almost eaten alive" by the competitive hostesses of Paris eager to feature her at their parties.[46] Lopes was the It Girl of the international jet set. While in France in 1938, Sir Victor visited stud farms in Normandy, met in Paris with French bankers and with the chairman of the US company General Electric. Travel to Paris and Deauville was among the pleasures of high finance, as were trysts with Lopes. The pair was seen at the Palais Royale together, and they enjoyed the gastronomic delights at the Ambassadors Club in Deauville. Eventually as Madame de Heeren, Aimée Lopes was considered one of the queens of Biarritz, the seaside town where she owned a villa and received her many admirers.

Italian baroness and socialite Giulia Coletti was another specimen in this celebrity whirl. Global capitalism was bathed in a social limelight of extraordinary power and influence. Fame and fortune bought access. Coletti was the widow of Sassoon's brother Hector and heiress to his fortune, mainly in Hong Kong real estate. The press bitingly dubbed her the "million pound widow." Soignée and elegant, she was known for her Titian hair and flamboyant guiles, and especially for strutting around town with her pet leopard on a leash. Her stunning wardrobe and jewels made the gossip columns: "Her pearls are said to be the largest in Mayfair . . . each pearl the size of a bird's egg. . . . All her jewelry is marvallous."[47] She later married Prince Cesare Ottoboni from one of the oldest patrician families of Italy. Sir Victor kept up a long-running friendship with his dazzling sister-in-law and stayed with her regularly at her palace in the cypress-covered hills above Monte Carlo.

Aimée de Heeren and Giulia Coletti were Sassoon's closest companions on the French Riviera. The habitués of London's clubland were well traveled across the Continent's most exclusive resorts. The 1930s were the heyday of the Riviera and its cosmopolitan scene of attention seekers and famous habitués. The first-class trains departing from London's Victoria Station and the Gare de Lyon in Paris deposited the social crush on the Côte d'Azur for their ritual summer holiday. Sassoon regularly joined them at Cannes and Monte Carlo, at Nice and Mentone. It was a seaside playground of the super-rich seduced by the idyllic retreat and imbibing the superfluous. Sir Victor spent mornings at the swimming pool with his movie camera trained on English starlet Wendy Barrie and the other young ladies drifting by. The Beach Restaurant on the seaside at Monte Carlo was the place to see and be seen. There, Victor chatted with Hollywood legend Douglas Fairbanks and with Olive, Lady Baillie, the Anglo-American heiress considered the smartest hostess on the coast. "If you can't say . . . 'I'm with Olave at Monte Carlo,' you're running serious social risks," the *Sketch* reported.[48] Evening dress was obligatory for the shows at the Casino, where Lady Baillie was known as a gambler and the portly Aga Khan dropped hundreds of pounds sterling in five minutes. Life on the Riviera was self-indulgently faux but altogether delightful for the very wealthy.

✵ 5 ✵
London, Capital of Finance

London is the chief abode of the great god Money.
CHARLES TURNER, "Money London," in Sims,
Living London (1902–1903)

Sir Victor Sassoon's globe-trotting and womanizing carried him across Europe's most exclusive watering holes. But his sojourns in London had more serious intent. In the high-risk world of global trade and banking, connections in the Foreign Office and privileged business circles were paramount. The hinge for the Sassoon financial apparatus was in the City of London. It was a ceremonial district known as the Square Mile in London's historic heart, with its own police force and its own pompous rituals. Despite the financial damage of the First World War, the City reemerged as the heart of the global economy. Its tentacles were everywhere in the interwar years. It reigned supreme in the currents of banking and insurance, the shipping and trading that greased the world's financial flows. It was the command-and-control center for the markets in gold and silver bullion. "London is the chief abode of the great god Money, whose throne, visible to all men, is in the heart of the City," urban explorer Charles Turner remarked. It was a jubilant comeback after the war years and the last hurrah, since capital-rich New York loomed as the emerging pivot of international finance. The giants ensconced in the City of London were well aware of the colossus rising on the other side of the Atlantic,[1] to which they were heavily indebted. Nevertheless, the City held sway as financier to the world, with all its famous hubbub in full glory.

A constant whirlwind of people and vehicles encircled the neoclassical eminences of the Bank of England and the Royal Exchange. The bevy of banks and brokerage houses on Lombard Street seemingly bowed to them like courtiers. There was a visual aesthetics that went along with the

FIGURE 7. The Bank of England and the Royal Exchange, City of London, ca. 1930s. (Heritage Image Partnership Ltd / Alamy Stock Photo)

financial goings-on in global helms, especially in London. The City was a monumental urban setting in the name of capital accumulation and the borrowing and exchange of money. The imposing colonnaded Bank of England complex, with its public bank halls and offices, courtyards and gardens, warehouses and vaults, was steeped in symbolism—strength, stability, permanence. The Bank of England was essentially a sovereign world power. Its vaults glittered with stacks upon stacks of gold and silver ingots—some good portion of which was shipped from Bombay.

Gold was fundamental to global finance and the symbol of British economic might. The Bank of England also regulated the payment of interest on India's public debt and commanded decisions on the fluctuating rupee. Although gold has received plenty of attention, the complex role of silver in the global economy has rarely been given its just due.[2] But silver determined the markets with India and China, and with it, imperial policy. The postwar boom sparked an orgy of speculation in foreign exchange and the commodity markets in gold and silver. The City's four private bullion houses had a long and fabled history and held iron-fisted control over the trade in these two precious metals. The fluctuating price of both gold and silver was calculated at a precise time daily in what was known as the "fixing."[3] The buying and selling then took place in frenzied cables and telephone calls between London, Shanghai, Bombay, and New York. The transactions flashed around the world with lightning speed. The fortunes made were spectacular in what amounted to the financialization of the global economy.

The City's reservoir of money seemed bottomless. Six of the world's ten largest banks were headquartered there. Most of the world's foreign investments were made in London. And a wave of mergers after the First World War resulted in the formation of five huge British banks that handled the boom times of the 1920s: Barclays Bank and Lloyds Bank on Lombard Street, the Midland Bank on Leadenhall Street, the Westminster on Lothbury Street, and the National Provincial Bank on Bishopsgate at the junction with Threadneedle Street. Although smaller in size, the merchant banks—long-established houses such as Habro, Lazard, Schroder—threw their hefty weight around the global marketplace. They were transforming into modern exchange banks that speculated on money markets. Moreover, there were some eighty foreign banks in the City. These commercial and joint-stock banks remained strong even during the Great Depression of the 1930s. "Each of these banks has its spacious strong-rooms in the basement, a large room crowded with clerks, special sanctums for manager and secretary, and somewhere upstairs a board-room," Turner continued. "The glossy hats, the well-conditioned black coats and trousers, the expensive waist-coasts, nearly every one of which supports a gold watchchain . . . if the thousands of busy feet do not actually tread on gold, you have a feeling that underneath are vaults and strong rooms guarding fabulous hoards."[4] The insurance industry had also gone through a spate of mergers that concentrated their head offices in the City, where they invested heavily in securities and kept a close eye on the London Stock Exchange. With new markets in motor and aviation coverage, even exchange banks began to expand into insurance brokering.

A thin slice of Britain's population owned virtually all this capital and property. In their privileged opinion, they preserved the integrity of London's global power. They cherished the pious conviction that the bounty of British trade and the influx of wealth would trickle down to the laboring classes and cure whatever social evils existed. They raked in profits and protected their commercial investments. Their beliefs in a free market and the stability of the pound sterling as the world's currency were held with religious fervor. Entry into this exclusive guild of gentlemanly capitalists relied on blue-blood family connections and wealth, a youth spent at Eton, and "clubbability." The agreeable hours in leather armchairs sipping whiskey at an exclusive gentleman's club were when and where deals were parlayed. An old-boy network upheld Britain's Establishment.

The highest positions in the Bank of England, the London Stock Exchange, and Lloyds were traditionally held by Etonians. The younger sons of this upper crust were installed in the City's firms. Their careers were spent inside this coterie that recruited from within. The pool of good fellows were sent out to bank branches in the colonies and beyond, where they extended the City's reach. British multinational banks operated more than 2,250 branches in cities across Latin America, Africa, Asia, and the Pacific.[5] The gossipy tabloid the *Sketch* offered a satirical chat in a first-class train carriage between a broker and a City editor about sons making good use of family connections. "Boys so often want to go abroad these days.... Banks are good in that way. The Anglo-Egyptian, Hong and Shanghai, Anglo-South American, and suchlike are often open to take a really good chap."[6] It was a pompous knot of formality with enormous power over successive British governments and the empire.

At the City's peak in the mid-1930s, some half a million people worked there.[7] It was at the zenith of its global power. Tens of thousands of accountants, actuaries, appraisers and solicitors, clerks and copyists, left their homes in the suburbs and clambered onto buses and Tube trains each day. They shuttled into the City, heads buried in the *Daily Express*, ready to oversee the trafficking in money and credit in the banks and brokerage houses installed on the maze of narrow streets. Banking and financial services were a growth industry, and office work swelled. The salaried masses eagerly took up positions behind the desks. British Liberal intellectual Charles Masterman described them spending "the best of their days in copying other men's letters, adding up other men's accounts.... They are all either clerks in banks or shipping companies, or accountants, or insurance officials. And they are all rearing children to be insurance officials, or accountants, or clerks in banks or shipping companies."[8] Be that as it may, journalist Collin Brooks was spot-on about "little Mr. Smith, of Surbiton, who may not look a particularly important person when he leaves home to catch the nine-fifteen train in order to fill his accustomed place in the office of one of the banks or discount houses in the money market." But it was because of the presence of Mr. Smith "that some adventurer is able to set to work a thousand black men in the tropics, whose labours will eventually enrich the tables of Smith with some once rare and now plentiful refreshing fruit, or with some contrivance for keeping the toast warm."[9]

The daily performance of global finance was carried out behind the monumental facades of the City's buildings. New communication and information technologies were transforming finance. Gone were the days when traders met daily to haggle out buying and selling on the floor of the Royal Exchange. The new world of high-speed messaging spelled the end of meeting in person and close relations between broker and client. Instead, the money market was conducted in company offices outfitted with high-tech switchboards, pneumatic tubes, and telegraphic instruments. It was an intelligence network that stretched across the globe. The bills of exchange, the flow of loans and credit, payments, and the "council bills" that all pumped money globally were made through telegraphic transfers. Currency rates were quoted throughout the day. Commission agents raced to read stock prices in New York as they rolled off ticker tapes and telex machines. They sat in front of switchboards with direct lines to brokers and special customers. The switchboard lights, known as doll's eyes, blinked on and off as the dealers plugged in the lines. Cylindrical logarithm calculators spun on their desks with a staccato drumming.[10] The new technologies increased the mobility of capital and handled transactions at lightning speed in a trading world with London at its apex. "Increasingly," historian Rob Harris remarked of the office economy, "merchants, brokers and agents gravitated to the City, organizing and controlling world trade, most of which never touched Britain's shores."[11] The centralized management in these head offices was the largest money market in the world and tied directly to Bombay and Shanghai. The new technologies made the competition cutthroat and predatory. Batteries of telephones rang off their hooks. Reuters radio bulletins blared out international news. Agents raced to seal their transactions. Troops of young women bent over their desks and clacked away at typewriters. Clerks and runners rolled documents into cylinders and stuffed them into pneumatic tubes, where they flew between offices.

Dealers gathered in the City's pubs and, drinks in hand, spilled out into the streets in the late afternoon to await the daily news from New York's Wall Street, hours behind them. After work, the financial minions indulged in Soho's restaurants and jazz clubs. London's nightlife was more popularly accessible in the interwar years. It was an established feature in the lives of the salaried workers. Smoking and a voguish cocktail in a West End nightclub were signs of their louche sophistication. Rifling through the *Sketch* and the *Tatler* gave them the latest gossip on what to wear and where best to be seen. They were young, making good money, in tune with the latest crazes, in search of the independent lifestyle portrayed in magazines and film. They shared in the cosmopolitanism evident across global cities—the new salaried class could just as well be seen in jazz clubs in Bombay and Shanghai.[12]

Both men and women indulged in the Twenties fashions that blurred class distinctions. In "Changing London," a series of articles in the *Sphere*, Irish novelist Shaw Desmond feigned shock on London Bridge as he "saw the pioneer of the collarless brigade—a man not of twenty but of forty, coatless, his sports-shirt thrown open to the London airs, as he went to his office."[13] The new middle class rushed to buy rayon clothes and cosmetics, gramophones and electric gadgetry. The Woolworth's and the Marks & Spencer department stores were packed with enticing things, some good portion imported from the colonies. Young people kicked up their heels doing the Charleston and black bottom on the crowded dance floors of the city's cabarets. Couples crammed into lavish movie theaters to see the latest Hollywood talkies. Glamour was in reach of almost everyone in the Twenties, even if only briefly on an evening out. For those with higher salaries, choosing between a Morris Minor, Austin Seven, or Ford motorcar was the ultimate high. Dreams of riches played out in the grandstands of the racetracks, where the crowds clutched their bets in anticipation as the horses thundered by.

The center of London became an administrative, financial, and services zone consummate with its role as a global powerhouse. The Colonial Office and the grand sweep of Whitehall were hectic with bureaucrats diligently administering the vast territorial realm. There were calls for London to be planned and beautified as an imperial capital in league with the great cities of the world. But large-scale planning on the scale of Paris or other European capitals eluded London. The city's development was largely given over to the happenstance of real estate speculation—as it was in Bombay and Shanghai—with massive amounts of the money for the task derived from overseas trade and investments. Real estate was one of the most conspicuous sectors in the dance between urbanization and global capitalism. A fine-tuned financial choreography turned global profits into glitzy edifices. With few checks by municipal authorities on profitable real estate deals, the encroachment on the city by commercial interests was unstoppable. Especially in the boom years of the Twenties, profiteering was rampant and the profits zany. Even in the dour 1930s, money was cheap and flowed into real estate in all three cities. The sale of land and buildings plumped bank accounts with every transaction, with maximum return on investments. Real estate speculation reduced big cities to a kind of flatness that made it easy to scrutinize and remove any complicating humanity. In London, commercial real estate agencies popped up in the West End on Maddox Street to handle the deals. Construction companies stood with equipment at the ready.

Property in London, especially in the exclusive neighborhoods of Mayfair, Belgravia, and Kensington, was at a premium. Despite the cost, development consortia bought up the fabric of once-distinguished neighborhoods for commercial exploitation. The creative destruction of this property market was astonishing. Outmoded mansions around Park Lane and Grosvenor Square were demolished to make way for hotels and modern apartments. Ancient buildings along the City's narrow streets met the wrecking ball, quickly replaced by spanking-new office buildings. Global corporations needed facilities to house the office machinery and communication technologies, the marketing and advertising departments for their sprawling operations. Major retailers such as Boots, Marks & Spencer, and F. W. Woolworth gobbled up property from small-time local shops. The profits to be made in High Street areas far exceeded the costs of redevelopment. Chain stores were sold to insurance companies and investment groups to generate financing for expansion into new districts.[14] It was a landscape of private capital that led to a general decline in inner London's population. Real estate investments went further afield, out to the suburbs where supermarkets and shopping malls followed the working classes setting up their lives in the new housing estates.

Even so, in the City the commercial response to modernity was distinctively traditional. The district underwent extensive transformation in the interwar years. Larger offices and expanded staffs were needed to oversee the myriad global operations in money and credit. These modernization projects were a tangible sign of the exorbitant wealth in the banking sector despite the economic crises of the 1920s and 1930s. Yet there was little interest in fashioning the City's financial precincts into the skyscraper canyons of New York. Four of the major banks (Lloyds, the Midland, the National Provincial, and the Westminster) together with the Bank of England draped their new headquarters in the classical past. If modernity found its spirit in art deco, the veneer of neoclassicism remained the visual language of Britain's empire of money. The City's rebuilding was explicitly constituted within this discourse of imperial finance.[15] The Bank of England itself was redesigned in a majestic classical vision by architect Herbert Baker, who was called back from India, where he had been working on the design of New Delhi. It resembled, according to urban explorer Harold Clunn, "a raised palace surrounded by a fortress."[16] Lloyds Bank celebrated its overseas expansion and mechanization of counting procedures with a headquarters secured with Roman columns and a temple-like banking hall. Midland Bank acted as the London bank for some 650 associated banks around the world, including the Hong Kong & Shanghai Bank. It built an imperial nerve center in the City designed along classical lines and filled with the newest managerial offices and operations equipment. National Provincial Bank and Westminster Bank followed suit in their neoclassical scale. Overall, the City's modernization projects yielded a monumental landscape that exuded global financial power.

In 1925, the King and Queen laid the foundation stone for the new Lloyd's Register of Shipping building on Leadenhall Street. The great marine insurance company's edifice was decorated in a concoction of Doric columns, pedimented windows, domed turrets, and marble-lined corridors. Lloyd's was a stodgy, conservative institution that tripped into a series of scandals in the 1920s, but it remained the hub of international shipping. It was the "watcher of the seas," with fifteen hundred agents worldwide and thousands of underwriters and brokers.[17] It was flanked on Leadenhall Street by a bevy of insurance companies, the head offices of the Cunard and the P&O shipping lines, and the newly built command center for the Port of London overlooking the Thames.

London dominated the movement of international shipping. As well as being a physical place, the City was an immense commercial intelligence network, "with all the information all the time."[18] Vessels from all over the world were chartered in the cathedral-like trading hall of the Baltic Exchange on St. Mary Axe. By telephone, shipowners were constantly kept informed about freight rates. Specialist firms emerged that concentrated on specific types of ships and cargoes. Indian and South American shipping companies launched. Erlebach Shipping, the New Zealand Steamship, and the Union Castle Mail Steamship companies straddled Fenchurch and Leadenhall Streets. In an article titled "The New London," the *Sphere* reported that Furness Shipping was constructing a massive building with "a cliff-like face" that would dominate the two streets.[19]

Inside this dense mass of global kingpins was the E. D. Sassoon & Company office on Fenchurch Street. It was the control center for the web of investments that made up Victor Sassoon's world. E. D. Sassoon was a well-heeled mercantile house, with operations throughout Asia and the Middle East. London's City was wedded to a long-standing idea of cosmopolitan commercial capitalism, and firms such as E. D. Sassoon were the maestros of global trade. There were some fifteen hundred merchant houses in London in the late 1920s specializing in the trade and shipping that kept goods flowing globally. If it did not reach the summits of enterprises such as the Lazards and Helbert Wagg, E. D. Sassoon was considered enviably prosperous and among the principal firms. There was undeniable anti-Semitic prejudice in the City, but some Jewish-led companies were too well established, too important to be shunned. That was the case for E. D. Sassoon & Company. Its long-established international networks were invaluable. These old-style merchant fiefdoms were the quintessence of the orthodox life of the City, and they were strictly run by family members. Sons succeeded fathers, and the businesses depended on descendants spread out across the globe to manage their affairs. Jacob Sassoon was the mastermind behind the expansion of E. D. Sassoon as a multinational enterprise in the late nineteenth and early twentieth centuries (see chapter 1). From its origins in Bombay, it had spread out globally, with offices in Manchester, the Persian Gulf ports, Calcutta, and Karachi as well as Japan. It had long been a distinguished presence in Hong Kong and Shanghai as well.

To finance his far-flung ventures, Sir Jacob had founded Eastern Bank in 1909 with capital of £2 million (see chapter 1). It functioned as the banking arm of the E. D. Sassoon enterprises and operated out of the company's headquarters on Fenchurch Street. From their command centers in London, exchange banks such as this did the entire work of financing India's foreign and seaborne trade. Eastern Bank appeared on the British Stock Exchange almost immediately. In short order, it was profiting mightily from the drive toward a world system of British Empire banks with money funneled through London and tentacles spread across the globe. Managers frequently moved from one branch and affiliate to another, one country to another. They nurtured a clannish banking culture tied directly to the City's coffers. The risk taking in global exchange banking was enormous. It depended on established networks and was no place for squeamish outsiders. "London was littered with the gravestones of stillborn initiative and murdered expectations," author Robert Sinclair remarked sardonically.[20] After currencies were unpegged from gold in 1919, a veritable orgy of dealings took place on the world's currency exchanges, which became one of the largest global businesses. There was no real central foreign exchange market. It was essentially an amalgam of bankers, brokers, and dealers connected to one another by the new information technologies and to foreign centers across the world, relying on their word as bond.[21] It was a high-stakes game, and the profits could be huge.

In the most basic sense, Eastern Bank allowed the Sassoons to get in on this bonanza. It also allowed their company to transfer its winnings quickly for profitable prospects wherever these could be found. By the early 1920s, the bank had moved to Crosby Square in London. It was making the transition from an old-style merchant bank to a twentieth-century commercial and industrial financier. The bank's clerks and agents made loans, issued telegraphic transfers and letters of credit. The bank purchased the coveted bills of exchange and shifted silver and gold around throughout the East. A profit was made on every one of these transactions. Banking practices at this level neutralized any sense of geography and distance. They made capital footloose across the globe as capitalists searched out new opportunities for investment. Lord Balfour of Burleigh was Eastern Bank's first chairman, one of many British titled peers who took up positions as ornamental directors in the City's banks and major companies. E. D. Sassoon & Company itself was the largest shareholder and held controlling interest in the bank, and there were other powerful investors. Two continental banks were shareholders and sat on the Eastern's board—the Société Générale of Paris and the Banque d'Outremer of Belgium. Both hungrily eyed ventures in China, and the bank was happy to facilitate the financing.

It was only a short jump for the British, and for that matter the French and the Belgians, to rely on exchange banks such as the Sassoons' Eastern Bank to tap the growing opportunities in the geopolitical landscape that emerged after the First World War.[22] The British invested millions in China, especially as part of international banking consortia that negotiated loans to the Chinese government. The hub of these loan operations lay in the City of London. It was a profit-making scheme that gave the global banking oligarchy extraordinary power over China's development. The British stakes went to massive public works projects—railroad construction and a communications network of cable, telegraph, and wireless in Hong Kong and Shanghai to facilitate business. Many were pie-in-the-sky projects cooked up by British adventurers greedy for profits. Millions went into public utilities, real estate, and warehousing in Shanghai's International Settlement as well as into its valuable leased property. It was precisely these dealings that made cities into cutting-edge modern helms in a global geography.

Muscling in on some of the lucrative Chinese investment opportunities led to vicious rivalries between the global banks. It led to Eastern Bank's failed takeover bid for the Hong Kong & Shanghai Bank's loan business in China. The majority of the shares in the latter were held by British investors who left the day-to-day operations to trusted compradors in the Crown colony and Shanghai. It was a major force in London's City, with palatial headquarters on Gracechurch Street that oozed marble and mahogany. It was banker to the British-managed Imperial Maritime Customs in China, and it worked closely with the Foreign Office. There was a simmering undertow of resentment in London's banking circles of the Hong Kong & Shanghai Bank and its near monopoly on loans to China. The bank was so powerful that it was handling gold, silver, and sterling trades on the global market and challenging the elite exchange banks on their own turf. Eastern Bank's bid to snatch its China business was quickly blocked by the Hong Kong & Shanghai grandees perched in their City offices. Undaunted, the Sassoons steered their bank into other lucrative fields of operation.

With the breakup of the Ottoman Empire, the French and the British took possession of Syria, Lebanon, Palestine, Jordan, and Iraq and offered a wealth of new prospects. Bankers and corporate moguls ensconced in the City hung greedily over the territorial reshuffling and colonial mandates that opened up regions on the cusp of development. With official British support and "thanks," Eastern Bank moved into the Middle East. It was, after all, where the Sassoons had begun their trading empire. It meant a windfall: bank chairman J. S. Haskell reported a "large increase in business," with dividends to its shareholders shooting upward.[23] After the British invasion of Iraq, the bank opened branches in Baghdad, Basra, and Bahrain. It negotiated with local potentates over cheap exchange rates, which gave it a monopoly on the money trade. Both aboveboard and contraband gold flowed into its coffers and was converted to silver-backed rupees—the preferred specie for Arabian Sea trade. Once the British Mandate in Iraq had been established, Eastern Bank branches opened in Mosul and Kirkuk. Haskell sat on Iraq's first Currency Board. Then, expansion into the Middle East with British sanction allowed the bank to funnel money into oil exploration and petroleum development. It bought up property throughout the Middle East as well as in Southeast Asia.[24] At its shareholder meeting, Haskell outlined the bounty about to cascade from striking oil near Kirkuk, plans for a railway from Baghdad to Haifa, and the development of Iraq's cotton-growing industry.[25] Eastern Bank continued its expansion in the 1920s into British possessions east of Suez in Colombo, Madras, Karachi, and Singapore. By the end of the decade, it was moving into the North American market. All told, it had some £5 million in assets.[26]

The power of Eastern Bank had waned by the 1930s, and no new branches were opened, although the Sassoon family maintained controlling interest well into the 1950s. Instead, the family's priority shifted to transforming E. D. Sassoon & Company from a family-controlled merchant house to an aggressive corporate firm that controlled a variety of overseas subsidiaries in trade, manufacture, and finance. The transition to modern global finance was in full swing: a cadre of international elites expanded control over how the world's resources and capital would be deployed. At E. D. Sassoon & Company, the changes were instigated by Sir Victor himself once he inherited it upon his father's death in 1924. In January 1921, it was converted into a limited liability company that combined the characteristics of private ownership with those of a corporation.

It was valued at £15 million. The directors were Sir Victor Sassoon and his brother Hector Sassoon, along with Abraham Jacob Raymond and Albert Raymond, who ran the Sassoon mills in Bombay and were taipans in the Hong Kong business community (see chapter 3). The office in Hong Kong on Queen's Road remained open. The new Sassoon House on the Bund became headquarters in Shanghai. In Bombay, the company moved into offices in Ballard Estate. Its corporate maneuvering was a case study in the kind of tactics that wove global cities together in a web of finance and trade.

In the shape-shifting advance of the Sassoon enterprises, Arnhold Brothers Limited, through which the Sassoons conducted much of their business in Hong Kong and Shanghai, was reconstituted as a British enterprise and renamed Arnhold & Company. Harry Arnhold was Victor Sassoon's closest business partner. Born in Hong Kong in 1879, he was eight years younger than Sir Victor. Arnhold was an enigmatic figure. Known for his irascible personality, he went through three wives, one of them only eighteen years of age when they married. The gossip mills were abuzz when he divorced American ingenue Daisy Grace for running up debts with her extravagant buying sprees and for committing adultery. But he was a master at global trade and had planted the Arnhold flag in Berlin, Zurich, London, and New York and assembled extensive assets in Hong Kong and Shanghai. After the First World War, however, anti-German hostility hampered Arnhold's maneuvers. Sensing the change in the business climate, he sold out to Victor Sassoon. Handing over the company to Sassoon meant integrating into a multinational conglomerate of properties and businesses with massive financial reserves. Sassoon became the majority stockholder, while Arnhold maintained management. Under their leadership, Arnhold & Company expanded into an array of real estate, engineering, and trade interests of extraordinary value—in both Hong Kong and Shanghai.

The hulking pace of these mergers and acquisitions typified global finance and trade in the interwar years. Such transactions intensified for Sassoon as he shifted his assets from Bombay to Shanghai. What historical imprint exists of him is usually about his womanizing and legendary parties. But in actuality, Victor Sassoon lived by calculation. An undercurrent of self-possession fed his ambitions, and his personal connections provided a wealth of chatter on tidy investment opportunities. E. D. Sassoon & Company continued to oversee the Sassoon cotton mills in Bombay. But there was no point in wasting money on sectors with diminishing returns. Instead, the London office in the City worked with the new Arnhold & Company on hotter opportunities in China. The company's financial reserves were transferred to the new E. D. Sassoon Banking Company, which became a separate entity. It was registered in Hong Kong with capital of £1 million and headquartered at the Gloucester Building. Hong Kong allowed Sassoon to put his money to work in new ventures while avoiding the British tax collector. Both Hong Kong and Shanghai were outside the British tax zone. Moreover, according to British law, the bank records could be kept confidential.

Essentially, the new bank freed Sassoon from the crisis-ridden cotton industry in Bombay and allowed investments to flow into other, more lucrative enterprises. It reflected his recognition that the center of gravity for global investment was shifting. Thus, through the E. D. Sassoon Bank, he transformed revenues from Bombay's cotton mills through the maze of currency speculation into real estate in Shanghai. The bank had one of the largest sterling covers on the market and crossed it with both US dollars and local Chinese currencies at massive profit. Vast loans at high interest rates were given to Chinese developers. Sir Victor had millions upon millions at his disposal, and Shanghai was a convenient tax haven. But it was not just tax avoidance that propelled him toward China. In 1926, Britain made the dramatic decision to reestablish the gold standard. This immediately overvalued both the pound sterling and the Indian rupee. By funneling his wealth to Shanghai, Sassoon could purchase untold amounts of silver-based Chinese currency, which was worth little in comparison but did quite nicely for local real estate speculation. He was awash in cash.

The new bank and its chain of intermediaries let Sassoon transfer assets and branch out into global ventures, from oil extraction to electric power and utilities, as well as new technologies such as the Photomaton Corporation. Photomaton was a start-up venture that Sassoon's close friend Carl Bendix, a London banker, also gambled on. A Photomaton was installed first in London's Leicester Square and at Selfridge's Department Store. Patrons could enter the booth, "drop their shilling in the slot, and in twenty seconds have pictures taken in eight different positions. . . . Eight minutes later, the machine delivers the photographs in a single strip."[27] Sassoon also invested in the Shanghai Exploration and Development Company in search of oil and gas reserves in China. Further, the Power Investment Corporation project for electricity generation in that country had the likes of Sassoon and the British head of the Shanghai Stock Exchange plunking down their money.

Wealthy capitalists roamed the world looking for speculative opportunities. An archipelago of exchange banks made financial capitalism globally footloose. These were glamorous, if risky, investments but well within the tradition of Sassoon finance and trade. After just two years, the E. D.

Sassoon Bank was issuing new shares to raise capital for a host of new business prospects, especially in Shanghai's red-hot real estate market. The bank moved its headquarters into the glitzy new Sassoon House on Shanghai's Bund.

The Docklands, Global Gateway

Men, money, and markets tied together Britain's empire of commerce. Adherence to the Britishness of trade and finance was the bedrock of shared prosperity across this colonial realm, muffling the chorus of claims for independence. Whatever the political proclivities, global trade depended on the financial machinations going on in the City and the voracious demand for goods in London. London was the helm of the British Empire and the largest port in the world. The major destination of goods from the imperial domains was the wharves of London's East End. Tons of tea, raw cotton, and farm products were shipped out through Bombay's port to Britain each year. Ships arrived at the London docks with over 20 percent of India's exports in 1929, increasing to 34 percent by 1938.[28] India's industries were wedded to this trade. Whether this caused a drain on the native economy and the country's hopes for independence was a heated controversy made worse as the terms of trade shifted ever more in Britain's favor during the 1920s and 1930s. It was the reality behind the blistering disputes over tariffs and currency ratios along with the calls for protecting India's homegrown industries that sent Victor Sassoon into such a tailspin. Bombay also re-exported tons of material from the Middle East on to Britain.[29] The long-standing British demand for Chinese luxuries, especially tea, silk, porcelain, and objets d'art, continued unabated. The value of tea exported through Shanghai's port to London was enormous. Raw silks and silk products arrived from Shanghai, as did oils and wood.[30] A new import into the Docklands at London's East End was plantation rubber destined for making tires fitted on automobiles manufactured in London. Tankers lined up to deposit imported petroleum at the terminal built for Esso. It joined the oil terminals of Shell, the Anglo-Iranian Oil Company, and Vacuum Oil. The reign of the automobile was beginning to dominate the global marketplace.

British exports were another matter. While the goods imported through the Docklands increased, exports dwindled. Among the biggest drops in British commodities being shipped out was cotton textiles. Another was the "re-export" or transshipment market for goods dispatched to Britain, with value added through assembly and manufacture before redistribution overseas. It was a sign that British industrial might was waning and becoming more dependent on empire. Increasingly, the colonies were the cushion for British exports through a system of preferential tariffs. Britain sent nearly 50 percent of its exports directly to the dominions, India, and the Crown colonies. Until 1935, India was the largest single market for British goods, and it remained among the top three afterward.[31] Cotton textiles, machinery, iron, and steel flowed from London's Docklands to Bombay as the major trading gateway into the Indian subcontinent. London's new consumer industries were whipping out motorcars, electrical appliances, broadcasting and wireless equipment, and film equipment that filled the holds of steamships docked along the East End wharves as they waited to sail for Bombay. Britain and the British Empire also shipped massive amounts of manufactured goods to Shanghai. The total value of specifically British imports was millions of dollars each year, with those same consumer products, machinery, and Lancashire cotton textiles the main merchandise piling up on the wharves along the Huangpu River. Only Japanese goods could reach these import summits in Shanghai.[32] It was a British world of trade until the late 1930s, when the flags of not only Japan but also the United States and Germany began to eclipse those of Britain and its colonies flying in the harbor.

The London Docklands were legendary. It was a vast panorama of wharves piled high with cargo, wholesale markets and exchanges, and warehouses and factories stretching from the Pool at London Bridge down the looping river Thames twenty-six miles to Tilbury Docks. A multitude of London's industries relied on the port. Jobs indirectly related to the port and goods distribution numbered in the hundreds of thousands and were among the foundations of London's economy. In the 1920s, over fifty thousand people turned up at the port gates for work in shipping and dock services, although their numbers declined as cargo handling became more efficient. Many dockworkers depended on the wretched system of casual labor and lived in the warren of streets and alleyways twisting out from the quaysides. The districts of Shadwell and Stepney were some of the poorest and most densely populated areas of the East End. Thousands eked out a living street hawking and name-your-price haggling at the markets on Petticoat Lane and Brick Lane. Poplar and Stepney were enclaves of Indian migrants, where Sikh dealers sold silk, herbal medicines, and trinkets and hawked cheap Japanese goods. Local gangs in the East End ran the black market and gambling. It was a world away from the wealth and glamour paraded in Victor Sassoon's West End whirl.

A kaleidoscope of vessels of every size bearing the flags of every nation filled the waterway. Some sixty thousand ships steamed into port each year loaded with tons of merchandise. A hundred cranes waited to lift the bounty onto the piers. The largest, called the British Mammoth, hauled up to 150 tons a swing. Products from the East were generally off-loaded at St. Katherine's Dock. The George the Fifth Dock in North Woolwich was the newest mooring. Over five hundred acres of warehouses lined the streets in what was by every measure a massive accretion of global goods. The total value of imports and exports was fantastic. It reached over a billion pounds sterling in the early 1920s.[33] Silks and carpets, teas and coffee, cotton piece goods, and chinaware were stored in the uptown warehouses on Cutler Street. Urban explorer A. H. Blake was agog as he toured one warehouse and walked "from room to room. . . . Vast chambers are filled with precious products. Tea and cotton from India, ivory, silk, feathers, carpets from the looms of Persia, fabrics from China—in fact, all the riches and colouring of the gorgeous East blaze in these dull dark rooms."[34]

London's East End had long been the single most important center of economic activity in Britain and the epicenter for manufacturing, especially in factory districts such as the Isle of Dogs and West Ham. But there were striking changes to the Docklands atmosphere so vividly present since the Victorian era. To be sure, there were still traces of the old untamed East End in districts where urban explorer Thomas Burke found

FIGURE 8. Merchant ships in the Royal Albert Dock, London, 1926–1927. (The Print Collector / Alamy Stock Photo)

"a grotesque allotment of toil, breathing and smoking and rumbling.... It is a wilderness shot with glowering colour and ringing with the voices of the pilgrims of the night."³⁵ The factories and workshops tucked away in cramped backstreets still throbbed with productive work. But they were in older manufacturing sectors such as shipbuilding and repair, textiles, furniture making, and printing. They were hit hard in bad times, especially during the economic slump of the 1930s, when exports suffered dramatic setbacks. The Docklands were aging, and so were its industries. Its Victorian prime and pulsating energies of the turn of the century had passed. It was losing its economic muscle to London's outskirts, a situation true for London as a whole. The time-honored daily rituals around industrial work in the inner city were drying up as factories closed their doors and left for the urban periphery.

The notorious social landscape of London's East End was also slipping away. The maze of mean streets with their poor and downtrodden, their prostitutes and street urchins was vanishing. The Eliza Doolittles and the Fagans that George Bernard Shaw and Charles Dickens had captured with such poignancy were few to be found. The East Enders who could packed their belongings and left to find better circumstances elsewhere. Many found new homes in the first of the great public housing estates in the suburbs. Many of the stevedores and dockhands migrated downriver as new docks opened up. But their politics remained ferocious. Enraged in 1923 over a proposed pay reduction from eight shillings to five shillings sixpence for four hours' work, some twenty-five to thirty thousand dockworkers walked out and brought the Port of London to a standstill. Over two hundred vessels sat at anchor in the river waiting to be offloaded. Among their cargo were London's wheat supplies, sitting in the holds while the city's mills stood idle. The wildcat strike undermined the Docker's Union, which accused communist agitators of instigating the trouble and hooking up with militant unemployed organizations. At a packed meeting of several thousand in Whitechapel, dockworkers and lightermen booed union leaders and "sacked" them as "bloodsuckers" and "traitors," then marched into the streets.³⁶ The dockers still wielded tremendous power.

Institutions such as the Dockland Settlements, the London Seamen's Mission, and the Seamen's Union Maritime Hall provided shelter and protection for "rightful" British stevedores and wayfarers. But the fierce competition for jobs boiled over into race riots. British seamen accused "bloody aliens" of stealing jobs and undercutting wages on the docks. *Alien* was a slippery term thrown at non-Britons or "colored" seamen regardless of their actual rights as British subjects. *Colored* was a synonym for African, West Indian, Chinese, South Asian, and Arab sailors. It was common knowledge that Indian *lascars,* or sailors, worked long hours for next to nothing. They represented nearly one-third of the crews employed on British ships alone—a staggering forty-two thousand seamen, while the number employed on the docks was huge. In London, they were sheltered in cramped boardinghouses or warehoused by shipping companies such as the P&O line, whose godown at Albert Dock was a notorious abyss of humanity.[37]

The Coloured Alien Seamen Order of 1925 required foreign seamen to register as aliens and regularly threatened them with deportation. Colored seamen were routinely stopped and searched by police. They were attacked by mobs as work grew scarce and grudges boiled over into violence. White and black seamen battled it out in the streets with guns and knives drawn. Boardinghouses for colored sailors were ransacked. "Malayans in seafaring garb, Indians with scarlet and yellow turbans, Chinese, and negroes in khaki" huddled inside the Strangers' Home for Asiatics in Limehouse, a refuge run by Christian missionaries for colored sailors. At any provocation, crowds hurled rocks through its windows, because "darkies have cash in their pockets, that's why they've got the girls," referring to a "certain type of Limehouse woman."[38] Chinese seamen set up *fong* meeting places as refuge from the abuse meted out. The Chi Kung Tong society organized gangs for protection.

The tiny Indian Seamen's Union in London attempted to organize the *lascars* with gatherings at the dock gates. Its leaders—Paddy Upadhyaya and Shapurji Saklatvala—were under surveillance and hunted by police for stirring up strikes and communist rowdyism in the streets. Upadhyaya— the radical extraordinaire—had worked at the Bombay Stock Exchange before coming to London. He immersed himself in the communist cause and led protests against the paltry pay and conditions on the ships. Saklatvala was a nephew of Bombay's J. N. Tata and arrived in England to manage the Tata Company offices in Manchester. After moving to London, he became an ardent Communist Party member and won election to Parliament from the industrial district of Battersea on the south bank of the Thames. Global connectivity was multilayered, both official and subversive. Saklatvala helped establish the Communist journal *Sunday Worker* and went on to form the League against Imperialism. In fiery speeches, "Comrade Sak" railed against the injustices shared by mill workers in Britain and India. His condemnation of the British Empire was unequivocal. Writing in the *Workers' Weekly,* he fumed that "the British Empire is made up of the aristocratic and cunning dirty dogs of Great Britain, who will assail anyone's country any time." At open-air meetings in "Red" Battersea, Saklatvala called for using the interest on the national debt to pay for cheap housing and measures "for the people's welfare."[39]

Urban observers never tired of unearthing the Docklands' menacing foreignness and racial exoticism. Novels and films, popular magazines about the strange, mysterious worlds tucked into the East End were nothing if not ubiquitous. They were also highly exaggerated. The East End was vilified by its detractors as a dreary wasteland of "Turks, Jews, infidels, and anarchists."[40] Drug dealing and sex trafficking were viewed as omens of the Yellow Peril. Chinese "scabs" from Hong Kong and Shanghai stayed around Pennyfields near West India Dock Road, just adjacent to Limehouse. Londoners soaked in the sensationalist descriptions of Pennyfields and Limehouse after dark, when "Every Chinese, stealing past you with cat-like tread, is a Fu Manchu. Every pale-faced girl is a Broken Blossom." The images percolated from the hugely popular Sax Rohmer *Fu Manchu* movies and the Thomas Burke stories of the East End made into film. Burke's Limehouse was a theater of social types hanging out at the Blue Lantern tavern, "where the missionaries love to prowl." His tales of Slippery Sam, Sing-a-Song Joe, and Katie the Kid ("She was a stunner. She was a Spanker. She was a jazz of a girl") were a sensation. Burke's Mrs. Raymond mutters that the "Chinks" were "dirty yeller boys. They eat rats, y'know. Yerce, they do. I seen 'em. And worship images. They never wash themselves. And treacherous—yeh never know wher y'are with 'em. Stick a knife in yer back fer tuppence, and think nothing of it."[41] The sinister portrayals were helped along by drug dealer Brilliant "Billie" Chang, who ran an empire in Limehouse with abundant quantities of cocaine and opium supplied to rich clients on the West End through his restaurant on Regent Street. The "dapper little Chinese" made the tabloid front pages for keeping Freda Kempton, a local dance hall girl who died of a cocaine overdose.[42] The police finally caught up with Chang in 1924 and he was deported.

But all this was rare, so Limehouse was a disappointment for anyone looking for titillation. By the late 1920s, there was little chance of stumbling into an opium den or running into "a fantastical Chinaman, with a yellow face, a gown decorated with dragons," as a journalist salaciously reported in the *Illustrated London News*.[43] The Thomas Cook travel agency organized bus tours for rubbernecking sightseers but was forced to hire Chinese to stage hatchet fights to make it worthwhile. The Chinese endured deportations and entry refusals under the 1919 Aliens Act, the 1920 Dangerous Drugs Act, and the 1925 Coloured Alien Seamen Order. Their numbers dwindled. As jobs on the wharves for coolies dried up, fewer remained in Limehouse. Many were dependent on the Chung Yee Tong

Benevolent Society. Some set up the Chinese laundries found across the capital, while others tried for chop suey shops or groceries. In 1931, only one thousand Chinese were living in London and less than two hundred in Limehouse, which was already undergoing slum clearance.[44] They had moved to the West End or out to the peripheries.

The Jewish neighborhoods also came under the magnifying glass in depictions of London's global underbelly and the East End's twisted streets shrouded in fog. The districts of Stepney, Whitechapel, and Hackney, once predominately Irish, became enclaves of religiously devout Yiddish families from eastern Europe. Over 90 percent of Jews in London lived in these districts, where life revolved around the synagogue, the Yiddish theater, and the market stalls lining the narrow lanes. They were a world apart from the West End high society inhabited by the Sassoons. For wealthy Jewish families, East End Jewry was a source of embarrassment and anxiety over rumors about its radical political proclivities. Anti-Semitism was rife in London and got patched onto fears of communist plots hatched in the ghettos of the East End.[45]

But those on the hunt for conspiracies would have been let down. By the early 1930s, the East End had become a place to escape from, especially for a young generation of Jews who were products of English schools and more secularized. Those who persisted in the old ways in Stepney and Whitechapel were older and eked out their lives in crowded and miserable hovels. The Poor Jews' Temporary Shelter helped refugees gain a foothold. This was a world to leave behind. Even the Ayah's Home for Indian and Chinese nannies moved from narrow old Jewry Street to more spacious premises in Hackney. Poverty and unemployment were particularly cruel for those who remained precisely because their traditional artisanal trades were rapidly disappearing. Jobs in tailoring, shoemaking, and cabinetmaking evaporated, especially during the Great Depression. The younger generation broadened their horizons and enjoyed weekends at the dance hall and the cinema. They moved east and northward, far beyond the county boundaries in search of jobs and decent housing. They worked in engineering and in ready-to-wear, and they manned the desks as clerks and typists in the offices of the City.

Working London, Global Enterprise

The lure of London was inescapable. Something like two-thirds of the new jobs in Britain were created in Greater London in the 1920s and 1930s. It was a boom town amid a declining British economy. The wealth of the City lubricated industrial development. Multinational companies opened branch operations. Although it was clearly the imperial metropole among the three, London shared with Bombay and Shanghai a panorama of global businesses taking advantage of local labor pools and new markets. It was part of their status as global helms and connected all three in a dense web of capitalist production.

The assembly-line plants and workshops of the twentieth century roared into action with electricity. In London, factories marched westward and northward, out past the old urban boundaries, landing in towns and villages rapidly gobbled up into the greater metropolitan fold. The new industrial belt was in the western suburbs, where most multinational factories in Britain were located. In her 1932 novel *To the North*, author Elizabeth Bowen described a train ride through the area, where "in the distance aërial glassy white factories were beginning to go up among forlorn may trees, branch lines and rusty girders: here and there one was starting to build Jerusalem."[46] Factories went to Lea Valley, where some forty thousand people were working in manufacturing by the 1930s, and to West Middlesex, with its seventy-five thousand employed and nearly a hundred foreign companies.[47] Land was cheap. Automated plants spread out along the main thoroughfares and train lines. This is where the high-demand products of the 1920s and 1930s were made—automobiles and tires, consumer goods, drugs and chemicals, glass and chromium plate, and electrical equipment. Londoners snapped up the radios and gramophones, the electric cookers and vacuum cleaners that rolled off the assembly lines and onto department store shelves.

Despite the Depression, the prosperity of London was remarkable in the 1930s. The heartbreaking vision of the jobless was a long way off from the capital. Thousands of destitute, unemployed men and women from the rest of Britain descended there in search of jobs in the new consumer industries, in aircraft and automobile plants. These were the sunrise industries of the interwar years. British Aircraft Manufacturing and Handley Page produced military and commercial planes. The Ford Motor Company and Briggs Motors churned out automobiles at Dagenham. The British firm Glaxo Laboratories moved its headquarters in inner London to a new facility, where it produced the newest pharmaceutical products. The Glaxo Building on Great West Road was state of the art, with offices and laboratories, a tennis court, and a canteen for workers. The Gramophone (EMI) Company was renovating its recording studios at Abbey Road while the Standard Telephones (owned by ITT) factory at Southgate supplied Londoners with radios and telephones.

Spanking-new plants in the northwest of London at Park Royal provided abundant job opportunities. About 250 firms employed some 20,000 people there.⁴⁸ Multinational corporations, especially American ones, expanded their operations worldwide. They jumped into the British market with the newest consumer products. In the late 1930s, a two-mile stretch of Great West Road to Park Royal known as the Golden Mile alone marshaled 53 factories employing 11,000 people.⁴⁹ The Golden Mile was a visual parade of new industries. Their streamlined art deco office and production facilities symbolized a modern way to work. These buildings were state-of-the-art showpieces built in steel and reinforced concrete. Architecture stood for a new world of consumer goods. A staff of some 1,600 people produced vacuum cleaners at the American Hoover Vacuum Company plant on Western Avenue near the Golden Mile. Like the Glaxo Building, the Hoover Building was designed by Wallis, Gilbert & Partners in the art deco style as a model factory and advertising brand for the company. The architectural firm was responsible for some of the finest "fancy"⁵⁰ industrial buildings along the Golden Mile. Its Firestone Tyre building on Great West Road was designed in art deco with Egyptian motif and floodlit at night for full effect. It was the US company's first overseas operation. US multinational conglomerates Gillette Razor and Heinz Foods established themselves on the Golden Mile as well. The Helena Rubinstein and the Coty laboratories on Great West Road fabricated the stylish cosmetics that were all the rage. Wallis, Gilbert & Partners designed the Coty facility with sparkling white walls and strip windows in the latest art deco style.

For outdated industries in London's fading East End, the city's vibrancy was gossamer thin. Hundreds of factories closed in the old districts. The split between London's traditional industries and its brand-new manufacturing meant intense social inequalities. It was symptomatic of globalization's impact on urban life. While salaried office workers in the City and employees in the new factories on the Golden Mile were on their way up, those stuck in low-wage work had few chances for a better life. Families struggled along the poverty line, and unemployment was a constant dread. The specter of two different urban worlds snowballed most dramatically into the 1926 General Strike. On the eve of the walkout, London prepared as if going to war. The city's police were reinforced. Hyde Park was turned into a massive distribution center, its trees strung with telephone wires to relay messages to the supply points. Whitehall was besieged by thousands of volunteers waiting to man essential services. Government ministers who saw a Bolshevik revolutionary in every striker made a special appeal over the wireless for volunteer constables for the stock exchange, Lloyds, and the Baltic and Corn Exchanges.⁵¹ They were ready to defend the City and the Crown. The *London Times* boastfully reported that "the

Stock Exchange and the Money Market showed great calmness . . . and it is doubtful whether in any country where a general strike has occurred has so little disturbance to the financial markets been experienced." Nonetheless, across the Thames, crowds surrounded the Houses of Parliament, singing in defiance and waiting for the stroke of midnight, when "a rather hysterical enthusiast yelled hoarsely 'Comrades, the hour has struck.'"[52]

On May 4, the docks closed down. The Tube, trams, and trains stopped running. London's bridges and the main routes into the city were besieged by masses of motortrucks, wagons, bikes, and cars jammed with dapper men and women from the suburbs struggling to make their way to their desks in the City's banks and offices. Traffic in Trafalgar Square, Parliament Square, Piccadilly Circus, and the Embankment was impassable.[53] London's power stations were manned by a skeleton crew and electricity rationed. Telegrams, mail, even telephone calls were restricted. The industrial heartland around the docks in the east and southeast was steadfast in support of the strike. Throngs of dockworkers blocked the gates onto the piers. Radio bulletins from the BBC kept followers apprised of events. Newspapers published only nominal daily editions. Even the *London Times* managed no more than a sheet or two, and its offices were struck by arson.

Strike waves and public protests were a shared experience in the 1920s across London, Bombay, and Shanghai. The city streets were alight with collective rage at the same moment Victor Sassoon and his cronies were whooping it up at the cabarets and fancy-dress balls that kept high society aflutter on London's West End, at charity balls in Bombay, and at the French Concession in Shanghai. The social disparities were dramatic across the three cities. Opulence and hardship existed side by side. The easy money and good times of the Roaring Twenties were relished by the privileged few. Their exploits were eagerly imitated by those in well-paid white-collar positions, in services work, and even in skilled manufacturing jobs. The salaried masses made their way on the crest of the new industries and their global reach. The anger of those left behind, their social frustration, simmered below the surface and broke out in unending marches and walkouts across the global urban panorama. London's General Strike mirrored these populist movements. Thousands amassed for huge marches organized by the Labour Party. Trafalgar Square and Hyde Park became a sea of people and banners, with labor leaders exhorting the throngs. As the strike wore on, buses and trains run by middle-class volunteers were invaded, taxis and private cars harassed. Troops and Grenadier Guards marched past picket lines and took charge of the docks. Motortrucks were loaded with essential supplies and sent by convoy to Hyde Park. But for all the emergency, London's cabaret shows, its playhouses and sporting events trundled on, and its movie theaters were packed. Then, after nine days of turmoil, the Trade Unions Congress called off the strike. Public transport resumed, and people drifted back to work.

London's Global Commerce

The City's moguls tried in vain to revive the glory years of the imperial economy after the First World War. But the General Strike was more than enough evidence that even in London, those days had waned. More important, the return to the gold standard in 1925 drastically reduced the ability of businesses to invest abroad. Overseas assets, trade, and exchange were falling off. Global trade was rapidly expanding, but the British share of world exports dropped from one-fourth before the war to only one-fifth by 1930. For all the cargo slung onto London's wharves, Britain's overseas business was imperceptibly flagging. Confidence in London as the world's financial center was never quite the same. But it wasn't just about the money. It was about the decline of British prestige. London could no longer settle the world's money affairs on its own. Eyes were shifting to New York's Wall Street and the American colossus. Moreover, US and German manufacturers were driving out British trade from its own colonies. Imported American products "from typewriters and pickles to comic operas" amounted to an "invasion"[54] that undermined homegrown manufacturers even in Britain itself. Fears about Americanization reverberated through the press. "The New Rich is essentially American. American in its tastes. American in its hopes. And certainly American in its bank balance," Shaw Desmond warned in the tabloid the *Sphere*.[55]

In response, the City bore down on the commercial web of empire to pump up its global economic influence. The imperial domain loomed large in the British psyche. Britain's foreign investments in its empire were massive. It was no wonder that politicians and policy makers were obsessed by these transactions. They were convinced that pumping up the flow of goods and capital from Britain to its territories would create economic progress, and in return the colonies would provide markets for British goods. At the Ottawa Conference in 1932, Britain negotiated seven separate bilateral trade agreements with Commonwealth countries, including India. Whitehall's policy became incessantly export oriented, with London as the central pivot in these imperial trading and financial transactions. It would guarantee the flow of money into the City. This was the rationale behind the British Empire Exhibition. It was meant to hustle trade with the empire and find new global markets.

A hastily organized Imperial Economic Committee was set up to improve the outdated promotion of goods across the British realm. London's old Imperial Institute in South Kensington was repurposed to promote economic ties with the colonies. The London Chamber of Commerce was the heart of a vast commercial network spread across British territories. It connected thousands of members, trade associations, and overseas chambers of commerce. The Federation of British Industries linked businesses across the realm and carried out trade missions.[56] There was an insiders' tone to these colonial networks. They were entirely British initiatives, and the racial divisions were stark. Imperial trade networks were white men's clubs, where face-to-face relations and informal negotiations took place over gin. Few native businessmen broke through the color line. Although the Bombay Chamber of Commerce was of mixed membership, relations had deteriorated between the European and Indian commercial magnates. Indian participation in these trade schemes was resisted in order to avoid the snarled tariff issues. In Shanghai, the International Settlement's Chamber of Commerce worked hand in hand with British companies, while Chinese businessmen had entirely separate commercial networks. In London, pressure groups such as the Empire Free Trade Crusade, the United Empire Party, and the Empire Marketing Board all pushed citizens to "Buy British" across what was imagined as a loyal and prosperous Commonwealth. Over four hundred organizations participated in the trade push. Billboards were unveiled across London exhorting consumers to make their purchases patriotically.

India was the principal trading possession of the British Crown and a captive market for British products and services. Some 40 percent of its imports came directly from Britain[57]—a huge market for the goods rolling out of London's factories. Nonetheless, British merchants were facing stiff competition from the United States, Japan, and the European continent to fill the insatiable demands of Indian consumers, especially for motorcars and motorcycles, drugs and medicines, and the newest domestic products. Even in Shanghai, British imports of heavy machinery and electrical equipment were slacking off, replaced by American and German wares.[58] British trade was not keeping up with the demand for automobiles, wireless and telecommunications gear, and electric appliances. In his reports on overseas trade, Senior Trade Commissioner Thomas Ainscough declared that "it is necessary that British manufacturers should realise the situation before it is too late. After 21 years' business and official experience in two of our greatest markets, India and China, I state with firm conviction that the marvellous industrial strength of the United Kingdom is to a large extent dissipated . . . owing to the fact that our marketing methods are not so scientific and carefully planned."[59] Manufacturers had to become salesmen to compete globally. The fact was that trade was expanding among the empire countries themselves. They were also looking to other external sources to fulfill their needs. The British Empire, including India with its entrepôt of Bombay, was becoming more and more integrated into the world economy but much less so with Great Britain. The long-standing British world of trade was fracturing.

Despite a fierce patriotic belief in cotton textiles as the symbol of British industrial might, the days were past when Albion supplied the world's clothing. A speculation craze hit Lancashire just after the war, when old textile mills were being bought and sold and new ones springing up in anticipation of an export boom. It mirrored the profiteering in Bombay at the same moment, when mills were being sold at fabulous prices and huge investments made in textile production. The boom was short-lived, however, and a staggering crash followed. By 1929, Lancashire's textile exports had fallen to one-third of their value in 1913 and never again reached anything near prewar levels. Worse, the sale of its piece goods to India, China, Japan, and Hong Kong declined by a staggering 90 percent between 1913 and 1937.[60] It was a shocking turnaround in the competition for global markets. Contenders in Bombay, Shanghai, and Osaka were decentering British economic dominion to the benefit of Asia.

The same complaints about Bombay's mills were being made in Lancashire to explain the precipitous decline in exports—overcapitalization, backward techniques, heavy taxation, middlemen at every turn, and high labor costs. India had been Lancashire's most important market, so the decline in exports reaching Bombay's wharves was the single most important factor in the textile region's downturn. India accounted for 76 percent of Lancashire's trade loss from the prewar high. Despite the complaints lodged against Bombay's stodgy mills and the endless strikes, the textile factories in Girangaon were supplying nearly half of India's consumption. Their homegrown success was an endless source of consternation for British mill owners. Lancashire's second-most-important market was China. But even here, the Chinese market was falling like a stone. The textile mills of Shanghai were eating into the British market across the Far East. Far more worrying, however, was Japan. Before the First World War, British cotton piece goods dominated the Chinese market. By 1929, Japan had taken over with a 75 percent ratio, in contrast to Lancashire's measly 25 percent.[61] Even the most lucrative textile mills in Shanghai were Japanese owned. Japan was the principal culprit for both Manchester's and Bombay's trade issues, and the mill owners in both places made themselves hoarse carping about Japanese cotton textiles flooding the global market.

Victor Sassoon laid out what he saw as the problem: "What British manufacturers must realise is that the cost of their goods in the East is too high. They are not such good value as they were. We used to talk of shoddy German and Japanese goods. They are no longer shoddy and if they are only 90 per cent as good as ours they are 50 per cent cheaper."[62] It was a tough lesson to learn. Then the Great Depression devastated the ailing textile industry. Trade plummeted; "disaster was starring Lancashire in the face."[63] The Lancashire lobby made the rounds of London's clubs, pressing its case for protection over private lunches with the commissioner of customs, members of the House of Commons, and the Board of Trade. The old-boy network was pursued with a vengeance. In an atmosphere of desperation, the Manchester Chamber of Commerce sent a textile delegation to India in 1933 to hammer out a trade agreement. The group was welcomed at the dock by the Bombay Chamber of Commerce and swiftly driven to the Taj Mahal Hotel. It was an "amazing affair," reported Sir Raymond Streat. "They do everything for you. . . . The Yacht Club has everything for the comfort of the white man in the East. Fans, large open spaces, cool polished floors and innumerable servants whose 'sole object in living is to watch out and approach when any of the lords of creation require a light for their cigars.'"[64]

Sassoon was among the hosts at the dinner for the Lancashire delegates at the Willingdon Sports Club. In an interview with the Associated Press, he emphatically insisted that the measures to ward off Japanese competition would be entirely beneficial to India.[65] Bombay's businessmen swung toward compromise with the Raj. In a sign of this conviction, the Bombay Millowners' Association bargained with Lancashire, triggering Indian nationalist opposition. The 1933 Lees-Mody Pact gave preference to British textiles in place of Japanese imports, and in return the Manchester merchants gave vague, airy promises to buy more Indian cotton. Homi Mody, one of Bombay's most noted Parsi businessmen and longtime president of the Millowners' Association, was excoriated in the Indian nationalist press as a Lancashire lackey. The British delegates fired back that it "required sacrifices on both sides" to stem the tide of Japanese imports.[66]

The compromise amounted to a Machiavellian move, but it did Lancashire little good. If there were any gains by way of the tariff policy, they were reaped by Bombay and Shanghai, which began offering cotton goods at a price as low as Japan's.[67] Even though the terms of trade were decidedly on the side of the British, their exports to both India and China continued to crash. The number of ships carrying British goods into Bombay's port were declining, while more ships from other countries were docking at the quayside. Trade with other British possessions, Europe, Asia, and the United States was on the rise.[68] The fierce protectionism of the Lancashire textile lobby had less appeal to a British government watching the growing economic supremacy of New York. Eyes turned toward London's new industries for deliverance. By the mid-1930s, a rising mood of economic nationalism was fixated on global finance and services as well as commodity trading, all now being governed by the speed of telecommunications and air transport.

※ 6 ※
Enigmatic Shanghai

> Shanghai is the Paris of the Far East ... where Unthinkable
> Degradations are Cloaked Beneath a Veil of Brilliant Gaiety and
> Hectic Pleasure-Seeking.
> "The Paris of the Distant Orient," *Sphere* (1927)

When Victor Sassoon moved himself and his wealth from Bombay to Shanghai in 1931, the situation was not promising. The global economy had crashed. And China was convulsed by war and revolution: Shanghai was being wracked by massive protests and labor strikes. Chinese workers had reduced the city's cotton mills to a daily battleground, its machinery ransacked and its managers assaulted. It was the same uproar, the same worker insurrection Sassoon had faced at his mills in Bombay. In Shanghai, the violence spiraled out of control in May 1925, when a Chinese worker was killed in the Japanese-owned Naigai Wata Mills. Anti-Japanese and anti-British protests broke out on Nanjing Road and ended with British-led police firing into the crowd. A litter of bodies was left in the ensuing mayhem. The incident galvanized the city against the foreigners. A fierce anti-imperialist uprising rocked Shanghai in what became known as the May Thirtieth Movement. Cotton mills and factories were shuttered. Ships sat idle in the harbor as dockworkers walked out. A yearlong boycott of foreign goods swept across the city. Roving gunfights between rioters and police turned the streets into combat zones.

Then in 1927, a communist uprising against the warlords controlling Shanghai ended in a bloody massacre. Next, the Nationalist forces of General Chiang Kai-shek arrived from Wuhan. Suddenly, their Kuomintang Party flags were flying over the city. Bedraggled Russian, Polish, and Ukrainian refugees from the Bolshevik Revolution and the Russian Civil War flooded into Shanghai in what was a full-scale humanitarian crisis. It was not a propitious moment for Sassoon to be sallying forth. If he was attempting to escape the political turmoil in Bombay, Shanghai was not a good choice, and ultimately it would be his undoing. Yet he remained optimistic as he sailed to the East. In a press interview during a short stop in Singapore, he defended his gamble on China, claiming that it was "emerging from her troubles." China was a better investment than India. Business was good, credit was solid.[1] Shanghai was the head of the Chinese dragon. Its population exploded from one to almost four million people in the space of twenty-five years (1910–1935). It was the largest city in the Far East and plump with possibilities. The fact was that Sir Victor was staggeringly rich, and his opinion counted. The press reported his company's wealth at 1 billion rupees and the E. D. Sassoon Bank at another 1 million.

For many in London perusing Sassoon's confident predictions, China remained an enigma. It was the subject of countless books, newspaper articles, and BBC Radio programs. Self-appointed experts, or "China hands," who may or may not have had any real experience in the country, kept up a litany of high-handed opinions. Foreign correspondents churned out a flood of reports from a pretentious British point of view. The *London Times* had close connections with the Shanghai English-language papers and relied on them for information, especially the *North China Daily News*, the official British organ and opinion leader for the foreign community. O. M. Green, editor of the *North China Daily News* and a correspondent for the *London Times*, was a diehard loyalist to British interests. The paper spewed nothing but scorn at Chinese nationalist aspirations, dismissing them as pure silliness. H. G. W. Woodhead was a prolific journalist working in Tientsin and Shanghai, writing for the *Shanghai Evening Post and Mercury* and spearheading his own journal, *Oriental Affairs*. His annual *China Year Book* was a standard reference in Britain, and his books, especially *The Truth about the Chinese Republic* (1925), were heavily reviewed in the London press. Woodhead was a staunch imperialist and blamed the chaos in China on Bolshevik agents and Soviet interference in the domestic affairs of the teetering republic.[2] It was an opinion echoed by Sassoon, who regularly pointed the finger at communist agents in Bombay and Shanghai as the culprits behind mill strikes and political turmoil.

In the press, China was either showered with the imperialist imagery of the British Empire Exhibition at Wembley or maligned with photos of civil strife. The country radiated the "spell of the Orient" and all the usual tropes of mystery and incomprehensible strangeness. But it was an opportunist's paradise where fortunes could be made, where adventurers lived the romance of the Far East. For British sojourners, both Hong Kong and Shanghai were baffling places, their streets filled with half-naked beggars and pigtailed coolies pulling rickshaws. The impressions they scrawled about Shanghai typically pointed to the medley of vitals and wares dangling in its markets. Paper lanterns swung in alleyways where sedan chairs teetered through the crowds. Depictions zeroed in on wing-tipped pagodas. Picturesque sampans and junks with their dragon-head carvings bobbed in the harbor, their billowing sails painted with the eye of the sea god for good luck. Suspicions quickly turned to Shanghai's seedy underworld, its bribery and corruption, prostitution and child slavery. The savagery shocked British sensibilities. The city's temptations—the opium dens with their earthy haze, the easy women and easier money, the gambling and dance halls—could unravel a British griffin suffering from loneliness. In the opinion of many, Shanghai was a city of depravities, especially the teahouses and bordellos on Fuzhou Road where the singsong girls offered respite.

Shanghai, Global Helm

These exotic hallucinations blotted out the modern city that unfolded as passengers arrived on steamers at the mouth of the Yangtze River and then glided up its Huangpu River tributary. There is "little that suggests the Orient," the Carl Crow tour guide warned tourists in 1921: "The river is crowded with shipping, the waters dotted with large and small steamers, tugs, lighters and sampans. The smoke stacks of many factories stand out in a skyline which recalls memories of Europe or America. On the shore there are huge shipbuilding plants, warehouses, cotton mills, silk filatures, oil tanks, docks and a busy line of railway." A *North China Herald* reporter marveled at the factories and mills lining the riverbank: "Chimneys, belching thick black smoke, rear their grotesque ugliness against the skyline. Chimneys! A never-ending stream of them.... One factory succeeds another, one mill begats a second."[3] Like London and Bombay, Shanghai was at the helm of global commerce. Some 40 to 50 percent of China's external trade flowed through it. The increase in trade at its port was meteoric between 1915 and 1930. The European belligerents in the First World War summoned both India and China to supply the battle fronts with clothing and materiel. Workers streamed into Shanghai for jobs in factories, generating equipment at a feverous pace. The city's population ballooned during the war from one to well over two million. With the return of peace, the demands of reconstruction kept Shanghai's factories running at high gear. Ships laden with exports steamed down the Huangpu to the Yangtze's deep swirls, out along the China coast, and then to the transoceanic lanes.

Shanghai was China's global marketplace. Fifty shipping companies operated the commercial traffic. The great bulk of it was in the hands of well-established Chinese hongs. Some twenty-two thousand riverboats, coastal steamers, and oceangoing vessels berthed each year at the fourteen miles of piers and pontoons extending up the Huangpu to its offshoot, the narrow brown Suzhou Creek.[4] Coolies swarmed the docks, stooped under enormous loads roped on their backs. Huge barrels and sacks were driven in wheelbarrows and slung on poles, then carted off to storerooms. Over three hundred godowns lined the riverfront, arranged by the geography of trade. They were jammed with the imports and exports, the transshipment of goods[5] that were the city's lifeblood. It was a scene that mirrored the docklands of London and Bombay. Traditional exports—farm products, tea, and silk—were declining in favor of locally manufactured goods and textiles. The smuggling rackets in opium and narcotics, in guns, in every conceivable commodity of value, were their own highly lucrative clandestine exchange.

Fortunes were there for the taking. Chinese entrepreneurs fled the political calamities of the country's interior and headed for the foreign concessions and industrial districts. With plenty of cash, they plowed capital into shipping and manufacturing, especially in the Yangtzepoo district along the river. Most factories were owned by Chinese. They were savvy players in a hard-edged game. Armed robberies and racketeering were scourges. Paying "squeeze" to the crime bosses and handing out cash for arms and munitions were the price of doing business. Merchants wielded political power through their professional alliances—the Chinese Millowners' Association, the Shanghai Bankers' Association, and the Chamber of Commerce. They organized boycotts against foreign competitors. There were no regulations on wages for work in factories, so only a pittance was paid. It left plenty of room for Shanghai's merchants to prey on its toilers. A corrupted hiring system and miserable pay were what awaited peasants escaping the wretchedness of the countryside. The abuse was scandalous and provoked the strikes that tore the city apart. The work stoppages became more aggressive with each passing year.

Some 50 percent of China's industrial workers were concentrated in Shanghai, and over half of those generated the city's massive output of cotton textiles. Although exact numbers are impossible, some 150,000 to 200,000[6] men, women, and children toiled away in dingy rooms reeling threads and manning looms for twelve hours a day. Many of them were indentured to labor contractors who fed off destitute families in the countryside. These were the minions that anthropologist Margaret Read had seen in Bombay and in the mills across Asia (see chapter 2). Their daily grind droned to the rhythms of global capitalism. Altogether, 76 Chinese cotton mills outfitted with British machinery operated in Shanghai. The three firms of Dafeng, Lixin, and Dacheng pioneered the manufacture of finished cotton cloth and made the city into a textile powerhouse. "Cotton and flour kings" such as Rong Zongjing built an industrial empire. His massive Shenxin textile mills employed 30,000 mill hands. The Rong family were the richest and most cutting-edge entrepreneurs in the country. Another 32 mills in Shanghai were owned by Japanese, and 5 were British. There were scores of smaller cotton, silk, and wool mills, dyeworks, and piece-goods plants. Reports from the early 1930s counted some 560 textile workshops in the International Settlement and another 600 in Greater Shanghai. Alongside were 46 cigarette factories and over 300 chemical works making soaps, drugs, and industrial chemicals.[7] The grimy maze of lanes along Suzhou Creek were packed with warehouses, machinery sheds and engineering works, and shipbuilding yards. Across the Huangpu River, the Pudong district was a continuous line of wharves and warehouses, behind which stood a scrabble of factories and spinning and weaving mills.

Shanghai was China's London. It was China's Bombay. Surveying the scene in 1925, French journalist Albert Londres declared that "Shanghai is for making money. It is the first and last aim." It was the same refrain heard on the streets of London and Bombay. "Bankers and moneychangers from everywhere threw themselves, belly down, on the promised city," Londres continued. "And so, Shanghai was born from a Chinese mother and an americo-anglo-franco-germano-hollando-italo-japono-judéo-espagnol father."[8] Some three hundred thousand shop clerks and desk workers kept the city's global commerce going each day.[9] A new class of bankers and stockbrokers worked in the Chinese and foreign banks that were financing Shanghai's merchant capitalism. The Maritime Customs Union employed hundreds of young, well-trained Chinese to manage import and export trade and gather the myriad statistical data merchants depended on. There was no doubt that China was heavily reliant on foreign private capital, and Shanghai was graced with the lion's share of foreign investments in the country. Western companies pounced on Shanghai as a new territory for speculation, for the China market was a gold mine for businesses willing to take risks. A rich world of compradors made the link between these foreign companies and the Chinese markets. They captured the city's spirit of enterprise but were sneered at by the Chinese for aping Europeans and denounced by the foreigners they served as "unscrupulous."[10] Business was rough and tumble, and it was cutthroat. Suspicions of crime and profiteering reigned on all sides.

In the 1920s and early 1930s, Britain was Shanghai's major trading and investment partner. Some 170 British firms opened local offices and managed this bonanza. By 1937, however, Japan, the United States, and Germany had all overtaken Britain as the city's major importers.[11] Even during the economic slump of the 1930s, the city remained a commanding global entrepôt. "Despite depressions, financial panics, retrenchments and the threatening loss of extraterritoriality," the *China Journal* reported, "the present year [1935] saw the greatest number of ships in seventy-five years lying in the Whangpoo River, and the highest total of tonnage in many months." In addition, foreign trade reached record high levels in 1936.[12] Altogether, sixteen foreign chambers of commerce had offices in Shanghai to promote business and help market products. Huge international trading firms governed the flow of goods. Their offices were filled with the bookkeepers, managers, and clerks who daily ran global trade. Both the E. D. Sassoon & Company and the David Sassoon enterprises were joined by merchant titans Jardine & Matheson, the German Carlowitz Company, and the Japanese Mitsui Bussan Kaisha Company. Butterfield & Swire, with headquarters in Shanghai and London, owned the China Navigation Company, with its fleet of vessels plying the China Sea littoral and the web of routes in the Far Eastern trade.[13] Parsi and Gujarati Indians got in on the moneymaking. Headquartered in Bombay, commission agents such as Abdoolally, Ebrahim & Company, and Tata & Company planted their affiliates in Shanghai. Altogether, the number of Indian companies in Shanghai increased in the 1930s to forty-nine firms.[14]

Ships steamed up the Huangpu River loaded with heavy machinery, electrical equipment, boilers, and turbines from Britain. The cargo was put to work building China's railroads, electric power stations, factories, and modern cotton mills.[15] The massive storage tanks of the Standard Oil Company and the British Shell-Royal Dutch Asiatic Petroleum Company (APC) towered over the Pudong district waterfront. The headquarters of the APC took up residence on the Bund, where its vast distribution networks were managed. The APC alone captured 44 percent of the Chinese petroleum market. British Imperial Chemical Industries opened palatial offices and showcased its products in a spectacular exhibit at the Majestic Hotel. Some five hundred Chinese employees installed in its offices supervised over a thousand Chinese agents spread throughout the country.[16] The extent to which global corporations and venture capitalists jumped into the Shanghai market was mind boggling. Even the city's stock index was put together by the US Oriental Finance Corporation.

The Chinese were hungry for electricity, the telegraph, and telephones. Foreign contracts were there for the taking. Shanghai's electric power station on the Huangpu was designed by British engineers and filled with imported American equipment. Although it was state of the art, it could barely keep up with demand. The city was ablaze with electric light. The equipment for the Electric Appliance Factory on Suzhou Creek was imported from Germany's Siemens Company. Telecommunications giants pounced on lucrative schemes to modernize Shanghai's global connectivity. Telegraph cables landed on Chinese soil directly under the Bund. Cable transmission to the rest of the world was in the hands of a consortium made up of the Danish Great Northern Telegraph Company, the British-owned China Telegraph Company, and the American Pacific Cable Company. Shanghai's International Wireless Station was equipped by the French Associated Wireless Company. The US-owned International Telephone &Telegraph Company ran the Shanghai Mutual Telephone Company, although the connections were scratchy and required screaming into the phone.

The city's blockbuster Auto-Fashion Show was a main event during the spring horse-racing extravaganza known as Race Week. The show introduced thousands of gawkers to the latest imported American and British motorcars. The Auto Palace on Avenue Edward VII flaunted Morris Minors, Austins, and Chevrolets in a showroom gleaming with plate-glass windows. Captivated by the demand for glitzy Western automobiles, Victor Sassoon bought the Auto Palace outright in 1928. He was among four hundred people crowded into the China Motors showroom to inspect British Standard automobiles direct from "the very heart of England."[17]

The magnitude of these European and American business ventures was striking. The enterprises swooped down on Shanghai en masse and entwined it in the widening network of global capitalism. When China slapped heavy tariffs on imported goods in 1929, foreign companies established themselves directly in the city or licensed brokers for their products—a windfall for multinational companies hunting out commodity markets. The booming British-American Tobacco Company churned out billions of the machine-made Ruby Queen cigarettes in its Pudong district factory. From its giant headquarters in London, Unilever formed its foreign affiliate (the China Soap Company) and introduced Chinese consumers to its popular Sunlight and Lux Soap brands. By the early 1930s, it was employing a thousand Chinese workers.

The old merchant house Jardine & Matheson spun off Jardine Engineering, while Arnhold & Company formed New Engineering and Shipbuilding Works (see chapter 5). The two subsidiaries fabricated heavy machinery and electric equipment and were responsible for some of the most important civic projects in Shanghai, including the double-decker omnibuses and municipal tram system. Jardine & Matheson and Arnhold & Company held near monopolies in the International Settlement and protected their interests by controlling local politics. They raked in

FIGURE 9. Chinese workers of a British business, Shanghai, early 1900s. (KGPA Ltd / Alamy Stock Photo)

profits and weathered the political storms that engulfed the city. Anderson, Meyer & Company was the largest electric machinery company in China. It partnered with General Electric to distribute and manufacture electric equipment for Shanghai's factories and power plants. Danish entrepreneur Vilhelm Meyer, its director, was one of the city's most flamboyant and influential foreigners, a man "who could easily have made a success on the grand opera stage." Meyer was knighted by the Danish king and awarded the highest decoration ever given to a foreigner in China — the Chia Ho.[18] US companies opened electric lamp factories and motorcar assembly plants, and they set up a venture partnership with the Chinese in the China National Aviation Corporation.

Shanghai was also the powerhouse of banking in China. There were twenty branches of foreign exchange banks and some forty native Chinese banks, many of the latter run by the money whizzes who had migrated to Shanghai from Ningbo.[19] They tied Shanghai to the London and New York money markets, and through an interlocking system of credit to the old-style Chinese banks that worked the country's interior. Chinese merchants ordering imported British goods paid for them in London in pounds sterling, but they sold them in Chinese taels, or silver dollars. The same situation faced Shanghai's exporters. The funds for these transactions were funneled through the banks. Everything depended on the exchange rate. The flow of capital was controlled entirely by globally connected financiers and shrewd local currency brokers.

Many a bright young Chinese with education sat behind the desks in the city's banks and mercantile houses servicing the elaborate operations of global finance and trade. They were Shanghai's new salaried class. Almost all the banks were within the International Settlement and the French Concession and concentrated around the Bund. The "Bund Banks" were lordly places, fortresses of global finance capitalism. The neoclassical Hong Kong & Shanghai Bank building with its striking dome overlooked the Bund. It was a temple of commerce and the financial arm of the British imperial government. "Spare no expense, but dominate the Bund," the bank's manager had ordered.[20] Further along the Bund were the Russo-Asiatic Bank, the Bank of Australia & China, and the Yokohama Specie Bank. Also standing on the Bund was a branch of the Mercantile Bank of India, headquartered in Bombay. The new Bank of China, a money stronghold built at the behest of Finance Minister H. H. Kung (Hsiang Hsi), rose on the Bund with $25 billion in capital. It opened a branch in London, where Chinese bankers chased British money and met with investors.[21]

In a world dominated by gold, silver was the heart of the Chinese monetary system. China was the only country on a total silver standard. There was no single national currency. Instead, exchange took place in silver coins or in the shoe-shaped, silver-backed tael (or sycee). Even after the tael was replaced in 1933 by the yuan, the new currency was still silver. "'Money' to the average peasant in the East means silver in some form or other," banker A. W. Pinnick reported.[22] Everyday exchange was just as apt to take place in Mexican silver pesos or even the mixture of silver-based paper banknotes that circulated simultaneously. In whatever form, silver reigned supreme. Shanghai was the world's leading silver market, followed by Bombay, London, and New York. The city's silver exchange determined the value of China's currency. The entire system of credit pivoted around Shanghai. Its stock of silver was enormous, about £16 million in 1930.[23]

Silver poured into the city with every violent disturbance in the countryside, then poured out again when a truce was called. Bank vaults were stuffed full of silver bullion. The Hong Kong & Shanghai Bank resorted to packing the ingots into garages and brick sheds at the back of its premises on the Bund. The city was littered with small-time money shops and loan shops jammed with people slipping gold, paper money, and banknotes across a barred counter for changing into silver. When the exchange rates whipsawed, wildcat gold bar exchanges sprang up where gamblers could bring gold jewelry and ornaments to exchange for Mexican silver dollars. Calculation and risk taking were ordinary practices. Every dealer had their scale. Silver bars were freely sold by local speculators. Chinese families hoarded silver plaques, trays, and jewelry, but not only as heirlooms. Just as in Bombay, they were wealth that guarded against volatile currencies. How much families were willing to bet their world on these transactions made them keen observers of the global metal and money markets.

Silver was an internationally traded commodity without any restrictions. What made foreign trade such treacherous territory was that the value of the tael in relation to the English pound sterling—or the American gold dollar, or any other foreign currency, for that matter—fluctuated wildly. It could lose half its value overnight. The global market in silver was a specimen of finicky overreaction to any piece of news. The Chinese were major purchasers of silver on the New York, London, and Bombay silver markets. The daily "fixing" of its value in the bullion houses of London's City determined profits and losses (see chapter 5). Anyone ready to buy or sell eyeballed the rates reported in all the major newspapers. They read out prices per ounce from ticker tapes and automatic transmitters in the Bund Banks and in Sassoon House. "There are times when Shanghai becomes the centre literally of 'frenzied finance,'" a journalist reported, "and everybody, from the Taipan or head of the firm down to the most junior clerk, has visions of wealth beyond the dreams of avarice as he puts his wad on the game."[24]

It was high stakes indeed. Speculators could be wiped out in an instant or land a fortune. It was why someone like Victor Sassoon, awash in riches from playing the financial markets, was treated like a mastermind. The frenzied speculation in Shanghai, the fluctuations in currencies and feverish gambling on both gold and silver left plenty of room for avarice. The river of money was easy pickings for shysters looking to make a killing. The city's financial waters were "teeming with sharks and other predaceous fishes."[25] It was no wonder, then, that the mighty Soong family of Chiang Kai-shek's wife and her Kung family relations quickly took control of four of Shanghai's largest banks. Harvard-educated T. V. Soong (Tzu-wen) had worked in New York for National City Bank and its international subsidiary. He was classy, had a Yankee style, and was a master at parlaying his stature into staggering riches. The Soongs dealt in a mesh of aboveboard and illicit currency speculation that added to catastrophic inflation and sped up the demise of the Kuomintang regime.

The delirium around financial speculation became all too apparent during the global silver crisis of the late 1920s and early 1930s, when the price of the metal on the world market collapsed. China bought up all the silver it could find. It was a major buyer from the United States, which along with Mexico was the world's largest miner of the precious metal. Silver from India's unwanted reserves from melted-down rupees was put up for sale. The amount of the metal was mind boggling. The Indian Treasury dumped 35 million ounces of it onto the global market in 1929, piled up on the Bombay quays to be sent across the waves. The strongboxes filled with bars and ingots arrived in Shanghai and were off-loaded onto the wharves, where they were guarded by Sikhs and then wheeled in carts by coolies to the banks. That same year, customs officials reported the import of 121 million ounces of silver from India and other countries.[26] Speculation reached frenzied levels. China's demand for silver bullion was insatiable, particularly because the plunge in the value of silver made Shanghai's hodgepodge of currencies a bargain in comparison to those of countries on the gold standard. Although the silver crisis was a disaster for import businesses, the falloff made the city's exports cheap on world markets. The one-up was plain to Indian textile merchants like Sassoon or the cotton barons of Lancashire, who all bemoaned the competition in Chinese fabrics that went for a song. The ships along the Yangtze were loaded up with cotton and silk textiles, cheap Chinese products bound for waiting markets overseas while the Bombay and Lancashire cotton barons looked on enviously.

Even during the early 1930s as the Great Depression hit, the city's bank vaults were stuffed with silver. The economic slump hit the interior of China hardest. The one hedge against penury for millions of rural families had lost 50 percent of its value. Anything left was forcibly taken in brutal taxation. They suffered devastating famine along with vicious banditry and violence at the hands of warlords. The bitter winters and floods on the Yangtze left a trail of heartbreak. John F. Darling, the director of the Midland Bank in London, translated what this meant for the global marketplace: "Here is a nation of 400 million labourers whose standard of existence is measured in bowls of rice. How can Lancashire compete with that wage? The mechanized output of such a country will bring ruin to the working classes of both Europe and America." The West had to understand that "silver is more important to the world than gold." The value of silver had to be restored to China to raise its wages and standard of living.[27]

But the Chinese response to the silver crisis was a traditional one. People hoarded whatever silver they had in Shanghai for safeguarding until it regained its value. By 1934, it was estimated that over half of China's bullion stockpile had been stuffed away in that city. The big banks along the Bund gorged on silver. Their profits ballooned. They had plenty of money to lend. When asked how business in Shanghai could be booming amid so much calamity, it was the surplus of silver that Victor Sassoon pointed to. Despite the turmoil in the countryside and a Chinese economy teetering on the edge of collapse, new banks opened their doors in Shanghai. An artificial prosperity propped up Shanghai's fortunes.

Then, as the Depression worsened, the world's biggest economies finally came off the gold standard—first Britain, then India with its silver rupee backed by gold. Germany, Japan, and finally the United States followed suit. The Roosevelt administration in Washington, DC, switched to a policy of buying silver at propped-up prices and storing it in the US Treasury until it constituted a full quarter of the US monetary supply. The price of the white metal jumped to record levels. Shanghai's financiers sold their silver holdings to the United States and raked in profits. Millions of dollars in silver poured out of China. The consequences were disastrous. The sale of government bonds collapsed. Interest rates in Shanghai shot skyward. Credit dried up. The real estate market slumped. China lost its competitive edge. Production was cut back, especially in textiles. The holds of the ships along the waterfront sat idle as Shanghai's exports dropped by more than half. Business failures swept across the city.[28] To unlock the credit markets, Sassoon proposed a temporary "Shanghai sterling" currency backed by the British until the Americans came to their senses. If he was not exactly eloquent—Sassoon was no politician—he was a powerful voice in global finance and was eagerly quoted in the newspapers. He saw his idea as a "lubricating oil" to grease the wheels of commerce and industry until they approached normalcy. Critics groused that the idea was a way for Sassoon to protect his investments. As long as the Americans were scooping up the metal, silver was worth far more abroad than it was on the local exchange markets. He irately suggested that the Americans buy their silver from India, which he had just left behind, to avoid the damage to China's finances and his own assets.[29]

As fast as the metal had poured into Shanghai, it now poured out to New York—by smuggling as much as by legal means. Facing near-certain collapse, the Nationalist government imposed an embargo to stem the tide. But it did little good. Even the banks slipped silver out of Shanghai right under the government's nose. Their bank vaults suddenly emptied out. By 1935, China's government had taken a momentous step and nationalized its silver stock, then sold it to the Americans in exchange for US dollars. China was divorced from the metal that had dominated exchange for over two thousand years. Some $84 million worth of silver bullion was shipped by way of Hong Kong, then through London, then finally to New York. It momentarily put the Chinese economy on a managed paper-currency basis. The Nationalist government now controlled the money supply. It forced speculators like Sassoon to exchange their silver for the new Chinese yuan. For all his supposed financial knack and his contacts among Chiang's financial elite, Sir Victor was caught flat-footed and called it a coup. But even under these strained circumstances, his empire had little to worry about. By that time, his silver trove had been transferred into Shanghai real estate. Foreign banks like E. D. Sassoon were also in the best position to take advantage of the inflated prices for silver in New York and London and continued to rake in profits.[30] Even under so much pressure in the global bullion market, Shanghai's freewheeling financial capitalism weathered the storm.

Shanghai Modern

Despite the financial volatility and the calamities, Shanghai was mesmerizing. It was a global entrepôt of nearly four million people. Journalist Lady Drummond-Hay, that "notable explorer of the light and dark places of the earth," wrote her impressions of the city for the London tabloid the *Sphere*. "Shanghai, whose very name sounds the clarion of adventure and romantic hazard, cosmopolitan hub of the 'other side of the world,' is to-day ... an international whirlpool of pulsating life and action," she enthused. It was the "Paris of the Far East ... where Unthinkable Degradations are Cloaked Beneath a Veil of Brilliant Gaiety and Hectic Pleasure-Seeking." She remarked that the city was a unique mixture of East and West: "Along the Bund ... hourly passes a kaleidoscopic procession of the peoples of the globe."[31] The breathtaking buildings rising along Nanjing Road (anointed the city's Great White Way) and along the Bund were pure urban spectacle. Writer Mao Tun was spellbound by the hallucinogenic electric signage in *Midnight*, his 1933 novel of Shanghai. Looking out over the cityscape, "one saw with a shock of wonder on the roof of a building a gigantic neon sign in flaming red and phosphorescent green: LIGHT, HEAT, POWER!"[32] The 1933 avant-garde montage film *City Nights* by director Fei Mu captured the blaze of light along the Bund and the dazzling advertising displays on that quartet of consumerism—the Wing On, the Sincere, the Da Sun, and the Sun Sun department stores along Nanjing Road.

The entrepreneurs risking it all on the city's celebrity department stores had Australian and Hong Kong roots. The Guo (Kwok) brothers' first Wing On department store opened in Hong Kong in 1907, and their colossal Shanghai emporium followed in 1918. Determined to bring modern management practices to China, the brothers expanded their web of Hong Kong and Shanghai holdings to include textile mills and machinery, fire and marine insurance, and banking. Along with real estate, these were the arenas that drove global investment and rewarded venture capitalists in Shanghai as well as in London and Bombay. Thoroughly Westernized, the Guo brothers lived in Tudor villas fronted by sweeping English-style lawns. Their wives and daughters flaunted the latest in the knee-skimming flapper style of the Roaring Twenties. Western influence was unambiguous for Shanghai's "Modern Girls." They were visible on the streets, strutting their bobbed hair and makeup. They scooped up popular magazines such as *Liangyou* (*The Young Companion*) and *LinLoon huabao* (*LinLoon Magazine*) that featured a modern lifestyle and advertisements for Western brand-name products.[33] The department stores on Nanjing Road boasted the latest in fashion and cosmetics from Paris, London, and New York. For some, the Modern Girl was the epitome of a dangerous modernity. But the cosmopolitanism of this archetype was a global phenomenon and opened an entirely new consumer market and outlet for global trade.

The Modern Girl was a member of Shanghai's newly formed middle class, many of whom found jobs as salaried workers in the city's banks, shipping and trading companies, and real estate industry. They were educated, had a command of English, and kept up with news and the parade of global trends. They reveled in Shanghai's cosmopolitanism and demanded the kind of lifestyle that earlier had been open only to Europeans and wealthy elites. The top floor of the sumptuous Wing On department store tickled customers with eateries and cabaret entertainment. Neon signs flashed The Customer Is Always Right. The Sincere department store

FIGURE 10. Nanjing Road, Shanghai, 1930s. (Historic Collection / Alamy Stock Photo)

also debuted in Hong Kong and was the first to employ women shop assistants. Its Shanghai branch was a baroque confection, its top floors a cavalcade of variety shows and Chinese and Hollywood films. Some fifty thousand foreigners and Chinese flew through the doors of the splendid Sun Sun on opening day; there they found the marvels of consumerism arrayed in profusion. The Sun Sun had its own radio station that broadcast sales as well as musical performances from its rooftop garden. The Da Sun was a lavish modernist colossus and the first to install escalators. There was nothing like Nanjing Road anywhere else in China. It was the country's most glamorous boulevard.

Shanghai had a notorious reputation as a wild, pleasure-mad place in the Twenties and Thirties. It indulged in the crazy years of that time to excess.[34] The highbrow Paramount Ballroom, the Sky Terrace at the Park Hotel, and the Ballroom at the Cathay Hotel were the leading hotspots for nighttime carousing. Like the Savoy in London and the Taj Mahal Hotel in Bombay, Shanghai's grand hotels were synonymous with the cosmopolitan glamour of the Jazz Age. Their stunning architecture and design made them instant urban landmarks. They were a rarefied form of dramatic theater for global elites. The Paramount Ballroom was known as the Gate of One Hundred Pleasures. It was a lavish display of Shanghai's self-indulgence. Russian and Filipino orchestras struck up wild syncopated rhythms for the riotous dancing on a glass floor lit by a rainbow of electric lighting. The city's celebrities cut a rug alongside local gangsters. They could eat, drink, and indulge every desire with little in their pockets. Shanghai's carousel of delights was entirely on credit, with little care of paying up at month's end. Few fell afoul of the law, though the wildest among them drank too much, indulged in loose morals, gambled on anything under the sun. The city was a global epicenter of commercial gambling, with slot machines and roulette wheels raking in millions. Bookmakers shouted the odds at the horse and greyhound races and at the jai alai courts. Garish dance halls, bars, and shady establishments vibrated until dawn, indulging the hedonism Shanghai was known for.

Along with Bombay, Shanghai was Asia's premier entertainment hub. The two cities were helms in the budding global media landscape. Shanghai's grand movie palaces were bathed in ornamental splendor. Hundreds of foreign films were imported. The Cathay Cinema on the Avenue Joffre was the favorite of the city's socialites and was owned by Victor Sassoon. Movie fans dripping in furs entered a lobby designed with opaque glass and bathed in a soft neon glow, climbed the ornamental staircase, and settled into the thousand seats to watch Hollywood blockbusters. Local motion picture studios produced a host of films and created the first

Chinese movie stars. Billboards advertising the latest blockbusters were plastered across the city's buildings. Cinema captured the imagination of Shanghai. In author Ding Ling's novella *Shanghai, Spring 1930*, the protagonist, Mary, buys tickets for a movie at a deluxe theater, where she and Wang Wei "climb the elegantly carved stairway, pass through the doors where handsome ushers were standing, and take their seats. Not far from her sat well-dressed foreign wives, and from time to time one could smell the fragrance of their superior perfume.... When the movie started, Mary was happy no matter what." The movie theaters were legion, "not a neighbourhood in Shanghai being without two or three," a journalist reported.[35]

The tram connected Nanjing Road to Great World, the city's spectacular amusement palace with its brilliantly lit landmark tower and six floors of merriment. Some twenty thousand visitors a day passed through its doors. The crowds were from all walks of life, from every race and ethnicity in the city. An entire entertainment district grew up around the complex. The filmmaker Josef von Sternberg visited during his stay in Shanghai in the 1930s: "On the first floor were gambling tables, singsong girls, magicians, pickpockets, slot machines, fireworks.... The third floor had jugglers, herb medicines, ice cream parlors.... The fifth floor featured girls whose dresses were slit to the armpits, a stuffed whale, storytellers, peep shows."[36] It was a sideshow replete with free beer and two-headed babies. Great World was opened by drugstore operator and impresario Huang Chujiu, who had made a fortune from his miracle potion for improving the brain. Huang ran the Day and Night Bank attached to the amusement center. It had some thirteen thousand small-time depositors before he went broke and the whole complex passed into the hands of Shanghai's notorious racketeers. But it put little dent in the Chinese appetite for entertainments. The Lou Wai Lou and New World amusement parks were run by real estate comprador and "King of Shanghai Land" Jing Runshan. Small World and Great Thousand Worlds were jammed with revelers. The amusement parks played a central role in urban life and tied Shanghai to the global culture of amusement.[37] The city gorged on the thrills and excitement.

Shanghai Peripheries

But Lady Drummond-Hay knew better than to be hypnotized by Shanghai's glamour; she recognized its sinister sides, like ominous clouds hanging over the city. It was run by a treacherous brew of criminal gangs and warlords. Extortion, kidnapping, and murder were their stock-in-trade. She admitted this stark reality in the *Sphere*: "Shanghai is a city of armed troops, shining guns, gleaming bayonets, miles of barbed-wire defences, sand-bag redoubts, concealed machine-guns." It was a "scene of subtle International diplomacy, crow's nest for Revolutionary Indian and Far Eastern conspirators, centre of Bolshevik activity, refuge for White Russians, and home of the slant-eyed Chinamen: in short Pandora's Box of the world's worst thrills."[38] The city, in short, was no haven of charity. Grinding poverty was as much on display as glittering wealth in it and other global cities. The slithering undercurrents of Shanghai were shamefully sordid and ugly, giving Bombay a run for its money on disrepute. "Gunmen, thugs, robbers, thieves, burglars, kidnappers, smugglers, dope agents, terrorists, assassins, con men, gamblers—all these Shanghai supports in profusion," the *China Press* reported. The teeming sex trade was as extensive as it was in Bombay. Thousands of young Chinese girls, many of them brought from Hangzhou and Suzhou, were sold into prostitution. They roamed Nanjing Road and the major commercial streets looking for tricks. International correspondent Harry Greenwall saw Shanghai as "a mad, mad city" of "drama in the streets, wealth galore and plenty of starvation . . . I do not think there is any place in the world where poverty and wealth rub shoulders so often and so closely."[39] But this was the reality of the global city in Asia, just as palpable in Bombay.

Shanghai's allures were far beyond the reach of the thousands of Chinese who descended on the city. *Shanghai ren* (Shanghai people) were inevitably from somewhere else. They made up the city's sea of humanity, its proletariat. They were the mobile labor force on which global capitalism hung and were just as recognizable in Bombay and London. In Shanghai, they found jobs on the docks, and in the textile mills and factories hugging the waterfront. Wide-eyed country bumpkins toting their satchels clamored off trains at the North Railway Station to pursue their "Shanghai dream." Migrants from the same place followed one another to the same districts and the same industries. Most of them came from the neighboring Jiangsu and Zhejiang provinces. Desperate refugees escaping violence in the countryside arrived with little more than hope. The devastating floods along the Yangtze in 1923 brought a deluge of evacuees. Deprivation at this scale was a tragedy shared with the millions in India who sought refuge in Bombay.

They carried out the tangle of their everyday lives in obscurity, far from the neon lights. It was a world the "foreign devils" feared to tread. The living conditions here were far more crowded than in London's East End. The boggy wastelands on the city's periphery filled up with straw-hut squatter camps that sheltered thousands. Others found shelter in their sampans and junks tied up along the banks of Suzhou Creek and the Huangpu River. Boat people numbered over fourteen thousand in the

1920s. Pawnbrokers and loan sharks took their pound of flesh from the indigent. Shanghai's famed cosmopolitanism never touched the coarseness of these badlands. Yaoshuilong and Fangualong, the city's largest shantytowns, were masses of crude hutments held together with bamboo.[40] Yaoshuilong, on a marshy curve of Suzhou Creek, housed some ten thousand people by the 1930s who were under the thumb of local gangs. Fangualong, near the North Railway Station, was just as large and just as wretched. Neither place had any basic necessities other than the water fetched from the polluted river. Fires raged through the slums as a matter of course, burning everything in their paths and leaving thousands homeless. Attempts by the authorities to demolish the shantytowns were met by organized resistance, as there were few other choices. By the 1920s, over ten thousand squatters were still camping out in the hut districts.[41]

Better-off workers found lodging in the *lilong* wards built by profit-hungry property developers along a grid of alleyways in the foreign concessions. This housing was a *shikumen* fusion of the Western-style rowhouse and the Chinese courtyard house, first in wood and then in brick, arranged into neighborhoods with distinctive arched stone gateways and auspicious names. The *lilong* buildings were a windfall for real estate developers. They were found all over Shanghai and housed some 40 percent of the city's population in some of the highest population densities in the world. They gave the city its two- and three-story brick structures and ordinary built fabric. Then, as gas, water, and electricity were installed, Shanghai's petty bourgeois and commercial classes moved in. Residents were jam packed, with multigenerational families living atop each other among people from all walks of life. The *lilong* were an everyman's tenement—a symbol of the workaday populace seeking its fortune. They were intimate neighborhoods, where news and gossip rebounded in a split second. Chinese essayist Lu Xun complained about the street vendors and prostitutes roaming the alleyways, the monks "beating their drums and clashing their symbols." Although "you may never have set eyes on your neighbours ... if you are separated by a flimsy partition only, you can hear practically everything they and their visitors say."[42]

The inhuman conditions and paltry salaries in Shanghai's factories were plenty of cause for bitterness. Rural migrants hunting for jobs in the textile mills were at the mercy of labor contractors or Number Ones, many of whom were members of Shanghai's notorious Green Gang crime syndicate. Coolie millhands, especially young women, were coerced into forced labor and indentured by a villainous hiring system. Pitiful wages meant laborers lived hand to mouth. Their anger was chiefly directed at foreign factory owners, especially the Japanese. Their treatment of millhands was notorious. Like the Sassoon textile mills in Bombay, the Japanese counterparts aggressively enforced fast-paced productivity drives to stay competitive on the global market. Bonded laborers were crowded into prison-like dormitories and regularly beaten for not following orders or trying to escape.[43] Grueling ten- to twelve-hour workdays and the surveillance of the mill hands by armed guards made the humiliation worse. The exploitation of China's laborers by foreign bullies became a political rallying cry. It boiled over into sabotage and work stoppages. The inequalities of global capitalism made Shanghai a tactical site of social conflict, just as they did in Bombay and London. Women mill hands went on a rampage, smashing machinery and setting fire to yarn. By 1926, Shanghai had descended into a vortex of strikes, demonstrations, and violence. Fiercely powerful, even if illegal, local labor unions bellowed against Japanese imperialism and Japanese cruelty to Chinese workers. Their demands were clear: carry through a Nationalist revolution against the imperialists, higher wages and an eight-hour day, equal pay for women, an end to corporal punishment and child labor, and unemployment insurance. Conditions in factories were a far cry from the dazzling gaieties in Shanghai's famous nightclubs.

It was all too easy for both Nationalist and communist agitators to represent the working world. Shanghai University was a hotbed of leftist activism, with students and staff heading into the alleyways to educate workers. The Socialist Youth League was a rallying point for communist sympathizers. In 1927, dockworkers and textile workers along with labor unions and local communist militants staged an armed insurrection and seized control of the Chinese district from local warlords.[44] It was a peevish alliance among erstwhile revolutionaries. The Soviet-controlled Comintern contributed vast organizational and financial assistance to the communist cause in Shanghai. Its operatives attempted to impose ideological correctness over the revolt. But local communist fighters steered an erratic course riddled with infighting. It was more a populist grassroots upheaval led by Shanghai's divisive labor unions than an organized insurrection. Some five hundred thousand workers staged two general strike waves. The city was brought to a standstill. Union militias cut the electricity, telephone, and telegraph lines. The trams stopped running. Ships weighed anchor in the harbor, their iron chains clanging. The department stores on Nanjing Road barricaded their doors. The street violence was appalling. Any strikers caught were immediately executed by garrison forces wielding broad swords. Dockworkers and seamen battled with warlords and gangsters in league with the police. Communist henchmen gunned down their enemies. The insurgents declared themselves a popular self-government. A citizen's assembly of thousands was held at the Public Recreation Grounds. For a moment, the city took on a festive atmosphere of liberation. Then the communists unleashed a Red Terror. The call "All power to the Soviets!" rang out crystal clear. Fires raged out of control. Looters roamed the streets. The slaughter went on.

Caught in the bloody chaos, ordinary people, businessmen, and foreigners looked to the Nationalist forces under Chiang Kai-shek and their underworld cronies for rescue. The city's wealthy handed him money in the hopes of some stability. Chiang and his vanguard Northern Expedition arrived in Shanghai to the acclaim of the Chinese population. But it did not take long for the euphoria to evaporate. The insurrection descended into treachery as Chiang staged his anti-Red bloodbath. When communists welcomed the Nationalist trains entering the city, they were met with a hail of bullets. A demonstration by more than one hundred thousand workers, students, and townspeople in the neighborhood of Zhabei was mowed down by machine guns. Hundreds were killed or wounded. Thousands of houses were consumed by fires during the fighting. Any attempt at armed resistance was met with summary executions. Within weeks, the people's movement was savagely liquidated by Chiang's forces and their sinister Green Gang henchmen, with the full support of the foreign concessions. Martial law was declared. Some five thousand victims were executed or vanished as the workers' revolution was decimated.

The mayhem in Shanghai made headlines in the London press, which gave sensational reports on the "Chinese outrages" and "Reign of Terror" on the city's streets. Editorials pounded on the brutalities committed against the British, who were spat on, looted, rounded up, and kidnapped. Rumors of atrocities against foreigners fueled panic among the Shanghailanders (European and American settlers) holed up in the International Settlement. Foreigners spoiled on the city's temptations suddenly found themselves barricaded behind barbed wire. Tanks manned by the Shanghai Volunteer Corps patrolled the streets. The arrival of British gunboats to defend the International Settlement was greeted with fanfare: "The whole foreign community is combining magnificently; strict martial law is now enforced, and at nightfall no Chinese are allowed in the streets." Over 22,000 foreign troops were stationed in Shanghai, 16,000 of whom were British, another 3,000 American, and 2,000 Japanese. Forty-two warships were moored in the harbor, overpowering giants alongside the sampans and junks. Fourteen of the ships were Japanese, thirteen were American, and another eight British.[45] Such was the military force required to maintain foreign interests in China. Colonial capitalism required naval fleets to sustain itself. Newspaper photos of the warships anchored in the Huangpu River and the machine gun company of the Volunteer Corps convinced readers that British interests were being protected. But such displays were a mixture of bluff and firepower.

The *London Illustrated News* plastered images of the battle-scarred city in full-page coverage along with photos of the Scottish brigade in kilts and the Sikh police force sent to protect British lives and property.[46] In the end, the accounts of the China crisis in the British press depended on political persuasion. The *Daily Herald*, Britain's Labour organ, appealed to British workers to think internationally and support the Chinese strikers as comrades in arms. The roots of the disturbances were not bolshevism but Chinese patriotism "against the humiliations which the country has been subjected by foreign nations." The paper slammed British aggression and detailed the terrible conditions and "hideous outrage" of child slave labor in the hellhole factories. The London Trades Council organized demonstrations "against the oppression of the Chinese people" and to "HELP the Chinese workers in their fight for Freedom."[47]

A *Times of India* headline echoed British outrage, blasting the "reign of terror" in Shanghai.[48] But revolutionaries across Asia were sowing their own version of global cosmopolitanism. The North China Sea was traversed continually by Chinese and Japanese leftist writers and intellectuals.[49] The affinities between the Indian *swaraj* cause and the Chinese revolutionary movement promised a new kind of Sino-Indian alliance, despite every effort by the British to squelch it. Indian rebels had long used Shanghai as a base of operations for fellow travelers and smuggling arms. The Indian revolutionary Barakatullah spearheaded an early anti-British campaign from Tokyo and dispatched his pan-Islamic pamphlets and *El Islam* newspaper from Shanghai into Bombay, exhorting Muslims to rise up against British despotism. A surge of Pan-Asian solidarity coalesced anticolonial sentiments and created a framework for conceptualizing Asian identity. The movement took place in Shanghai, Tokyo, Bombay, and Calcutta, with accompanying debates eagerly covered by local media. Poet-philosopher Rabindranath Tagore's visit to China in 1924 was a watershed moment in Sino-Indian relations and "called forth such a welcome as has been given to few visitors in recent years." He was enthusiastically greeted by Chinese students and admirers on his stop in Shanghai, where he urged them to rise above the materialism of life and become dreamers: "The dreamer and the worker must go hand in hand."[50]

Mahatma Gandhi and Jawaharlal Nehru castigated the British for using Indian sepoys and Sikh police against the Chinese popular uprising and the pro-independence rebels. The condemnation found impassioned support among the Sikhs serving the British military and security forces abroad. Shanghai was a center for the insurrectionary plots of the Indian-led Ghadar Party that had a robust following among the Indian troops and Sikh police stationed there. The Ghadarites had received training and weapons overland through Tashkent from the Soviet Union as part of Lenin's call for a worldwide battle against imperialism. They gave their full support to Chiang Kai-shek's Nationalist Revolutionary Army as it marched through China in the mid-1920s, and they urged Indians to desert the British and join the Chinese Revolution. Word spread that Indian police and soldiers refused to obey British orders to repress Chinese protests.[51] If caught, they were charged with sedition and imprisoned.

Trailblazing intellectuals and political rebels crisscrossed the globe in search of a common cause. This was indicative of the global brand of cosmopolitan leftism. The World Congress against Colonial Oppression and Imperialism held in 1927 in Brussels was the occasion for a more direct alliance between the Indian National Congress leaders and the Chinese Kuomintang. The Indian and Chinese delegates issued a joint manifesto dedicated to their anti-imperialist struggle and inaugurated the League against Imperialism. Nehru called for a boycott of Japanese goods in sympathy with the Chinese people enduring foreign occupation. In London, the India League organized mass rallies in Trafalgar Square, where portraits of Chinese and African leaders in the struggle for freedom were paraded alongside those of Nehru and Gandhi. Although it appeared that Chinese and Indian nationalists had aligned, by the late 1930s the Shanghai Indian community began to shift its allegiance to the Indian Independence League. In a move anathema to the Chinese nationalists, the league campaigned for the support of Japan in the Indian freedom movement. Undaunted, in 1933 the Chinese Communist Party organized an "anti-imperialism anti-war congress" in Shanghai that was publicly announced and attended by left-wing activists from across China, along with delegates from the European socialist parties and the British Labour Party.

Hong Kong Redoubt

Despite the troubles and the naysayers, Victor Sassoon had reason for optimism as he contemplated his future. The Sassoon family had a long history in China and were deeply entrenched in both Shanghai and Hong Kong. The two places operated together as beachheads for foreign interests in the Far East. Understanding Shanghai within the context of global history requires witnessing Hong Kong as the British Crown colony. After Britain, Japan, and the United States, Hong Kong was Shanghai's most important trading partner, mainly for the re-export of British goods.[52] Hong Kong was thoroughly British, with "fine shops and public buildings, with splendid roadways, with hotels and clubs, with everything that modern civilization could produce," Londoner and travel writer Ethel Tweedie reported in the 1920s. Some eight thousand British controlled the island, most of them entrepreneurs indulging in its unbridled capitalism and officials engaged in the imperial service. The Chinese population there reached well over half a million. With the addition of Kowloon and the new territories as part of the Crown colony, some eight hundred thousand Chinese lived under British rule. By 1938, the total population of Hong Kong had exceeded one million. Teas and silks as well as a myriad of goods were exported from its "wondrous harbour, which at night twinkles with a thousand lights as if the stars had descended," Tweedie recounted.[53] It was already one of the largest shipping ports in the world.

Jewish merchant families—the Sassoons, the Kadoorie and Ezra families, the Gubbays—along with Jardine & Matheson and Arnhold & Company all had deep roots in Hong Kong that matched those in Shanghai. These were the merchant blue bloods whose hands guided Hong Kong's development and the "civilizing effects" of British colonial authority. Their authority amounted to a stabbing racial segregation, with European districts strictly separated from the Chinese and the rabble of peoples filtering through the colony. Mountain Lodge, the governor of Hong Kong's summer residence, was secluded atop Victoria Peak. Living above May Road was the mark of British social status. Behind the deep verandas, the British stuffed their villas with Chinese blackwood and porcelain and the precious oriental treasures they collected. The Chinese themselves were left to the squatter settlements and packed tenements on the barren rock below. Class and ethnicity were essential definers of British occupation, although segregation could never be carried out strictly.[54] A handful of wealthy Chinese, Jews, and Parsees broke through this barrier and entered the world of stultifying snobbishness, at least on business terms. Yet for all their wealth and sway, the doors of the prestigious Hong Kong Club were still barred shut. For the Sassoons, as well as for other Parsee and Jewish businessmen, Hong Kong's Happy Valley racecourse and Jockey Club were the venues for acquiring social standing.

The Sassoons' huge earnings from their trading empire were turned into finance, insurance, and real estate—the triad of capitalist investment in urban development put to good use for both profits and political power. Their antennae spread out into a web of influence over Hong Kong's future. Taking full advantage of imperial rule, they were everywhere in the Crown colony. Members of the family held shares and were board members of the city's most important businesses, including the Hong Kong & Shanghai Bank. The bank was the acknowledged powerhouse in the global money market, with commodity prices and currency movements charted daily at its magisterial head office on Queens Road. E. D. Sassoon & Company in Hong Kong was under the supervision of Abraham Jacob Raymond and Albert Raymond (see chapter 3). The Raymonds were members of the global capitalist oligarchy that flouted borders and pulled the levers of global finance. They traveled between Bombay, London, Shanghai, and Hong Kong on behalf of Sassoon interests. The former was on the board of the Hong Kong & Shanghai Bank, while the latter was director at China Light & Power and the Hongkong Land Investment Company. Their positions were the mechanisms for amassing wealth and property. The China Light & Power plant in Kowloon could not keep up with the Crown colony's voracious demand for electric light. Its profits soared. The Hong Kong Land Investment Company was the most powerful development arm on the island. It was the vehicle for taipans such as the Jardines and the Sassoons to acquire large swaths of central Hong Kong. Hong Kong Land Investment was behind the island's first modern tall buildings—the Alexandra and Gloucester apartments, Marina House, and Holland House. As they ventured into the flourishing insurance industry, the Sassoons were part owners and on the board of directors of the China Fire Insurance Company and the Canton Marine Insurance Company.

Hong Kong was the dragon head for all Chinese labor abroad. Throngs of people from across Asia used the island as a jumping-off point for prospects across the world. This sea of humanity crossing the oceans was huge. It was the mobile workforce that underpinned the global economy. These nameless wayfarers followed ethnic networks in vast migration chains. They lived in and identified with multiple places. Hong Kong was a never-ending drift of people, a watery flow of travelers and goods. "Crimp" recruiters set up operations to meet contracts for cheap Chinese and Indian labor on plantations and in timber and mining operations across Asia and Australia and in South Africa, and for railroad construction in the Americas. Thousands were packed into steerage on tramp steamers for the journeys each year. Global migration at this scale was big business in Hong Kong. Companies specialized in providing overseas contacts, lodging, and provisions, and passing on the remittances. The possibilities for villainous mistreatment of coolies were endless. Many a criminal ring made a killing fabricating false identities and smuggling illegal Guangdong coolies to the Straits Settlements, the Dutch Indies, and Thailand, where they worked in the mines and cleared jungles. Chinese middlemen took care of transmitting goods, letters, cash, and paychecks from Chinese abroad to their villages back home. Silver and gold moved easily in and out of Hong Kong as well. The flow of all these monetary and metal transfers was tremendous.

But the payments were not just stuffed away. They were another opportunity to speculate on currency exchange.[55]

Indians crossed the Bay of Bengal and landed in Shanghai and Hong Kong to either find work in southern China or obtain passage to the Straits Settlements or the west coast of North America. By the mid-1930s, some seven to eight thousand Hindu and Muslim Indians were in Hong Kong and over three thousand in Shanghai.[56] They were a plentiful and cheap labor force. Some made a pittance hawking goods on the streets. Others went into retail and sold exotic luxury imports. They worked as middlemen handling long-distance trade for major companies. Still others found jobs as watchmen guarding offices and warehouses from theft.[57] Cheap lodging houses and fleabag hostels for migrants littered both cities. The Sikh *gurudwaras* and shared bed spaces in the tenements were filled with destitute Indian men hunting for odd jobs and facing vague futures or trying to find passage to North America through smugglers. British authorities eyed them suspiciously as the contagion of disaffection and militant nationalism took hold among the Indian diaspora. Any hint of resentment at their plight was immediately branded as Bolshevik-inspired antiforeignism.

Nevertheless, the tapestry of migration was integral to the social landscape of global cities. Migrants and working nomads congregated in these global hubs precisely because of the opportunities offered there. The sheer numbers of peoples on the move in the interwar years were sights in themselves. Migrant networks knit London, Shanghai, and Bombay together at a myriad of levels, both formal and informal, legal and illegal. These were the itinerants' own version of cosmopolitanism marked by racial, ethnic, and gender hierarchies and shaped by ingrained patterns of inclusion and exclusion. There was another industry, however, that was shifting Hong Kong's global connectivity by the late 1930s. Flights from Kai Tak Airport were more than doubling each year, from 3,600 passengers in 1937 to nearly 10,000 arrivals and departures by 1938, along with tons of mail. Imperial Airways connected the island to London. Air services went to Paris, San Francisco, and through China National Aviation Corporation to Shanghai.[58] The 1930s were a prescient moment in the collapsing of global space. Harbors were jammed with cruise ships with the likes of Victor Sassoon and his coterie aboard, skirting around excited tourists. Steamers packed with Chinese, Indians, and people from across the Far East sailed out to sea. Airplanes flew over Hong Kong en route to global destinations.

✳ 7 ✳
Global Shanghai

> And then looming in the hazy late afternoon, we made out the famous
> Bund, a half-mile-long rampart of granite and marble.
>
> SAM GINSBOURG, *My First Sixty Years in China* (1982)

It was, however, Shanghai that captured Victor Sassoon's fancy. The freewheeling possibilities for his millions there were enticing. The International Settlement was the firmament in which he starred. In 1925, its population was over 840,000, some 96 percent of whom were Chinese. By 1937, the numbers had ballooned to 1.2 million. This human mass was jammed into an irregularly shaped nine-square-mile cocoon carved out of Shanghai and under the authority of the British and US delegations. The British Shanghailanders were jealous guardians of the privileges granted by this extraterritoriality and their semi-independent existence. There was no omnipotent viceroy as there was in Bombay. No colonial bureaucracy hamstrung business dealings. Foreigners with "extra" status could not be arrested or tried by Chinese authorities. Foreign companies in the Settlement were exempt from Chinese laws and taxes. Anyone could start a bank or a business without any formalities. British capital investments in Shanghai were enormous, and the Shanghailanders were ferocious lobbyists on behalf of their assets.

The Settlement's municipal council was the citadel of British power. It was ruled over by an oligarchy of good-fellow businessmen, whose chairmen were the likes of Harry Arnold and John Hellyer Liddell, both close allies of Victor Sassoon's. They were every inch taipans, with hands open for financial assistance from the Hong Kong & Shanghai Bank.[1] There were no doubts of the personal gains to be made by shining in the municipal council's limelight. It gave plenty of ammunition to taxpayers who accused it of avarice and a sinister secrecy around financial dealings. Its members were "either crooks, nit wits, or merely dumb," the most fed-up fumed.[2] The powerful coterie brushed off these complaints and "got on with the job" of managing the fifteen-hundred-strong Volunteer Corps, the police force, even the fire brigade. The public works department oversaw the Settlement's gaslight, electricity, and running water. Residents enjoyed a rare telephone service. These were the first modern services in China.

The Bund, the fabulous boulevard along the Huangpu riverfront, was the International Settlement's jewel. It lay at the heart of British expatriate life and was the symbol of imperial might. It also was undergoing unprecedented transformation, with monumental banks, luxurious hotels, and stately buildings rising from the mudflats. Sam Ginsbourg escaped Russia with his mother and recounted his first view of the Bund as they reached the city by ship: "Thousands of junks and sampans, packed with sweating men, screaming women and squealing children, lined the banks of the river. Strung out in a mile-long line, bow to stern, were anchored warships of all nations. And then looming in the hazy late afternoon, we made out the famous Bund, a half-mile-long rampart of granite and marble."[3] This sense of wonder at a city blazing with activity and commotion was what struck onlookers. The Bund was a vision of the global metropolis. Gazing on the river scene, a *North China Herald* reporter saw the Huangpu "curling like a gigantic yellow worm and carrying on its back hundreds and hundreds of ships . . . tiny sampans crawling in and out amongst proud liners . . . ungainly, sailess junks, shuffling along clumsily against the tide."[4]

The Bund was the ceremonial space of global finance. Rising up out of the haze were the Yokohama Specie Bank, the Agricultural Bank of China,

FIGURE 11. The Bund (Waitan), Shanghai, 1930. (CPA Media Pte Ltd / Alamy Stock Photo)

and the powerful Bank of China, this last designed in art deco style by the British firm of Palmer & Turner. The firm's moderne style and especially its neoclassical designs were the preferred symbols of the British imperium. Neoclassicism was a conservative aesthetic that exuded pomposity and matched the urban fabric of London's City as well as the colonial monuments in Bombay. Originally based in Hong Kong, Palmer & Turner had so many projects in Shanghai that the branch office eventually took over as headquarters under architect George Wilson. The firm's Hong Kong & Shanghai Bank on the Bund was an austere neoclassical palace in granite, with its crouching bronze lions guarding the entranceway. *Wayfoong*, as the British pronounced the bank's Chinese name, was the most celebrated foreign bank in China. Despite its sumptuous offices in both Shanghai and Hong Kong, it was managed from London by the chief officer and the London Committee. Massively wealthy, it financed British trade and effectively set the foreign exchange rate in China's money markets.[5] When it was grandly opened with an honor guard of Sikh and Chinese police, its Shanghai headquarters was considered the finest building east of the Suez Canal. The lobby was decorated with mosaic panels depicting the eight world cities where the bank's branches were located.

Next to the Hong Kong & Shanghai Bank, the clock tower of the neoclassical Customs House (also designed by Palmer & Turner) overlooked the city. The two buildings stood alongside the Chartered Bank of India, Australia and China as well as the Banque de l'Indochine in a phalanx of international finance that included the Russo-Asiatic Bank and the Mercantile Bank of India. The exclusive Shanghai Club on the Bund was the watering hole of the toffs—British dynasts and old China hands who gathered nightly at its Long Bar for gin and whiskey. The Bund headquarters of the long-established *North China Daily News* was the tallest building in Shanghai. Americans met at the Astor House Hotel, where businessmen made their deals. According to John B. Powell, the editor of the *China Weekly Review*, "At one time or another, one saw most of the leading residents of the port at dinner parties or in the lobby ... and all the crooks who hang out on the China coast."[6] Crowds along the Bund dodged swanky automobiles and clanging tram cars flashing up and down the esplanade. The sampans of the wharf coolies extended into the river, with wooden planks connecting them to the shore. The Bund announced Shanghai in all its stunning, disputatious, and conflicted garb.

The races hardly mixed at all. For most Shanghailanders, the Chinese were vulgar and selfish. The British maintained unwavering distain for Orientals, as they called them, and steadfast loyalty to British routines as if they were still in England. They took their cues from London. It was a cultural politics suited to the traditions of empire. They had their clubs, their charity events, their ponies and golf. English author Somerset Maugham attended one of their parties during his stay in Shanghai. The formalities were excruciating. The guests "talked of racing and golf and shooting. They were all persons of consequence. There was number one at Jardine's and his wife, and the manager of the Hong-Kong and Shanghai Bank and his wife, the A.P.C. man and his wife.... They were bored to death with one another."[7]

The Shanghai branch of the Royal Empire Society was financed by the Sassoons and Jardine Matheson. It was a league of gentlemen dedicated to the British Commonwealth. Empire Day and royal events were feted with gusto. For the Silver Jubilee of King George V's ascension to the throne, the Royal Navy fleet in Shanghai's harbor was festooned in a rainbow of flags. The Shanghai racecourse was fitted out in British pageantry, with military bands, mounted Sikh police on parade, and a moonlight steeplechase by the light horse cavalry. The Bund was awash in illumination for the coronation of George VI in May 1937. The celebration went on for three days. Performers of every stripe emerged from a castle set up in the center of the racecourse. Beams of light pierced the twilight while sailors and soldiers paraded in their dress liveries. All this was going on as thousands of Japanese troops were massing toward the city and Shanghai was preparing for war. Regardless, the British remained blissfully confident in their authority. They stayed with their own kind and practiced well-guarded isolation from what they saw as racially inferior Asians as well as from Russians and Jews. They peered out the windows of their Packard motorcars for forays onto the streets, where the automobiles lumbered through the crowds and rickshaws.

The Parade of Nationalities

Although they flocked into the foreigners' redoubt, the Chinese were daily wounded by a thousand racist cuts. The concessions were overwhelmingly Chinese. But they took no part in governance until they were finally given a few token seats on the municipal council in 1927. The first Chinese member was Pei Tsuyee, one of China's most prominent bankers, with a slew of contacts in the London and New York banking worlds. The Pei family invested a fortune in the International Settlement's real estate. But even this grudging consent to some municipal council representation took place only after the Chinese organized into street unions. Nor did they have much representation as rent payers. The Chinese residents paid the lion's share of taxes. Regardless, the Settlement's revenues were spent for the benefit of its foreigners.[8] Its churches, libraries, and schools were open only to Shanghailanders.

Although the British relied entirely on Chinese labor in the countless transactions of everyday life, they practiced an abusive bigotry. The *tai-tai*'s (the taipan's wife) daily interactions with a retinue of servants were carried on in barely tolerated pidgin English. British homes were walled compounds forbidden to Chinese except for the retinue of coolies, amahs, and chauffeur. Even the incomparable Chinese cuisine rarely appeared at mealtime—it was considered fit only for natives. The nuances of Chinese ethnicity and dialect were deemed incomprehensible. The Chinese were barred from British clubs, although they were tolerated at the American Club and the Circle Sportif Français. They were banned from European cabarets and brothels. The Settlement's parks were off limits to them as well as to Indians and Japanese until 1928, when they were finally open to all residents.

Nonetheless, the lure of Western-style comforts and relative freedom made the foreign concessions a magnet for Chinese who had made their fortunes. Wealthy elites moved in to provide a secure haven for their families and their investments. Chinese businessmen owned cotton and railway shares and controlled the local banks as well as the shipping and merchant trades in what historian Marie-Claire Bergère has called the "golden age of Shanghai capitalism."[9] They were the captains of industry and commerce, with their finger on the pulse of Shanghai. Although their fortunes had been made in alliance with foreign business, they were united in their nationalism. Just as in Bombay, they were members of a new bourgeoisie, a business elite whose identity expanded far beyond the status of compra-dor, and one that was patriotic and steadfast in modernizing the nation. Private capitalist enterprises contributed to the wealth of the Chinese nation, in their way of thinking. The rewards would include a good life of material comforts. Travel, newspapers, and modern initiative framed their professional lives in a promising global perspective.[10] Chinese capitalists soaked up news and information at the Shanghai Chamber of Commerce, their guilds, the Chinese Ratepayers Association; on the golf course; and at charity events. These formal and informal circles were crucial to how business was done.[11]

Lieu Ong Sung (O. S. Lieu) was one of the city's great industrialists living in the International Settlement and a member of the Shanghai Municipal Council. He financed the Shanghai Cement Works and the China Match Company, and he was a board member of the city's prominent bank and insurance companies. His most authoritative title was General Manager of the China Merchants' Steam Navigation Company. Schooled at Shanghai's St. John's University, he eventually became its director and a generous educational philanthropist. Li Ming was one of China's most prominent bankers and served as chairman of the Bank of China as well as a board member of Victor Sassoon's Yangtze Finance Company and the Shanghai Power Company. Li was among the most influential Chinese financiers in Western banking circles and spearheaded the joint purchase of the International Settlement's electric power system and the Shanghai Mutual Telephone Company. Banking executive Ling Kong-hou was a leading light of the Shanghai Chamber of Commerce and the Bankers' Association, and he served on the Education Board of the Shanghai Municipal Council.[12]

For Chinese business elites such as these, a mansion in the International Settlement on Bubbling Well Road alongside the Europeans was the ultimate sign of success. Bubbling Well Road was the patrician quarter of Shanghai. It was one of the first roads to receive fresh water and electricity. Tree-shaded and lined with stately mansions and villas, it was the kind of bucolic garden-city ambiance that appealed to the wealthy. As the value of land reached astronomical levels, the Chinese monied class poured cash into real estate. They indulged in exotic Western trappings—electric lighting, radios and gramophones, and luxury motorcars. Perfumed wives and daughters paraded the avenue in the latest silks and satins, expensive furs coiled around their shoulders. The best schools for Chinese boys were in the Settlement, donated by philanthropic Chinese. Older children traveled to Europe or the United States to be educated; a Western education was a ticket to wealth and status. Even the homes of Chinese workers living in the Settlement's *shikumen lilongs* were outfitted with enamel washbasins, electric cooking pots and alarm clocks, and bicycles, even if the items were recycled or locally produced knockoffs.

Across the Avenue Edouard VII, the French Concession was wedged in between the International Settlement and the old Chinese City. It was entirely under the thumb of the French Consul General, although its police force, partly made up of Vietnamese, was known to be in cahoots with the Green Gang crime syndicate and generally turned a blind eye to illegalities. Frenchtown was a small territory with a population density far exceeding anything in London or Bombay. It was a snarl of some five hundred thousand people in the 1930s,[13] the vast majority of whom were Chinese. The remainder was a wild amalgam of foreigners. Avenue Joffre was a stylish boulevard lined with shops and cafés nestled under trees imported from France.

There was another side to the French Concession that was enticing in the illicit sense. If the British-led International Settlement was known for its priggish respectability, Frenchtown had a reputation for wickedness.[14] The sounds of jazz spilled from its cabarets and dance halls. Voluptuous singsong girls and Russian hostesses held their hands out for customers' dance tickets. Gigolos worked the crowds. Drugs and sex were for sale. The legalized brothels were a scintillating draw. The Rue Chau Pao San alone, better known as Blood Alley, had some fifteen cabarets and seedy fleshpots where anything could be bought and sold. Having drunk their fill and more, sozzled patrons stumbled past the tables and out into the Shanghai night.

The foreign concessions' extraterritorial status put them outside all normal constraints. The boundaries between colonial elites, Chinese, and the masses of people of all ethnicities were blurred on the surface of the city. Anyone could disembark and head into the area without passports or identity papers. It was an El Dorado for foreign adventurers and shady characters skimming along the edge of criminality. "You can start a bank single-handed.... You can form a mining company or an oil company or any old company, issue and sell stock without one penny's worth of assets," a denizen of the concessions reported.[15] Bandits and warlords hid out in the foreign concessions as a haven. Just beneath the surface lay a cloak-and-dagger world of political plotters, conspiracies, and secret societies. The indulgent atmosphere also made the concessions a moraine of refugees, the dislocated, and the stranded. Shanghai was truly a helm of the world for those caught in the maelstrom of war and political calamity. Its global status made it a sanctuary for a multitude of displaced people.

Thousands of White Russians escaping czarist persecution and the Bolshevik Revolution bore the curse of refugees. Fleeing in caravans, they endured the bitter Siberian winds and found their way to Shanghai, with a first wave arriving between 1905 and 1917. Others remained in Manchuria until the Japanese invasion in 1931. Then, some fifty thousand destitute civilians and remnants of the White Army and the Far Eastern Cossacks boarded ships in Vladivostok and Harbin for the passage to Shanghai. All these people had been driven by desperation to Shanghai because of political circumstance. Trotskyites planning the downfall of capitalism were stuck alongside czarists dreaming of a return to their palaces. Nobles and heiresses hocked their jewels; Shanghai's pawnshops were filled with their priceless baubles. Stateless, they were all left to their own devices. Many lived hand to mouth. A bevy of relief organizations emerged that served meals and helped find shelter and work. Former Cossacks became bodyguards for wealthy Chinese or joined the International Settlement's Volunteer Corps.[16] Russians worked as chauffeurs and labored on the docks and in construction. They were regarded with loathing when they filled in at jobs during Chinese strikes. For some, the hardships drove them into the sex trade or the criminal underworld. Taxi dancers and prostitutes claimed to be descendant from czars. Hundreds of brothels littered the foreign concessions. Prostitution became so prevalent that a League of Nations Commission investigating the trafficking of women and children in the East arrived in Shanghai in 1930 as part of its Asian tour. The white slavery trade was a source of constant alarm for the British, who saw it as a moral threat and a mark of Shanghai's depravities.

The flood of refugees from the collapsing Russian Empire to Shanghai also carried Ashkenazi Jews.[17] They far outnumbered the city's small Sephardic community, which had roots in Baghdad and Bombay. Even at its height, the city's Baghdadi Jewish population probably numbered no more than eight hundred. Although vagabonds and adventurers were among them, the Baghdadis were known for their illustrious merchants— the Hardoon, the Kadoori, the Ezra, and the Sassoon families. They had been in Shanghai since its opening as a treaty port. But even those Baghdadi Jews who were not tycoons were still entrenched in Shanghai's commercial life. They represented close to 40 percent of the membership in the Shanghai Stock Exchange. In contrast, the Ashkenazi refugees from Russia, Poland, and the Ukraine never attained this kind of wealth and status, and the animosity between the two groups was exasperating. Russian Jews complained bitterly about the better-off "Arabs." The Committee for the Assistance of Jewish Refugees attempted to mediate the raucous disagreements between the newly arrived and the deep-rooted Jewish communities. By the late 1930s, the Ashkenazi community had already neared eight thousand. They settled in cheap lodgings in the Hongkou and Chapei districts, where the Jewish Club became the heart of their community. But many remained destitute, and their political battles followed them. Ukrainian Jews put down roots in the French Concession and demanded that the authorities treat them separately from the Russians or anyone else.

Over twenty thousand Japanese, the city's largest contingent of foreigners, far outnumbered the British and Americans. They were centered in Hongkou, north of Suzhou Creek, in what was known as Little Tokyo. Here, Japanese was the language of daily life. Wu Song Road was filled with Japanese stores, their Rising Sun flags fluttering in the breeze. Music from Japanese theaters, bars, and dance halls bellowed into the night. Families visited Buddhist temples and Shinto shrines. The Japanese Club was the watering hole for factory managers and bankers. Branches of Japanese banks moved in as the country expanded its economic interests in China. Mitsui, Mitsubishi, and the Yokohama Specie Bank were all located on the Bund. Social ordering in the community was strict. The Company

Clique was made up of the heads of large corporations, directors of bank branches, and wealthy entrepreneurs in Shanghai. The Native Clique were lower-class Japanese working in small-scale businesses and restaurants.[18] The former were sojourners in Shanghai, the latter were settlers.

The Japanese were buying up failing Chinese and British cotton mills and had owned some thirty mills in the city by the late 1920s. Thousands of bales of Osaka-made cotton textiles and cheap sundry goods from Japan were also off-loaded on the docks and dumped onto the Shanghai market, eating away at profits for local Chinese entrepreneurs and adding to the festering hostilities between the two peoples. Japan maintained a naval force of 3,500 in Shanghai to protect its interests, and local paramilitary units stood at the ready against Chinese attacks. They were known for their brutality. With the Japanese invasion of Manchuria in 1931, the hatred between the Chinese and Japanese became ruthless. By 1932, protests against Japanese aggression had spread throughout the city. Chinese hoodlums stoned Japanese in the streets while mobs looted Japanese-owned shops. Japan responded by attacking Shanghai with artillery and aerial bombing. Some 50,000 Chinese battled 100,000 Japanese troops and left Chapei and Hongkou in ruins. Machine-gun fire blasted through the streets. Japanese planes rained bombs on Chapei. The North Railway Station was engulfed in flames. Thousands were killed.

Fighting was close enough to the International Settlement for the British and the Americans to rush in troops for its defense. Fierce battles raged near the British Embassy while Japanese warships trained their guns on Garden Bridge. Rooftops in the International Settlement were packed with gawkers watching the toxic clouds of smoke over Chapei and the North Railway Station. Ensconced in his Cathay Hotel on the Bund, Sir Victor scribbled in his diary about the combat, the "bomb [that] exploded by Jap consulate," and the "dead bodies." He pasted in snapshots of barbed wire and sandbags surrounding the Settlement, of the soldiers and desperate refugees. "It really is a war,"[19] he wrote, and he offered his services and two Royal Air Force planes for the fight. From the Cathay's rooftop roost, he snapped Japanese soldiers marching down Nanjing Road. The walls of the Cathay were peppered with bullets and shrapnel. He made the rounds checking for damage as the building shook from the bomb blasts. Venturing out to film the action, a bullet whizzed past, perilously near his head, then smashed into a nearby window. A Chinese soldier had mistaken him for a Japanese sniper. When the Chinese general in charge heard about the close call, he sent over sweets and his profound regrets. Not to be outdone, the Japanese offered their apologies for the damage inflicted on the "Honorable Cathay." Sir Victor downplayed the whole incident and called the apologies "most gentlemanly." The League of Nations chose his Cathay Hotel as the site of negotiations to end the conflict. Sassoon kept up the delegates' spirits by ordering pink champagne for them at the hotel's bar.[20] Although Japanese forces never entered the foreign concessions, the stress took its toll on the normally unflappable Sassoon. He had bet his fortune on a city that was now under siege.

The British Cocoon

Lady Drummond-Hay was sharply sardonic about the British living their lives in their cocoon, "blissfully going round and round like a merry squirrel in its cage. The round is quite a large and giddy one, if you keep it all up. Dancing, mah-jongg, bridge, and gossip for the women, club life for the men."[21] But it was an increasingly difficult act to uphold. The parties were in full swing, but Republican China and the viciousness of the Japanese invasion were beginning to penetrate the social whirl. Arthur Ransome, the Shanghai correspondent for the *Guardian* of Manchester, castigated the "Shanghai mind" that would have Britain go to war rather than adjust itself to changing circumstances. The British seem "to have lived in a comfortable but hermetically sealed and isolated glass case.... They look round on their magnificent buildings and are surprised that China is not grateful to them for these gifts," he declared.[22] Global city Shanghai may have been, but it was tightly bound in the straitjacket of colonialism. Despite the witless distain Shanghailanders had for "inferior races," the foreign concessions were a polyglot of peoples who rarely shared in the caste-like privileges the British defended with such ferocity. It was also a strange paradox that over a million Chinese residing on Chinese soil lived under Western governments. The cruel tensions between globalization and imperium were on full view in Shanghai's harbor. Only British, US, and French warships anchored majestically in the Huangpu River safeguarded foreign lives and their millions invested in property. A constant bone of contention, the boundaries of the International Settlement encroached on more and more Chinese territory, with foreign troops stationed at some forty-three miles of surrounding road.

It was no surprise, then, when the conflict over extraterritorial jurisdiction came to a head. It was impossible for the British to carry the flag of extraterritoriality indefinitely. They bitterly cursed that China was going to hell. In a tactic meant to stave off rendition, outside observer Richard Feetham of the South African Supreme Court was invited to prepare recommendations on the future of extraterritoriality. The Feetham Report (1931) was an exhaustive study that arrived at a predictable imperial conclusion: The immediate handing over of the International Settlement was neither practical nor desirable. It would be a disastrous loss to global commerce. The Chinese were inexperienced in self-government. Until the Chinese had the capacity for the rule of law and a stable constitutional government—which would take decades—the British would continue as trustees of the International Settlement.[23] They were its natural ruling class. The fact was that the British had enormous monetary investments to protect—half of their millions plowed into China were in Shanghai, in the bricks and steel of the city and in its trade, with all of it accomplished by the money-spinners in London.

A storm of protest by Chinese interests immediately followed public notice of the Feetham Report. The condemnation was echoed by the Labour and the Communist press in London.[24] The nationalist Kuomintang threw out Feetham's recommendations as a boldface insult and refused to include them in negotiations over the "future of Shanghai"—an oft-used phrase that seemed to encapsulate the knotted complexities of the city. Instead, the nationalists looked forward to an immediate surrender of the foreign concessions and the development of Shanghai's sprawling metropolitan area.

In 1927, the Kuomintang outwitted the foreigners and established a municipal government for Greater Shanghai. It took in the old Chinese city with its labyrinth of passageways and zigzag bridges and spread amoeba-like through the modern city and the Yangtze River Valley. It was a chaotic mixture of densely built-up neighborhoods spreading out to hamlets woven through rice paddies and mosquito-infested canals, with rutted trails and towpaths the only connective tissue. There were still areas not far beyond the city center where a one-wheeled taxi or sedan chair was the only means of getting around. The shantytowns spread out on desolate wastelands were barely controlled by the local authorities. The expanse was riddled with vice and the dirty work of the crime syndicates. Brigands, floods, and epidemics were a constant threat. But it was fertile ground for real estate development, especially by wealthy Chinese eager to expand their investments beyond the constricted foreign territories.

The Nationalist government's Greater Shanghai Plan sketched out the region's growth along the Huangpu with a model government and business center. The heart of the project was the Civic Center on the flat plain of the Jiangwan district. It was the Kuomintang's thrilling monument to progress. American-trained Chinese architect Dong Dayou adapted the latest Western urban planning ideas to modern China, and he would be behind the 1936 Shanghai Architectural Exhibition that introduced a Chinese interpretation of international modernism and the blueprints for the

Greater Shanghai Plan.²⁵ As for the Civic Center, Dong designed it as a grand crossing of boulevards and gardens with a lofty pagoda at its juncture. The mayor's building, a museum, and a library boasted upswept rooflines and pillared facades in a novel fusion of classical Chinese and art deco styles. A Central Railway Station was planned along with a medical school and a hospital. Dong created a sumptuous art deco headquarters for China's new Civil Aviation Association in the shape of an airplane. Overall, the plan was an extraordinary vision for Shanghai with meticulous residential districts, tidy streets and canals, and parks and open spaces laid out on a tree-lined grid.²⁶ It was a direct challenge to the foreign domination of the city and even more remarkable given the savage conflicts engulfing Shanghai. Buyers scrambled for the choice lots.

The Sassoon Real Estate Empire

Victor Sassoon found himself in an ambiguous position in Shanghai. The arrival in the city "of this almost legendary creature" in 1931 triggered enormous gossip and speculation.²⁷ He was fabulously wealthy and head of one of Shanghai's most powerful foreign companies. He was an instant celebrity, but he was not a Shanghailander. Sir Victor was never fully accepted in the International Settlement world any more than he was in London. It mattered little that he played golf with the Prince of Wales. Regardless of his British pedigree, Sassoon was Jewish and dark skinned. The snide racist remarks by Shanghai's upper crust were relentless. In their minds, he was a subject of the Raj, marked as an overcivilized Oriental from Baghdad. Loutish young men sent up chants of "Back to Baghdad" when Sassoon entered the British clubs. The jeers were even more biting because Sir Victor was always ambivalent about his background. Although he continued the Sassoon tradition of patronage, he avoided the Jewish religious observances his family once cherished. He had no association with the Middle East other than lucrative business deals. Sir Victor saw himself as a custodian of fine culture, a cosmopolitan blue blood as comfortable in Bombay or Shanghai as he was in London, or anywhere else in the world he traveled to.

Besides, Sha Sun (Sassoon's name in Chinese) regularly associated with Chinese business magnates, among whom were Chiang Kai-shek's brother-in-law T. V. Soong (Tzu-wen) and H. H. Kung (Hsiang Hsi). These men controlled the finances of the Nationalist government, and Kung was reportedly the richest man in China. Both were regular guests at Sir Victor's lavish receptions at the Cathay Hotel. The severe color barriers could be scaled by Chinese luminaries at these heights, which was politically expedient and good for business. Sir Victor pledged his troth to Chiang Kai-shek and the Nationalists to protect his investments. His backing was greased with financial donations to the Nationalist cause. Chiang's Nationalist government mounted an extraordinary campaign to win over power brokers like Sassoon. It played on his fear of communism and offered lucrative investments in government bonds. But rubbing elbows with the Chinese was a practice the British disdained. It was deemed un-British of Sassoon, as was his tax evasion. Under their breath, the Shanghailanders called Sir Victor a tax dodger who had skipped out on his British taxes by moving his fortune from Bombay to Shanghai. Though it had been a clever move, it fueled the bigotry against him. Racism, jealousy, and snooty arrogance made a vicious stew. But the Shanghailanders could not ignore Sir Victor. He had more money than anyone else.

Regardless of the sneers, Sassoon was in full company with an entourage of the most powerful members of the British Settlement. With the levers of politics and trade in their hands, they grabbed up everything worth taking—money, companies, real estate, and rents. Harry Arnhold, who ran his myriad business interests from the Arnhold Building on Kiukiang Road and then from Sassoon House on the Bund, was a constant companion. He had merged his company with Sassoon's far-flung enterprises and become a key figure to their success (see chapter 5). Arnhold was a shrewd observer of the political winds and succeeded in gaining the chairmanships of both the British Chamber of Commerce and the Shanghai Municipal Council. He was Sassoon's insider, with his ear to the ground regarding the goings-on in the Settlement, ready to steer policy in the Sassoon direction.

Jack and Billie Liddell were among Sir Victor's most familiar cronies, and they shared his epicurean tastes (see chapter 4). Jack Liddell also served as chairman of the Shanghai Municipal Council. An avid horsewoman, Billie Coutts Liddell was a born-and-bred Shanghailander and an immensely popular figure in the British horse-racing world. She owned We Two Stable with Vera McBain, the wife of local magnate William McBain. The McBain family had made their fortune in the East in shipping, rubber, and oil and were among Shanghai's wealthiest tycoons. Their three-story mansion in the International Settlement was surrounded by ten acres of manicured garden. "Willie" McBain was behind the development of the city's zanily popular Luna Park as well as Building No. 1 on the Bund that was leased to the British Shell-Royal Dutch Asiatic Petroleum Company for its headquarters. McBain was on the boards of dozens of the city's companies, including Sassoon's Yangtze Finance and the Cathay Hotel investment group. Like Sir Victor, he was an avid fan of aviation. McBain founded the Aeroclub of Shanghai and owned the city's first privately owned plane. To house it, he built his own landing field at Hongqiao.

This was the privileged air the global oligarchy breathed. Its members carried out the routines of global finance as a peripatetic cosmopolitanism between London, Shanghai, and Bombay. They conducted their business over cocktails and at the racetrack, undeterred by the gross inequities and social turmoil around them. Sir Victor's friend Arthur Henchman was manager of the Hong Kong & Shanghai Bank on the Bund. Known as a financial wizard, he was one of the most powerful men in China and steered the bank through the shoals of the silver crisis and the Great Depression. "Hench" and wife Mary were an institution in Shanghai.[28] The couple joined in the bragging rights of horse ownership and were regulars at the Shanghai Race Club. The club was the consummate social whirl for the international financial elite with connections to London and New York. John and Peggy Reed were also members of this genteel migration between global places. John "Red" Reed headed the National City Bank of New York's offices in China and Japan (see chapter 4). Another National City Bank partner was American Lewis Holt Ruffin. Ruffin was a regular at Sassoon's parties in both Shanghai and Bombay. It was with the aid of these allies at National City Bank that Sassoon could save some portion of his fortune by shifting it out of Shanghai ahead of both the Japanese and then the communist takeover of the city.

The winnings from global finance were poured into Shanghai's property boom. The land occupied by the foreign concessions represented only a fraction of the city's territory, and it was outrageously valuable. The adamant refusal of the Kuomintang to expand its boundaries meant that the price of its real estate skyrocketed. Outside Shanghai, China was in acute political turmoil. Chinese investors rushed into the city to shelter their financial reserves. Compradors, local merchant bankers, and entrepreneurs parked their money in property and real estate. Family clans owned thousands of buildings in Shanghai: some were extravagant villas in the International Settlement, others were hotels, *lilong* districts, and tenements. Shanghai and global cities like it were a topography of real estate speculation. Given the political instability of the Kuomintang takeover, mortgaging land in the concessions was also the best way to raise funds for businesses. Land there was legally protected and widely accepted as collateral by foreign and Chinese banks alike. It was sold and resold at exorbitant prices. Financial sorcery turned buildings into liquid cash or socked fortunes away. The astronomical price tags for real estate on the Bund were the highest in China. Property prices on Nanjing Road and Fuzhou Road as well as in the French Concession were astonishing.

In the meantime, Shanghai's silver-based currency plummeted. There was a direct connection between the silver bust and the building boom. Foreign investors rushed to take advantage of the exchange rates and then plowed their money into the real estate market. Somehow, amid global disaster, when China's countryside fell deep into depression, Shanghai was not only buoyant but booming. Credit was easy. The stock market was up.[29] For those with command over the liquidity of capital, the instability was a source of speculative profits. Cities were spaces of global flows. A flood of foreign money, including the fabulous reserves of Victor Sassoon, arrived from abroad to catch the wave of China's devalued silver-based currency. Once the currency was converted, Sir Victor was awash in cash. He and foreign investors like him then dumped their funds into real estate and infrastructure projects that were making Shanghai into a beacon of modernity. Land and buildings were lucrative financial assets added to global investment portfolios. Even after the turmoil of the May Thirtieth Movement in 1925, *Looking Ahead*, a promotional brochure by the Asia Realty Company, was predicting an "exceedingly bright" future for Shanghai's real estate. Just two years later, Asia Realty was paying shareholders sky-high dividends of 12 percent. From 1928 to 1932, the largest property boom in modern Shanghai took place.[30] The real estate bonanza was not just limited to the foreign concessions. The scramble for buildings and land pushed steadily westward, where properties changed hands "among the wealthier class of the city's working men."[31]

Early on, the top clans of British-based merchants, mostly Jewish families long involved in the opium trade, had scooped up the choicest property in the foreign concessions and beyond. The wealthy Ezra family controlled many of the city's finest hotels and owned most of the land north of Suzhou Creek, which it sold off to developers as the prices rose. Silas Hardoon owned some sixteen properties along Nanjing Road, including the land on which the Wing On and Sincere department stores stood. Thanks to Hardoon's shrewdness during his years as the Sassoon agent, E. D. Sassoon & Company owned twenty-nine prime properties by the early 1920s. When Sassoon bought out Arnhold & Company, he gained its most valuable assets—the Cathay Land Company and the Shanghai Land Investment Company. The transaction gave Sir Victor control over even more apartment buildings and hotels in the International Settlement as well as choice housing estates in the French Concession. The Arnhold inventory included breweries and laundries, lumber and transport companies, and the Oriental Cotton Mill. It also owned the omnibus lines in the International Settlement. An even more breathtaking coup was Sassoon's acquisition of Silas Hardoon's lavish landholdings upon the tycoon's death. When Hardoon passed away in 1931, the city celebrated his legacy with an extraordinary funeral. Some five thousand mourners gathered to celebrate his spirit at his estate gardens, which were draped in white silk. Sassoon quickly swooped in and formed an investment vehicle that acquired Hardoon's most valuable sites on Nanjing Road.

At the same time, Sassoon built up even more capital for his real estate empire by issuing a large quantity of corporate bonds through the Shanghai Stock Exchange. He set up two trust companies—the International Investment Trust Company and the Yangtze Finance Company, each with dizzying amounts of capital in Chinese taels. They were modeled after the powerful trust companies in London and meant to assure a healthy return on the shares. It was a stunning move. Given Sassoon's fame, the issues on the Shanghai Stock Exchange were swept up immediately. The money poured in. The trusts were managed by Sassoon's right-hand partners, Harry Arnhold, Lucien Ovadia, Frederick Davey, Ellis Hayim, and Vilhelm Meyer.[32] These capitalist oligarchs appeared again and again on the boards of Sassoon's banks and enterprises. Ellis Hayim, head of the Shanghai Stock Exchange, looked like "a forbidding Arab sheikh... Anglo-Saxon women were mad for him," as his son recalled. A true cosmopolitan, Sir Victor's cousin Lucien Ovadia was born in Egypt and educated in France. He was as comfortable in Europe as he was in Asia. Ovadia had a long stint in the Sassoon enterprises and had worked in the company offices in Manchester. He had also put his financial skill to good use at the Banque Belge pour l'Etranger in London. Banker Frederick Davey presided over the annual meeting of both trusts in 1934 and reported that "few, if any, investment trust companies in the world can claim to have done so well during so difficult a period." They had weathered the Great Depression by "taking advantage of favourable opportunities."[33] The trust companies worked in tandem with the new E. D. Sassoon Bank that was registered in Hong Kong and then opened offices in Shanghai (see chapter 5). Together they created a tight investment circle that generated nonstop profits.

The success pushed Sassoon further into one luxury property scheme after another. He issued corporate bonds at an annual interest rate of 6 percent for his Cathay Land Company. A cascade of investors swooped in to grab a slice of the riches. The share price skyrocketed. The Feetham Report of 1931 encouraged the powerful land companies to invest even further. The China Investment & Trust Company was set up. Between 1930 and 1934, Sir Victor floated at least seven lots of corporate bonds worth 12 million taels through the various companies under his wing.[34] Profits from the real estate and financial entities allowed Sassoon to pounce on the most sought-after properties in Shanghai—on the Bund, at the corner of Foochow and Kiangse Roads across from the Shanghai Municipal Council. Just on their own, Sassoon's astounding ventures kept Shanghai's real estate red hot. By 1935, land prices had increased to triple their 1927 level.[35] The Sino-Japanese War had the perverse effect of worsening the city's already severe property shortage. Sassoon's real estate office at Sassoon House was flooded with requests for apartments, shops, and offices at any price. Many of the Sassoon companies were still raking in jaw-dropping profits in 1940, when the good times were teetering on collapse. The Shanghai Land Investment Company's profits that year were the largest in its history. In sum, the book value of Sassoon's real estate holdings was estimated at nearly ¥87 million.[36]

With land prices at epic levels, the best option was to build taller. As the *North China Herald* reported, "Indications are that Shanghai is destined to become an apartment city just as are New York and London."[37] Not even the Depression silenced the thump of the pile drivers, the pouring of concrete, and the raising of steel beams. From the late 1920s, some thirty tall buildings mounted on deep stilts rose over the neoclassical colonial edifices on the Bund, many of them based on American building techniques and dressed in art deco—"modern genies that, on a flat mud bank, rear cement and concrete palaces to the sky," reported the *North China Daily News*.[38] They were bank buildings, hotels, department stores. Sinuous apartment buildings appeared on the skyline, their flats outfitted with the latest modern conveniences. They were icons to a global money machine run by banks, by currency markets, by international investors, and by a municipal council all too willing to share in the riches. With little oversight and even fewer taxes, Shanghai was a gold mine for developers ready to capitalize on the city's growth. It was one of the largest property markets in the world. The global financial machinations there materialized on its horizon as an opulent skyline of art deco towers. The visual effect of the new style was stunning. It possessed the extraordinary power and excitement of globalization's built form.

The most sumptuous of all the towers was Sassoon House, which occupied the choicest piece of property in Shanghai—the corner of the Bund and Nanjing Road. Sassoon established the Cathay Hotel Company in Hong Kong as a vehicle for the project. George "Tug" Wilson, the Palmer & Turner architect chosen for the building's design, was also a company director. His interest in the project's success, then, was more than just aesthetic—it was also pecuniary. Urban property was a speculative market, tied to the rhythms of finance across the globe. Sassoon House was the ultimate prize. It rose eleven stories over the city as an art deco masterpiece and instantly became an icon of luxury and sophistication. It exuded the surface glitter and hedonistic tastes of the age. The interior was an extravagant parade of luminous Lalique glass imported from Paris. The fantastic designs and colors, the "riot of beauty," stunned reporters on the opening tour.[39] In the ground-floor arcade were the finest in luxuries imported from London, Paris, and New York.

Passing through the Lalique-laced doors of Sassoon House, the public found telegraph and telephone exchanges. Ticker tapes read out currency rates and quotations on the price of silver. The building was Shanghai's command center for telecommunications and the information flows vital to global capitalism. The new communication technologies were contracting space and making international business a fast-moving operation. The "Radio Central of China" was located on the first floor of Sassoon's sumptuous building "in the very heart of the business and financial district ... where may be seen in operation the latest perforators, automatic transmitters, printers, recorders and telegraph typewriters." Direct radio was established with London in 1934. The ground and first floors were jam packed with electronic equipment, where "messages are being dispatched to and received from all parts of the world." Mezzanine accounting offices handled billing for "the hundreds of messages sent and received daily."[40] Sassoon House was a prestigious address for the sales offices of foreign companies. And the various arms of the Sassoon empire moved their headquarters to the third floor, next to Sir Victor's private offices.

The Cathay Hotel installed in the building welcomed the international jet set that Shanghai was famous for. It was one of the most luxurious hotels in the world. Everyone, from Hollywood movie stars to Russian oligarchs, Italian aristocrats and Japanese ambassadors, imbibed its luxury. American superstar Will Rogers stopped by for lunch. Rogers dubbed Sassoon the "J. P. Morgan" of the East, "who knows more about China and India than any man. . . . We have to get his O.K. to see if we can have sugar with our coffee."[41] Stays at the hotel and dinners with Sassoon were a must for a long list of colonial elites and global celebrities. Sir Victor welcomed film stars Greer Garson and Laurence Olivier to the Cathay. English writers W. H. Auden and Christopher Isherwood were amazed at the sophisticated atmosphere of the hotel, which was among "the biggest animals [that] pushed their way down to the brink of the water. . . . You can dance at the Tower Restaurant on the roof of the Cathay Hotel [whose jazz orchestra came directly from New York], and gossip with Freddy Kaufmann, its charming manager, about the European aristocracy or pre-Hitler Berlin." It was the pinnacle of Shanghai's cosmopolitan whirl, a place where the "jeweller and the antique dealer await your orders, and their charges will make you imagine yourself back on Fifth Avenue or in Bond Street."[42] E. Carrard, the manager of the Taj Mahal Hotel in Bombay, came to oversee the opening of the Cathay. Sassoon persuaded Louis Suter, the general manager of Claridge's, London's most elegant hotel, to manage his new property.

Endless likenesses of Sassoon House appeared in photos and illustrations. With its Chinese-style art deco facade and patina-green pyramidal roof, the building, along with its Cathay Hotel, became the city's most recognizable landmark. Sassoon was rhapsodic about its success and basked in the hosannas of praise. His diary records his first stay in his eleventh-floor penthouse, next to photos of the airy view of the Bund and Nanjing Road.[43] As soon as Sassoon House became the heart of Shanghai's legendary social whirl, it was jammed with people. "All one's friends were there," the *North China Herald* gushed. Writer Vicki Baum captured the atmosphere in her novel *Shanghai '37*: "Dance music could be heard through every wall.... The clatter of bottles and glasses, the subdued murmur of many conversations, the cigarette smoke, the scent of women, the almost inaudible sound of the felt soles of Chinese waiters and page boys shuffling on the thick sand-colored carpets—all gave an indefinable impression of elegance and the great world."[44]

Victor Sassoon owned Shanghai. In the afterglow of the Cathay Hotel, his development companies built the luxurious Metropole Hotel and its mirror image, Hamilton House, both designed by Palmer and Turner, on an intersection of Foochow Road. These towers set Shanghai abuzz with their 16 stories and curved facades. Grosvenor House, with its jutting 21-story modernist tower, was financed by Sassoon's Cathay Land Company in the French Concession. The nearby Cathay Mansions, also a project of the Cathay Land Company, was built by Arnhold & Company. It was a deluxe 18-story residential hotel around the corner from the Canidrome greyhound track. These were the choicest, priciest locations in Shanghai. The buildings were art deco citadels with steel-frame construction and ample use of aluminum. Sassoon's towers introduced Otis elevators, air-conditioning and central heating, automatic sprinklers, and fire alarm systems. The sprawling, curved Embankment Building alongside Suzhou Creek was the largest residential building in Asia. The monumental Broadway Mansions was long the most impressive building in the Hongkou district. The 22-story modernist icon was another Palmer and Turner design and financed by the Shanghai Land Investment Company. Like many of Sassoon's real estate ventures, it was leased as a combination of offices, shops, and luxury apartments.

Yet Sassoon's freewheeling social life in Shanghai is what is best known about him, and it has been recounted by many writers. This narrative reached an epic scale, forming an indelible part of the myth of the city. Sassoon's fancy-dress balls and madcap parties were the highlights of Shanghai's social season. He choreographed his costume parties at the Cathay with the opulence and trickery of an opera set. Their themes swung from a shipwreck party to a circus party, which had guests dressed as animals and Sir Victor as the ringmaster dressed in top hat, scarlet coat, and riding whip. In fact, he became utterly dependent on surrounding himself with pleasure-seeking people. He was not alone in his terror of boredom. High society in the Twenties and Thirties meant seeking constant amusement and mingling with the right people, all the while feigning the dullness of it all. Shanghai was a playground for the ultraconnected.

Snubbed at the Paramount Ballroom for being a Jew, Sir Victor retaliated by building his own sumptuous venue. He spared no expense on his Ciro's nightclub on Bubbling Well Road. It was an art deco sensation, with a steel-and-glass tower flashing its name in neon lights. It was the classiest, costliest club in Shanghai, with the hottest dance floor and jazz orchestras. Guests arrived like movie stars in chauffeur-driven limousines. They entered a door framed by flaming-red lacquered columns. Strips of neon laid alongside a reflecting pool led the way to the ballroom, where patrons drank gin slings and danced until dawn. There was never a time when Sassoon did not combine his flamboyant social life with business, however. His table at Ciro's opening night was graced with consul-generals and trade commissioners. Entertainment was the space in which vital information was passed and deals cut. The competition between Ciro's and the glamorous Paramount Ballroom was fierce. Inevitably, though, thrill seekers succumbed to Ciro's siren call and left the Paramount facing bankruptcy.

Ultimately, Sassoon's world revolved around the Shanghai Race Club, the epicenter of Shanghailander high society. Situated on some of the choicest property in the International Settlement, the Shanghai's racecourse and grandstand were among the world's largest and its facilities second to none. The fenced grounds covered seventy-two acres smack in the middle of the city and constituted an extravagant spatial intrusion of Western culture. A sumptuous new six-story clubhouse with an imposing orientalist art deco tower opened in 1934. It symbolized colonial power and was one of the city's most impressive landmarks. The club became the wealthiest foreign corporation in China except for the banks and shipping companies. And it was rigidly segregated. Prominent Chinese could join only as members of the club's appendage for staff.[45] Regardless of the insulting bigotry, all Shanghai was addicted to the races, regardless of nationality or social class. It was a civic religion. The Chinese were fascinated by the turf. The racecourse was the city's most prominent public arena. Upward of a million people each year flowed into the grandstands. It was a setting for every fantasy and pure urban spectacle. Shanghai closed at midmorning for the grand race festivals that went on for days in the fall and the spring. Even the brutal battles for political control in 1927 did not stop the meets. Two other racetracks—the International Recreation Club in Kiangwan and the Chinese Jockey Club at Yangtzepoo—fed Shanghai's passion for the races. Hundreds of horses spun around the tracks each weekend. "There was nothing like it in the world," American writer Emily Hahn declared.[46]

Sir Victor's other passion was the Royal Air Force Association (RAFA), which he headed in Shanghai. He was a pivotal force in the development of aviation clubs in India. And in Shanghai, the RAFA was a means to keep up with news in the rarefied world of aviation and promote its development in China. Air travel was a pioneering vision. It was contracting space and transforming the map of the world. The competition to build up air routes and connect cities globally was fierce. The RAFA held its weekly luncheons and ceremonial dinners under the celestial canopy of the Hong Kong & Shanghai Bank on the Bund. A keen ally of the city's early aviation, Sir Victor championed the Aero Club of Shanghai, which repeated the tactic he had successfully applied in Bombay in training pilots and introducing the public to flight. The Shanghai version allied with the Michigan-based Detroit Aircraft Export Company, which sold planes in China and provided test pilots and flight training along with the Boeing Company. Crowds welcomed the world-circling *Spirit of Detroit* airplane as it touched down on the grounds of the racecourse.

Early on, Shanghai had the densest aviation network in China. The Hongjao airport served military planes, while the aerodrome at Longhua was headquarters for China National Aviation and Eurasia Aviation. By the mid-1930s, passenger flights linked some forty cities throughout China. Airplanes and seaplanes flew to distant parts of the country and hooked up with Russian aircraft for flights to Europe.[47] By 1933, the Eurasia Aviation Junker planes put Shanghai within seventy-two hours of London. Plans were afoot for flights hopping the Pacific to California.

The End of the Party

Air defense was indeed on the minds of many as the war with Japan arrived in the city in 1937. The foreign community in Shanghai had largely lived complacently on the edge of this volcano. Yet try as they might, it was impossible for the Shanghailanders to ignore the thousands of Japanese troops massing toward the city. An armada of Japanese cruisers and destroyers streamed toward the harbor. The International Settlement was ringed with barbed wire and sandbags, the Volunteer Corps at the ready. The murder of Japanese officers at Hungjao airport in August 1937 had triggered the violent eruption by Japan. Thousands of Chinese fled the districts of Hongkou and Chapei as rumors spread of an imminent Japanese attack. They poured into the foreign concessions, carrying their worldly possessions and their children with them. The streets were jammed with desperate refugees as the bombs began to fall. In the fierce air attack, incendiary bombs wreaked havoc on Chapei, Hongqiao, and Yangtszepoo, while antiaircraft batteries set the sky ablaze. Houses and factories were laid to waste. Thousands were slaughtered.

The battle reached the International Settlement and the French Concession. Naval guns off the harbor and aerial shelling resounded across the city. Smoke and debris filled the air. With planes skimming the tops of buildings, two massive bombs were dropped on thousands of families massed at a relief center set up near the Great World amusement center. Mangled bodies and charred remains heaped around the building. Chinese aircraft attacking the Japanese battleship *Idzumo* missed their mark and dropped massive bombs on Nanjing Road. These ripped through the Sincere and Wing On department stores, leaving hundreds of casualties. The Palace Hotel burst into flames. The entrance of the Cathay Hotel was hit, its Lalique glass shattered into glittering shards. Hundreds of wounded and dead were strewn across Nanjing Road in the simmering heat. The racecourse was turned into a makeshift morgue, with scores of bodies wrapped in cheap matting.

British and US defense forces arrived and took up positions on the sandbagged perimeter of the International Settlement. Women and children were hurriedly evacuated to ships waiting at sea. The once-glittering windows along the city's famed commercial avenues were boarded up. Cabarets were converted into emergency hospitals. But the battle was lost. An evil red glow and heavy smoke filled the whole of Shanghai's northern sky. Hordes of refugees fled across Soochow Creek. The Japanese pushed south through the city and into the Pudong district despite fierce Chinese resistance. By November, they had taken over the post office and all radio and telegraph communication. Some six thousand Japanese troops paraded through the International Settlement in a victory march. Sir Victor pasted his photos of the procession in his diary and scribbled, "several incidents, bomb thrown."[48] An onlooker had heaved a bomb into the phalanx of troops as it passed the Sun Sun department store.

Japanese occupying forces took control of Shanghai. They purchased Sassoon's Broadway Mansions for cash and made it into their military headquarters. "Broadway Mansions is the 'brain' of all Japanese control in Shanghai," a US Congress subcommittee reported. "Here most of the important combined policy meetings are held."[49] Barricades and blockhouses with Japanese sentries surrounded the foreign concessions. A curfew was strictly enforced. In a symbolic gesture of Japanese supremacy, the new Mitsui Bank building rose on Kiukiang Road. The Japanese yen became the city's currency. Chinese businesses were reorganized into cartels to further Japanese production. Factories were taken over by Japanese monopolies. Seized machinery piled up on the wharves, awaiting shipment to Tokyo. Only a fraction of Shanghai's industrial laborers was brought back to work. Instead, jobs were taken by the burgeoning Japanese population, which had reached some seventy thousand by 1940. Gambling houses, opium dens, and brothels sprang up like weeds. Japanese smugglers ran a lucrative racket in opium, heroin, and morphine. The powerful Mitsui family conglomerate distributed its opium-laced Golden Bat cigarettes throughout China. Ships of the Japanese navy shamelessly delivered them to Shanghai, where the tar-filled smokes flooded the city.

The savageries of Japanese occupation made life unbearable for the city's Chinese. The atrocities meted out were horrifying. The International Settlement was comparatively protected, although it was bloated with people fleeing the cruelties of war. Its municipal council kept its authority reasonably intact in a delicate dance with the Japanese overseers. Shanghai's famed real estate market stumbled. But a purely Japanese Central China Development Company painted a rosy picture of Shanghai's future under Japanese control. The cooperation of foreign companies was welcomed but would not be requested. People stomached their qualms and went about their business. Some foreign firms collapsed or fled; others carried on. The big mills made a profit. For some, the Japanese were "honorary Westerners" and good for business. The great banks on the Bund continued operation. A panic flight of capital fueled a black market in high-priced foreign currency. Massive amounts of gold and silver ingots, bars, and coins were stuffed into strongboxes and loaded onto ships for the voyage to London and Hong Kong for safekeeping.[50] Although the Japanese controlled the harbor, ships continued to unload their cargoes along the Bund. But foreign trade was only a pale specter of what it had been in the city's halcyon days. "Shanghai was living on its capital," the Shanghai correspondent for the *London Times* reported glumly. It was one of the world's tragic cities, and its future was ominous.[51]

Like many foreigners watching their paradise crumble, Victor Sassoon retained his largesse and was outwardly polite to the Japanese. But his efforts to somehow ride out the storm by mollifying the new masters of Shanghai were deemed untenable. He was eventually accused of collaboration with the Japanese (see epilogue). In the meantime, Shanghailanders continued their social rounds in an act of either defiance or oblivion to the disaster unfolding around them. Sir Victor invited his coterie to cocktail parties and evenings at Ciro's, where the music and laughter drowned out the dread. But his sanguine demeanor did little to hide his mounting anxieties about his far-flung conglomerate of investments and property. The glory years were over, and Sir Victor was too shrewd not to know it. What was left was merely a residue of what had been. He prepared to make his exit from Shanghai.

✳ EPILOGUE ✳

Almost every time a Japanese shell exploded, it took a little nick off the Sassoon fortune.

China Weekly Review (1938)

Sassoon was not in Shanghai when a bomb hit his Cathay Hotel and the city fell to the Japanese. He had embarked in April 1938 on an around-the-world tour, much of it soaring aloft in the aircraft he had revered his entire life. He held one of the most expensive tickets ever issued by Pan American Airways, covering nearly thirty thousand miles to twenty-seven countries. It was an aviation buff's dream. His purpose for this journey was to salvage his wealth by shifting it out of China. His group left Hong Kong aboard a Pan Am Hawaii clipper in the pouring rain. They flew to Honolulu and then San Francisco, where Sassoon met with Bank of America executives. A diversion to Los Angeles was the occasion for mingling with movie moguls and kissing cheeks with glamorous stars. The conveyor belt of cocktail parties was peppered with more bank meetings and chats about bankrolling the motion picture industry. From California, the group flew down the west coast of South America. In Brazil, Sir Victor viewed the Sassoon coffee plantations and cruised the Amazon River. At each stop, he was greeted by executives of National City Bank's branches in Latin America along with carefully selected local businessmen and shipping magnates. He was on the hunt for attractive investments outside the sterling arena, and the local elites fell over themselves wooing him. He had already begun steps to establish a powerful financial trust in Latin America with his surplus assets. Crossing the Andes, the group flew to Buenos Aires, Rio de Janeiro, and then on to New York.

Sir Victor's American acquaintances and the whirlwind of New York's financial scene became increasingly familiar parts of his charmed circle.

Global financial supremacy was shifting from London to New York. While there, Sassoon opened a branch office and met with National City Bank. He took in Broadway shows and clubbed at the Rainbow Room atop Rockefeller Center. *Fortune* magazine printed a lavish article on the "Shanghai Boom," describing it as the "cradle of the new China," with "the tallest buildings outside the American continent; the biggest hoard of silver in the world."[1] It featured Sir Victor as the kingpin behind the city's good fortune. By June, he was in London, then went on to Paris. He attended the Palais Royale with Aimée Lopes and dined at Maxim's. From there, his French coterie descended to Monte Carlo to enjoy the Riviera's indulgent party scene for the last time. In November 1938, Sassoon left London aboard the fabled *Normandie* ocean liner and returned to New York. The Atlantic crossing was loaded down with stage and screen celebrities. Sir Victor hobnobbed with Lawrence Olivier, Noël Coward, and Leslie Howard. The ship was met at the Brooklyn piers by a sleek white yacht to take the beautiful people into Manhattan. It was a whirlwind of a world tour.

"Almost every time a Japanese shell exploded, it took a little nick off the Sassoon fortune," a reporter for the *China Weekly Review* scribbled in 1938 as Sir Victor was preparing for his trip. "Almost every Chinese shell smacked into the Sassoon purse for pounds, shillings and pence."[2] Sassoon and other prominent Western businessmen who had ridden the waves of British colonial capitalism were transferring their millions out of Shanghai. The pathos and violence of the Japanese takeover and the city's misery were left behind by global entrepreneurs. They skirted the treacherous undertow of urban unrest. These mandarins had carved out a global economy of financial flows that made shifting assets remarkably easy. As early as 1936, Sassoon had merged his various currencies—rupees, yuan, sterling, and silver—into a trust known as the Victoria Holding Company. It allowed him to sell half his assets in India and China.[3] The fortune left plenty for enticing investments. He bought a huge block of lucrative Australian bonds and acquired controlling interest in the Société de Banque Parisienne. He shifted his fortune to the United States, with investments in technology start-ups and the manufacture of plastics and synthetic fibers. Sir Victor was preparing for the day when the capital exchanges and foreign trade that were his lifeline in Shanghai would be cut off completely. He had lost his bet on China. The only solution he could think of was to "withdraw every Britisher from China including civilians from Hong Kong."[4] The disheartening reality hit home when he began selling off his stable of racing ponies.

The Japanese negotiated carefully with Sassoon. They had collected plenty of intelligence on Shanghai's so-called Jewish *zaibatsu*, the powerful web of business interests in real estate, banking, and global trade that worked against Japanese policies in China. The espionage specifically targeted Victor Sassoon as the key figure and instigator of anti-Japanese maneuvers. He was the "white boss of Shanghai," and the Japanese knew it. When they attempted to increase their membership in the International Settlement's municipal council, an "unknown" individual with vast holdings manipulated the council's qualifications to increase British dominance. Sassoon was shattering the dream of a Japanese empire in China. One Japanese confidential report claimed to have exposed the anti-Japanese conspiracy headed by Sassoon's "Nanking Road headquarters . . . to exploit and exercise a financial stranglehold on China." Sassoon ran the *zaibatsu* in East Asia, the report went on, with its other headquarters on Prince Street in London and at the National City Bank in New York.[5]

The new bosses of Shanghai launched an enticing campaign to dissuade Sir Victor's anti-Japanese mindset or at least keep him neutral enough toward their occupation policies. Lunch and dinner parties with Japanese merchants and entrepreneurs became routine. Sassoon took tea at the Imperial Hotel with steel magnate Shibusawa Eiichi, who spearheaded the introduction of Western-style capitalism to Japan. He met with Tsutomu Nishiyama, the Japanese financial commissioner and board member of the Yokohama Specie Bank. Suspicions about these overtures circulated immediately. Sassoon's seeming acquiescence to Japanese occupation and boldface attempts to shield his assets fueled accusations of collaboration. A US newspaper slammed the war in China as nothing more than a bitter battle between the Mitsuis, the richest merchant family in Japan, and the Sassoons for trade domination. Sassoon traveled to Yokohama and Tokyo in March 1939 to lobby on behalf of British business. "And now Sir Victor has been trying slyly to cajole the Japanese financiers and business men," newspapers reported.[6] Officials from Japan's top banks and corporations redoubled their efforts to win his support. But he had few illusions about the Sino-Japanese conflict. He saw neither victory nor defeat for either side. He was increasingly stoic about the realities and predicted that once the war was over, "no man will be rich anymore. . . . I am quite reconciled to that situation myself."[7]

Victor Sassoon had profited handsomely from Bombay, London, and Shanghai in their glory years. As one of the era's leading global tycoons, he was involved in many of their achievements. His career captures the moment of the deep transition from an imperial economy to the contemporary practices of global business—from the gentlemanly capitalism associated with traditional merchant trade to modern forms of capital management. The attention paid to what Sir Victor said and did reveals a collective process of global capitalism and its impact on urban life. The economies of Bombay, London, and Shanghai were entangled in colonial enterprise. They were dominated by aggressive global businesses in the interwar years. These processes of globalization continued even during the economic slump of the 1930s. The three cities were mutually dependent places in a multiform global system rooted in colonial empire and yet increasingly entangled in world-spanning networks that made for shared constituency.

Cities were key to these globalizing processes. Observing the links between London, Shanghai, and Bombay provides us with multiple perspectives on both globalization and urbanization in the mid-twentieth century. Each city was at the leading edge, at the helm of the world in the last glory years of the British Empire. All three entered an interwar "golden age" at the nexus in the cultural, socioeconomic, and technological circuits that crisscrossed the globe. These were places of global power and colonial encounter. A myriad of interconnections existed between them — formal and informal, lawful and illicit. The exchange of peoples and goods set the chaotic rhythm of their urban life. The three cities were connected by a dense circuit of global business and finance. They were major hubs for labor migration and diaspora. They were crucibles of cultural and ideological transmission. London, of course, was the imperial capital of a vast empire. But more than just colonial peripheries, Bombay and Shanghai were economic powerhouses in their own right during the 1920s and 1930s. Global functions were deeply embedded in the urban tissue of each city. They were beacons of modernity. Their wealth and glamour flaunted all the showiness of the Roaring Twenties. Urban citizens saw their connection with people across the globe intensify — through the commonalities of city life, through politics, culture, sports. The salaried masses consumed stylish global fashions from luxury shops and department stores. Cabarets and nightclubs throbbed with the glitz and glamour the 1920s and even the 1930s were known for. This cosmopolitan ethos at myriad levels was a counterpart to globalization.

At the same time, the contradictions and inequalities of tradition, of colonial policy, and of globalization made each place a tinderbox of social conflict. The three cities were deeply cosmopolitan and inclusive but just as much places of exclusion. The practices of global capitalism were highly racialized and socially segregating. Incessant strikes and protests echoed through the streets. By the late 1930s, nationalist agendas were transforming the globalizing force of the British Empire, with all its benefits and drawbacks. The omen of war made things even more explosive.

The glory years slid into the horrid realities of the Second World War. The war fractured London's imperial authority and diminished its global role. Shanghai was cut off by the Communist Revolution while Bombay endured the throes of Indian independence. The backlash of nationalism and authoritarianism altered the cosmopolitan atmosphere that had infused so much of urban life.

These gyrations make clear that globalization has a history. The interwar years are most often known for cultural glitz, for political and economic instability, and ultimately for the Great Depression. This book argues that despite the political volatility and economic crises, globalization was in full swing in the interwar decades. The circulation of money, trade, people, and information was higher than ever before. It was a period of increasing internationalization and worldwide exchange. Millions of people were on the move. Multinational corporations, banking, and financialization all expanded their global reach. Then the junctures and disjunctures of the Second World War altered these interchanges. The world-spanning trade and finance that had been so vital to urban development were siphoned off by the ferocious hostilities. The networks that had fused global geography were shape-shifted by mass conflict, the flight of peoples, and the overwhelming forces of wartime resource allocation. Postwar reconstruction, the Bretton Woods institutions, and the liberalization of trade added further to the dynamic processes of globalization. These ebbs and flows were altered yet again by the neoliberal economic order of the late twentieth century. Yet the cities that gained global status as the twenty-first century appeared on the horizon shared much with interwar Bombay, London, and Shanghai. They were marked by massive wealth accumulations, obsessive quests for status and high-end luxury consumption, and an information revolution, along with growing inequalities and deprivation as well as precarious systems of financialization and commercial exchange.

Sassoon faithfully continued brief sojourns in Bombay to visit his racing stable and his catalog of friends and acquaintances. But he increasingly became a foreigner in a city that had been as much built by his family as anyone else. By the late 1930s, the approaching war clouds had reengaged him with Bombay. In the press, Sassoon hammered on India to join the effort to win the war and defeat the Nazis: "Every Indian must realise that this country can avoid being a slave nation only if we beat Hitler."[8] In an interview with the Associated Press in early 1942, Sassoon called for power to be handed over to the viceroy, who would declare a national emergency and rule India as a temporary dictator. The disapproving response from India's government was expected. Sir Victor's views "were not helpful."

"God save the British from such friends," one official retorted. The loss of Shanghai and Hong Kong has "shattered Sir Victor Sassoon's nerves." One response accused him of becoming frantic now that his vast possessions were in Japanese hands. He was "flitting from one country to another with his money bags."[9]

Sassoon was branded a "war monger" by US politicians anxious to stay out of the wartime debacle,[10] and he was accused of making money off all sides in his currency trading. He pushed for British and American economic collaboration in a flood of press interviews, "rambling on and on. . . . If his object is to bewilder by his rapid flow of words," a journalist retorted, "he accomplished his goal." There was little evidence that Sassoon influenced American public opinion. But that did little to stop him. Addressing the Advertising Club in New York, he claimed that Japan did not want war with the United States, and "they wouldn't have a chance and they know it." It would be sheer suicide.[11] At a luncheon for motion picture executives in Hollywood, he called for a federal alliance between Britain and the United States. It would be the ultimate democracy of the future and would preserve world peace.[12] Sir Victor's hopes for the merging of Britain, Australia, the United States, and Canada in a world federation met with scathing criticism in London. Conservatives raised hues and cries of "nonsense" and "shame" in the House of Commons. But Prime Minister Winston Churchill hedged his bets amid the uproar. He was himself pressuring for an Anglo-American entente.

Sir Victor was on the high seas when the Japanese attacked Pearl Harbor on December 7, 1941. From Singapore, the American vessel had made the coast of Borneo with flags flying, its lights ablaze. It was blissfully unaware that the United States was now at war. Japanese radio reported the ship sunk. But it made port and began defensive preparations. For safety, the voyage was forced off course in a circuitous journey around the world. In his diary, Sassoon noted passing the wreckage of torpedoed ships along with incoming reports of the war at sea.[13] "So the ten thousand pro-German-war men in Japan have dragged the millions of their compatriots to certain destruction," he reflected.[14] The die had been cast. Finally reaching New York, Sassoon was peppered with questions by reporters about his fabled wealth. "If China goes I'll be way down," he joked. "If India goes, I shall be around asking for a job."[15] But he was far too high profile for US federal agents to take any chances that he might be picked off by Japanese gunmen. Despite his protests, Sassoon was given an FBI security detachment in New York.

The news of the communist takeover of Shanghai reached him while he was in his office in New York. "Well there it is," he famously quipped.

"I gave up India and China gave me up." The Japanese took over all foreign banks in Shanghai and emptied their vaults. Lucien Ovadia, his cousin and partner in Sir Victor's trust companies, had been left behind to manage the Sassoon properties and attempt to unload them. He was kept under house arrest in Grosvenor House, where local officials demanded absurdly high taxes on the properties to milk Sassoon dry. Finally, Ovadia was given forty-eight hours to leave the country while the state took over what was left of Sassoon's Shanghai real estate empire without any compensation. Harry Arnhold was interned by the Japanese for the duration of the war. A number of the Sassoon employees were accused of being spies and sent to prison. Some escaped to Hong Kong, while others collaborated with the communists and went about their business. The Sassoon textile mills in Bombay worked triple shifts during the war with over forty thousand workers. They were eventually closed or sold off at the war's end. During the war years, Victor Sassoon divided his time between Bombay at the Taj Mahal and London at the Ritz, seeing to his companies. Even with the devastating losses in Shanghai, he was still worth millions. He eventually withdrew to the Bahamas, where he continued his passion for horse racing.

Acknowledgments

This book is a product of the Covid pandemic. Writing it kept me sane during the long weeks and months of confinement in a small apartment in Midtown Manhattan, a place emptied of its normal crowds, noise, and exasperating hubbub, all of which I sorely missed as soon as they were gone. Sitting quietly while writing about other places on the globe in other times was a saving grace. Luckily, as it turns out, I was able to complete archival research for the project just before the lockdown began.

Producing a book about three cities in distinct parts of the world requires substantial support. That came from a Fulbright Global Scholar Grant in 2019–2020, which allowed me to carry out research in Mumbai, Shanghai, and London. In each place, I was privileged to work with scholars at distinguished urban institutions. My sincere thanks to the School of Media and Cultural Studies at the Tata Institute of Social Sciences in Mumbai; to the History Department at the University of London's Birkbeck College and the Centre for Urban History at the University of Leicester; and to the College of Architecture and Urban Planning at Tongji University in Shanghai for their sponsorship. Taking part in seminars, discussions with colleagues, and presentations on this project allowed me to flesh out ideas and understand the global relationships I was seeking in each of the cities. My sincere thanks to K. P. Jayasankar at the Tata Institute, Jerry White at Birkbeck, Simon Gunn at the University of Leicester, and Yingchun Li and Placido Gonzalez Martinez at Tongji University for their support for this project and for sharing their insightful advice and extraordinary knowledge of urban history. In particular, the invitation as guest editor for a special issue on Shanghai for Tongji University's *Built Heritage* journal was the opportunity to meet the most influential scholars of that city and to profit immensely from their knowledge and expertise.

I was also fortunate to receive support from Fordham University in the form of faculty fellowships and the History Department's O'Connell Initiative in the Global History of Capitalism. Funding from Fordham's Office of Research was essential to developing the project at its early stages. The O'Connell Initiative grant allowed me to carry out research at the Victor Sassoon Archives held in the DeGolyer Library at Southern Methodist University in Dallas.

A host of archives provided the evidence for this book. The venerable Royal Asiatic Society, founded in 1823 for the colonial study of science, literature, and the arts in Asia, was a gold mine of materials not only in London but at its satellite organizations in Mumbai and Shanghai. Its libraries are housed in some of the most iconic buildings in these cities. It was a pleasure to spend time among the society's extraordinary collections in the old Town Hall at Mumbai's Horniman Circle, the House of Roosevelt on the Bund in Shanghai, and the library on Stephenson Way in London. The British Library Archives hold a treasure trove of materials on all three cities. Time spent in its Asian and African Studies Reading Room is this historian's idea of research paradise. Similar time at the University of London's SOAS Library (School of Oriental and African Studies) provided the opportunity to mine its outstanding resources on India and China. Collections at the London Metropolitan Archives (especially the E. D. Sassoon archives) and at the Museum of London Docklands were a bedrock for this project, as was the Bhau Daji Lad Mumbai City Museum in Mumbai. In Shanghai, collections at the Shanghai Municipal Library and the archive materials of the Fairmont Peace Hotel provided essential materials. A host of other, shorter archival soundings also provided resources, for example the Archives at Girton College, Cambridge, the RIBA Drawings and Archives Collections, and the Maharashtra State Archives. Poring over Victor Sassoon's diaries, struggling to decipher his tiny, scribbly handwriting, and identifying the people in his photos were the cost for doing this project. Luckily, the expert archivists at the Victor Sassoon Archives at the DeGolyer Library guided me through this thicket of materials. Portions of his diaries have now been digitized. Lastly, and as always, the New York Public Library's Stephen A. Schwarzman Building has been my home research base for as long as I can remember. Its research collections and support were vital to the research on all three cities and the processes of global exchange that lie at the heart of this study.

Historians can now readily access a plethora of online archival materials without traveling to distant locations. For this project, the British Newspaper Archive and ProQuest Historical Newspapers were essential resources. The Asiatic Society of Mumbai's Granth Sanjeevani project and the Virtual Shanghai platform have digitized an abundance of archival materials central to this book. The National Archives of India Abhilekh

PATAL digital portal, the Parliament of India Lok Sabha Digital Library, and Art Deco Mumbai online databases provided access to resources on Bombay. Digitized archival sources are now also available on the government of India's Indian Culture website. Bristol Archives, British Empire and Commonwealth Collection and the Hong Kong Public Libraries' Old HK Newspapers database supplied other materials. Lastly, but just as importantly, the Internet Archive and the many film and photographic online collections offered vital primary written and visual texts on Bombay, Shanghai, and London.

Pulling a biographical thread through the histories of Bombay, London, and Shanghai was a new challenge. I have the greatest respect for authors who work in this genre. Following the trail of Victor Sassoon brought me to unexpected places. It meant traipsing through what is left of the Sassoon mills in Girangaon, which are now part of Mumbai's "intangible heritage." Sensing the atmosphere of Sassoon's Bombay meant taking tea in the Sea Lounge at the Taj Mahal Hotel where he held court and a day at the races at Mahalaxmi. Locating the E. D. Sassoon Building in Ballard Estate brought me to the Alexandra Dock and the old Café Britannia, one of the few Parsi eateries left in Mumbai. Luckily, I also fell upon Hamilton Studios at the E. D. Sassoon Building. This incomparable photography shop was opened by Victor Sassoon, who was a lifelong shutterbug, and run by Ranjit Madhavji. It is now managed by his daughter Ajita Madhavji. The studio's archive of glass-plate negatives captured the city's elite in all their glory and is now part of the British Library's Endangered Archives project.

The tour of Sassoon's buildings in Shanghai was a step into the city's art deco past. My thanks to colleagues Li Hou and Yingchun Li for treating me to dinner at the Dragon Phoenix Restaurant atop Sassoon's Cathay Hotel. Tracing the outline of the Shanghai Race Club meant walking today's People's Square and the Shanghai Art Museum. Sassoon's London home at Grosvenor Place near Buckingham Palace has been demolished. Only a few photographs of its sumptuous interior remain. The building on Gracechurch Street in London's City where the E. D. Sassoon Bank was located has been razed and the site redeveloped as a mixed-use office complex and swank public courtyard. The building that housed the E. D. Sassoon & Company offices on Fenchurch Street also fell to the wrecking ball and is now the site of the "Walkie-Talkie" glass office tower that won the dreaded Carbuncle Cup as the ugliest building of the year in 2015.

Discussions with colleagues are the foundation for historical research and writing. My genuine thanks to the many scholars who offered ideas and suggestions with such generosity during the gestation of this book.

They include Dorothee Brantz of the Center for Metropolitan Studies Program at Technische Universität Berlin, Edward Denison of the Bartlett School of Architecture at University College London, James Farrer of Sophia University in Tokyo, Andrew Field in Shanghai, Mark Frazier of the New School for Social Research in New York, Li Hou of Tongji University, Alistair Kefford at Leicester, Julia Lovell at Birkbeck, Abigail McGowan of the University of Vermont, Sujata Patel of the Indian Institute of Advanced Study, Gabor Sonkoly of Eötvös Loránd University Budapest, Chandak Sengoopta at Birkbeck, and Florian Urban of the Glasgow School of Art. Discussions with members of the Global Urban History Project, especially Carl Nightingale, Alexia Yates, and the Urban Theory group, provided critical insights into the processes of globalization and the impact on cities.

My sincere thanks as always to colleagues and students at Fordham University. The Interlibrary Loan staff at the university library, especially Charlotte Labbé, works miracles in finding material, in this case crumbling hard copy of the elusive *Finance & Commerce* newspaper published in Shanghai. Lastly, Dylan Montanari, Fabiola Enríquez, and Mary Al-Sayed at the University of Chicago Press made this book happen. All my thanks to them for seeing it through.

Notes

Introduction

1. Population data from Tertius Chandler, *Four Thousand Years of Urban Growth, an Historical Census* (New York: St. David's University Press, 1987), 534. Phrase from Tim Harper, *Underground Asia: Global Revolutionaries and the Assault on Empire* (Cambridge, MA: Belknap Press of Harvard University Press, 2021), 65. An overview of cities and urban culture from a global perspective is given in chap. 1, "'30s Modern," in *The Global 1930s: The International Decade*, by Marc Matera and Susan Kingsley Kent (London: Routledge, 2017).

2. See the excellent analysis in Simon J. Potter and Jonathan Saha, "Global History, Imperial History and Connected Histories of Empire," *Journal of Colonialism and Colonial History* 16, no. 1 (2015), https://doi.org/10.1353/cch.2015.0009. Potter and Saha cite Lynn Hunt on "globalization from below" in Lynn Hunt, *Writing History in the Global Era* (New York: W. W. Norton, 2014), 59.

3. The scholarship on global cities is voluminous. For a recent review of the field and the interpretative debates, see Ugo Rossi, *Cities in Global Capitalism* (Cambridge: Polity Press, 2017), as well as Xuefei Ren and Roger Keil, eds., *The Globalizing Cities Reader*, 2nd ed. (Abingdon, UK: Routledge, 2018). A study of the global cities of Shanghai and Mumbai in comparative context is Klaus Segbers, ed., *The Making of Global City Regions: Johannesburg, Mumbai/Bombay, São Paulo, and Shanghai* (Baltimore: Johns Hopkins University Press, 2007).

4. World exports grew by about 80 percent from 1921 to 1929, which made up for the disastrous war years. The volume of seaborne trade increased by over 50 percent in the 1920s before declining during the Great Depression. After the worst years from 1929 to 1932, it climbed again by 80 percent. M. Stopford, *Maritime Economics* (London, 1997), as quoted in John Darwin, *Unlocking the World: Port Cities and Globalization in the Age of Steam, 1830–1930* (London: Allen Lane, 2020), 335.

5. Giovanni Arrighi, *The Long Twentieth Century: Money, Power, and the Origins of Our Times* (London: Verso, 1994), 229–30.

6. Daniel Gorman, *The Emergence of International Society in the 1920s* (Cambridge: Cambridge University Press, 2012), 2.

7. Jeffrey N. Wasserstrom, *Global Shanghai, 1850–2010: A History in Fragments* (London: Routledge, 2009), 20; Andrew B. Liu, *Tea War: A History of Capitalism in China and India* (New Haven, CT: Yale University Press, 2020), 4. Also useful is Michael D. Bordo, Alan M. Taylor, and Jeffrey G. Williamson, eds., *Globalization in Historical Perspective* (Chicago: University of Chicago Press, 2003).

8. Edward Ross Dickinson, *The World in the Long Twentieth Century: An Interpretive History* (Berkeley: University of California Press, 2018), 42.

9. This term is used by Tani Barlow, "Debates over Colonial Modernity in East Asia and Another Alternative," *Cultural Studies* 26, no. 5 (2012): 622. See also the broader historical arguments in Sanjay Subrahmanyam, *Connected History: Essays and Arguments* (London: Verso Books, 2022).

10. See in particular Matthias Middell and Katja Naumann, "Global History and the Spatial Turn: From the Impact of Area Studies to the Study of Critical Junctures of Globalization," *Journal of Global History* 5, no. 1 (2010): 149–70.

11. The most recent study of the Sassoons (by a member of the family) is Joseph Sassoon, *The Sassoons: The Great Global Merchants and the Making of an Empire* (New York: Pantheon, 2022). The definitive Sassoon family biography is Stanley Jackson, *The Sassoons* (London: Heinemann, 1968). Also important is the earlier Cecil Roth, *The Sassoon Dynasty* (London: R. Hale, 1941). An earlier description is given by Ernest O. Hauser, "The Fabulous Sassoons," *American Mercury* (January 1940), 60–67.

12. Excellent sources on twentieth-century Bombay are Gyan Prakash, *Mumbai Fables* (Princeton, NJ: Princeton University Press, 2010), and Prashant Kidambi, Manjiri Kamat, and Rachel Dwyer, eds., *Bombay before Mumbai: Essays in Honour of Jim Masselos* (New York: Oxford University Press, 2019). See also the older volume by Sujata Patel and Alice Thorner, eds., *Bombay, Metaphor for Modern India* (New Delhi: Oxford University Press, 1995), as well as Gillian Tindall, *City of God: The Biography of Bombay* (Gurgaon, India: Penguin Random House India, 1992), and Sharada Dwivedi and Rahul Mehrotra, *Bombay: The Cities Within* (Bombay: India Book House, 2001).

13. On Shanghai's built form, see Cole Roskam, *Improvised City: Architecture and Governance in Shanghai, 1843–1937* (Seattle: University of Washington Press, 2019), as well as Edward Denison and Guang Yu Ren, *Building Shanghai: The Story of China's Gateway* (Chichester, UK: John Wiley, 2006). See also Christian Henriot, *Shanghai, 1927–1937: Municipal Power, Locality, and Modernization* (Berkeley: University of California Press, 1993), and Isabella Jackson, *Shaping Modern Shanghai: Colonialism in China's Global City* (Cambridge: Cambridge University Press, 2017). On Shanghai's Jazz Age, see Andrew David Field, *Shanghai's Dancing World: Cabaret Culture and Urban Politics, 1919–1954* (Hong Kong: Chinese University of Hong Kong, 2010), as well as Harriet Sergeant, *Shanghai: Collision Point of Cultures, 1918–1939* (New York: Crown, 1990); Leo Ou-fan Lee, *Shanghai Modern: The Flowering of a New Urban Culture in China 1930–1945* (Cambridge, MA: Harvard University Press, 1999); and Marie-Claire Bergère, *Shanghai: China's Gateway to Modernity* (Stanford, CA: Stanford University Press, 2009). See also the excellent Robert A. Bickers, *Empire Made Me: An Englishman Adrift in Shanghai* (New York: Columbia University Press, 2003).

14. The most comprehensive study of twentieth-century London is Jerry White, *London in the Twentieth Century* (London: Bodley Head, 2001). See also Roy Porter, *London: A Social History* (Cambridge, MA: Harvard University Press, 1995); Mara Arts, *Interwar London after Dark in British Popular Culture* (Cham, Switzerland: Palgrave Macmillan, 2022); and Lindsey German and John Rees, *A People's History of London* (London: Verso, 2012). More narrowly focused are Marc Matera, *Black London: The Imperial Metropolis and Decolonization in the Twentieth Century* (Berkeley: University of California Press, 2015), and Judith Walkowitz, *Nights Out in Cosmopolitan London* (New Haven, CT: Yale University Press, 2012).

15. Excellent examples of urban history from a global perspective are Andrew Lees, *The City: A World History* (Oxford: Oxford University Press, 2015), and A. K. Sandoval-Strausz and Nancy H. Kwak, eds., *Making Cities Global: The Transnational Turn in Urban History* (Philadelphia: University of Pennsylvania Press, 2018). Also see the wide-ranging Carl H. Nightingale, *Earthopolis: A Biography of Our Urban Planet* (Cambridge: Cambridge University Press, 2022). Shane Ewen, *What Is Urban History* (Cambridge: Polity Press, 2015), is an insightful examination of the field. The Cambridge Elements in Global Urban History series offers outstanding analysis by leading scholars: https://www.cambridge.org/core/publications/elements/global-urban-history.

16. See the migration figures and debates on interwar global migration in Adam M. McKeown, "Global Migration, 1846–1940," *Journal of World History* 15, no. 2 (2004), esp. pp. 172–77, as well as his "A World Made Many: Integration and Segregation in Global Migration, 1840–1940," in *Connecting Seas and Connected Ocean Rims: Indian, Atlantic, and Pacific Oceans and China Seas Migrations from the 1830s to the 1930s*, ed. Donna R. Gabaccia and Dirk Hoerder (Leiden: Brill, 2011), 46.

17. See the work of Michael Peter Smith, most recently in the collection by Adrian Favell and Michael Peter Smith, eds., *The Human Face of Global Mobility* (New York: Routledge, 2006).

18. On the urban role of ports, see Lasse Heerten, "Mooring Mobilities, Fixing Flows: Towards a Global Urban History of Port Cities in the Age of Steam," *Journal of Historical Sociology* 34, no. 2 (2021): 350–74, as well as the outstanding analysis by Su Lin Lewis, *Cities in Motion: Urban Life and Cosmopolitanism in Southeast Asia, 1920–1940* (Cambridge: Cambridge University Press, 2016), 58.

19. David Harvey, "The Right to the City," *New Left Review* 53 (September/October 2008): 25–26.

20. Malcolm Muggeridge, *The Thirties: 1930 1940 in Great Britain* (London: Hamish Hamilton, 1940), 8.

21. An excellent source on business culture is chap. 5, "Culture," in *Europe and the Maritime World: A Twentieth Century History*, by Michael B. Miller (New York: Cambridge University Press, 2012). See also Gary Magee and Andrew Thompson, *Empire and Globalisation: Networks of People, Goods and Capital in the British World, c. 1850–1914* (Cambridge: Cambridge University Press, 2010).

22. See Siegfried Kracauer, *The Salaried Masses: Duty and Distraction in Weimar Germany*, trans. Quintin Hoare (London: Verso, 1998), esp. the chapter "Unknown Territory."

23. Lewis, *Cities in Motion*, 12–13.

24. Emily S. Rosenberg, ed., *A World Connecting, 1870–1945* (Cambridge, MA: Belknap Press of Harvard University Press, 2012), 3–4.

25. Harry J. Greenwall, "Shanghai—City of Paradox," *Sphere* (London), 28 August 1937.

26. Ananya Roy and Aihwa Ong, eds., *Worlding Cities: Asian Experiments and the Art of Being Global* (Chichester, UK: Wiley-Blackwell, 2011), 3.

27. Among the best studies of social and political conflict in Shanghai and Bombay is Mark W. Frazier, *The Power of Place: Contentious Politics in Twentieth-Century Shanghai and Bombay* (Cambridge: Cambridge University Press, 2019). Another excellent resource is Anindita Ghosh, *Claiming the City: Protest, Crime, and Scandals in Colonial Calcutta, c. 1860–1920* (New Delhi: Oxford University Press, 2016). See

also Sandip Hazareesingh, *The Colonial City and the Challenge of Modernity: Urban Hegemonies and Civic Contestation in Bombay City, 1900–1925* (Hyderabad: Orient Longman, 2007).

28. Richard Harris, *How Cities Matter*, Cambridge Elements in Global Urban History, ed. Michael Goebel, Tracy Neumann, and Joseph Ben Prestel (Cambridge: Cambridge University Press, 2021), 15–16. See also, in the same Cambridge series, Alexia Yates, *Real Estate and Global Urban History* (Cambridge: Cambridge University Press, 2021).

Chapter 1

1. Jean Cocteau, *My Journey round the World*, trans. W. J. Strachan (London: Peter Owen, 1958), 132.

2. Cocteau, 142.

3. Newspaper clipping, no newspaper title, article author, or date, Victor Sassoon Diary, 3 June 1936; Sir Ellice Victor Elias Sassoon Papers and Photographs, series 1: Diaries and Correspondence, DeGolyer Library, Southern Methodist University, Dallas.

4. *Straits Times* (Singapore), 24 October 1937.

5. G. E. Miller [pseud.], *Shanghai, the Paradise of Adventurers* (New York: Orsay, 1937), 60.

6. Ken Cuthbertson interview with Emily Hahn as recounted in Ken Cuthbertson, *Nobody Said Not to Go: The Life, Loves, and Adventures of Emily Hahn* (Boston: Faber and Faber, 1998), 135. Rothschild quote recounted in Harriet Sergeant, *Shanghai* (London: John Murray, 1991), 132.

7. Pan Ling, *In Search of Old Shanghai* (Hong Kong: Joint Publishing, 1982), 44.

8. Cocteau, *Journey round the World*, 142.

9. Walter J. Fischel, "Bombay in Jewish History in the Light of New Documents from the Indian Archives," *Proceedings of the American Academy for Jewish Research* 38/39 (1970–1971): 132.

10. See Sunil S. Amrith, *Crossing the Bay of Bengal: The Furies of Nature and the Fortunes of Migrants* (Cambridge, MA: Harvard University Press, 2015). Also useful in relation to Bombay are Nile Green, *Bombay Islam: The Religious Economy of the West Indian Ocean, 1840–1915* (Cambridge: Cambridge University Press, 2011); A. Alpers and Chhaya Goswami, *Transnational Trade and Traders: Situating Gujarat in the Indian Ocean from Early Times to 1900* (New Delhi: Oxford University Press, 2019); and Thomas R. Metcalf, *Imperial Connections: India in The Indian Ocean Arena, 1860–1920* (Berkeley: University of California Press, 2008). See also the classic study by Janet L. Abu-Lughod, *Before European Hegemony: The World System A.D. 1250–1350* (New York: Oxford University Press, 1991).

11. Among the histories of the opium trade, see Hunt Janin, *The India-China Opium Trade in the Nineteenth Century* (Jefferson, NC: McFarland, 2014), as well as Timothy Brook and Bob Tadashi Wakabayashi, eds., *Opium Regimes: China, Britain, and Japan, 1839–1952* (Berkeley: University of California Press, 2000), and Mary L. Kienholz, *Opium Traders and Their Worlds*, vol. 2, *A Revisionist Exposé of the World's Greatest Opium Traders* (Bloomington, IN: iUniverse, 2008).

12. On Bombay's merchant families, see Lakshmi Subramanian, *Three Merchants of Bombay: Pioneers of the Nineteenth Century* (New York: Penguin, 2016). See also John R. Hinnells and Alan Williams, eds., *Parsis in India and the Diaspora* (Abingdon,

UK: Routledge, 2008), and T. M. Luhrmann, *The Good Parsi: The Fate of a Colonial Elite in a Postcolonial Society* (Cambridge, MA: Harvard University Press, 1996). Finally, on the Parsi community in Bombay, see Christine E. Dobbin, *Asian Entrepreneurial Minorities: Conjoint Communities in the Making of the World-Economy 1570–1940* (London: RoutledgeCurzon, an imprint of Taylor and Francis Group, 1996), 77–103.

13. On the early history of Shanghai, see Toby Lincoln, *An Urban History of China* (Cambridge: Cambridge University Press, 2021), 141–44, as well as Denison and Ren, *Building Shanghai*, chap. 1.

14. Betty Peh-T'i Wei, *Old Shanghai* (New York: Oxford University Press, 1993), 12–13.

15. Christian Henriot, Lu Shi, and Charlotte Aubrun, *The Population of Shanghai (1865–1953): A Sourcebook* (Leiden: Brill, 2019), 13. See also Robert F. C. A. Nield, *China's Foreign Places: The Foreign Presence in China in the Treaty Port Era, 1840–1943* (Hong Kong: Hong Kong University Press, 2015), 200–208.

16. See Claude Markovits, "Bombay as a Business Centre in the Colonial Period: A Comparison with Calcutta," in Patel and Thorner, *Bombay, Metaphor*, 41–42.

17. For an excellent analysis of the shift from opium to cotton and the role of the Sassoons in the India-China trade, see Chen Zhilong, "Shanghai: A Window for Studying Sino-Indian Relations in the Era of Colonialism and Imperialism," in *India and China in the Colonial World*, ed. Madhavi Thampi (Abingdon, UK: Routledge, 2017), 33–51.

18. Sven Beckert, *Empire of Cotton: A Global History* (New York: Vintage, 2014), 256.

19. For an excellent history of silver in the global commodity market, see Jürgen Osterhammel, *The Transformation of the World: A Global History of the Nineteenth Century*, trans. Patrick Camiller (Princeton, NJ: Princeton University Press, 2015), 731–33; quotation is from p. 732.

20. Fernand Braudel, *The Perspective of the World*, trans. Siân Reynolds, vol. 3 of *Civilization and Capitalism, 15th–18th Century* (New York: Harper and Row, 1984), 66.

21. John Smith, "Hong Kong: A Study in British Far-Eastern Diplomacy," *Foreign Affairs* (June 1926): 361. On the history of the Hong Kong & Shanghai Bank, see Zhaojin Ji, *A History of Modern Shanghai Banking: The Rise and Decline of China's Finance Capitalism* (Armonk, NY: M. E. Sharpe, 2003), 45–50. On monetary fragmentation in China and the role of the Western banks, see Niv Horesh, *Shanghai's Bund and Beyond: British Banks, Banknotes Issuance, and Monetary Policy in China, 1842–1937* (New Haven, CT: Yale University Press, 2009), 24–30.

22. Osterhammel, *Transformation of the World*, 737.

23. Gregory Clark and Robert C. Feenstra, "Technology in the Great Divergence," in Bordo, Taylor, and Williamson, *Globalization in Historical Perspective*, 295.

24. Lincoln, *Urban History of China*, 141.

25. "Ducks" referred to a strong-smelling dried fish.

26. The Sephardic Jewish community favored English over local languages and readily adapted to anglicized circles. Sarah Abrevaya Stein, "Protected Persons? The Baghdadi Jewish Diaspora, the British State, and the Persistence of Empire," *American Historical Review* 116, no. 1 (2011): 91. See also Joan G. Roland, *The Jewish Communities of India: Identity in the Colonial Era*, 2nd ed. (New Brunswick, NJ: Transaction, 1998).

27. On this point, see Rajnarayan Chandavarkar, *The Origins of Industrial Capitalism in India: Business Strategies and the Working Classes in Bombay, 1900–1940* (Cambridge: Cambridge University Press, 1994), 242.

28. Karl Polanyi, *The Great Transformation: The Political and Economic Origins of Our Time*, 2nd ed. (Boston: Beacon Press, 2001), 11.

29. A. S. J. Baster, *The Imperial Banks* (London: P. S. King and Son, 1929), 120. See also Magee and Thompson, *Empire and Globalisation*, 198–200.

30. Christine E. Dobbin, *Urban Leadership in Western India: Politics and Communities in Bombay City, 1840–1885* (London: RoutledgeCurzon, an imprint of Taylor Francis Group, 1996), 158.

31. Sidney Low, *A Vision of India* (New York: E. P. Dutton; London: Smith, Elder, 1907), 9.

32. A. B., *Old and New Bombay: An Historical and Descriptive Account of Bombay and Its Environs* (Bombay: G. Claridge, 1911), 56; Walter Crane, *India Impressions, with Some Notes of Ceylon during a Winter Tour, 1906–7* (New York: Macmillan, 1907), 25.

33. See Homi Bhabha, "Of Mimicry and Man: The Ambivalence of Colonial Discourse," *October* 28 (Spring 1984): 127.

34. For a definitive analysis of imperial London, see Jonathan Schneer, *London 1900: The Imperial Metropolis* (New Haven, CT: Yale University Press, 1999).

35. George R. Sims, ed., *Living London: Its Work and Its Play, Its Humour and Its Pathos, Its Sights and Its Scenes* (London: Cassell, 1902-03), 1:6. For a general history of Edwardian London, see Simon Heffer, *The Age of Decadence: A History of Britain; 1880–1914* (New York: Pegasus, 2021), and Felix Barker, *Edwardian London* (London: L. King, 1995).

36. Zhilong, "Shanghai," 42.

37. Quoted in Stanley D. Chapman, *The Rise of Merchant Banking* (London: Routledge, 2006), 131.

38. Jackson, *The Sassoons*, 138.

39. Good recent sources on this Jewish merchant network in China are S. R. Goldstein-Sabbah, *Baghdadi Jewish Networks in the Age of Nationalism* (Leiden: Brill, 2021), and Jonathan K. Kaufman, *The Last Kings of Shanghai: The Rival Jewish Dynasties That Helped Create Modern China* (London: Penguin Books, 2021).

40. *Aeronautics*, 15 June 1915.

41. "The Wheel and the Wing," *Sketch* (London), 26 April 1916.

42. Victor Sassoon's biography and plane crash are described in detail along with photos in Jackson, *The Sassoons*, 210–16.

43. *Pioneer Mail and India Weekly News* (Allahabad) 47 (19 November 1920), 18.

44. Jackson, *The Sassoons*, 204.

Chapter 2

1. On the First World War, see Sarah Ansari, "The Bombay Presidency's 'Home Front,' 1914–1918," in *India and World War I: A Centennial Assessment*, ed. Roger D. Long and Ian Talbot (Abingdon, UK: Routledge, 2018), 60–78.

2. Sir Stanley Reed, *The India I Knew, 1897–1947* (London: Odhams Press, 1952), 100.

3. C. W. Cursetjee, *The Land of the Date* (Bombay: Dhanjibhoy Dosabhoy, 1918), 4, and Edwin S. Montagu, *An Indian Diary* (London: William Heinemann, 1930), 2. For descriptions of Bombay in 1919, see Indian Science Congress, *Bombay Past and Present: A Souvenir of the Sixth Meeting of the Indian Science Congress Held in Bombay*

in January 1919 (Bombay: Times Press, 1919). For British perceptions of Bombay ethnography, see Stephen Meredyth Edwardes, *By-Ways of Bombay* (Bombay: Times of India Office, 1912), esp. chap. 12, "Citizens of Bombay," as well as Percival Strip and Olivia Strip, *The Peoples of Bombay* (Bombay: Thacker, 1944).

4. Harry James Greenwall, *Storm over India* (London: Hurst and Blackett, 1933), 28–29.

5. S. M. Rutnagur, *Bombay Industries; the Cotton Mills; a Review of the Progress of the Textile Industry in Bombay from 1850 to 1926 and the Present Constitution, Management and Financial Position of the Spinning and Weaving Factories* (Bombay: Indian Textiles Journal, 1927), 188.

6. Victor Trench, *Lord Willingdon in India* (Bombay: Karnatak, 1934), 62–63.

7. Rutnagur, *Bombay Industries; the Cotton Mills*, 55; Harold James, "Finance Capitalism," in *Capitalism: The Reemergence of a Historical Concept*, ed. Jürgen Kocka and Marcel Van der Linden (London: Bloomsbury Academic, 2016), 139.

8. Robert S. Baker and James Sexton, eds., *Aldous Huxley: Complete Essays*, vol. 2, *1926–1929* (Chicago: Ivan R. Dee, 2000), 410–11.

9. Charles Trevelyan and Humphrey Trevelyan, *The India We Left: Charles Trevelyan, 1826–65, Humphrey Trevelyan, 1929–47* (London: Macmillan, 1972), 108. On the institution of the club, see David Gilmour, *The British in India: A Social History of the Raj* (New York: Farrar, Straus and Giroux, 2018), 394–97.

10. Vivian Stevenson-Hamilton, *Yes, Your Excellency* (London: Harmsworth, 1985), 41–42.

11. *Times of India* (Bombay), 29 November 1928. For engaging descriptions of club life, see Dennis Kincaid, *British Social Life in India, 1608–1937* (London: Routledge, 1938), 278–85. Also see Mrinalini Sinha, "Britishness, Clubbability, and the Colonial Public Sphere: The Genealogy of an Imperial Institution in Colonial India," *Journal of British Studies* 40, no. 4 (October 2001): 489–521.

12. Louis Bromfield, *Night in Bombay* (New York: Grosset and Dunlap, 1939), 79.

13. O. U. Krishnan, *The Night Side of Bombay* (Bombay: Krishnan, 1923), 1.

14. Bakhtiar K. Dadabhoy, *Barons of Banking: Glimpses of Indian Banking History* (Haryana, India: Penguin Random House India, 2013), 121; *London Times*, 6 November 1925.

15. Mike Huggins, *Horseracing and the British, 1919–39* (Manchester: Manchester University Press, 2003), 1–6.

16. "The Outstanding Thoroughbreds of 1927," *Illustrated Sporting and Dramatic News*, 11 February 1928; "Winners by Their Beautiful Heads," *Sketch* (London), 9 May 1934; cover illustration, *Bystander* (London), 6 July 1927.

17. *Times of India* (Bombay), 23 July 1925.

18. Kincaid, *British Social Life in India*, 285.

19. *Times of India* (Bombay), 12 and 13 March 1925.

20. Labor statistics from A. R. Burnett-Hurst, *Labour and Housing in Bombay: A Study in the Economic Conditions of the Wage-Earning Classes in Bombay* (London: P. S. King, 1925), 3–6. See also Dick Kooiman, *Bombay Textile Labour: Managers, Trade Unionists and Officials, 1918–1939* (Amsterdam: Free University Press, 1989).

21. See Sheetal Chhabria, *Making the Modern Slum: The Power of Capital in Colonial Bombay* (Seattle: University of Washington Press, 2019), and Prashant Kidambi, *The Making of an Indian Metropolis: Colonial Governance and Public Culture in*

Bombay, 1890–1920 (London: Routledge, 2007). See also Preeti Chopra, *A Joint Enterprise: Indian Elites and the Making of British Bombay* (Minneapolis: University of Minnesota Press, 2011).

22. Sir Frederick Sykes, *From Many Angles: An Autobiography* (London: George G. Harrap, 1942), 359.

23. Margaret Read, *The Indian Peasant Uprooted: A Study of the Human Machine* (London: Longmans, Green, 1931), 1. Also see the excellent study of Bombay's social and ethnographic fabric by Meera Kosambi, *Bombay in Transition: The Growth and Social Ecology of a Colonial City, 1880–1980* (Stockholm: Almqvist and Wiksell International, 1986), esp. pp. 66–83.

24. See Ashwini Tambe, *Codes of Misconduct: Regulating Prostitution in Late Colonial Bombay* (Minneapolis: University of Minnesota Press, 2009), xviii–xx.

25. On Bombay's connection with Zanzibar and East Africa, see Sifra Lentin, *Mercantile Bombay: A Journey of Trade, Finance and Enterprise* (Abingdon, UK: Routledge, 2022), 49–57.

26. Bombay Presidency, *A Review of the Administration of the Presidency* (Bombay: Government Central Press, 1930), ii.

27. Read, *Indian Peasant Uprooted*, 2–3, 19.

28. Bombay Presidency, *Annual Factory Report of the Presidency of Bombay for the Year 1919* (Bombay: Government Central Press, 1919), 1–2. On the Afghanistan connection, see Arun Coomer Bose, *Indian Revolutionaries Abroad, 1905–1922: In the Background of International Developments* (Patna: Bharati Bhawan, 1971), 196–208, and Gene D. Overstreet and Marshall Windmiller, *Communism in India* (Berkeley: University of California Press, 2020), 87 and 370. See also Nicholas Owen, "Alliances from Above and Below: The Failures and Successes of Communist Anti-Imperialism in India, 1920–1934," in *Workers of the Empire, Unite: Radical and Popular Challenges to British Imperialism, 1910s–1960s*, ed. Yann Béliard and Neville Kirk (Liverpool: Liverpool University Press, 2021), 81–115.

29. Government of Bombay, *Annual Report of the Police of the City of Bombay for the Year 1920* (Bombay: Government Central Press, 1920), 20–21.

30. Frazier, *Power of Place*, 90.

31. *Graphic* (London), 17 December 1921.

32. *Bombay Chronicle*, 1 August 1921; Dinyar Patel, "Beyond Hindu-Muslim Unity: Gandhi, the Parsis and the Prince of Wales Riots of 1921," *Indian Economic and Social History Review* 55, no. 2 (2018): 221–47. See also Frazier, *Power of Place*, 93–96, and Hazareesingh, *Colonial City*, 159–66. See also Usha Thakkar and Sandhya Mehta, *Gandhi in Bombay* (New Delhi: Oxford University Press, 2017), chap. 4 on the Prince of Wales riots.

33. Ben Diqui, *A Visit to Bombay* (London: Watts, 1927), 59.

34. Christof Dejung, David Motadel, and Jürgen Osterhammel, "Worlds of the Bourgeoisie," in *The Global Bourgeoisie: The Rise of the Middle Classes in the Age of Empire*, ed. Christof Dejung, David Motadel, and Jürgen Osterhammel (Princeton, NJ: Princeton University Press, 2019), 17.

35. Nikhil Rao, *House, but No Garden: Apartment Living in Bombay's Suburbs, 1898–1964* (Minneapolis: University of Minnesota Press, 2013), 71–73.

36. Baker and Sexton, *Aldous Huxley*, 2:413.

37. *Times of India* (Bombay), 25 July 1919; R. S. Deshpande, *Cheap and Healthy*

Homes for the Middle Classes of India (Poona: Aryabhushan Press, 1935), vii and 11. Also see Hazareesingh, *Colonial City*, 26–36.

38. Charlotte Benton and Tim Benton, "The Style and the Age," in *Art Deco 1910–1939*, ed. Charlotte Benton, Tim Benton, and Ghislaine Wood (New York: Bulfinch, 2003), 12–27.

39. On the expansion plans for Bombay, see Mariam Dossal, *Theatre of Conflict, City of Hope: Bombay/Mumbai; 1660 to Present Times* (Oxford: Oxford University Press, 2010), 163–74. See also Jyoti Hosagrahar, *Indigenous Modernities: Negotiating Architecture and Urbanism* (London: Routledge, 2005).

40. Swati Chattopadhyay, *Unlearning the City: Infrastructure in a New Optical Field* (Minneapolis: University of Minnesota Press, 2012), xvi and 79. See Dilip Parameshwar Gaonkar, "On Alternative Modernities," in *Alternative Modernities*, ed. Dilip Parameshwar Gaonkar (Durham, NC: Duke University Press, 2001), 1–23, and Prashant Kidambi, "Consumption, Domestic Economy and the Idea of the 'Middle Class,'" in *Towards a History of Consumption in South Asia*, ed. Douglas E. Haynes et al. (New Delhi: Oxford University Press, 2010), 108–35. See also Homi K. Bhabha, *The Location of Culture* (London: Routledge, 1994), and Marwan M. Kraidy, *Hybridity: On the Cultural Logic of Globalization* (Philadelphia: Temple University Press, 2005).

41. Rotary Club of Bombay, ed., *Bombay, the Gateway to India: The Advantages It Offers to Industrialists* (Bombay: E. M. Gilbert-Lodge, 1936), 33.

42. *Capital*, 10 November 1937.

43. *Times of India* (Bombay), 3 November 1937. A *zanana* was the women's quarters in a Hindu or Muslim household in India. On the Ideal Homes Exhibition and Bombay's domestic modernism, see Abigail McGowan, "Domestic Modern: Redecorating Homes in Bombay in the 1930s," *Journal of the Society of Architectural Historians* 75, no. 4 (2016): 424–46. On the new Bombay flat, see Rao, *House, but No Gardens*, chap. 3.

44. *Graphic* (London), 16 June 1923. On the role of Bombay's industrialists in city politics and urban development, especially the Back Bay, see A. D. D. Gordon, *Businessmen and Politics: Rising Nationalism and a Modernising Economy in Bombay, 1918–1933* (New Delhi: Manohar, 1978), 124–28.

45. Navin Ramani, *Bombay Art Deco Architecture: A Visual Journey (1930–1953)* (New Delhi: Roli Books, 2016), 40, and Mustansir Dalvi, "'Domestic Deco' Architecture in Bombay: G. B.'s Milieu," in *Buildings That Shaped Bombay: Works of G. B. Mhatre*, ed. Kamu Iyer (Mumbai: Kamala Raheja Vidyanidhi Institute of Architecture, 2000); quotation is from p. 14. See also Amin Jaffer, "Indo-Deco," in Benton, Benton, and Wood, *Art Deco 1910–1939*, 383–84.

46. On the significance of the interwar grand hotel in the work of Kracauer and the interwar avant-garde, see Marc Katz, "The Hotel Kracauer," in *Differences: A Journal of Feminist Cultural Studies* 11, no. 2 (Summer 1999): 134–52.

47. Naresh Fernandes, *Taj Mahal Foxtrot: The Story of Bombay's Jazz Age* (New Delhi: Roli Books, 2012), 33–39.

48. Greenwall, *Storm over India*, 56. See Priti Ramamurthy, "The Modern Girl in India in the Interwar Years: Interracial Intimacies, International Competition, and Historical Eclipsing," *Women's Studies Quarterly* 34, no. 1/2 (2006): 197–226. See also Alys Eve Weinbaum et al., *The Modern Girl around the World: Consumption, Modernity, and Globalization* (Durham, NC: Duke University Press, 2008).

49. *Times of India* (Bombay), 2 July 1921, and *Bombay Chronicle*, 24 December 1924.
50. Debashree Mukherjee, *Bombay Hustle: Making Movies in a Colonial City* (New York: Columbia University Press, 2020), 68–69.
51. Kincaid, *British Social Life in India*, 290.
52. *Daily Mail* (London), 22 September 1926.
53. *Bombay Chronicle*, 5 December 1924.

Chapter 3

1. A comprehensive study of dockworkers was conducted by Rasiklal P. Cholia, *Dock Labourers in Bombay* (Calcutta: Longmans, Green, 1941); statistic is from p. 5.
2. Bromfield, *Night in Bombay*, 13.
3. On the expansion of Bombay's port facilities depicted in maps, see Port of Bombay, "The Gateway of India," in Rotary Club of Bombay, *Bombay*, 5–7. See the description of coastal shipping in E. J. K., "Bombay's Coastal Trade Ships," in the pamphlet *Modern Bombay and Her Patriotic Citizens* (Bombay: Who's Who, 1941), 47–53, and Kenneth McPherson, "Port Cities as Nodal Points of Change: The Indian Ocean, 1890s–1920s," in *Modernity and Culture: From the Mediterranean to the Indian Ocean*, ed. Leila Fawaz and C. A. Bayly (New York: Columbia University Press, 2002), 87.
4. Trade statistics are taken from Bombay Presidency, Customs Administration, *Report on the Sea-Borne Trade and Customs Administration of the Bombay Presidency, excluding Sind for the Official Year 1923–24* (Bombay: Government Central Press, 1924), 4–5, 12, and from the *Report on the Sea-Borne Trade and Customs Administration of the Bombay Presidency, excluding Sind . . . for the Official Year Ending 31st March 1935* (Delhi: Manager of Publications, 1935), 20.
5. Bombay Presidency, Customs Administration, *Report on the Sea-Borne Trade of the Bombay Presidency, excluding Sind for the Official Year Ending 31st March 1930* (Calcutta: Government Central Press, 1930), 17–18.
6. Government of India, Indian Tariff Board, *Report of the Indian Tariff Board Regarding the Grant of Protection to the Oil Industry* (Calcutta: Central Publication Branch, 1928), 91.
7. *Financial Times* (London), 11 December 1929.
8. Bombay Presidency, *Report on the Sea-Borne Trade and Customs Administration . . . Official Year Ending 31st March 1935*, 4–5.
9. Bombay Presidency, 25.
10. Rutnagur, *Bombay Industries; the Cotton Mills*, 457–64.
11. Utsa Patnaik, "India in the World Economy 1900 to 1935: The Inter-War Depression and Britain's Demise as World Capitalist Leader," *Social Scientist* 42, no. 1/2 (2014): 20; G. Findlay Shirras, *Indian Finance and Banking* (London: Macmillan, 1920), 382–84; Basaarsu Ramachandra Rau, *Present-Day Banking in India* (Calcutta: University of Calcutta, 1938), 127–35. For a discussion of the impact of India's reliance on overseas banks, see Gopalan Balachandran, "Colonial India and the World Economy, c. 1850–1940," in *A New Economic History of Colonial India*, ed. Latika Chaudhary et al. (London: Routledge, 2016), 86–89.
12. Sugata Bose, *A Hundred Horizons: The Indian Ocean in the Age of Global Empire* (Cambridge, MA: Harvard University Press, 2006), 204 and 207.
13. See the detailed study of Indian immigration by C. Kondapi, *Indians Overseas*

1838–1949 (New Delhi: Indian Council of World Affairs and Oxford University Press, 1951), and Amarjit Kaur, "Indian Ocean Crossings: Indian Labor Migration and Settlement in Southeast Asia, 1870–1940," in Gabaccia and Hoerder, *Connecting Seas and Connected Ocean Rims*, 135–39.

14. Author unknown, undated note, *Anecdotes of Smuggling into and out of the Port of Bombay during the late 1930s and the Second World War*, MSS Eur C446, 1936–1945, India Office Records and Private Papers, British Library. See also Jonathan Hyslop, "Guns, Drugs and Revolutionary Propaganda: Indian Sailors and Smuggling in the 1920s," *South African Historical Journal* 61, no. 4 (2009): 845.

15. Dinkar D. Desai, *Maritime Labour in India* (Bombay: Servants of India Society, 1940), 20.

16. Desai, 120–32; F. J. A. Broeze, "The Muscles of Empire: Indian Seamen under the Raj, 1919–1939," *Indian Economic and Social History Review* 18, no. 1 (1981): 43–67; Holger Weiss, "The International of Seamen and Harbour Workers—a Radical Global Labour Union of the Waterfront or a Subversive World-Wide Web?," in *International Communism and Transnational Solidarity: Radical Networks, Mass Movements and Global Politics, 1919–1939*, by Holger Weiss (Boston: Brill, 2017), 290.

17. Coll 7/10 China (Yunnan): Export of Arms to China via Burma, IOR/LPS/12/2179, Political and Secret Department Records, India Office Records and Private Papers, British Library.

18. *Times of India* (Bombay), 5 January 1923.

19. Tirthankar Roy, *India in the World Economy: From Antiquity to the Present* (Cambridge: Cambridge University Press, 2012), 210.

20. See Aashish Velkar, "Swadeshi Capitalism in Colonial Bombay," *Historical Journal* 64, no. 4 (September 2021): 1010.

21. Chandavarkar, *Industrial Capitalism in India*, chap. 6. See also Claude Markovits, *Merchants, Traders, Entrepreneurs* (New York: Palgrave Macmillan, 2008).

22. Roy, *India in the World Economy: From Antiquity to the Present*, 218; A. D. Shroff, "What Is the Industrial Future of Bombay?," in *Bombay Looks Ahead*, ed. Clifford Manshardt (Bombay: D. B. Taraporevala, 1934), 86–87.

23. Reed, *India I Knew*, 129.

24. David Washbrook, "The Cambridge History of Capitalism: India," in *Capitalisms: Towards a Global History*, ed. Kaveh Yazdani and Dilip M. Menon (New Delhi: Oxford University Press, 2020), 133–35.

25. A. B., *Old and New Bombay*, 56. See also A. N. Joshi, *Life and Times of Sir Hormusjee C. Dinshaw* (Bombay: D. B. Taraporevala, 1939), 71. On the Tata family, see Girish Kuber, *The Tatas: How a Family Built a Business and a Nation* (New York: Harper Business, 2019).

26. *Times of India* (Bombay), 7 March 1924.

27. *Times of India*, 7 March 1924; *Report by the Commissioner for India for the British Empire Exhibition* (Calcutta: Government of India Press, 1925), 53–54.

28. *Times of India* (Bombay), 7 and 23 January 1924. For photos of the exhibit, see *Souvenir of the Indian Pavilion and Its Exhibits* (Wembley: British Empire Exhibition, 1924). Daniel Stephen, *The Empire of Progress: West Africans, Indians, and Britons at the British Empire Exhibition, 1924–25* (New York: Palgrave Macmillan, 2013), 61, 85–89; quotation is from p. 88. See also Deborah L. Hughes, "Kenya, India and the British Empire Exhibition of 1924," *Race and Class* 47, no. 4 (April–June 2006): 66–85.

29. Letter from E. D. Sassoon Manchester Office, 22 November 1927, Standard Chartered Bank, E. D. Sassoon Limited, CLD/B/207/ES03/01, Administration, General Correspondence, London Metropolitan Archives.

30. See Simon J. Potter, *Wireless Internationalism and Distant Listening: Britain, Propaganda, and the Invention of Global Radio, 1920–1939* (Oxford: Oxford University Press, 2020), esp. chap. 5 on the BBC Empire Service.

31. *Times of India* (Bombay), 7 April 1925 and 19 June 1928; S. R. Kantebet, "Communication Facilities of Bombay," in Rotary Club of Bombay, *Bombay*, 44–45.

32. See the essay by Maya Sorabjee, "Swadeshi Moderne: Aesthetics, Politics and Appropriation in Bombay's Deco," at Art Deco Mumbai, accessed September 11, 2023: https://www.artdecomumbai.com/research/swadeshi-moderne-aesthetics-politics-and-appropriation-in-bombays-deco/. On Bombay's art deco, see also Ramani, *Bombay Art Deco Architecture*.

33. *Times of India* (Bombay), 15 August 1919.

34. *Times of India* (Bombay), 1 March 1918 and 9 March 1920; P. A. Wadia and G. N. Joshi, *The Wealth of India* (London: Macmillan, 1925), 341–42; and Stuart Tappin, "The Early Use of Reinforced Concrete in India," *Construction History* 18 (2002): 79–98. Gyan Prakash discusses art deco and concrete as design material in Prakash, *Mumbai Fables*, 97–100.

35. Philip Sassoon, *The Third Route* (London: William Heinemann, 1929), 6–14, 155. See also Sir Frederick Sykes, "Imperial Air Routes," *Geographical Journal* 55, no. 4 (1920): 241–62.

36. Martin Pugh, *We Danced All Night: A Social History of Britain between the Wars* (London: Vintage, 2009), 313–14.

37. *Times of India* (Bombay), 12 September 1927 and 26 January 1928.

38. *Straits Times* (Singapore), 24 February 1931.

39. *Bombay Flying Club Display* and *"At Home," Juhu Air Park*, 3 December 1929. Pamphlet in Aero Club—Membership, Annual Reports, Minutes, Aero Club of India & Burma Ltd and the Bombay Flying Club, 1931; M. R. Jayakar Private Papers, National Archives of India Abhilekh PATAL digital portal, accessed September 3, 2023, https://www.abhilekh-patal.in/jspui/.

40. *Bombay Chronicle*, 25 January 1928.

41. *Times of India* (Bombay), 8 May 1929.

42. *Times of India* (Bombay), 21 September 1926. See also Priyanka Srivastava, *The Well-Being of the Labor Force in Colonial Bombay* (New York: Palgrave Macmillan, 2018), 139. On the Sassoon Welfare Institute, see Rutnagur, *Bombay Industries; the Cotton Mills*, 512. See also the detailed study of the "millhands and their city" in Richard Newman, *Workers and Unions in Bombay, 1918–1929: A Study of Organisation in the Cotton Mills* (Canberra: Australian National University, 1981), 8–28.

43. Letter from V. Sassoon to Giulia Ottoboni, 1 May 1936, Sir Ellice Victor Elias Sassoon Papers and Photographs, series 1: Diaries and Correspondence, DeGolyer Library, Southern Methodist University, Dallas.

44. *Bombay Chronicle*, 15 February 1927, and *Singapore Free Press*, 3 October 1927.

45. Parliament of India, *Legislative Assembly Debates*, 3 April 1939, p. 3244; Parliament of India Lok Sabha Digital Library, https://eparlib.nic.in/.

46. Marguerite Dupree, ed., *Lancashire and Whitehall: The Diary of Sir Raymond Streat*, vol. 1, *1931–39* (Manchester: Manchester University Press, 1987), 46.

47. The conflicts between Indian cotton magnates and the colonial state over tariff

policy are recounted in Beckert, *Empire of Cotton*, 418–26. See also Tirthankar Roy, *A Business History of India: Enterprise and the Emergence of Capitalism from 1700* (Cambridge: Cambridge University Press, 2018), 76–80.

48. Sir Leslie Wilson, governor of Bombay, quoted in Neil Charlesworth, "The Problem of Government Finance in British India: Taxation, Borrowing and the Allocation of Resources in the Inter-war Period," *Modern Asian Studies* 19, no. 3 (1984): 537.

49. Parliament of India, *Legislative Assembly Debates*, 19 March 1923, p. 3702 as well as 17 March 1923, p. 3634, and 27 February 1923, p. 2893.

50. Reed, *India I Knew*, 130–31.

51. Chien Tsai and Yu-Kwei Cheng, *Statistics of Foreign Trade of Different Chinese Ports with Various Countries (1919, 1927–1931)* (Shanghai: Commercial Press, 1936), 250–55.

52. *Bombay Chronicle*, 18 March 1925.

53. Parliament of India, *Legislative Assembly Debates*, 19 March 1923, p. 3702.

54. *Times of India* (Bombay), 7 December 1926.

55. A. N. Joshi, *Plea for Impartial Investigation into the Bombay Textile Industry* (Bombay: All-India Trade Union Congress Office, 1925), 6–12.

56. Joshi, 6–12; *China Mail* (Hong Kong), 8 September 1927; *Times of India* (Bombay), 23 August 1927. See also Government of India, Indian Tariff Board, *Report of the Indian Tariff Board (Cotton Textile Industry Inquiry) 1927* (Bombay: Government Central Press, 1927), 21–24.

57. John Maynard Keynes, *Indian Currency and Finance* (London: Macmillan, 1924), 196. See P. A. Wadia and G. N. Joshi, *Money and the Money Market in India* (London: Macmillan, 1926), 221–24. See also G. Balachandran, "Towards a 'Hindoo Marriage': Anglo-Indian Monetary Relations in Interwar India, 1917–1935," *Modern Asian Studies* 28, no. 3 (July 1994): 615–47.

58. See Johan Mathew, *Margins of the Market: Trafficking and Capitalism across the Arabian Sea* (Berkeley: University of California Press, 2016), 123, as well as B. R. Ambedkar, *The Problem of the Rupee: Its Origin and Its Solution* (London: P. S. King and Son, 1923), 87.

59. Bombay Presidency, Customs Administration, *Report on the Sea-Borne Trade and Customs Administration . . . 1923–24*, 4. See also A. W. Pinnick, *Silver and China* (Shanghai: Kelly and Walsh, 1930), 40–41.

60. *Hearing before the Committee on Coinage, Weights, and Measures*, House of Representatives, 72nd Cong., 1st Sess. on H. Res. 72, A Resolution to Investigate the Cause and Effect of the Present Depressed Value of Silver, 7–11 March 1932 (statement of S. R. Bomanji) (Washington, DC: US Government Printing Office, 1932), 152.

61. On the silver crisis of 1918, see chap. 8, "Currency and Exchange," in Vaman Govind Kale, *India's War Finance and Post-war Problems* (Poona: V. G. Kale, 1919).

62. Patnaik, "India in the World Economy," 21–22. See also G. Balachandran, *John Bullion's Empire: Britain's Gold Problem and India between the Wars* (Abingdon, UK: Routledge, 2006).

63. Quoted in Dadabhoy, *Barons of Banking*, 98.

64. *Times of India* (Bombay), 7 August 1926. On the political debates and evolution of the industrial bourgeoisie in India, see chaps. 5–6 in David Lockwood, *The Indian Bourgeoisie: A Political History of the Indian Capitalist Class in the Early Twentieth Century* (London: Bloomsbury Academic, 2020).

65. *Bombay Chronicle*, 13 October 1926.

66. *Bombay Chronicle*, 3 February 1927.
67. *Times of India* (Bombay), 7 December 1926.
68. Kooiman, *Bombay Textile Labour*, 35.
69. Fred Stones, "The Employer and the City," in *Bombay Today and Tomorrow*, ed. Clifford Manshardt (Bombay: D. B. Taraporevala, 1930), 71.
70. Committee of Assistance to the Textile Workers, "Injustice to the Bombay Textile Workers. Government's and Millowners' Attitude towards the Settlement of the Dead-Lock," Servants of India Society's Home (Girgaon, Bombay: Vaibhav Press, 1925), 30.
71. *Times of India* (Bombay), 13 September 1928 and 10 October 1928 as well as 6 February 1929.
72. *Labour Monthly* 12 (1930): 188; *Straits Times* (Singapore), 18 October 1930.
73. Victor Sassoon Diary, 28 January 1930, 5–6 and 13 February, 30; Sir Ellice Victor Elias Sassoon Papers and Photographs, series 1: Diaries and Correspondence, DeGolyer Library, Southern Methodist University, Dallas. On the Whitley Commission, see Amerdeep Panesar et al., "J. H. Whitley and the Royal Commission on Labour in India 1929–31," in *Liberal Reform and Industrial Relations: J. H. Whitley (1866–1935), Halifax Radical and Speaker of the House of Commons*, ed. John A. Hargreaves, Keith Laybourn, and Richard Toye (Abingdon, UK: Routledge, 2018).
74. *Times of India* (Bombay), 4 December 1929; Royal Commission on Labour in India and John Henry Whitley, *Report of the Royal Commission on Labour in India: Written Evidence*. Vol. 1, pt. 1, *Bombay Presidency including Sind* (London: His Majesty's Stationery Office, 1931), multiple pages.
75. *Daily Mail* (London), 10 October 1928.
76. Bombay Presidency, *Textile Labour Inquiry Committee, 1938–40*. Oral Evidence, vol. 16. File 72-C, Maharashtra State Archives, India.
77. S. D. Mehta, *The Cotton Mills of India, 1854 to 1954*, quoted in Chandavarkar, *Industrial Capitalism in India*, 264.
78. *Times of India* (Bombay), 10 October 1928; Stones, "Employer and the City," 59.
79. *Financial Times* (London), 20 March 1928.
80. *Times of India* (Bombay), 21 March 1928.
81. *Times* (London), 18 July 1931.
82. Newspaper clipping, Morris Gilbert, "Europe Day by Day" (no newspaper title, date), Victor Sassoon Diary, 26 October 1931.
83. *Times of India* (Bombay), 23 November 1932.

Chapter 4

1. Arthur Mee, *London: Heart of the Empire and Wonder of the World* (London: Caxton, 1937), 1.
2. J. B. Priestley, *English Journey* (London: William Heinemann, 1934), 401.
3. Shaw Desmond, "Changing London, 3: Speeding-up London," *Sphere* (London), 12 October 1929. See city descriptions of the interwar years, such as A. H. Blake, *Things Seen in London* (London: Seeley, 1921), esp. chap. 7, "Life of the Streets."
4. Robert Sinclair, *Metropolitan Man: The Future of the English* (London: George Allen and Unwin, 1937), 17.
5. Paul Cohen-Portheim, *The Spirit of London* (London: B. T. Batsford, 1935), v. An up-to-date discussion of London's migrant communities with excellent historical

background is Panikos Panayi, *Migrant City: A New History of London* (New Haven, CT: Yale University Press, 2020), esp. chap. 8, "Christians, Hindus, Jews, Muslims, and Sikhs."

6. James A. Jones, *Wonderful London Today* (London: John Long, 1934), 131–33.

7. Min-Ch'ien T. Z. Tyau, *London through Chinese Eyes* (London: Swarthmore, 1920), 311–13.

8. This moniker was used throughout the British popular press. See for example *Daily Standard* (London), 14 July 1932, and *Aberdeen (Scotland) Press and Journal*, 14 July 1932.

9. Jones, *Wonderful London Today*, 259; H. V. Morton, *H. V. Morton's London*, 12th ed. (London: Methuen, 1945), 186.

10. The strikes were regularly reported in London's daily newspapers. On the Tube and electrician strikes, see the *Globe* (London), 3 February 1919, and *Times* (London), 4 February 1919.

11. The protest marches were covered extensively in London's daily newspapers. On the rail strike, see the *Globe* (London), 27 September 1919.

12. H. Llewellyn Smith, *The New Survey of London Life and Labour*, 9 vols.; vol. 1, *Forty Years of Change* (London: P. S. Kind and Son, 1930), 29.

13. *Daily Herald* (London), 3 May 1920. See also *Labour's May Day Demonstrations (1920)*, British Pathé, Gaumont Graphic Newsreel (Reuters), accessed September 1, 2023, https://www.britishpathe.com/asset/118644. On the protests and hunger marches, see German and Rees, *People's History of London*, 194–96.

14. *Daily Herald* (London), 19 October 1920.

15. Huggins, *Horseracing and the British*, 50.

16. "Great Owners—but Poor Tipsters," *Illustrated Sporting and Dramatic News*, 4 June 1927; Vartash, "Talk of the Turf," *Sketch* (London), 9 May 1928; *Manchester (England) Guardian*, 31 May 1927.

17. Newspaper clipping, Morris Gilbert, "Europe Day by Day" (no newspaper title, date), Victor Sassoon Diary, 30 March 1931; Sir Ellice Victor Elias Sassoon Papers and Photographs, series 1: Diaries and Correspondence, DeGolyer Library, Southern Methodist University, Dallas.

18. In London, Victor's cousin Philip Sassoon was the family's luminary. Fabulously rich, he was a member of Parliament and served as private secretary to Prime Minister David Lloyd George and as undersecretary for the Air Ministry. Philip's sister Sybil Sassoon was one of London's stellar society hostesses and patron of the arts. Flora Sassoon took over the David Sassoon business upon her husband's death and was a leading Jewish scholar and philanthropist. Siegfried Sassoon found the family's most enduring fame as a writer and poet of the soldier's experience during the First World War.

19. See Martin Conboy, *Tabloid Britain: Constructing a Community through Language* (London: Routledge, 2006), 9–14; Arts, *Interwar London after Dark*, 6–7.

20. See for example "White's Club Members on the Green," *Sketch* (London), 10 June 1931, and the "Miss Peeps" column, *Bystander* (London), 2 September 1936. See also the "And the World Said" column in the *Tatler* (London), 24 November 1937. On the influence of London's society rags, see Sallie McNamara, *"Tatler"'s Irony: Conspicuous Consumption, Inconspicuous Power and Social Change* (Cham, Switzerland: Palgrave Pivot, 2018).

21. Muggeridge, *The Thirties*, 8.

22. This term is used by D. J. Taylor, *Bright Young People: The Rise and Fall of a*

Generation, 1918–1940 (London: Chatto and Windus, 2007). See in particular chap. 6, "Party-Going," pp. 123–44.

23. Beverley Nichols, *All That I Could Never Be* (London: Jonathan Cape, 1949), 41.

24. See the examples in Walkowitz, *Nights Out in Cosmopolitan London*, 209–13.

25. Sidney Theodore Felstead, *The Underworld of London* (London: John Murray, 1923), 4–5.

26. "Sir Victor Sassoon Amuses Himself with His Camera at the Winter Garden, Snapping 'Rhyme and Rhythm,'" *Sketch* (London), 5 October 1932.

27. Charles Graves, *The Price of Pleasure* (London: Ivor Nicholson and Watson, 1935), 8.

28. Hon. Evelyn Fitzhenry and her friend the Lady Betty Berkshire, "The Letters of Eve," *Tatler* (London), 27 August 1930. On the "bottle party belt" and West End redoubts, see Juliet Gardiner, *The Thirties: An Intimate History* (London: Harper Press, 2011), 623–30. On the cultural influence of the Prince of Wales and the London West End, see Stella Margetson, *The Long Party: High Society in the Twenties and Thirties* (London: Cremonesi, 1976), 27–39.

29. Mee, *London*, 210.

30. *Times* (London), 9 July 1930.

31. See the introduction in Felix Driver and David Gilbert, eds., *Imperial Cities: Landscape, Display and Identity* (Manchester: Manchester University Press, 1999), 3–12. See also the outstanding discussion in Schneer, *London 1900*.

32. Morton, *H. V. Morton's London*, 20.

33. *Sphere* (London), 19 July 1924.

34. A good overview of the intense debates about British attitudes to empire is given in Bernard Porter, *Empire Ways: Aspects of British Imperialism* (London: I. B. Tauris, 2016), chap. 21. On the relationship between labor and the anti-colonial struggle, see the introduction in Béliard and Kirk, *Workers of the Empire, Unite*.

35. Anne Reinhardt, *Navigating Semi-Colonialism: Shipping, Sovereignty, and Nation-Building in China, 1860–1937* (Cambridge, MA: Harvard University Press, 2018), 148–52. On interwar tourism in the age of steam, see Lorraine Coons and Alexander Varias, *Tourist Third Class: Steamship Travel in the Interwar Years* (New York: Palgrave Macmillan, 2003).

36. Gordon Pirie, *Cultures and Caricatures of British Imperial Aviation: Passengers, Pilots, Publicity* (Manchester: Manchester University Press, 2012), 5. See also his "Incidental Tourism: British Imperial Air Travel in the 1930s," *Journal of Tourism History* 1, no. 1 (March 2009): 49–66.

37. John Murray, *A Handbook for Travellers in India, Burma and Ceylon, including All British India, the Portuguese and French Possessions, and the Indian States* (London: John Murray, 1924), 5, 7.

38. An Indian Student, "Social Disabilities of Indians in England," *Britain and India* 1, no. 3 (March 1920): 86–87.

39. *Kensington (England) Post*, 17 October 1930; India League, *Condition of India: Being the Report of the Delegation Sent to India by the India League in 1932* (London: Essential News, 1932), 471. On Manon and the India League, see Rozina Visram, *Ayahs, Lascars and Princes: Indians in Britain, 1700–1947* (London: Pluto, 1986), 159–64.

40. Austin Coates, *China Races* (Oxford: Oxford University Press, 1983), 178. Billie Coutts also opened her own Miss Billie Coutts Stable in 1926. On her influence

in Shanghai, see Ning Jennifer Chang, "Women in the Chase: Sports, Empire, and Gender in Shanghai, 1860–1945," *Chinese Studies in History* 54, no. 2 (2021): 130–48.

41. Magee and Thompson, *Empire and Globalisation*, 46.

42. On the history of National City Bank and its international role, see Peter James Hudson, *Bankers and Empire: How Wall Street Colonized the Caribbean* (Chicago: University of Chicago Press, 2017), especially the introduction.

43. "Grosvenor-Mayfair," *Bystander* (London), 1 April 1931, and "At Home in Sussex, Mrs. Carl Bendix and Her Son," *Tatler* (London), 6 August 1930.

44. Cover photo montage, *Bystander* (London), 4 March 1931.

45. Letters from Victor Sassoon to Yvonne Fitzroy, n.d. *Empress of Britain*, Meridian Day and 12 January 1933, Cathay Hotel, IOPP/MSS Eur E312, India Office Records and Private Papers, British Library.

46. Bettina Ballard, *In My Fashion* (New York: David McKay, 1960), 81.

47. *Straits Times* (Singapore), 24 September 1928.

48. Pamela Murray, "Monte Carlo Asides," *Sketch* (London), 22 August 1934. On the French Riviera in the 1930s, see Anne De Courcy, *Chanel's Riviera: Glamour, Decadence, and Survival in Peace and War, 1930–1944* (New York: St. Martin's Press, 2020). Most recently, see Jonathan Miles, *The Once upon a Time World: The Dark and Sparkling Story of the French Riviera* (New York: Pegasus, 2023).

Chapter 5

1. David Kynaston, *The City of London*, vol. 3, *Illusions of Gold, 1914–1945* (London: Pimlico, 2000), 143–44.

2. The role of silver in the global economy is reviewed in Dennis O. Flynn, "Silver, Globalization, and Capitalism," in Yazdani and Menon, *Capitalisms*, esp. pp. 42–52. Also useful is William L. Silber, *The Story of Silver: How the White Metal Shaped America and the Modern World* (Princeton, NJ: Princeton University Press, 2019).

3. Robert Gibson-Jarvie, *The City of London: A Financial and Commercial History* (Cambridge: Woodhead-Faulkner, 1979), 53–55.

4. Charles C. Turner, "The City at High Noon," in Sims, *Living London*, 2:122–23; Charles C. Turner, "Money London," 3:88; Mark Billings and Forrest Capie, "Financial Crisis, Contagion, and the British Banking System between the World Wars," *Business History* 53, no. 2 (April 2011): 195.

5. Dickinson, *Long Twentieth Century*, 73.

6. "City Notes: Finance in a First-Class Carriage," *Sketch* (London), 29 October 1924.

7. Ranald C. Michie, *The City of London: Continuity and Change, 1850–1990* (Basingstoke, UK: Macmillan, 1992), 14.

8. Charles F. G. Masterman, *England after War: A Study* (London: Hodder and Stoughton, 1922), 52.

9. Collin Brooks, *Something in the City: Men and Markets in London* (London: Country Life, 1931), 39–40.

10. H. W. Phillips, *Modern Foreign Exchange and Foreign Banking* (London: Macdonald and Evans, 1926), 54–55 and 67–68. See S. W. Dowling, *The Exchanges of London* (London: Butterworth, 1929), 212–13. See also Michael John Law, *1938: Modern Britain; Social Change and Visions of the Future* (London: Bloomsbury, 2018), 71–73.

11. Rob Harris, *London's Global Office Economy: From Clerical Factory to Digital Hub* (Abingdon, UK: Routledge, 2021), 155.

12. Judith Walkowitz uses "louche cosmopolitanism" to describe the Soho scene in Walkowitz, *Nights Out in Cosmopolitan London*, 214. See Arts, *Interwar London after Dark*, 5. On social class and white-collar workers in the interwar years, see Noreen Branson, *Britain in the Nineteen Twenties* (Minneapolis: University of Minnesota Press, 1976), 91–96.

13. Shaw Desmond, "Changing London: 5: Manners and Mannequins," *Sphere* (London), 26 October 1929.

14. Peter Scott, *The Property Masters: A History of the British Commercial Property Sector* (London: E. and F. N. Spon, 1996), 50–51, 68–69.

15. Ian Black, "Rebuilding 'The Heart of the Empire': Bank Headquarters in the City of London, 1919–1939," *Art History* 22, no. 4 (November 1999): 600–601.

16. Harold P. Clunn, *The Face of London: The Record of a Century of Changes and Development*, 7th ed. (London: Simpkin Marshall, 1937), 26.

17. A good description of Lloyd's is found in Brooks, *Something in the City*, 213–24.

18. Michie, *City of London*, 39.

19. W. F. T., "The New London: The Rebuilding of a City," *Sphere* (London), 24 December 1921.

20. Sinclair, *Metropolitan Man*, 173.

21. Kynaston, *City of London*, 3:345.

22. The history of Eastern Bank is recounted in the archives of Standard Chartered Bank, Eastern Bank Limited, 1909–1972, collection CLC/B/207-5, London Metropolitan Archives.

23. *Times* (London), 26 March 1920.

24. Eastern Bank Limited, 1909–1972, collection CLC/B/207-5. Property holdings in collection CLC/B/207/CH09/01/001 and 002, London Metropolitan Archives.

25. *Financial Times* (London), 29 March 1928.

26. Articles of Association and Board of Directors, *Second Annual Report*, E. D. Sassoon Banking Company Limited, 1931. Standard Chartered Bank, Eastern Bank Limited, 1909–1972, collection CLC/B/207/ED03, London Metropolitan Archives.

27. *Times* (London), 3 December 1928, and *Daily Mail* (London), 27 March 1928.

28. R. O. Buchanan, "Empire and World Trade," in *Britain and Her Export Trade*, ed. Mark Abrams (London: Pilot Press, 1945), 131.

29. Bombay Presidency, *Report on the Sea-Borne Trade... Official Year Ending 31st March 1930*, 30 and 39.

30. Tsai and Cheng, *Statistics of Foreign Trade*, pt. 5, "Statistics of Principal Exports of Each Port to Different Countries," multiple tables.

31. Walter Hill, "Why Export?," in Abrams, *Britain and Her Export Trade*, 13–14, 16.

32. Tsai and Cheng, *Statistics of Foreign Trade*, 17 and 21; *Maritime Customs, Shanghai Annual Trade Report and Returns 1926* (Shanghai: Statistical Department of the Inspectorate General of Customs, 1927), 5.

33. Port of London Authority, *London, the Premier Port and Market of the World* (London: Port of London Authority, 1924), 48.

34. Blake, *Things Seen in London*, 54. See also Fiona Rule, *London's Docklands: A History of the Lost Quarter* (Gloucestershire: History Press, 2019), esp. chaps. 19–20.

35. Thomas Burke, *The London Spy* (New York: George H. Doran, 1922), 245.

36. *Times* (London), 23 July 1923. On social banditry and the mythical imagery of

the East End in the interwar years, see John Marriott, *Beyond the Tower: A History of East London* (New Haven, CT: Yale University Press, 2011), 295–98.

37. Laura Tabili, "The Construction of Racial Difference in Twentieth-Century Britain: The Special Restriction (Coloured Alien Seamen) Order, 1925," *Journal of British Studies* 33, no. 1 (1994): 68; Rozina Visram, *Asians in Britain: 400 Years of History* (London: Pluto, 2002), 228.

38. *Daily Herald* (London), 17 April and 30 May 1919.

39. *Times* (London), 29 November 1923 and 24 October 1924. On the backlash against Indian seamen, Uphadhaya, and Saklatvala, see Robert Winder, *Bloody Foreigners: The Story of Immigration in Britain* (London: Abacus, 2013), 287–91. On Saklatvala, see also Arup K. Chatterjee, *Indians in London: From the Birth of the East India Company to Independent India* (London: Bloomsbury Academic, 2021), 242–48.

40. Blake, *Things Seen in London*, 60.

41. Thomas Burke, *More Limehouse Nights* (New York: George H. Doran, 1921); quotations are from pp. 49, 118–19, and 133.

42. *Pall Mall Gazette and Globe* (London), 24 April 1922.

43. *Illustrated London News*, 26 September 1925.

44. Population figures from John Seed, "Limehouse Blues: Looking for Chinatown in the London Docks, 1900–40," *History Workshop Journal* 62, no. 1 (2006): 63–64. Jones, *Wonderful London Today*, 137.

45. Tony Kushner, "The End of the 'Anglo-Jewish Progress Show': Representations of the Jewish East End, 1887–1987," in *The Jewish Heritage in British History: Englishness and Jewishness*, ed. Tony Kushner (New York: Frank Cass, 1992), 81.

46. Elizabeth Bowen, *To the North* (New York: Anchor, 2006), 79.

47. Gavin Weightman and Steve Humphries, *The Making of Modern London, 1914–1939* (London: Sidgewick and Jackson, 1984), 49; Douglas Hector Smith, *The Industries of Greater London: Being a Survey of the Recent Industrialisation of the Northern and Western Sectors of Greater London, Etc.* (London: P. S. King, 1933), 171. See also chap. 8 in Peter Hall, *The Industries of London since 1861* (London: Hutchinson, 1962).

48. See Hall, *Industries of London*. See also *Report of the Royal Commission on the Distribution of the Industrial Population (Barlow Report)* (London: His Majesty's Stationery Office, 1940), 49, 163–67. Also, John Armstrong, "The Development of the Park Royal Industrial Estate in the Interwar Period," *London Journal* 21, no. 1 (1996): 64–79.

49. White, *London in the Twentieth Century*, 179.

50. Joan S. Skinner, *Form and Fancy: Factories and Factory Buildings by Wallis, Gilbert & Partners, 1916–1939* (Liverpool: Liverpool University Press, 1997), 110. See also Elain Harwood, *Art Deco Britain: Buildings of the Interwar Years* (London: Batsford, 2009), 224–39.

51. Julian Symons, *The General Strike: A Historical Portrait* (London: Cresset, 1957), 101.

52. *Times* (London), 4 May 1926; Wilfrid Harris Cook, *The General Strike: A Study of Labor's Tragic Weapon in Theory and Practice* (Chapel Hill: University of North Carolina Press, 1931), 389.

53. See for example the photos in the *Illustrated London News*, 8 May 1926.

54. *New York Times*, 14 August 1921.

55. Shaw Desmond, "Changing London, 6: London's 'New Poor' and 'New Rich,'" *Sphere* (London), 2 November 1929.

56. These organizations are discussed in David Thackeray, *Forging a British World of Trade: Culture, Ethnicity, and Market in the Empire-Commonwealth, 1880–1975* (Oxford: Oxford Scholarship Online, 2019), 12–13 and chap. 2.

57. Buchanan, "Empire and World Trade," 132.

58. Tsai and Cheng, *Statistics of Foreign Trade*, 278–83; British Consulate General, Commercial Counsellor, Shanghai, *Report on Trade Conditions in China* (London: Department of Overseas Trade, July 1932), 11. See also the Maritime Customs annual trade statistics and summaries that evidence the falloff in British trade, for example Maritime Customs, *Shanghai Annual Trade Report and Returns 1925 and 1926* (Shanghai: Maritime Customs, 1926 and 1927), 5–7.

59. Thomas Martland Ainscough, *Report on the Conditions and Prospects of British Trade in India, 1927–28* (London: His Majesty's Stationery Office, 1928), 20–23, 26.

60. Alfred E. Kahn, *Great Britain in the World Economy* (New York: Columbia University Press, 1946), 94. For the interwar crisis of the British cotton industry, see Steven Toms, *Financing Cotton: British Industrial Growth and Decline, 1780–2000* (Woodbridge, UK: Boydell Press, 2020), 219–33.

61. Freda Utley, *Lancashire and the Far East* (London: George Allen and Unwin, 1931), 74, 230, 277; *Finance & Commerce* (Shanghai), 18 November 1936. Japan represented 26 percent of trade with China; the United States, 17.6 percent; and the United Kingdom, only 9 percent. Charles Frederick Remer, *Foreign Investments in China* (New York: H. Fertig, 1968), 58.

62. *Singapore Free Press*, 30 May 1931.

63. Quoted in Arthur Redford, *Manchester Merchants and Foreign Trade*, vol. 2, *1850–1939* (Manchester: Manchester University Press, 1956), 283.

64. Dupree, *Lancashire and Whitehall*, 1:255–56.

65. Associated Press, *Statesman* (Calcutta),17 July 1933.

66. *Times of India* (Bombay), 30 October 1933.

67. F. V. Meyer, *Britain's Colonies in World Trade* (London: Oxford University Press, 1948), 80–81.

68. Bombay Presidency, *Report on the Sea-Borne Trade and Customs Administration of the Bombay Presidency, excluding Sind for the Official Year Ending 31st March 1938* (Delhi: Manager of Publications, 1938), 18.

Chapter 6

1. *Singapore Free Press*, 30 May 1931.

2. See the review of Woodhead's *The Truth about the Chinese Republic* in the *Illustrated London News*, 26 December 1925. An excellent early British source on the treaty ports of China is Arnold Wright and H. A. Cartwright, eds., *Twentieth Century Impressions of Hongkong, Shanghai, and Other Treaty Ports of China* (London: Lloyd's Great Britain, 1908). See also Smith Middleton, *The British in China and Far Eastern Trade* (London: Constable, 1920).

3. Carl Crow, *The Travelers' Handbook for China (including Hong Kong)*, 3rd ed. (New York: Dodd Mead, 1921), 106; *North China Herald* (Shanghai), 30 June 1931.

4. Reinhardt, *Navigating Semi-Colonialism*, 149.

5. Transshipment, or re-export, of goods through Shanghai constituted one of the most important elements in the city's port economy, as it did in Bombay. See

Rhoads Murphey, *Shanghai, Key to Modern China* (Cambridge, MA: Harvard University Press, 1953), 130–32.

6. Murphey, 168–69.

7. Statistics are from Murphey, 166–69. The Rong family also owned the sixteen Maoxin and Fuxin flour mills.

8. Albert Londres, *La Chine en folie* (Paris: A. Michel, 1925), 192–93.

9. Wen-hsin Yeh, *Shanghai Splendor: Economic Sentiments and the Making of Modern China, 1843–1949* (Berkeley: University of California Press, 2008), 4–5.

10. Ling, *In Search of Old Shanghai*, 67–68.

11. *Finance & Commerce* (Shanghai), 3 February 1937; Tsai and Cheng, *Statistics of Foreign Trade*, pt. 4.

12. "Shanghai, the Commercial Centre of the Orient," *China Journal of Science and Arts* 22, no. 5 (May 1935): 248; *Finance & Commerce* (Shanghai), 1 September 1937.

13. See Robert Bickers, *China Bound: John Swire & Sons and Its World, 1816–1980* (London: Bloomsbury Business, 2020). Also, Maggie Keswick, ed., *The Thistle and the Jade: A Celebration of 175 Years of Jardine, Matheson & Co.* (London: Francis Lincoln, 2008).

14. Shanghai Academy of Social Sciences, as given in Zhilong, "Shanghai," in Thampi, *India and China*, 48.

15. E. M. Gull, *British Economic Interests in the Far East* (London: Oxford University Press, 1943), 112–14.

16. On the training and employment of Chinese in foreign companies, see Sherman Cochran, *Encountering Chinese Networks: Western, Japanese, and Chinese Corporations in China, 1880–1937* (Berkeley: University of California Press, 2000), esp. chap. 2 on Standard Oil.

17. *China Press* (Shanghai), 10 January 1932.

18. "Anderson, Meyer & Co. Achievements during Twenty-Five Years," *North China Herald* (Shanghai), 7 April 1931.

19. On the golden age of Shanghai banking, see Ji, *History of Modern Shanghai Banking*, chap. 4.

20. Richard Roberts and David Kynaston, *The Lion Wakes: A Modern History of HSBC* (London: Profile Books, 2015), 12. On architecture on the Bund, see Denison and Ren, *Building Shanghai*, 136–45.

21. Ming Li, "Development of Modern Banks in China," *Far Eastern Review* 26 (1930): 608; *North China Herald* (Shanghai), 13 June 1931. See also Horesh, *Shanghai's Bund and Beyond*, 31–38.

22. Pinnick, *Silver and China*, 26.

23. "Sport, Society, and Silver: Interview of James Caldwell by Frank H. H. King," in *Shanghai: Electric and Lurid City*, ed. Barbara Baker (Hong Kong: Oxford University Press, 1998), 174; Richard Feetham, *Report of the Hon. Richard Feetham . . . to the Shanghai Municipal Council*, vol. 1 (Shanghai: North-China Daily News and Herald, Ltd., 1931), 302.

24. "Finance, Currencies and Exchange in Shanghai," *China Journal of Science and Arts* 12, no. 6 (June 1930): 263.

25. "Finance, Currencies," 232.

26. Data from Pinnick, *Silver and China*, 29 and 33. See also the data in Boris Torgasheff, "Silver in the Far East," *China Weekly Review*, 5 January 1929.

27. "Rehabilitation of Silver: Banker's Scheme for New Empire Currency," *Times of India* (Bombay), 4 March 1931.

28. A good discussion of the economic and political implications of the downturn is given in Bergère, *Shanghai*, 165–69.

29. *North China Herald* (Shanghai), 3 April 1935; "Sir Victor Sassoon Suggests that U.S. Buy Silver from India," *China Weekly Review*, 22 December 1934.

30. Parks M. Coble, *The Shanghai Capitalists and the Nationalist Government, 1927–1937*, 2nd ed. (Cambridge, MA: Harvard University Press, 1986), 144–48.

31. Lady Drummond-Hay, "The Paris of the Distant Orient," *Sphere* (London), 16 July 1927. Grace Margaret Hay, or Lady Drummond-Hay, later boarded a zeppelin for the first round-the-world trip by a woman.

32. Mao Tun, *Midnight* (Amsterdam: Fredonia Books, 2001), 1, 8. Descriptions of Nanjing Road and the atmosphere of the department stores can also be found in the novel by Vicki Baum, *Nanking Road* (London: Geoffrey Bles, 1939).

33. Sarah E. Stevens, "Figuring Modernity: The New Woman and the Modern Girl in Republican China," *NWSA Journal* 15, no. 3 (2003): 82–103.

34. Among the many descriptions of the mythical Shanghai, see the excellent Bickers, *Empire Made Me*, esp. chap. 9; Yeh, *Shanghai Splendor*, chap. 3.

35. Ling Ding, Tani Barlow, and Gary Gjorge, *I Myself Am a Woman: Selected Writings of Ding Ling* (Boston: Beacon Press, 1989), 154–55. Second quote is from "Shanghai at Play," *China Journal* 22 (1935): 230.

36. Josef von Sternberg, *Fun in a Chinese Laundry* (New York: Macmillan, 1965), 82–83. A description of Great World can also be found in Maurine Karns and Pat Patterson, *Shanghai: High Lights, Low Lights, Tael Lights* (Shanghai: Tridon, 1936), 7–8.

37. Meng Yue, *Shanghai and the Edges of Empires* (Minneapolis: University of Minnesota Press, 2006), 187. The relationship to global entertainment is made by Catherine Yeh, "Guides to a Global Paradise: Shanghai Entertainment Park Newspapers and the Invention of Chinese Urban Leisure," in *Transcultural Turbulences: Towards a Multi-Sited Reading of Image Flows*, ed. Christiane Brosius and Roland Wenzlhuemer (Berlin: Springer Berlin Heidelberg, 2011), 97–131, cited in Nga Li Lam, "Women as Pleasure Seekers: Courtesans, Actresses, and Female Visitors in the Amusement Halls of Early Republican Shanghai," *Journal of Urban History* 45 (2019): 671–92.

38. Drummond-Hay, "The Paris of the Distant Orient," *Sphere* (London), 16 July 1927.

39. LaSelle Gilman, "Shanghai Alive with News in 1934," *China Press* (Shanghai), 1 January 1935; Harry J. Greenwall, "Shanghai—City of Paradox," *Sphere* (London), 28 August 1937.

40. Lu Xun, *Lu Xun: Selected Works*, trans. Yang Xianyi and Gladys Yang, 3rd ed., vol. 4 (Beijing: Foreign Language Press, 1980), 118–19; Hanchao Lu, "Creating Urban Outcasts: Shantytowns in Shanghai, 1920–1950," *Journal of Urban History* 21, no. 5 (1995): 563–96. See more recently Christian Henriot, "Slums, Squats or Hutments? Constructing and Deconstructing an In-Between Space in Modern Shanghai (1926–1965)," *Frontiers of History in China* 7, no. 4 (December 2012): 499–528.

41. Henriot, Shi, and Aubrun, *Population of Shanghai*, 23–24.

42. Xun, *Lu Xun*, 4:4, 80, 180.

43. On the treatment of Shanghai's millhands, see Wai Kit Choi, "Making Capitalism with Gangsters: Unfree Labor in Shanghai's Cotton Mills, 1927–1937," *International Labor and Working-Class History* 94 (Fall 2018): 107–32.

44. On leftist activism at Shanghai University, see Harper, *Underground Asia*, 523–24. On the protests and political movements in Shanghai, see chaps. 2–3 in Frazier, *Power of Place*. Also see S. A. Smith, *A Road Is Made: Communism in Shanghai, 1920–1927* (Honolulu: University of Hawai'i Press, 2000).

45. Jean Chesneaux, *The Chinese Labor Movement, 1919–1927* (Stanford, CA: Stanford University Press, 1968), 349.

46. *London Illustrated News*, 29 January and 16 April 1927 as well as 6 February 1932.

47. *Daily Herald* (London), 4 June, 6 August, and 14 November 1925.

48. *Times of India* (Bombay), 4 June 1925.

49. Leo Ou-fan Lee, "Shanghai Modern: Reflections on Urban Culture in China in the 1930s," in Gaonkar, *Alternative Modernities*, 105–6.

50. *Chinese Recorder* (Shanghai), 1 July 1924; Tansen Sen, *India, China, and the World: A Connected History* (New York: Rowman and Littlefield, 2017), 106–7, 123. See as well Madhavi Thampi, "The Indian Community in China and Sino-Indian Relations," in Thampi, *India and China*, 66–82.

51. On the Ghadar Party, see B. R. Deepak, *India-China Relations in the First Half of the 20th Century* (New Delhi: A. P. H., 2001), 70–74; Isabella Jackson, "The Raj on Nanjing Road: Sikh Policemen in Treaty-Port Shanghai," *Modern Asian Studies* 46, no. 6 (March 2013): 1–13; as well as Cao Yin, *From Policeman to Revolutionaries: A Sikh Diaspora in Global Shanghai, 1885–1945* (New York: Brill, 2017).

52. Tsai and Cheng, *Statistics of Foreign Trade*, 2–11.

53. Mrs. Alec-Tweedie, *An Adventurous Journey: Russia-Siberia-China* (London: Thornton Butterworth, 1926), 223. On the history of Hong Kong, see Steve Tsang, *A Modern History of Hong Kong* (London: I. B. Tauris, 2007), as well as Frank Welsh, *A History of Hong Kong* (London: HarperCollins, 1997), and Colin N. Crisswell, *The Taipans: Hong Kong's Merchant Princes* (Hong Kong: Oxford University Press, 1991). See also Chan Lau Kit-ching, *China, Britain and Hong Kong 1895–1945* (Hong Kong: Chinese University Press, 1990).

54. Cecilia L. Chu, *Building Colonial Hong Kong: Speculative Development and Segregation in the City* (Abingdon, UK: Routledge, 2022), 50–54. On racial segregation in Hong Kong, see also John M. Carroll, *Edge of Empires: Chinese Elites and British Colonials in Hong Kong* (Cambridge, MA: Harvard University Press, 2005), 90–96.

55. On the role of Hong Kong in the migrant middleman business, see Adam M. McKeown, "From Opium Farmer to Astronaut: A Global History of Diasporic Chinese Business," *Diaspora* 9, no. 3 (2000): 317–60. See also his "Chinese Emigration in Global Context, 1850–1940," *Journal of Global History* 5 (2010): 95–124. On the currency exchanges through remittances, see Elizabeth Sinn, "Hong Kong as an In-between Place in the Chinese Diaspora, 1849–1939," in Gabaccia and Hoerder, *Connecting Seas and Connected Ocean Rims*, 243. See also Elizabeth Sinn, *Pacific Crossing: California Gold, Chinese Migration, and the Making of Hong Kong* (Hong Kong: Hong Kong University Press, 2013).

56. These figures are given by Claude Markovits in "Indian Communities in China, c. 1842–1949," in *New Frontiers: Imperialism's New Communities in East Asia, 1842–1953*, ed. Robert Bickers and Christian Henriot (Manchester: Manchester University Press, 2000), 59.

57. On Indian businesses in Hong Kong, see Madhavi Thampi, *Indians in China, 1800–1949* (New Delhi: Manohar, 2005), 100–104, 165.

58. *Finance & Commerce* (Shanghai), 24 May 1939.

Chapter 7

1. Frank H. H. King, *The History of the Hong Kong and Shanghai Banking Corporation*, 4 vols., vol. 3, *The Hong Kong Bank between the Wars and the Bank Interned, 1919–1945: Return from Grandeur* (Cambridge: Cambridge University Press, 1988), 388–90.

2. *Finance & Commerce* (Shanghai), 4 November 1936. The Municipal Council is described in George Woodcock, *The British in the Far East* (New York: Atheneum, 1969), 155–61. More recently, see the excellent discussion of the council in Jackson, *Shaping Modern Shanghai*, esp. chap. 2.

3. Sam Ginsbourg, *My First Sixty Years in China* (Beijing: New World Press, 1982), 35.

4. *North China Herald* (Shanghai), 30 June 1931.

5. On the machinations of banking in China, see Clarence B. Davis, "Financing Imperialism: British and American Bankers as Vectors of Imperial Expansion in China, 1908–1920," *Business History Review* 56, no. 2 (Summer 1982): 236–64. A detailed description of the bank building on the Bund is given in the *North China Herald* (Shanghai), 17 January 1920.

6. John B. Powell, *My Twenty-Five Years in China* (New York: Macmillan, 1945), 7.

7. W. Somerset Maugham, *On a Chinese Screen* (New York: George H. Doran, 1922), 31–32. See also Nanad Djordjevi, "British Clubs and Associations in Old Shanghai," *Journal of the Royal Asiatic Society* 74, no. 1 (2010): 123–38. An excellent description of British Settlement life is given in Bickers, *Empire Made Me*, esp. chap. 3, "Shanghai 1919," as well as his earlier *Britain in China: Community, Culture and Colonialism 1900–1949* (Manchester: Manchester University Press, 1999), esp. chap. 3.

8. The debates around rates and racial segregation in the concessions are reviewed by Manley O. Hudson, "An Analysis of the 'International Settlement' at Shanghai," *China Weekly Review*, 29 October 1927, 21–26.

9. Bergère, *Shanghai*, 147.

10. Yeh, *Shanghai Splendor*, 1–2; Sabine Dabringhaus and Jürgen Osterhammel, "Chinese Middle Classes between Empire and Revolution," in Dejung, Motadel, and Osterhammel, *Global Bourgeoisie*, 331–32.

11. On this point, see Jeffrey N. Wasserstrom, "Cosmopolitan Connections and Transnational Networks," in *At the Crossroads of Empire: Middlemen, Social Networks, and State-Building in Republican Shanghai*, ed. Nara Dillon and Jean Oi (Palo Alto, CA: Stanford University Press, 2007), 206–66.

12. Biographical information on Chinese businessmen is found in George F. Nellist, ed., *Men of Shanghai and North China, a Standard Biographical Reference Work* (Shanghai: Oriental Press, 1933).

13. Henriot, Shi, and Aubrun, *Population of Shanghai*, 30.

14. See the descriptions of Shanghai's fleshpots in Karns and Patterson, *Shanghai*, 26–38.

15. Miller, *Shanghai*, 38.

16. On Shanghai's Russian community, see Marcia Reynders Ristaino, *Port of Last Resort: The Diaspora Communities of Shanghai* (Stanford, CA: Stanford University Press, 2001), 81–83.

17. On Shanghai's Jewish refugees, see Kevin Ostoyich and Yun Xia, eds., *The History of the Shanghai Jews: New Pathways of Research* (New York: Palgrave Macmillan, 2022), esp. pt. 2, "Cultural Life of Refugees."

18. Zu'en Chen, "Japanese People in Modern Shanghai," *Journal of the Royal Asiatic Society* 74, no. 1 (2010): 112–21.

19. Victor Sassoon Diary, 28–29 January 1932; Sir Ellice Victor Elias Sassoon Papers and Photographs, series 1: Diaries and Correspondence, DeGolyer Library, Southern Methodist University, Dallas.

20. This incident was described in interviews with Sassoon and his family by Stanley Jackson in Jackson, *The Sassoons*, 230–31.

21. Lady Drummond-Hay, "The Paris of the Distant Orient," *Sphere* (London), 16 July 1927.

22. Arthur Ransome, "The Shanghai Mind," *Manchester (England) Guardian*, 2 May 1927. See also Robert Bickers, *Changing Shanghai's "Mind": Publicity, Reform and the British in Shanghai, 1927–1931* (London: China Society, 1992).

23. Feetham, *Report of the Hon. Richard Feetham*, 1:1, e.g. 68–69, 77, 264, 301. See also "The Future of Shanghai" in the *North China Herald* (Shanghai), 29 September 1931.

24. On Chinese reactions to the Feetham Report, see C. Y. W. Meng, "A Chinese Viewpoint on Shanghai," *China Weekly Review* (Shanghai), 12 September 1931, and the *North China Herald* (Shanghai), 8 September 1931. On negative British reaction to extraterritoriality, see the *North China Herald* (Shanghai), 19 September 1925.

25. Roskam, *Improvised City*, 200–205.

26. See Dayu Doon, "Greater Shanghai—Greater Vision," *China Heritage Quarterly* 10, no. 5 (1935): 103–6, as well as Stuart Lillico, "The Civic Centre at Kiangwan," *China Journal* 22 (1935): 225–28. Also, Arthur De C. Sowerby, "Greater Shanghai," *China Journal* 16 (May 1932): 215–17. See also the detailed study of Shanghai's modernization by Henriot, *Shanghai, 1927–1937*.

27. Sergeant, *Shanghai: Collision Point*, 131.

28. *North China Herald* (Shanghai), 27 December 1933.

29. "Shanghai Stocks Climbing," *Far Eastern Review*, September 1931, 540.

30. See for example "Shanghai's Land Values," *North China Herald* (Shanghai), 15 August 1925, and "The Real Estate Market: Extraordinary Building Activity," *North China Herald* (Shanghai), 31 December 1929. On Asia Realty Company profits, "Asia Realty Company Gives Full Details of Recent Activities in Local Real Estate Market," *China Press* (Shanghai), 14 October 1930. See also Edward Denison and Guang Yu Ren, *Modernism in China: Architectural Visions and Revolutions* (Chichester, UK: John Wiley, 2008), 153.

31. *China Press* (Shanghai), 25 May 1933.

32. *North China Herald* (Shanghai), 25 March 1930.

33. *North China Herald* (Shanghai), 9 May 1934.

34. On the details of Sassoon's real estate deals, see Stephanie Po-yin Chung, "Floating in Mud to Reach the Skies: Victor Sassoon and the Real Estate Boom in Shanghai, 1920s–1930s," *International Journal of Asian Studies* 16 (2019): 1–31.

35. Nicholas R. Clifford, *Spoilt Children of Empire: Westerners in Shanghai and the Chinese Revolution of the 1920s* (Hanover, NH: Middlebury College Press, 1991), 273.

36. "British Realty Firms Earn Largest Profits in History," *China Weekly Review* (Shanghai), 17 February 1940. See also William Parker, "Progressive Future Seen for Shanghai," *China Press* (Shanghai), 16 September 1936. See also Yuezhi Xiong, *Shanghai Urban Life and Its Heterogeneous Cultural Entanglements*, trans. Lane J. Harris (Boston: Brill, 2022), 38.

37. *North China Herald* (Shanghai), 31 December 1929.
38. "Modern Genies," *North China Daily News* (Shanghai), 14 November 1932. See also Ernest O. Hauser, *Shanghai: City for Sale* (New York: Harcourt, Brace, 1940), 112, 120–21.
39. *North China Herald* (Shanghai), 3 August 1929.
40. George F. Shecklen, "Shanghai, the Radio Central of China," *Far Eastern Review*, June 1930, 290; M. Pavlovsky and H. Sauve, "French Equipped International Wireless Station in Shanghai," *Far Eastern Review*, March 1931, 182; *China Press* (Shanghai), 1 January 1935.
41. *New York Times*, 14 April 1932.
42. W. H. Auden and Christopher Isherwood, *Journey to a War* (London: Faber & Faber, 1939), 237–38.
43. Sassoon Diary, 10 and 12 April 1931.
44. *North China Herald* (Shanghai), 25 January 1933; Vicki Baum, *Shanghai '37* (Hong Kong: Oxford University Press, 1986), 319.
45. On these details and on the Shanghai races in general, see James Hugh Carter, *Champions Day: The End of Old Shanghai* (New York: W. W. Norton, 2020). See also Coates, *China Races*.
46. Emily Hahn, *China to Me: A Partial Autobiography* (Philadelphia: Blakiston, 1945), 22.
47. "Shanghai as an Aviation Center," *China Journal of Science and Arts* 22, no. 5 (May 1935): 243–47. In addition, see the *North China Herald* (Shanghai), 14 January 1930, and "Aeronautical Progress in China," *Far Eastern Review*, September 1930, 498–99. See also Lincoln, *Urban History of China*, 165.
48. Sassoon Diary, 6 and 9 November 1937 and 3 December 1937.
49. US Congress, Senate Committee on the Judiciary, Subcommittee to Investigate the Administration of the Internal Security Act and the Other Internal Security Laws, *The Amerasia Papers: A Clue to the Catastrophe of China*, vol. 1 (Washington, DC: US Government Printing Office, 1970), 279. See also the essays in Christian Henriot and Wen-hsin Yeh, eds., *In the Shadow of the Rising Sun: Shanghai under Japanese Occupation* (Cambridge: Cambridge University Press, 2004).
50. *Finance & Commerce* (Shanghai), 1 September and 15 September 1937. For the impact of the fighting and the Japanese takeover of Shanghai's industry, see Shanghai Municipal Council, *Report for the Year 1937 and Budget for the Year 1938* (Shanghai: North China Daily News and Herald, 1938), 21–23.
51. *Finance & Commerce* (Shanghai), 13 April 1938.

Epilogue

1. "The Shanghai Boom," *Fortune*, January 1935, 31–40.
2. Milton Bronner, "Sassoons, Greatest Boosters of Shanghai, Seriously Affected by Japanese War," *China Weekly Review* (Shanghai), 29 January 1938.
3. The details on Sassoon's financing are described in Jackson, *The Sassoons*, 251.
4. Letter to Derek Fitzgerald, 11 January 1938, Sir Ellice Victor Elias Sassoon Papers and Photographs, series 1: Diaries and Correspondence, DeGolyer Library, Southern Methodist University, Dallas.
5. Japanese intelligence gathering is detailed in Ristaino, *Port of Last Resort*, 150.
6. *North China Herald* (Shanghai), 15 March 1939.

7. Newspaper clipping, "Shanghai's Richest Man Sees Finish to Fortune" (no newspaper title, article author, date), Victor Sassoon Diary, 8 April 1941; Sir Ellice Victor Elias Sassoon Papers and Photographs, series 1: Diaries and Correspondence, De-Golyer Library, Southern Methodist University, Dallas.

8. Newspaper clipping, "'Congress Has Committed Suicide,' Sir V. Sassoon's Plea, 'Freedom Lies in Nazi Defeat'" (no newspaper title, article author, date), Victor Sassoon Diary, 9 October 1940.

9. Newspaper clipping, "Sir V. Sassoon's Views Not Helpful" (no newspaper title, article author, date), Victor Sassoon Diary, 20 January 1942, and "Concentration Camp!" (no newspaper title, article author, date), Sassoon Diary, 7 February 1942.

10. Newspaper clipping, "War Dooms Vast Fortunes, Says Orient's 'J. P. Morgan'" (no newspaper title, article author, date), Sassoon Diary, 3 March 1941.

11. Newspaper clipping, Ward Archer, "Shanghai's Richest Man Visits Memphis after Auto Accident" (no newspaper title, date), Sassoon Diary, 8 April 1941.

12. Newspaper clippings, "American-British Alliance Urged by English Visitor," 17 June 1941, and "'Britain Should Join the U.S.,'" Sassoon Diary, 18 June 1941 (no newspaper titles, article authors, dates); *Rangoon Gazette*, "'Japan Will Not Fight in S.E. Asia,' Sir V. Sassoon's Arrival in Rangoon" (no article author, date), Sassoon Diary, 25 August 1941.

13. Sassoon Diary, 20 March 1942.

14. *Times of India* (Bombay), 18 December 1941.

15. Newspaper clipping, "Ship Twice Sunk by Jap Radio Arrives with 175 Passengers" (no newspaper title, article author, date), Sassoon Diary, 28 March 1942.

Selected Bibliography

It would be impossible to account for all the outstanding histories of Bombay, London, and Shanghai in this bibliography, much less the corpus of research on cities and globalization. This list comprises the most instrumental publications in the research and writing of this book. I have also emphasized those written in the 1920s and 1930s as primary source material.

Abend, Hallett. *My Years in China 1926–1941*. London: John Lane, 1944.
Abrams, Mark, ed. *Britain and Her Export Trade*. London: Pilot Press, 1945.
Ainscough, Thomas Martland. *Report on the Conditions and Prospects of British Trade in India, 1927–28*. London: His Majesty's Stationery Office, 1928.
Alec-Tweedie, Mrs. *An Adventurous Journey: Russia-Siberia-China*. London: Thornton Butterworth, 1926.
Ambedkar, B. R. *The Problem of the Rupee: Its Origin and Its Solution*. London: P. S. King and Son, 1923.
Amrith, Sunil S. *Crossing the Bay of Bengal: The Furies of Nature and the Fortunes of Migrants*. Cambridge, MA: Harvard University Press, 2015.
Arrighi, Giovanni. *The Long Twentieth Century: Money, Power, and the Origins of Our Times*. London: Verso, 1994.
Arts, Mara. *Interwar London after Dark in British Popular Culture*. Cham, Switzerland: Palgrave Macmillan, 2022.
Baker, Barbara, ed. *Shanghai: Electric and Lurid City*. Hong Kong: Oxford University Press, 1998.
Balachandran, G. *John Bullion's Empire: Britain's Gold Problem and India between the Wars*. Abingdon, UK: Routledge, 2006.
Ballantyne, Tony, and Antoinette Burton. *Empires and the Reach of the Global, 1870–1945*. Cambridge, MA: Belknap Press of Harvard University Press, 2012.
Baster, A. S. J. *The Imperial Banks*. London: P. S. King and Son, 1929.
Baum, Vicki. *Nanking Road*. London: Geoffrey Bles, 1939.
———. *Shanghai '37*. Hong Kong: Oxford University Press, 1986. Originally published 1939.
Beckert, Sven. *Empire of Cotton: A Global History*. New York: Vintage, 2014.
Béliard, Yann, and Neville Kirk, eds. *Workers of the Empire, Unite: Radical and Pop-

ular Challenges to British Imperialism, 1910s–1960s. Liverpool: Liverpool University Press, 2021.
Benton, Charlotte, Tim Benton, and Ghislaine Wood, eds. Art Deco 1910–1939. New York: Bulfinch, 2003.
Bergère, Marie-Claire. Shanghai: China's Gateway to Modernity. Stanford, CA: Stanford University Press, 2009.
Bickers, Robert. China Bound: John Swire and Sons and Its World, 1816–1980. London: Bloomsbury Business, 2020.
———. Britain in China: Community, Culture and Colonialism 1900–1949. Manchester: Manchester University Press, 1999.
———. Empire Made Me: An Englishman Adrift in Shanghai. New York: Columbia University Press, 2003.
Bickers, Robert, and Christian Henriot, eds. New Frontiers: Imperialism's New Communities in East Asia, 1842–1953. Manchester: Manchester University Press, 2000.
Blake, A. H. Things Seen in London. London: Seeley, 1921.
Bordo, Michael D., Alan M. Taylor, and Jeffrey G. Williamson, eds. Globalization in Historical Perspective. Chicago: University of Chicago Press, 2003.
Bose, Arun Coomer. Indian Revolutionaries Abroad, 1905–1922: In the Background of International Developments. Patna, India: Bharati Bhawan, 1971.
Bose, Sugata. A Hundred Horizons: The Indian Ocean in the Age of Global Empire. Cambridge, MA: Harvard University Press, 2006.
Bowen, Elizabeth. To the North. New York: Anchor, 2006.
Branson, Noreen. Britain in the Nineteen Twenties. Minneapolis: University of Minnesota Press, 1976.
Braudel, Fernand. The Perspective of the World. Translated by Siân Reynolds. Vol. 3 of Civilization and Capitalism, 15th–18th Century. New York: Harper and Row, 1984.
Bromfield, Louis. Night in Bombay. New York: Grosset and Dunlap, 1939.
Brook, Timothy, and Bob Tadashi Wakabayashi, eds. Opium Regimes: China, Britain, and Japan, 1839–1952. Berkeley: University of California Press, 2000.
Brooks, Collin. Something in the City: Men and Markets in London. London: Country Life, 1931.
Burke, Thomas. The London Spy. New York: George H. Doran, 1922.
———. More Limehouse Nights. New York: George H. Doran, 1921.
Burnett-Hurst, A. R. Labour and Housing in Bombay: A Study in the Economic Conditions of the Wage-Earning Classes in Bombay. London: P. S. King, 1925.
Carroll, John M. Edge of Empires: Chinese Elites and British Colonials in Hong Kong. Cambridge, MA: Harvard University Press, 2005.
Carter, James Hugh. Champions Day: The End of Old Shanghai. New York: W. W. Norton, 2020.
Chandavarkar, Rajnarayan. Imperial Power and Popular Politics: Class, Resistance and the State in India, c. 1850–1950. New York: Cambridge University Press, 1998.
———. The Origins of Industrial Capitalism in India: Business Strategies and the Working Classes in Bombay, 1900–1940. Cambridge: Cambridge University Press, 1994.
Chandler, Tertius. Four Thousand Years of Urban Growth, an Historical Census. New York: St. David's University Press, 1987.

Chapman, Stanley D. *The Rise of Merchant Banking*. London: Routledge, 2006.
Chatterjee, Arup K. *Indians in London: From the Birth of the East India Company to Independent India*. London: Bloomsbury Academic, 2021.
Chattopadhyay, Swati. *Unlearning the City: Infrastructure in a New Optical Field*. Minneapolis: University of Minnesota Press, 2012.
Chaudhary, Latika, Bishnupriya Gupta, Tirthankar Roy, and Anand V. Swamy, eds. *A New Economic History of Colonial India*. London: Routledge, 2016.
Chesneaux, Jean. *The Chinese Labor Movement, 1919–1927*. Stanford, CA: Stanford University Press, 1968.
Chhabria, Sheetal. *Making the Modern Slum: The Power of Capital in Colonial Bombay*. Seattle: University of Washington Press, 2019.
Cholia, Rasiklal P. *Dock Labourers in Bombay*. Calcutta: Longmans, Green, 1941.
Chopra, Preeti. *A Joint Enterprise: Indian Elites and the Making of British Bombay*. Minneapolis: University of Minnesota Press, 2011.
Chu, Cecilia L. *Building Colonial Hong Kong: Speculative Development and Segregation in the City*. Abingdon, UK: Routledge, 2022.
Clifford, Nicholas R. *Spoilt Children of Empire: Westerners in Shanghai and the Chinese Revolution of the 1920s*. Hanover, NH: Middlebury College Press, 1991.
Clunn, Harold P. *The Face of London: The Record of a Century of Changes and Development*. 7th ed. London: Simpkin Marshall, 1937.
Coates, Austin. *China Races*. Oxford: Oxford University Press, 1983.
Coble, Parks M. *The Shanghai Capitalists and the Nationalist Government, 1927–1937*. 2nd ed. Cambridge, MA: Harvard University Press, 1986.
Cochran, Sherman. *Encountering Chinese Networks: Western, Japanese, and Chinese Corporations in China, 1880–1937*. Berkeley: University of California Press, 2000.
Cocteau, Jean. *My Journey round the World*. Translated by W. J. Strachan. London: Peter Owen, 1958.
Cohen-Portheim, Paul. *The Spirit of London*. London: B. T. Batsford, 1935.
Conboy, Martin. *Tabloid Britain: Constructing a Community through Language*. London: Routledge, 2006.
Cook, Wilfrid Harris. *The General Strike: A Study of Labor's Tragic Weapon in Theory and Practice*. Chapel Hill: University of North Carolina Press, 1931.
Coons, Lorraine, and Alexander Varias. *Tourist Third Class: Steamship Travel in the Interwar Years*. New York: Palgrave Macmillan, 2003.
Crane, Walter. *India Impressions, with Some Notes of Ceylon during a Winter Tour, 1906–7*. New York: Macmillan, 1907.
Crisswell, Colin N. *The Taipans: Hong Kong's Merchant Princes*. Hong Kong: Oxford University Press, 1991.
Crow, Carl. *The Travelers' Handbook for China (including Hong Kong)*. 3rd ed. New York: Dodd, Mead, 1921.
Cursetjee, C. W. *The Land of the Date*. Bombay: Dhanjibhoy Dosabhoy, 1918.
Cuthbertson, Ken. *Nobody Said Not to Go: The Life, Loves, and Adventures of Emily Hahn*. Boston: Faber and Faber, 1998.
Dadabhoy, Bakhtiar K. *Barons of Banking: Glimpses of Indian Banking History*. Haryana, India: Penguin Random House India, 2013.
Darwin, John. *Unfinished Empire: The Global Expansion of Britain*. London: Bloomsbury, 2013.

---. *Unlocking the World: Port Cities and Globalization in the Age of Steam, 1830–1930*. London: Allen Lane, 2020.
De Courcy, Anne. *Chanel's Riviera: Glamour, Decadence, and Survival in Peace and War, 1930–1944*. New York: St. Martin's Press, 2020.
Deepak, B. R. *India-China Relations in the First Half of the 20th Century*. New Delhi: A. P. H., 2001.
Dejung, Christof, David Motadel, and Jürgen Osterhammel, eds. *The Global Bourgeoisie: The Rise of the Middle Classes in the Age of Empire*. Princeton, NJ: Princeton University Press, 2019.
Denison, Edward, and Guang Yu Ren. *Building Shanghai: The Story of China's Gateway*. Chichester, UK: John Wiley, 2006.
---. *Modernism in China: Architectural Visions and Revolutions*. Chichester, UK: John Wiley, 2008.
Desai, Dinkar D. *Maritime Labour in India*. Bombay: Servants of India Society, 1940.
Dickinson, Edward Ross. *The World in the Long Twentieth Century: An Interpretive History*. Berkeley: University of California Press, 2018.
Dillon, Nara, and Jean Oi, eds. *At the Crossroads of Empire: Middlemen, Social Networks, and State-Building in Republican Shanghai*. Palo Alto, CA: Stanford University Press, 2007.
Ding, Ling, Tani Barlow, and Gary Gjorge. *I Myself Am a Woman: Selected Writings of Ding Ling*. Boston: Beacon Press, 1989.
Diqui, Ben. *A Visit to Bombay*. London: Watts, 1927.
Dobbin, Christine E. *Asian Entrepreneurial Minorities: Conjoint Communities in the Making of the World-Economy 1570–1940*. London: RoutledgeCurzon, an imprint of Taylor and Francis Group, 1996.
Dossal, Mariam. *Theatre of Conflict, City of Hope: Bombay/Mumbai; 1660 to Present Times*. Oxford: Oxford University Press, 2010.
Dowling, S. W. *The Exchanges of London*. London: Butterworth, 1929.
Driver, Felix, and David Gilbert, eds. *Imperial Cities: Landscape, Display and Identity*. Manchester: Manchester University Press, 1999.
Dupree, Marguerite, ed. *Lancashire and Whitehall: The Diary of Sir Raymond Streat*. Vol. 1, *1931–39*. Manchester: Manchester University Press, 1987.
Dwivedi, Sharada, and Rahul Mehrotra. *Bombay: The Cities Within*. Bombay: India Book House, 2001.
Edwardes, Stephen Meredyth. *By-Ways of Bombay*. Bombay: Times of India Office, 1912.
Farrer, James, and Andrew David Field. *Shanghai Nightscapes: A Nocturnal Biography of a Global City*. Chicago: University of Chicago Press, 2015.
Favell, Adrian, and Michael Peter Smith, eds. *The Human Face of Global Mobility*. New York: Routledge, 2006.
Fawaz, Leila, and C. A. Bayly, eds. *Modernity and Culture: From the Mediterranean to the Indian Ocean*. New York: Columbia University Press, 2002.
Felstead, Sidney Theodore. *The Underworld of London*. London: John Murray, 1923.
Fernandes, Naresh. *Taj Mahal Foxtrot: The Story of Bombay's Jazz Age*. New Delhi: Roli Books, 2012.
Field, Andrew David. *Shanghai's Dancing World: Cabaret Culture and Urban Politics, 1919–1954*. Hong Kong: Chinese University of Hong Kong, 2010.

Frazier, Mark W. *The Power of Place: Contentious Politics in Twentieth-Century Shanghai and Bombay*. Cambridge: Cambridge University Press, 2019.
Frieden, Jeffry A. *Global Capitalisms: Its Fall and Rise in the Twentieth Century*. New York: W. W. Norton, 2007.
Gabaccia, Donna R., and Dirk Hoerder, eds. *Connecting Seas and Connected Ocean Rims: Indian, Atlantic, and Pacific Oceans and China Seas Migrations from the 1830s to the 1930s*. Leiden: Brill, 2011.
Gaonkar, Dilip Parameshwar, ed. *Alternative Modernities*. Durham, NC: Duke University Press, 2001.
German, Lindsey, and John Rees. *A People's History of London*. London: Verso, 2012.
Ghosh, Anindita. *Claiming the City: Protest, Crime, and Scandals in Colonial Calcutta, c. 1860–1920*. New Delhi: Oxford University Press, 2016.
Gibson-Jarvie, Robert. *The City of London. A Financial and Commercial History*. Cambridge: Woodhead-Faulkner, 1979.
Gilmour, David. *The British in India: A Social History of the Raj*. New York: Farrar, Straus and Giroux, 2018.
Ginsbourg, Sam. *My First Sixty Years in China*. Beijing: New World Press, 1982.
Goldstein-Sabbah, S. R. *Baghdadi Jewish Networks in the Age of Nationalism*. Leiden: Brill, 2021.
Gordon, A. D. D. *Businessmen and Politics: Rising Nationalism and a Modernising Economy in Bombay, 1918–1933*. New Delhi: Manohar, 1978.
Gorman, Daniel. *The Emergence of International Society in the 1920s*. Cambridge: Cambridge University Press, 2012.
Graves, Charles. *The Price of Pleasure*. London: Ivor Nicholson and Watson, 1935.
Green, Nile. *Bombay Islam: The Religious Economy of the West Indian Ocean, 1840–1915*. Cambridge: Cambridge University Press, 2011.
Greenwall, Harry James. *Storm over India*. London: Hurst and Blackett, 1933.
Grescoe, Taras. *Shanghai Grand*. New York: St. Martin's Press, 2016.
Gull, E. M. *British Economic Interests in the Far East*. London: Oxford University Press, 1943.
Hahn, Emily. *China to Me: A Partial Autobiography*. Philadelphia: Blakiston, 1944.
Hall, Peter. *The Industries of London since 1861*. London: Hutchinson, 1962.
Harper, Tim. *Underground Asia: Global Revolutionaries and the Assault on Empire*. Cambridge, MA: Belknap Press of Harvard University Press, 2021.
Harris, Richard. *How Cities Matter*. Cambridge Elements in Global Urban History, edited by Michael Goebel, Tracy Neumann, and Joseph Ben Prestel. Cambridge: Cambridge University Press, 2021.
Harris, Rob. *London's Global Office Economy: From Clerical Factory to Digital Hub*. Abingdon, UK: Routledge, 2021.
Harwood, Elain. *Art Deco Britain: Buildings of the Interwar Years*. London: Batsford, 2009.
Hauser, Ernest O. *Shanghai: City for Sale*. New York: Harcourt, Brace, 1940.
Haynes, Douglas E., Abigail McGowan, Roy Tirthankar, and Haruka Yanagisawa, eds. *Towards a History of Consumption in South Asia*. New Delhi: Oxford University Press, 2010.
Hazareesingh, Sandip. *The Colonial City and the Challenge of Modernity: Urban Hegemonies and Civic Contestation in Bombay City, 1900–1925*. Hyderabad: Orient Longman, 2007.

Henriot, Christian. *Shanghai, 1927–1937: Municipal Power, Locality, and Modernization*. Berkeley: University of California Press, 1993.
Henriot, Christian, Lu Shi, and Charlotte Aubrun. *The Population of Shanghai (1865–1953): A Sourcebook*. Leiden: Brill, 2019.
Henriot, Christian, and Wen-hsin Yeh, eds. *In the Shadow of the Rising Sun: Shanghai under Japanese Occupation*. Cambridge: Cambridge University Press, 2004.
Horesh, Niv. *Shanghai's Bund and Beyond: British Banks, Banknotes Issuance, and Monetary Policy in China, 1842–1937*. New Haven, CT: Yale University Press, 2009.
Hosagrahar, Jyoti. *Indigenous Modernities: Negotiating Architecture and Urbanism*. London: Routledge, 2005.
Huggins, Mike. *Horseracing and the British, 1919–39*. Manchester: Manchester University Press, 2003.
Indian Science Congress. *Bombay Past and Present: A Souvenir of the Sixth Meeting of the Indian Science Congress Held in Bombay in January 1919*. Bombay: Times Press, 1919.
Iyer, Kamu, ed. *Buildings That Shaped Bombay: Works of G. B. Mhatre*. Mumbai: Kamala Raheja Vidyanidhi Institute of Architecture, 2000.
Jackson, Isabella. *Shaping Modern Shanghai: Colonialism in China's Global City*. Cambridge: Cambridge University Press, 2017.
Jackson, Stanley. *The Sassoons*. London: Heinemann, 1968.
Jones, James A. *Wonderful London Today*. London: John Long, 1934.
Joshi, A. N. *Life and Times of Sir Hormusjee C. Dinshaw*. Bombay: D. B. Taraporevala, 1939.
Kahn, Alfred E. *Great Britain in the World Economy*. New York: Columbia University Press, 1946.
Kale, Vaman Govind. *India's War Finance and Post-war Problems*. Poona: V. G. Kale, 1919.
Karns, Maurine, and Pat Patterson. *Shanghai: High Lights, Low Lights, Tael Lights*. Shanghai: Tridon, 1936.
Kaufman, Jonathan K. *The Last Kings of Shanghai: The Rival Jewish Dynasties That Helped Create Modern China*. London: Penguin Books, 2021.
Keynes, John Maynard. *Indian Currency and Finance*. London: Macmillan, 1924.
Kidambi, Prashant. *The Making of an Indian Metropolis: Colonial Governance and Public Culture in Bombay, 1890–1920*. London: Routledge, 2007.
Kidambi, Prashant, Manjiri Kamat, and Rachel Dwyer, eds. *Bombay before Mumbai: Essays in Honour of Jim Masselos*. New York: Oxford University Press, 2019.
Kienholz, Mary L. *Opium Traders and Their Worlds*. Vol. 2, *A Revisionist Exposé of the World's Greatest Opium Traders*. Bloomington, IN: iUniverse, 2008.
Kincaid, Dennis. *British Social Life in India, 1608–1937*. London: Routledge, 1938.
King, Anthony D. *Global Cities: Post-imperialism and the Internationalization of London*. London: Routledge, 2015.
———. *Writing the Global City: Globalisation, Postcolonialism and the Urban*. Abingdon, UK: Routledge, 2016.
King, Frank H. H. *The History of the Hong Kong and Shanghai Banking Corporation*. 4 vols. Vol. 3, *The Hong Kong Bank between the Wars and the Bank Interned, 1919–1945: Return from Grandeur*. Cambridge: Cambridge University Press, 1988.

Kocka, Jürgen, and Marcel Van der Linden, eds. *Capitalism: The Reemergence of a Historical Concept*. London: Bloomsbury Academic, 2016.
Kondapi, C. *Indians Overseas 1838–1949*. New Delhi: Indian Council of World Affairs and Oxford University Press, 1951.
Kooiman, Dick. *Bombay Textile Labour: Managers, Trade Unionists and Officials, 1918–1939*. Amsterdam: Free University Press, 1989.
Kosambi, Meera. *Bombay in Transition: The Growth and Social Ecology of a Colonial City, 1880–1980*. Stockholm: Almqvist and Wiksell International, 1986.
Kracauer, Siegfried. *The Salaried Masses: Duty and Distraction in Weimar Germany*. Translated by Quintin Hoare. London: Verso, 1998.
Krishnan, O. U. *The Night Side of Bombay*. Bombay: Krishnan, 1923.
Kuroda, Akinobu. *A Global History of Money*. Abingdon, UK: Routledge, 2020.
Kushner, Tony, ed. *The Jewish Heritage in British History: English and Jewishness*. New York: Frank Cass, 1992.
Kynaston, David. *The City of London*. Vol. 3, *Illusions of Gold, 1914–1945*. London: Pimlico, 2000.
Lau Kit-ching, Chan. *China, Britain and Hong Kong 1895–1945*. Hong Kong: Chinese University Press, 1990.
Law, Michael John. *1938: Modern Britain; Social Change and Visions of the Future*. London: Bloomsbury, 2018.
Lees, Andrew. *The City: A World History*. Oxford: Oxford University Press, 2015.
Lentin, Sifra. *Mercantile Bombay: A Journey of Trade, Finance and Enterprise*. Abingdon, UK: Routledge, 2022.
Lewis, Su Lin. *Cities in Motion: Urban Life and Cosmopolitanism in Southeast Asia, 1920–1940*. Cambridge: Cambridge University Press, 2016.
Lincoln, Toby. *An Urban History of China*. Cambridge: Cambridge University Press, 2021.
Ling, Pan. *In Search of Old Shanghai*. Hong Kong: Joint Publishing, 1982.
Liu, Andrew B. *Tea War: A History of Capitalism in China and India*. New Haven, CT: Yale University Press, 2020.
Lockwood, David. *The Indian Bourgeoisie: A Political History of the Indian Capitalist Class in the Early Twentieth Century*. London: Bloomsbury Academic, 2020.
Londres, Albert. *La Chine en folie*. Paris: A. Michel, 1925.
Long, Roger D., and Ian Talbot, eds. *India and World War I: A Centennial Assessment*. Abingdon, UK: Routledge, 2018.
Low, Sidney. *A Vision of India*. New York: E. P. Dutton; London: Smith, Elder, 1907.
Magee, Gary, and Andrew Thompson. *Empire and Globalisation: Networks of People, Goods and Capital in the British World, c. 1850–1914*. Cambridge: Cambridge University Press, 2010.
Manshardt, Clifford, ed. *Bombay Looks Ahead*. Bombay: D. B. Taraporevala, 1934.
———, ed. *Bombay Today and Tomorrow*. Bombay: D. B. Taraporevala, 1930.
Margetson, Stella. *The Long Party: High Society in the Twenties and Thirties*. London: Cremonesi, 1976.
Markovits, Claude. *Merchants, Traders, Entrepreneurs*. New York: Palgrave Macmillan, 2008.
Marriott, John. *Beyond the Tower: A History of East London*. New Haven, CT: Yale University Press, 2011.

Masterman, Charles F. G. *England after War: A Study*. London: Hodder and Stoughton, 1922.
Matera, Marc. *Black London: The Imperial Metropolis and Decolonization in the Twentieth Century*. Berkeley: University of California Press, 2015.
Matera, Marc, and Susan Kingsley Kent. *The Global 1930s: The International Decade*. London: Routledge, 2017.
Mathew, Johan. *Margins of the Market: Trafficking and Capitalism across the Arabian Sea*. Berkeley: University of California Press, 2016.
Maugham, W. Somerset. *On a Chinese Screen*. New York: George H. Doran, 1922.
McGowan, Abigail. *Crafting the Nation in Colonial India*. New York: Palgrave Macmillan, 2020.
McNamara, Sallie. *"Tatler"'s Irony: Conspicuous Consumption, Inconspicuous Power and Social Change*. Cham, Switzerland: Palgrave Pivot, 2018.
Mee, Arthur. *London: Heart of the Empire and Wonder of the World*. London: Caxton, 1937.
Metcalf, Thomas R. *Imperial Connections: India in the Indian Ocean Arena, 1860–1920*. Berkeley: University of California Press, 2008.
Meyer, F. V. *Britain's Colonies in World Trade*. London: Oxford University Press, 1948.
Michie, Ranald C. *The City of London: Continuity and Change, 1850–1990*. Basingstoke, UK: Macmillan, 1992.
Middleton, Smith. *The British in China and Far Eastern Trade*. London: Constable, 1920.
Miller, G. E. [pseud.]. *Shanghai, the Paradise of Adventurers*. New York: Orsay, 1937.
Miller, Michael B. *Europe and the Maritime World: A Twentieth Century History*. New York: Cambridge University Press, 2012.
Montagu, Edwin S. *An Indian Diary*. London: William Heinemann, 1930.
Morton, H. V. *H. V. Morton's London*. 12th ed. London: Methuen, 1945.
Muggeridge, Malcolm. *The Thirties: 1930–1940 in Great Britain*. London: Hamish Hamilton, 1940.
Mukherjee, Debashree. *Bombay Hustle: Making Movies in a Colonial City*. New York: Columbia University Press, 2020.
Murphey, Rhoads. *Shanghai, Key to Modern China*. Cambridge, MA: Harvard University Press, 1953.
Nellist, George F., ed. *Men of Shanghai and North China, a Standard Biographical Reference Work*. Shanghai: Oriental Press, 1933.
Newman, Richard. *Workers and Unions in Bombay, 1918–1929: A Study of Organisation in the Cotton Mills*. Canberra: Australian National University, 1981.
Nichols, Beverley. *All That I Could Never Be*. London: Jonathan Cape, 1949.
Nield, Robert F. C. A. *China's Foreign Places: The Foreign Presence in China in the Treaty Port Era, 1840–1943*. Hong Kong: Hong Kong University Press, 2015.
Nightingale, Carl H. *Earthopolis: A Biography of Our Urban Planet*. Cambridge: Cambridge University Press, 2022.
Osterhammel, Jürgen. *The Transformation of the World: A Global History of the Nineteenth Century*. Translated by Patrick Camiller. Princeton, NJ: Princeton University Press, 2015.
Ostoyich, Kevin, and Yun Xia, eds. *The History of the Shanghai Jews: New Pathways of Research*. New York: Palgrave Macmillan, 2022.

Ou-fan Lee, Leo. *Shanghai Modern: The Flowering of a New Urban Culture in China 1930–1945.* Cambridge, MA: Harvard University Press, 1999.
Overstreet, Gene D., and Marshall Windmiller. *Communism in India.* Berkeley: University of California Press, 2020.
Panayi, Panikos. *Migrant City: A New History of London.* New Haven, CT: Yale University Press, 2020.
Patel, Sujata, and Alice Thorner, eds. *Bombay, Metaphor for Modern India.* New Delhi: Oxford University Press, 1995.
Phillips, H. W. *Modern Foreign Exchange and Foreign Banking.* London: Macdonald and Evans, 1926.
Pinnick, A. W. *Silver and China.* Shanghai: Kelly and Walsh, 1930.
Pirie, Gordon. *Cultures and Caricatures of British Imperial Aviation: Passengers, Pilots, Publicity.* Manchester: Manchester University Press, 2012.
Polanyi, Karl. *The Great Transformation: The Political and Economic Origins of Our Time.* 2nd ed. Boston: Beacon Press, 2001.
Porter, Bernard. *Empire Ways: Aspects of British Imperialism.* London: I. B. Tauris, 2016.
Porter, Roy. *London: A Social History.* Cambridge, MA: Harvard University Press, 1995.
Potter, Simon J. *Wireless Internationalism and Distant Listening: Britain, Propaganda, and the Invention of Global Radio, 1920–1939.* Oxford: Oxford University Press, 2020.
Powell, John B. *My Twenty-Five Years in China.* New York: Macmillan, 1945.
Prakash, Gyan. *Mumbai Fables.* Princeton, NJ: Princeton University Press, 2010.
Priestley, J. B. *English Journey.* London: William Heinemann, 1934.
Pugh, Martin. *We Danced All Night: A Social History of Britain between the Wars.* London: Vintage, 2009.
Ramani, Navin. *Bombay Art Deco Architecture: A Visual Journey (1930–1953).* New Delhi: Roli Books, 2016.
Rao, Nikhil. *House, but No Garden: Apartment Living in Bombay's Suburbs, 1898–1964.* Minneapolis: University of Minnesota Press, 2013.
Rau, Basaarsu Ramachandra. *Present-Day Banking in India.* Calcutta: University of Calcutta, 1938.
Read, Margaret. *The Indian Peasant Uprooted: A Study of the Human Machine.* London: Longmans, Green, 1931.
Redford, Arthur. *Manchester Merchants and Foreign Trade.* Vol. 2, *1850–1939.* Manchester: Manchester University Press, 1956.
Reed, Sir Stanley. *The India I Knew, 1897–1947.* London: Odhams Press, 1952.
Reinhardt, Anne. *Navigating Semi-colonialism: Shipping, Sovereignty, and Nation-Building in China, 1860–1937.* Cambridge, MA: Harvard University Press, 2018.
Remer, Charles Frederick. *Foreign Investments in China.* New York: H. Fertig, 1968.
Ren, Xuefei, and Roger Keil, eds. *The Globalizing Cities Reader.* 2nd ed. Abingdon, UK: Routledge, 2018.
Ristaino, Marcia Reynders. *Port of Last Resort: The Diaspora Communities of Shanghai.* Stanford, CA: Stanford University Press, 2001.
Roberts, Richard, and David Kynaston. *The Lion Wakes: A Modern History of HSBC.* London: Profile Books, 2015.

Roland, Joan G. *The Jewish Communities of India: Identity in the Colonial Era*. 2nd ed. New Brunswick, NJ: Transaction, 1998.
Rosenberg, Emily S., ed. *A World Connecting, 1870–1945*. Cambridge, MA: Belknap Press of Harvard University Press, 2012.
Roskam, Cole. *Improvised City: Architecture and Governance in Shanghai, 1843–1937*. Seattle: University of Washington Press, 2019.
Rossi, Ugo. *Cities in Global Capitalism*. Cambridge: Polity Press, 2017.
Rotary Club of Bombay, ed. *Bombay, the Gateway to India: The Advantages It Offers to Industrialists*. Bombay: E. M. Gilbert-Lodge, 1936.
Roth, Cecil. *The Sassoon Dynasty*. London: R. Hale, 1941.
Roy, Ananya, and Aihwa Ong, eds. *Worlding Cities: Asian Experiments and the Art of Being Global*. Chichester, UK: Wiley-Blackwell, 2011.
Roy, Tirthankar. *A Business History of India: Enterprise and the Emergence of Capitalism from 1700*. Cambridge: Cambridge University Press, 2018.
———. *India in the World Economy: From Antiquity to the Present*. Cambridge: Cambridge University Press, 2012.
Rule, Fiona. *London's Docklands: A History of the Lost Quarter*. Gloucestershire: History Press, 2019.
Sandoval-Strausz, A. K., and Nancy H. Kwak, eds. *Making Cities Global: The Transnational Turn in Urban History*. Philadelphia: University of Pennsylvania Press, 2018.
Sassoon, Joseph. *The Sassoons: The Great Global Merchants and the Making of an Empire*. New York: Pantheon, 2022.
Sassoon, Philip. *The Third Route*. London: William Heinemann, 1929.
Schneer, Jonathan. *London 1900: The Imperial Metropolis*. New Haven, CT: Yale University Press, 1999.
Scott, Peter. *The Property Masters: A History of the British Commercial Property Sector*. London: E. and F. N. Spon, 1996.
Segbers, Klaus, ed. *The Making of Global City Regions: Johannesburg, Mumbai/Bombay, São Paulo, and Shanghai*. Baltimore: Johns Hopkins University Press, 2007.
Sen, Tansen. *India, China, and the World: A Connected History*. New York: Rowman and Littlefield, 2017.
Sergeant, Harriet. *Shanghai: Collision Point of Cultures, 1918–1939*. New York: Crown, 1990.
———. *Shanghai*. London: John Murray, 1991.
Shaikh, Juned. *Outcast Bombay: City Making and the Politics of the Poor*. Seattle: University of Washington Press, 2021.
Shirras, G. Findlay. *Indian Finance and Banking*. London: Macmillan, 1920.
Sims, George R., ed. *Living London: Its Work and Its Play, Its Humour and Its Pathos, Its Sights and Its Scenes*. 3 vols. London: Cassell, 1902–3.
Sinclair, Robert. *Metropolitan Man: The Future of the English*. London: George Allen and Unwin, 1937.
Sinn, Elizabeth. *Pacific Crossing: California Gold, Chinese Migration, and the Making of Hong Kong*. Hong Kong: Hong Kong University Press, 2013.
Skinner, Joan S. *Form and Fancy: Factories and Factory Buildings by Wallis, Gilbert and Partners, 1916–1939*. Liverpool: Liverpool University Press, 1997.
Smith, Douglas Hector. *The Industries of Greater London: Being a Survey of the*

Recent Industrialisation of the Northern and Western Sectors of Greater London, etc. London: P. S. King and Son, 1933.
Smith, H. Llewellyn. *The New Survey of London Life and Labour.* 9 vols. Vol. 1, *Forty Years of Change.* London: P. S. Kind and Son, 1930.
Smith, S. A. *A Road Is Made: Communism in Shanghai, 1920–1927.* Honolulu: University of Hawai'i Press, 2000.
Srivastava, Priyanka. *The Well-Being of the Labor Force in Colonial Bombay.* New York: Palgrave Macmillan, 2018.
Stephen, Daniel. *The Empire of Progress: West Africans, Indians, and Britons at the British Empire Exhibition, 1924–25.* New York: Palgrave Macmillan, 2013.
Sternberg, Josef von. *Fun in a Chinese Laundry.* New York: Macmillan, 1965.
Stevenson-Hamilton, Vivian. *Yes, Your Excellency.* London: Harmsworth, 1985.
Strip, Percival, and Olivia Strip. *The Peoples of Bombay.* Bombay: Thacker, 1944.
Subrahmanyam, Sanjay. *Connected History: Essays and Arguments.* London: Verso Books, 2022.
Sykes, Sir Frederick. *From Many Angles: An Autobiography.* London: George G. Harrap, 1942.
Symons, Julian. *The General Strike: A Historical Portrait.* London: Cresset, 1957.
Taylor, D. J. *Bright Young People: The Rise and Fall of a Generation, 1918–1940.* London: Chatto and Windus, 2007.
Thackeray, David. *Forging a British World of Trade: Culture, Ethnicity, and Market in the Empire-Commonwealth, 1880–1975.* Oxford: Oxford Scholarship Online, 2019.
Thakkar, Usha, and Sandhya Mehta. *Gandhi in Bombay.* New Delhi: Oxford University Press, 2017.
Thampi, Madhavi, ed. *India and China in the Colonial World.* Abingdon, UK: Routledge, 2017.
———. *Indians in China, 1800–1949.* New Delhi: Manohar, 2005.
Tindall, Gillian. *City of God: The Biography of Bombay.* Gurgaon, India: Penguin Random House India, 1992.
Toms, Steven. *Financing Cotton: British Industrial Growth and Decline, 1780–2000.* Woodbridge, UK: Boydell Press, 2020.
Trench, Victor. *Lord Willingdon in India.* Bombay: Karnatak, 1934.
Trevelyan, Charles, and Humphrey Trevelyan. *The India We Left: Charles Trevelyan, 1826–65, Humphrey Trevelyan, 1929–47.* London: Macmillan, 1972.
Trocki, Carl A. *Opium, Empire and the Global Political Economy: A Study of the Asian Opium Trade, 1750–1950.* London: Routledge, 1999.
Tsang, Steve. *A Modern History of Hong Kong.* London: I. B. Tauris, 2007.
Tyau, Min-Ch'ien T. Z. *London through Chinese Eyes.* London: Swarthmore, 1920.
Utley, Freda. *Lancashire and the Far East.* London: George Allen and Unwin, 1931.
Visram, Rozina. *Asians in Britain: 400 Years of History.* London: Pluto, 2002.
———. *Ayahs, Lascars and Princes: Indians in Britain, 1700–1947.* London: Pluto, 1986.
Wadia, P. A., and G. N. Joshi. *Money and the Money Market in India.* London: Macmillan, 1926.
———. *The Wealth of India.* London: Macmillan, 1925.
Walkowitz, Judith. *Nights Out in Cosmopolitan London.* New Haven, CT: Yale University Press, 2012.

Wasserstrom, Jeffrey N. *Global Shanghai, 1850–2010: A History in Fragments*. London: Routledge, 2009.
Wei, Betty Peh-T'i. *Old Shanghai*. New York: Oxford University Press, 1993.
Weightman, Gavin, and Steve Humphries. *The Making of Modern London, 1914–1939*. London: Sidgewick and Jackson, 1984.
Weiss, Holger. *International Communism and Transnational Solidarity: Radical Networks, Mass Movements and Global Politics, 1919–1939*. Boston: Brill, 2017.
Welsh, Frank. *A History of Hong Kong*. London: HarperCollins, 1997.
White, Jerry. *London in the Twentieth Century*. London: Bodley Head, 2001.
Woodcock, George. *The British in the Far East*. New York: Atheneum, 1969.
Wright, Arnold, and H. A. Cartwright, eds. *Twentieth Century Impressions of Hongkong, Shanghai, and Other Treaty Ports of China*. London: Lloyd's Great Britain, 1908.
Xiong, Yuezhi. *Shanghai Urban Life and Its Heterogeneous Cultural Entanglements*. Translated by Lane J. Harris. Boston: Brill, 2022.
Xun, Lu. *Lu Xun: Selected Works*. Translated by Yang Xianyi and Gladys Yang. 3rd ed. Vol. 4. Beijing: Foreign Language Press, 1980.
Yates, Alexia. *Real Estate and Global Urban History*. Cambridge Elements in Global Urban History, edited by Michael Goebel, Tracy Neumann, and Joseph Ben Prestel. Cambridge: Cambridge University Press, 2021.
Yazdani, Kaveh, and Dilip M. Menon, eds. *Capitalisms: Towards a Global History*. New Delhi: Oxford University Press, 2020.
Yeh, Wen-hsin. *Shanghai Splendor: Economic Sentiments and the Making of Modern China, 1843–1949*. Berkeley: University of California Press, 2008.
Yin, Cao. *From Policeman to Revolutionaries: A Sikh Diaspora in Global Shanghai, 1885–1945*. New York: Brill, 2017.
Yue, Meng. *Shanghai and the Edges of Empires*. Minneapolis: University of Minnesota Press, 2006.
Zahra, Tara. *Against the World: Anti-globalism and Mass Politics between the Wars*. New York: W. W. Norton, 2023.

Index

Page numbers followed by *f* refer to figures.

airports, 108, 168, 189–90. *See also* aviation
anti-Semitism, 30, 135
Apollo Bunder, 22, 34, 40, 42, 43f, 45, 52, 59, 61, 75
Arnhold, Harry, 127, 169, 181, 184, 199
Arnhold & Company. *See under* companies
art deco, 5, 8, 11; in Bombay, 56, 58, 61–62, 76–77; in London, 99, 108, 122, 137; in Shanghai, 171, 180, 185, 187–88, 203
Asiatic Petroleum Company (APC). *See under* companies
associations, 12, 97, 140, 147, 173–74, 189; East India Cotton Association, 56; Millowners' Association, 42, 81, 89, 142, 147
automobiles, 56, 64–65, 129, 136, 149, 150, 171–72
Avenue Joffre, 158, 174
aviation, 35–36, 73, 77–79, 82, 118, 189, 193; aero clubs, 35, 77–78, 189; air shows, 35, 77. *See also* airports; companies

Back Bay, 11, 58, 73, 79, 83, 108
Ballard Estate, 11, 56, 69–70, 74, 76, 81, 127, 203
ballrooms, 59, 61; Ballroom at the Cathay Hotel, 158; Paramount Ballroom, 158, 188. *See also* nightclubs

banking, 3–4, 9, 11, 13, 16, 19, 25–26, 29–30, 32, 36, 41, 44, 197; in Bombay, 71–72, 86–88; in London, 110, 116, 118–19, 122–25; in Shanghai, 148, 151–52, 156, 172–74, 195, 199
banks: Bank of China, 28, 152, 171, 174; Bank of England, 32, 116–17, 117f, 119, 122; Chartered Bank of India, Australia, and China, 66, 152, 171; Eastern Bank, 27, 32, 66, 124–26; E. D. Sassoon Bank, 95, 110, 128–29, 145, 156, 184, 203; Hong Kong & Shanghai Bank, 26, 28, 66, 81, 110–11, 122, 125–26, 152, 166–67, 169, 171–72, 182, 189; Lloyds Bank, 118, 122; Mitsui Bank, 176, 191; National City Bank, 66, 111, 153, 182, 193–95; Yokohama Specie Bank, 152, 170, 176, 195. *See also* banking; Bund: "Bund Banks"; exchange banks
BBC, 75, 99, 102, 105, 108, 138, 145. *See also* telecommunications
Bendix, Carl, 104, 111–12, 128
Bendix, Daisy, 111–13
Bombay Port Trust, 56, 63, 69, 81
British Empire Exhibition, 72–73, 105–6, 108, 139, 145
Bund, 11, 35, 110, 127, 129, 149–50, 152, 156, 170–72, 170f, 176–77, 181–82, 185, 187, 189, 191; "Bund Banks," 152–54, 171, 191

cabarets: in Bombay, 48, 59–60; in London, 104, 110, 121, 138–39; in Shanghai, 157, 173, 175, 190, 196. *See also* theaters

capitalism: colonial, 52, 90, 163, 194; financial, 128, 156; gentlemanly, 31, 71, 80, 112, 195; global, 2–5, 8–9, 12–15, 17, 22, 24, 28, 50, 74–75, 83, 109, 114, 121, 123, 147, 150, 152, 160, 162, 166, 186, 196; Indian, 71; merchant, 9, 26, 148

Cathay Hotel. *See under* hotels

Chamber of Commerce, 82, 142, 174; of Bombay, 41, 71, 140, 142; British, 181; Indian, 72, 109; of International Settlement, 140; London, 140; of Shanghai, 147, 173–74

Chapei, 176–77, 190

chawls, 48–50, 56, 87, 92. *See also* slums

Chiang Kai-shek, 144, 153, 155, 163, 165, 180–81

clubs, 12, 29, 34, 42, 45, 59, 105–6, 112, 114, 119, 140, 142, 172–73, 178, 180; Bombay Yacht Club, 29, 42–44, 142; Byculla Club, 28–29, 53; Circle Sportif Français, 173; Jockey Club, 102, 166, 189; Royal Western Indian Turf Club, 47; Shanghai Race Club, 34–35, 182, 188; Willingdon Sports Club, 42–44, 89, 142

communism, 51–52, 69, 91–92, 98, 100–101, 109, 132–33, 135, 144–45, 162–63, 179, 182, 197–99; Comintern, 51, 162; Communist Party, 133, 165

companies: Anderson, Meyer & Company, 151; Arnhold & Company, 69, 127, 150, 166, 183, 187; Asiatic Petroleum Company (APC), 149, 181; Bombay Talkies, 60, 72; British Burmah Oil, 65; British Imperial Chemical Industries, 64, 149; British India Steam Navigation Company, 70; British Petroleum, 99; Cathay Land Company, 183–84, 187; China Light and Power Company, 81, 167; China National Aviation Corporation, 151, 168, 189; David Sassoon & Sons, 30–33, 93, 149; E. D. Sassoon & Company, 31, 33–37, 41, 70, 72, 74, 79, 80, 91, 93, 110, 123, 125–27, 149, 167, 183; Hongkong Land Investment Company, 167; Jardine & Matheson, 149–50, 166; Kohinoor Film Company, 60; P&O Steam Navigation Company, 26, 45, 70, 84, 107, 123, 133; Scindia Steam Navigation Company, 70, 72; Shanghai Land Investment Company, 183, 185, 187; Standard Oil, 65, 149; Tata Iron and Steel Company, 72–73, 149; Unilever, 64, 98, 150; Universal Aviation Company, 36

concrete, 56, 61, 65, 69, 76–77, 137, 185

cosmopolitanism, 12, 14, 16, 45, 57, 59, 62, 76, 110–11, 113, 120, 157, 161, 164, 168, 182

cotton, 2, 14, 21–25, 50, 56, 60, 126; excise duties, 84–85; industry, in Bombay, 7, 16, 24, 28, 32, 34, 40, 48, 72–73, 79–80, 82–83, 85, 88–91, 93–95, 127–28, 142; industry, in Japan, 84–85, 89, 92, 141–42; industry, in Lancashire, 6, 70, 93, 141–42; industry, in Shanghai, 23, 142, 144, 146–49, 173, 177, 183; trade, 32–33, 64–67, 74, 84–85, 88, 129–31, 154, 177. *See also* associations; Lancashire; millowners

currency ratios, 86, 89–90, 93, 129

David Sassoon & Sons. *See under* companies

department stores, 13, 59, 66, 100, 156–57, 162, 183, 185, 190, 196; Evans & Fraser, 58; Marks & Spencer, 121; Sincere, 156, 183, 190; Sun Sun, 156; Whiteaway, 58; Wing On, 156–57, 183, 190

Dinshaw-Petit family, 60, 72, 77

Docklands, 31, 129–32, 134, 147, 202

East End (London), 31, 98, 109, 129–32, 134–35, 137, 160

E. D. Sassoon & Company. *See under* companies

E. D. Sassoon Bank. *See under* banks

European Group, 82, 94, 110

exchange banks, 27, 66, 86, 118, 124–25, 128, 151. *See also* banking; banks

INDEX   247

Feetham Report, 178–79, 184
film. *See* motion pictures
First World War, 3–6, 9–10, 38, 45, 52, 58, 70, 84, 87, 96, 99–100, 116, 118, 125, 127, 139, 141, 146
French Concession, 34, 138, 152, 174, 176, 182–83, 187, 190

Gandhi, Mohandas, 52–53, 82, 93, 98, 164–65
Girangaon, 39, 41, 51–52, 79, 141, 203
globalization, 2–5, 7–9, 11, 13–15, 17, 83–84, 137, 178, 185, 196–97
gold, 5, 25, 32, 75, 116–18, 125, 152–54; standard, 27, 87–89, 124, 128, 139, 155; trade in, 21, 64, 66, 68, 111, 126, 167, 191. *See also* speculation
Great Depression, 3–5, 10–11, 56, 64, 70–71, 83, 93, 118, 135–36, 142, 154, 182, 184–85, 197
Greater Shanghai Plan, 179–80
Great West Road, 136–37
Great World, 159, 190

Hardoon, Silas, 34–35, 176, 183–84
Hong Kong & Shanghai Bank. *See under* banks
horse racing, 12–14, 34–35, 43, 46–47, 101–2, 111, 150, 181, 189, 199. *See also* clubs
hotels, 8, 12, 19, 35, 43, 59, 122, 158, 166, 170–71, 182–83, 185–87, 190; Cathay Hotel, 19, 177–78, 180–81, 185–88, 190, 193; Green's Hotel, 59; Majestic Hotel, 149; Park Hotel, 112, 158; Savoy, 104, 112, 158; Watson's Hotel, 39. *See also* Sassoon House; Taj Mahal
Huangpu River, 23–24, 84, 130, 146–49, 160, 163, 170, 178–79

Imperial Airways, 77, 107–8, 168. *See also* airports; aviation
Imperial Maritime Customs, 24, 125, 148
India House (London), 104–5
India League (London), 100, 109–10, 165
Indian Currency League, 89–90. *See also* currency ratios

Indian National Congress, 52, 57, 165
insurance, 5, 11, 13, 30, 34, 55, 71, 73, 116, 118–19, 122–23, 156, 162, 166, 173; in Hong Kong, 167; in India, 75–76; in London, 123
Iraq, 38, 64, 126

Japan, 2, 24, 28, 32, 64–65, 68–69, 148, 155, 163–64, 173, 185–86; anti-Japanese protests, 144, 161–62, 165; competition with, 84–86, 89, 92–93, 130, 140–42, 149, 177; Japanese people in Shanghai, 172, 175–78, 189–93; Sassoon's relations with, 124, 182, 194–95, 198–99
jazz, 1, 12–13, 17; in Bombay, 40, 47, 59–61; in London, 104, 120, 134; in Shanghai, 158, 175, 186, 188
Jewish people, 7, 21–22, 27–31, 33–36, 43, 45, 123, 135, 166, 176, 180, 183, 195; Ashkenazi, 176; Baghdadi, 27, 30, 35, 176; Sephardic, 21, 45, 176

Kamathipura, 48–50
Karachi, 2, 32, 64, 67, 72, 78, 107, 124, 126
Kuomintang, 51, 144, 153, 165, 179, 182

labor. *See* workers
Labour Party, 100, 138, 165
Lancashire, 21, 24–25, 28, 33, 41, 70, 81–82, 84, 88, 91, 93, 130, 141–43, 154. *See also* cotton; millowners
lascars, 69, 133
Liddell, Billie Coutts, 111, 181
Liddell, John (Jack) Hellyer, 110–11, 169, 181
lilong (neighborhoods), 161, 174, 182
Limehouse (London), 31, 133–35

Mahalaxmi Racecourse, 37, 47–48, 203. *See also* horse racing
Malabar Hills, 29, 40, 44, 56, 72, 76
Mayfair (London), 33–34, 103, 114
May Thirtieth Movement, 144, 183
Mazagaon, 28, 31, 38, 50, 63–65, 69
Menon, V. K. Krishna, 109–10
middle class, 1, 13, 40, 54–57, 107, 121, 138, 157

migration, 2–3, 9–10, 23, 49–50, 67, 167–68, 182, 196
millowners, 47, 85
Millowners' Association, 42, 81, 89, 142, 147
Mitsui, 85, 149, 176, 191, 195. *See also* banks; Japan
motion pictures, 12, 18, 59–61, 70, 72, 102, 104, 120, 130, 134, 156, 158, 186. *See also* companies; theaters
Municipal Council, Shanghai, 24, 111, 169, 172–74, 181, 185, 191

Nanjing Road, 32, 35, 144, 156–60, 157*f*, 162, 177, 182–85, 187, 190
newspapers, 4, 12–14, 18–20, 34, 36, 46, 55, 57–58, 64, 81–82, 90, 99, 102–4, 108, 138, 145, 153, 155, 163–64, 173, 195. *See also* press
New Woman, 59, 79, 113
nightclubs, 5, 12–13, 104, 162, 196; Ciro's Club, 104, 188, 192

oil, 29, 38, 50, 64–65, 67, 91, 126, 128–29, 146, 149, 175, 181. *See also* companies; petroleum
opium, 7, 21–24, 26, 28, 34–35, 50, 68, 84, 134, 146–47, 183, 191
Osaka, 2, 50–51, 84–85, 141, 177. *See also* cotton; Japan
Ottawa Agreements, 93, 139

Palmer & Turner, 171, 185
P&O Steam Navigation Company. *See under* companies
Park Royal, 136–37
Parsi people, 21–22, 24, 29, 51, 53–54, 57–58, 61, 71–72, 76, 87, 108, 142, 149, 203
petroleum, 24, 29, 65, 70, 99, 126, 129, 149, 181. *See also* companies; oil
Port Trust, Bombay, 56, 63, 69, 81
press, 4, 11–12, 20, 42, 47, 52, 85–86, 90, 101–3, 107, 114, 139, 142, 145, 163–64, 179, 197–98; *Bombay Chronicle*, 51, 55, 87, 90; *Bystander*, 46, 103, 112; *China Weekly Review*, 171, 194; *Daily Mail*, 61, 99; *London Times*, 137–38, 145, 191;

North China Daily News, 145, 171, 185; *Sketch*, 103–4, 115, 119–20; *Sphere*, 121, 123, 139, 156, 159; *Tatler*, 103–4, 111–12, 120; *Times of India*, 39, 47, 55, 57, 76, 84, 89–91, 95, 164. *See also* newspapers

radio, 4, 13–14, 38, 46, 57, 59, 74–75, 99, 102, 107, 120, 136, 138, 145, 158, 174, 186, 190. *See also* telecommunications
Raymond, Abraham Jacob, 81, 127, 167
Raymond, Albert, 81, 127, 167
real estate, 2, 5, 8–9, 11, 14, 16–17, 19, 111, 156; in Bombay, 21, 56, 58, 71, 73, 75; in Hong Kong, 114, 127, 166; in London, 121–22; in Shanghai, 34, 125, 127–29, 155–57, 159, 161, 172, 174, 179–85, 187, 191, 195, 199. *See also* companies
Reed, John (Jack), 111, 182
Reed, Peggy, 111, 182
Reed, Stanley, 39–40, 71, 84
riots, 2, 15, 36, 40, 50–51, 53, 93, 100–101, 103, 132, 144. *See also* strikes
Royal Air Force, 78, 82, 177, 189. *See also* aviation
Royal Commission on Labour (Whitley Commission), 91–92, 110
Russians, 172, 175–76; White, 160, 175

Saklatvala, Shapurji, 52, 133–34
Sassoon House, 127, 129, 153, 181, 185–87
Sassoons: Albert, 27, 30–31; David, 20–24, 27; Edward Elias, 32–33; Elias David, 23, 58; Ellice Victor Elias, 16*f*, 20; Hector, 37, 114, 127; Jacob, 32–34, 36, 124; Mozelle, 37; Philip, 77–78; Reginald, 37
Second World War, 1, 5–6, 197
Sewri, 28, 63–66, 77, 85, 91, 93
Shanghai Municipal Council, 24, 111, 169, 172–74, 181, 185, 191
shipping, 3, 7, 10–11, 22–23, 27, 50, 70–74, 116, 119, 123, 130, 133, 146–47, 157, 173, 181, 188
silver, 23, 86–89, 93, 128, 151–53, 194; bullion, 25–26, 66, 116–17; crisis, 5, 153–56, 182–83; standard, 26–27, 86, 118, 186; trade in, 21, 32, 64, 67–

69, 111, 124–26, 167, 191, 194. *See also* speculation
slums, 31, 39, 48–49, 54, 56–57, 92, 99, 135, 161. See also *chawls*
Soong, T. V., 153, 180
speculation, 66, 99, 141, 148; in currency, 4–5, 27, 117, 128, 153–54; in real estate, 16, 32, 56, 111, 121, 182
sports, 5, 13–14, 46, 101–2, 107, 139, 196
steamers, 10–11, 23, 31, 33, 60, 64, 67, 75, 146–47, 167–68. *See also* steamships
steamships, 24, 50, 107, 130. *See also* companies
Stones, Fred, 81, 91–93
strikes, 2, 15, 17, 138; in Bombay, 36, 50–53, 69, 80, 85, 91–93, 141; in London, 100, 132–33; 1926 General Strike, 137–39; in Shanghai, 144–45, 147, 162, 164, 176, 196
Suez Canal, 10, 27, 40, 45, 74, 171
Suzhou Creek, 24, 147–48, 150, 160–61, 176, 183, 187
swadeshi cause, 53, 57, 70–71, 76–77, 85
Sykes, Sir Frederick, 49, 82

Taj Mahal, 34, 37, 39, 43, 43*f*, 44, 59, 73, 75, 78, 82, 106, 108, 142, 156, 158, 187, 199
Tata, 60, 77–79, 90, 133, 149. *See also* companies
telecommunications, 73–74, 99, 140, 143, 150, 159, 186. *See also* radio; telegraph; telephones; wireless technology
telegraph, 4, 27, 35, 63, 66, 74, 99, 120, 124–25, 149–50, 162, 186, 190. *See also* telecommunications
telephones, 4, 35, 57, 59, 75, 99, 118, 120, 123, 136–38, 149–50, 162, 170, 174, 186. *See also* telecommunications
Thakurdas, Purshotamdas, 82, 88–89, 94

theaters, 13, 53, 60–61, 72, 102, 112, 121, 135, 139, 158–59, 176. *See also* cabarets; motion pictures
Tokyo, 2, 111, 164, 176, 191, 195. *See also* Japan
tourism, 59, 107

unemployment, 92, 98, 100, 135, 137, 162
unions, 51, 69, 98, 100, 109, 132, 133, 139, 148, 172; clerk, 55; labor, 80, 85, 93, 132, 162; millworker, 51, 93; seamen, 69, 132–33, 148; student, 98, 109; trade, 51, 85, 91–92, 100, 139. *See also* workers
Upadhyaya, Paddy, 133

Volunteer Corps (Shanghai), 163, 170, 175, 190

West End (London), 103–4, 120–21, 130, 134–35, 138
Whitley Commission, 91–92, 110
wireless technology, 4, 74–75, 78, 96, 99, 125, 130, 137, 140, 150. *See also* telecommunications
Wittet, George, 61, 69
workers, 50–52, 67, 80, 97, 136, 146–47, 150, 151*f*, 161–64, 174; dockworkers, 11, 67–69, 68*f*, 130, 132, 138, 144, 162; *lascars*, 69, 133; millworkers, 41, 47, 51–52, 54, 66, 82–83, 85–86, 90–92, 133, 144, 162, 199; office, 13, 54, 137, 148; railway, 39, 69; salaried, 120, 137, 157; seamen (sailors), 67–69, 132–34, 162, 172; white-collar, 54, 138. *See also* unions
World War I. *See* First World War
World War II, 1, 5–6, 197

Yangtze River, 23, 146, 154, 160, 179